Living
Water

Living *Water*

a creative resource for the Liturgy

Complete Resource Book
YEAR A

Susan Sayers

with Father Andrew Moore

Kevin Mayhew

First published in 1998 by
KEVIN MAYHEW LTD
Rattlesden
Bury St Edmunds
Suffolk IP30 0SZ

0 1 2 3 4 5 6 7 8 9

ISBN 1 84003 217 0
Catalogue No. 1500199

The other titles in the *Living Water* series are

Prayer of the Faithful	ISBN 1 84003 221 9	Cat. No. 1500203
Treasure Seekers	ISBN 1 84003 218 9	Cat. No. 1500200
Pearl Divers	ISBN 1 84003 219 7	Cat. No. 1500201
Gold Panners	ISBN 1 84003 220 0	Cat. No. 1500202

Cover photographs:
Family group – courtesy of Comstock Photo Library
Background – courtesy of Images Colour Library Limited, London
Cover design by Jaquetta Sergeant
Edited by Katherine Laidler
Typesetting by Louise Selfe
Illustrations by Arthur Baker
Printed in Great Britain

FOREWORD

Living Water is designed to help you make the most of the possibilities of the three-year lectionary, particularly in parishes which are concerned to meet the needs of all ages and stages.

My aim is to spark ideas and start you off. The demands on those leading worship and preparing teaching are enormous, and I hope you will find here materials and suggestions which help take the strain and free you to enjoy the work of enabling people's faith to grow and of deepening their relationship with the living God.

As I was writing, I tried to keep these principles in mind:

- All-age worship needs to be just that, and not children's worship at which adults happen to be present.

- Different age groups need some teaching suited to their particular stage of development, but all benefit from studying the same passages of scripture on the same day. The whole parish is then able to grow together and share insights and discoveries.

- Separate children's ministry for part of the service is there to develop the children's faith now, and also to prepare them for taking a full part in your church's Sunday worship when they are older. Their age-appropriate worship and activities should aim to ease them gradually into full participation with the adults in church, rather than creating a completely separate culture which makes the transition difficult.

- We sell our children and young people short if we only teach them facts about our faith; what they need is to be introduced to a real relationship with God, in which the foundations are laid for life-long habits of prayer, study of the Bible and an openness to God's Spirit.

- We journey into faith, so all our worship and teaching must respect the diversity of stages reached, and the emotional and cultural luggage brought along. Any resource material should therefore be flexible, easily adapted, and accessible at a number of different levels.

- The cerebral and the academic approaches cherished by many in positions of leadership are not the only, nor necessarily the most effective ways to explore and express our faith! Unless we also make use of the senses and the emotions, we shall be shutting doors through which our God could reach the people he loves.

Let us worship the Lord in the beauty of holiness.

SUSAN SAYERS
with Father Andrew Moore

This book is dedicated to my family and friends,
whose encouraging support has been wonderful,
and to all those whose good ideas are included here for others to share.

ACKNOWLEDGEMENTS

The publishers wish to express their gratitude to the following for permission to use copyright material in this book:

The Iona Community, Pearce Institute, Govan, Glasgow, G51 3UU, for verse 1 from *Heaven shall not wait* by John L. Bell and Graham Maule, © Copyright WGRG and used by permission from the *Heaven shall not wait* collection (Sixteenth Sunday of the Year), and verse 1 of *Christ's is the world* by John L. Bell and Graham Maule, © Copyright 1989 WGRG and used by permission from the *Love from Below* collection (Twenty-fifth Sunday of the Year).

Kingsway's Thankyou Music, PO Box 75, Eastbourne, East Sussex BN23 6NW, for the extract from *You laid aside your majesty* by Noel Richards, © 1985 (Palm (Passion) Sunday); the chorus from *Meekness and majesty* by Graham Kendrick, © 1986 (Seventh Sunday of Easter); the chorus from *The heart of worship* by Matt Redman, © 1997 (Tenth Sunday of the Year); the chorus from *There is none like you* by Lenny Leblanc, © 1991 Integrity's Hosanna! Music (Seventeenth Sunday of the Year), and the extract from *5000+ hungry folk* by Ian Smale, © 1985 (Eighteenth Sunday of the Year).

All other material contained in this publication is © Kevin Mayhew Ltd.

CONTENTS

SPECIAL FEASTS

HOW TO USE THIS BOOK

PLANNING

You can select from the week's material as much as you find useful for your particular needs on any one week, as all the ideas are independent of one another, although they are all linked to the weekly readings.

All-age worship is not about the entertainment business, nor is it child-centred worship, or 'watered-down' worship. Neither need it be noisy and extra-hassle worship. There are usually many other age groups represented in our churches as well as children and our aim must be to provide for the middle-aged and elderly as well as for the young, for the stranger as well as the regulars.

Since God is in a far better position to know the needs of your congregation than anyone, it is naturally essential to prepare for Sunday worship in prayer. I don't mean asking God to bless what we have already planned, but to spend time discerning God's priorities and listening as he tunes in to the needs of those who will be there. Think about gathering a group of all ages to commit themselves to this each week, either together in church or separately at an agreed time. All the ideas in this book and other resource books are only secondary to this prayerful preparation.

Each week is set out as follows:

Thought for the day

Use this on the weekly handout, or as an initial focus when starting your planning.

Reflection on the readings

There are ideas here for getting your mind going when sermon preparation jams. Or the reflection can be used for individual and group Bible study.

Discussion starters

These are provided for adult group work and could sometimes be used for adults in the sermon slot while toddlers, children and young people follow their own programmes. Small group work within a service is rarely contemplated, but it can be a valuable way of involving everyone, avoiding the automatic pilot syndrome, and bringing the readings to life.

Some churches have parents present during the children's liturgy; consider providing a parents' class within that programme for a short time as a way of reaching those who are wary of actually 'going to church'.

All-stage talk

In my experience the difference in faith stages is more important than the age differences, so these talks aim to present the teaching in ways that people of all ages and stages can relate to. There are so many ordinary experiences which are common to all of us and these can be used and enjoyed without anyone being excluded. Abstract thinking and reading skills are not necessarily common to all, but deep and abstract concepts can often be grasped if explained through concrete images, like three-dimensional parables.

In all these talks I want to encourage adaptation, so that the talks come across as fresh and owned by you, rather than another person's jacket, stiffly worn. Get the ideas, and then enjoy yourself!

All-age ideas

I have suggested particular worship ideas for each week, but here are some more general guidelines to use to get your own ideas flowing.

Dramatised readings

Having read and prayed the readings, I find it helps to imagine myself sitting in the congregation, seeing and hearing the readings creatively expressed. If I imagine I am a child, a young adult, an elderly person and so on, I am more likely to pick up on what *won't* be helpful, and what *will* really make me think.

- Have a narrator to read, and simply mime what is read. Anyone not involved in the action at any one time freezes in his/her last position, like 'statues'.

- Give individuals their words to say. During the narration the characters act their parts and speak their own words.

- Have one or two instruments (guitar and flute, for instance, or organ) to play quietly as a background to the reading.

- Use a few materials as props and costumes. They need not be elaborate, just enough to aid imagination.

- Use live or taped music and depict not only the actions, but also the atmosphere, through mime or dance. Keep it natural, simple and controlled, and do make sure all types and ages are involved.

- There may be times, not just Palm Sunday, for involving the whole congregation in the telling of a story, either by writing their words on the weekly sheet, or by displaying their words, noises and actions at appropriate places in the narration.

Acts of worship

Sometimes something very simple will speak deeply to people. As you prepare try to give the cerebral a break for a while, and listen to what the readings make you feel. Then translate this into some music, communal action (or stillness), which will help people respond to God with their hearts as well as their minds.

Church decoration

The church building speaks. Our churches are visited and admired by many, and it is important that visitors see evidence of the living church of today as well as the beauty of the past. During services the mind and heart can be steered quietly towards the message of the day by means of a particular flower arrangement, exhibition of pictures, display or banner.

If those who arrange the flowers so faithfully, week by week, have access to the *Thought for the day* and the *Reflection on the readings*, they will be able to express these themes in an arrangement.

Prayer of the Faithful

The main aim of those who lead the people's intercessions is to provide a climate for prayer, so that the congregation are not just listening passively, but are actively involved in the work of prayer. I suggest times of silence at each section, rather than pauses, so as to allow for this, and you could have music playing quietly during these times, open prayer or prayer clusters as well as individuals praying fervently together in the stillness of their Father's company.

During this time the young children can be praying through pictures, following a prayer trail, praying in pairs with an adult, or singing some quiet worship songs.

Music

Music, played or sung well, drawn from a range of traditions, always sensitive to the liturgy of the day or season and appropriate to the resources available, can provide a 'landscape for worship' in which people are helped to focus their attention on God, and lift their hearts to him.

Both recorded and live music can be used in worship to help people settle to an inner stillness, give them space for reflection, and provide the environment for spiritual attentiveness. Use whatever gifts your congregation offers; organ music is lovely but need not be used exclusively. Consider a small ensemble of string and wind instruments with piano; a single instrument such as recorder, flute or trumpet; or a selection of percussion instruments such as shakers, triangles and bells. Many churches develop a music group of voices and instruments to provide a different sound for certain services each month. Welcome and involve young people and children, not necessarily as a separate group.

Choose recorded music from a wide range of traditions and styles, bearing in mind the people who are likely to be present. Keep a notebook handy to record titles of suitable pieces that you hear, and ask members of the congregation for their ideas.

There is now such a richness of material available that an attempt at an exhaustive list would be foolish and impractical. Whatever books you use at your parish, make the most of the choice they provide.

Treasure Seekers
3-5 year olds

I have included suggestions for a programme which picks up on some of the important truths of the weekly readings which form a foundation to build on. For the youngest children this teaching can slot into a general play session, where the care, good humour and friendliness of those in charge of the children will continue to help them realise how much God loves them, and enable them to develop trust – the beginning of faith.

Parents are encouraged to pray with their children during the week, using the worksheet prayers.

Pearl Divers
6-10 year olds

When planning for children's work it is advisable to read through the Bible passages prayerfully. You are then in a better position to see how the programme relates to the readings, and also to enable you to supplement and vary the programme as a result of your own insights and the specific needs of your group.

You may prefer to split your Pearl Divers group into two age groups, adapting the suggestions and worksheets accordingly.

The children are encouraged to pray during the week, using the suggestions on their worksheet. These can be built into a collection of prayers and made into a personal prayer book.

A few general ideas about story-telling:

- Tell the story from the viewpoint of a character in the situation. To create the time-machine effect, avoid eye contact as you slowly put on the appropriate cloth or cloak, and then make eye contact as you greet the children in character.

- Have an object with you which leads into the story – a water jug, or a lunch box, for instance.

- Walk the whole group through the story, so that they are physically moving from one place to another; and use all kinds of places, such as broom cupboards, under the stairs, outside under the trees, and so on.

- Collect some carpet tiles – blue and green – so that at story time the children can sit round the edge of this and help you place on the cut-outs for the story.

Gold Panners
11 years and over

Many churches are concerned about this age group feeling too old for children's liturgy but not able to relate to what the adults are doing in church. We have a wonderful resource here which we tend to ignore; many young people are happy to be involved with a music or drama group, and are excellent at preparing role-play material with a wit and challenge that is good for everyone.

As they move towards owned faith, it is vital that the church provides plenty of opportunity for questions and discussion, in an atmosphere which is accepting and willing to listen. Although many will be very valuable on the children's liturgy teams, I am convinced that they need feeding at their own level as well.

The factfiles on each week's worksheet can be collected into a book so that the course becomes a reference manual.

The Gold Panners material provides a transitional course from separate ministry for children to full participation in the service with adults.

RECOMMENDED BIBLES

It is often a good idea to look at a passage in several different versions before deciding which to use for a particular occasion, especially if you plan to involve several people in the reading. As far as children are concerned, separate Bible stories, such as those published by Palm Tree Press and Lion, are a good introduction for the very young. Once children are reading, a very helpful version is the *International Children's Bible* (New Century version) published by Word Publishing. Here children have a translation based on experienced scholarship, using language structure suitable for young readers, with short sentences and appropriate vocabulary. There is a helpful dictionary, and clear maps and pictures are provided.

For young people the New Century version is called *The Youth Bible*, and the layout includes various anecdotes and Bible studies which are inviting and challenging. A vivid version of the New Testament and parts of the Old Testament in contemporary language is Eugene Peterson's *The Message*. This catches the imagination and aids understanding. It is particularly good for reading aloud.

ADVENT

FIRST SUNDAY OF ADVENT

Thought for the day

We are to wake up and make sure we stay ready for the second coming.

Reflection on the readings

Isaiah 2:1-5
Psalm 121:1-2, 4-5, 6-9
Romans 13:11-14
Matthew 24:37-44

The Church begins its new year on Advent Sunday with the alarm clock jerking us out of sleep. There isn't even a snooze button. There is rather a sense of urgency as we listen to the readings.

First we have the vision seen by Isaiah of the last days, with the holy hill of Jerusalem a centre of pilgrimage for people from every nation. It is a picture of two-way traffic; the pilgrims streaming towards the city from all directions in order to understand and know God better, and the Word of God pouring out from Jerusalem in all directions to teach, explain and transform lives.

From our position in time we can appreciate the typical and extraordinary nature of such prophecy, since in Jesus the Word of God has indeed been pouring out from Jerusalem to the rest of the world, and to the rest of time during this last age before the end of all. And it is to him that the people come in every generation to have their lives transformed.

The Isaiah passage ends with a summons and an invitation to walk in the light of the Lord, and Paul takes this up in his letter to the Romans. The armour of light that will protect us from evil is the life of love spelt out by Jesus both in teaching and example. So, as we begin our preparation for Christmas, we are reminded of Jesus' humility in coming to live among us and show us the Way, and also of the future, when he will return in glory as righteous judge.

In the Gospel we have Jesus' own teaching about the last days, and discover that one thing we can be certain of is that the second coming cannot be predicted. No last-minute revision will be possible, then, and the regular coursework format is a more helpful model. We have to live our lives in constant readiness so that we are not taken by surprise. This is partly so that we can be prepared for death or the

second coming, and partly so that we can enjoy that quality of eternity which means God is constantly coming to us even while we live out our earthly lives. We need to be ready to receive him at every moment of every day.

Discussion starters

1. In what ways is the historical site of Jerusalem still a centre of pilgrimage? Why are so many people drawn to it?

2. Why do you think the timing of the second coming is known only to God the Father? How might it affect us if we knew all the details in advance?

All-stage talk

Begin by explaining that today is Advent Sunday, the first Sunday of the year as far as the Church is concerned. Advent means 'coming', and over the next four weeks we will be getting ourselves ready for the coming of Jesus which we celebrate on Christmas Day.

Today's readings tell us to keep ourselves ready and alert for God's coming, which happens all the time and will happen in a very dramatic way at the end of time when Jesus returns in all his glory. The children will be helping to show us all how to make sure we don't miss out by being unprepared for this.

Invite all the children and young people to walk quickly around the centre aisle, changing direction every time you clap your hands or blow a whistle. Two claps or whistle blows means stand still and listen to a new instruction. Give them a few goes at changing direction, and then make the standing-still and listening signal. Explain that one clap will now mean change direction, two will mean walk backwards, and three will mean stand still and listen. Try this out for a short while and then, when they are standing still and listening, thank them for their demonstration and ask them to sit down where they are.

Explain that if we are to keep ourselves ready and alert while we get on with our lives, it will mean listening out all the time for the good and loving direction that God whispers to us to follow, just as the children were doing so well. As they walked about their lives, they were listening out, so that whenever there was a need to change direction, they were ready to do it straightaway. If they hadn't listened so carefully, they wouldn't have been able to do it nearly so well.

Tell the children that this time when they hear the signal it will mean 'Go back to your seat'. As you start them moving about the aisle again, remind everyone to keep listening to God's loving direction as they walk about through life, so they are always ready. Make the last signal, and thank the children for their help as they go back to their seats.

All-age ideas

- At the beginning of the service tell everyone that at some point the first candle of the Advent ring will be lit. It won't be announced, so everyone is to watch out for it. When anyone sees it happening, they raise their hand, until everyone has noticed. (Arrange beforehand for the candle to be lit at an appropriate time, and as soon as everyone has raised their hand the usual short prayer can be said.)

- Read the Isaiah passage chorally, using the voices of men, women and children. Work through the reading together, trying out different voice combinations, and finish with verse 5 spoken all together.

- As an introduction to the Gospel reading, have small groups of people miming various everyday activities in different parts of the church during the Gradual hymn, and have the Bible, or book of the readings, held high just before the Gospel is read. Some of those miming notice straightaway and turn to face the reader, walking towards them and standing attentively. Gradually the others follow.

Prayer of the Faithful

Celebrant
Let us pray to the God of all time and space,
in whose love we exist
and by whose love we are saved.

Reader
As we prepare ourselves
for the time when Christ comes again in glory,
we pray for the grace and honesty
to see what needs transforming
in our lives as individuals
and as members of the Church of God.

Silence

O come:
let us walk in the light of the Lord.

May all church leaders, pastors and teachers
be directed, inspired and upheld
by the living Spirit of God,
and may there be a deepening
of love and commitment
in all Christians the world over.

Silence

O come:
let us walk in the light of the Lord.

May the leaders of this nation
and of all the nations
be drawn increasingly to understand
God's ways of justice and righteousness,
and be filled with the longing
to do what is right and honest and good.

Silence

O come:
let us walk in the light of the Lord.

May all the families on earth
be blessed with mutual love
and caring consideration one of another;
may arguments and misunderstandings
be properly resolved,
and difficult relationships refreshed and healed.

Silence

O come:
let us walk in the light of the Lord.

May those for whom the days and nights
creep past in pain or sorrow
be given comfort and hope;
may the frightened find reassurance
and the anxious find peace of mind.

Silence

O come:
let us walk in the light of the Lord.

May those who have reached the point of death
be given the knowledge of God's closeness
on that last journey;
and may those who have died
know the eternal peace and joy of heaven.

Silence

O come:
let us walk in the light of the Lord.

Mary's response prepared the way
for our salvation;
we make our prayer with her:
Hail, Mary . . .

In the silence of God's stillness
we name any we know
who especially need our prayer.

Silence

Celebrant
Father, trusting in your mercy,
we lay these prayers before you,
through Jesus Christ our Lord.
Amen.

TREASURE SEEKERS

Aim: To learn the importance of being alert to God all the time.

Starter

Play this version of 'musical bumps'. Tell the children that when you show the red sign they stand still. Whenever the music stops they sit down. This will mean that they have to keep watching, as well as listening, while they jump up and down.

Teaching

Praise everyone for watching and listening so well in the game. It was because they were watching and listening so well that they knew when to stop and when to sit down. Explain that Jesus told his friends to watch and listen carefully – he will be pleased to see how well the children at (your town) can do it already!

Explain that you are going to tell them a story. Every time they hear the word 'Jesus', they put their hand up.

Now tell them this story.

The world God had made was very beautiful. It had blue sea and green grass, and flowers of red and yellow and pink and purple. There were furry animals, and shining fish, birds which sang songs, and frogs which croaked. There were people. There were clouds. There was sunshine and rain and snow. God loved the world he had made. But he saw that people were spoiling the world; they were choosing to hate one another instead of loving one another. Sometimes they chose well and were happy. Sometimes they chose to be selfish and made themselves and each other very unhappy.

'The people I have made need saving and rescuing,' thought God. 'I will come to save and rescue them.'

He got his people ready. 'Watch and listen carefully!' he told them. 'Then when I come to save you, you will recognise who I am.'

Some of the people kept listening and watching. As they grew old they passed the message on to their children. And they passed it on to *their* children – 'Keep watching and listening. One day God will come to us to save and rescue us.'

At last, God kept his promise and came among his people in person to save and rescue them. The people had been expecting a rich and powerful king, but God came among his people as a tiny baby, who was born in a stable and put to bed in the animals' hay. This baby, whose name was Jesus, was God's Son, who had come into the world to save and rescue us.

Not everyone recognised him, because he wasn't what they were expecting. But the ones who were used to listening out for the loving words of God, and the ones who were used to watching out for the loving kindness of God – they knew exactly who Jesus was, and they were very pleased to meet him!

Praying

Dear God,
the world is full of your love. *(trace big circle)*
Help us to listen out for it. *(cup ears)*
Help us to watch out for it. *(shade eyes and look around)*
Thank you for all the goodness and love
that we can hear and see. Amen.

Activities

On the worksheet they can draw small and big things they enjoy seeing and hearing. These can all be cut out and stuck on to a group picture, or hole-punched and hung on to a coat hanger mobile, like this:

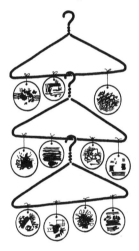

PEARL DIVERS

Aim: To look at the importance of watching and listening in readiness.

Starter

Give half the children a team band, and designate one leader from each group. Mix everyone up together, put on a praise tape and dance or move around to it. Everyone has to do whatever their team leader is doing, changing whenever they change. They will have to concentrate, as people around them will be doing something different.

Teaching

Talk about the way they were very watchful and alert during the dancing, so that they picked up on what their team was doing. We have to be watchful in life as well.

Explain that today is the first Sunday in Advent, and Advent means 'coming'. We are getting ready for Jesus' coming, both remembering him being born at Christmas, and also getting ready for when he comes again in glory. To be ready we need to be watchful and alert. As Christians we will sometimes find that we are living a different way from those around us (like we did in the dancing), but that is because we are following our leader, Jesus, and living his way. That's the best way for us, and the only way to make sure we are ready and don't miss any important instructions, even though it may mean living differently from other people sometimes.

When Jesus had been walking around on earth, teaching, healing and listening to people, he told them a little bit about what would happen at the end of time, so that they, and those who came after them, would be ready for it.

Look together at the Gospel for today, displaying these signs or pictures as you go along:

Praying

Lord, help us to see
the signs of your love today
in the world around us
and in the people we meet.
Train us to be ready to see you
and recognise you
when you come in glory. Amen.

Activities

Have some magnifying glasses so that the children can focus on things and see them in more detail. They can draw what they see on the sheet. There are also some things to look out for which show God at work. The first of the Advent candles will also be lit today, and the children can make the Advent calendar shown on the sheet.

GOLD PANNERS

Aim: To look at why we are to be ready and watchful.

Starter

Sit in a circle round a table or on the floor. Explain that you are going to give them a coded word and they have to try and crack the code. This is the code. For each letter you say something beginning with it – for S you might say, 'So you have to watch carefully'. For vowels you tap on the floor or table one, two, three, four or five times (for E you tap twice). The confusing thing is that you don't draw attention to either the speaking or the tapping, but to arranging some knives and forks in different and complex ways in front of you. This distracts them from seeing what is really important!

When you have made a word, tell them the word you have said, and then do it in code again (using different sentences). If no one guesses, try another word. If someone thinks they have cracked the code let them try doing a word themselves. If no one guesses the secret, give increasingly obvious clues until they do.

Teaching

Talk about how necessary it was to pay attention to the right things in order to crack the code. In our life there are lots of things we are pressured into thinking are important, and if we aren't careful we can end up giving our attention to them and ignoring what is really important.

Read Romans 13:11-14 together, to see what Paul has to say to help us in this. What kind of behaviour in our society would Paul call 'living in the darkness'? How do they think we can live today 'in the light'? (You can record their suggestions on a large sheet, placed under a table lamp, or they can use the worksheet.)

Now look at what Jesus told us about the time when he will return to earth in glory (Matthew 24:37-44). Draw attention to what we don't know and what we do: no one will know the time or date in advance, but we do know that things will carry on as normal right up to when it happens. Show them a front door key and talk about burglar alarms. When is the best time for a burglar to be unnoticed? When the people in the house are too busy to check their doors and windows before they go out; when they're asleep; or when they're deeply into their favourite video.

Place the key on another sheet of paper, and record here their ideas on ways we can make sure we are not taken by surprise, totally unprepared.

Praying

Lord our God,
make us watchful and keep us faithful
as we wait for the coming of your Son our Lord;
that, when he appears,
he may not find us sleeping in sin
but active in his service
and joyful in his praise. Amen.

Activities

On the sheet there are guidelines for them to create a short piece of drama based on being prepared and active. They may like to share this with those in church.

SECOND SUNDAY OF ADVENT

Thought for the day

Get the road ready for the Lord!

Reflection on the readings

Isaiah 11:1-10
Psalm 71:1-2, 7-8, 12-13, 17
Romans 15:4-9
Matthew 3:1-12

Before any real changes can take place in our spiritual development, we have to come to the point of recognising where we are and wanting it to be better. All addicts and their families are painfully aware of the necessity to acknowledge the addiction and find it unbearable, before there is any real hope of kicking the habit. It is at the point when a situation finally becomes intolerable that we are galvanised into taking action to change things.

Living in exile, the people of Israel became acutely aware of their nation's need for good leadership, justice, integrity and peace. In today's passage from Isaiah we sense their longing, as they look forward to God providing what they know they need. Typically, the prophecy was fulfilled in far greater measure, since the kingdom of justice, peace and love – the kingdom of God proclaimed by Jesus – is still growing throughout the entire world.

John the Baptist's message of repentance once again recovered the urgency for people sorting their lives out, since the coming of the Messiah was imminent and they wanted to put things right and be ready, much as we might rush round clearing up the house just before guests are due to arrive – especially those guests we want to impress, or those who we know will notice the clutter! Often the clearing will be something we know has needed doing for ages; the arrival of guests simply reminds us that it has to be done.

So what about all that spiritual clutter and grime which we know needs sorting? Today the Gospel helps to nudge us into urgent action, recognising that we don't want things to stay as they are, and the effort of changing whatever needs changing is well worth it. God comes and knocks at the door of our hearts all the time – not just at the end of the world.

Discussion starters

1. Does our church's outreach reflect a belief that God's good news is for all, or for the few who 'do it our way'?

2. Is Isaiah's righteous, just and compassionate living realistic, or simply a pipe-dream which can disillusion us?

All-stage talk

In the aisle lay down some 'holes' (cut from black paper) and some blocks (chairs with cardboard boxes or trays leaning against them).

Talk about John the Baptist coming out of the desert and urging everyone to 'Get the road ready!' Some people may have seen a new road being built, with some parts being banked up and others tunnelled through, in order to cut out the steep hills. Most people will at some time have been stuck in traffic jams while roads are being mended, or widened.

John the Baptist was imagining us getting a nice new road ready so that God can travel straight into our lives without finding any holes to fall down, or blocks in the way. He was saying to the people, 'You need to get yourselves ready like a good straight road.'

Ask a couple of volunteers to inspect the 'road' in the aisle, finding all sorts of blocks and holes along it that need putting right. This is a bit like our lives, and the lives of the people John was talking to nearly two thousand years ago. There are 'holes' of selfishness and meanness, and gaping holes in our loving. They need to be filled in with loving kindness and thoughtfulness. Perhaps there are gaps in our honesty, because we don't always tell the truth, or live the truth. These holes need filling up with truthfulness and integrity. There are perhaps holes of superiority, because we sneer at people who aren't like us, or as clever or handsome or rich as us.

Then there are those roadblocks which block God from getting through to us: blocks such as 'I don't need God', 'I'm fine as I am, thanks', 'I don't want to change', and 'It's not my fault I'm bad tempered so you'll have to put up with it'. (The blocks can have these labels written on them clearly.)

When today we hear John the Baptist rushing out of the desert and shouting, 'Get the road ready for our God!', it's a good idea to listen to him, look at our own life-road, see where the holes and blocks are, and ask God to help us put them right straightaway, so that God can come to us easily without any hold-ups.

All-age ideas

- For the Penitential Rite, give everyone a piece of paper and a pencil so they can draw their road and ask God to help them make it ready. Other people will only see the holes and blocks; what these stand for will be known only by the person drawing them.

- Read the Isaiah passage chorally. This helps to bring out both the meaning and the poetry.

- Act out the Gospel with someone dressed up as John the Baptist. This person can then light this week's Advent candle.

Prayer of the Faithful

Celebrant
Our God is always ready to hear our prayers.
Let us be still, and pray to him now.

Reader
Heavenly Father,
we thank you for all those who remind us
to be kind and loving by their words and example.
We pray for the Church throughout the world
and for our own community,
that we may be ready to welcome you
and put right whatever blocks us from your love.

Silence

Come to us, Lord:
we know our need of you.

We pray that the lines of communication
between people and nations
may be kept open, respected and honoured,
and that where communication
has broken down
there may be a new desire for healing.

Silence

Come to us, Lord:
we know our need of you.

Heavenly Father,
we pray for all those making and repairing roads,
travelling on them and stuck in traffic jams;
we pray for the towns and villages linked by roads,
for a public transport system
that protects the environment,
and serves the community.

Silence

Come to us, Lord:
we know our need of you.

We pray for those we see and talk to
every day or every week;
for those we often argue with
or misunderstand;
for those who brighten our lives
and make us smile;
for a greater thankfulness and appreciation
of those we usually take for granted.

Silence

Come to us, Lord:
we know our need of you.

We pray for those we have hurt or upset;
for those who feel isolated and alone;
for the ill, the frail, the stressed and the bitter.

Silence

Come to us, Lord:
we know our need of you.

We pray for the dying
and those who have died to this earthly life.
May they know the eternal peace
of your heaven,
and may those who miss them be comforted.

Silence

Come to us, Lord:
we know our need of you.

We make our prayer with Mary,
whose willing obedience
made our salvation possible:
Hail, Mary . . .

Together in silence
we make our private petitions
and thanksgivings.

Silence

Celebrant
Father of all time and place,
accept these prayers
through Jesus Christ.
Amen.

TREASURE SEEKERS

Aim: To think about getting ready for Jesus at Christmas.

Starter

Ready, steady, go! Give the children different tasks to do (such as running to the back wall, jumping round a chair, hopping to a leader). Having explained the task, they have to wait until you say, 'Ready, steady, go!' before they start.

Teaching

Talk about getting ready for Christmas, and all the things going on at home and in the shops. Everyone has long lists of jobs to do and cards and presents to make or buy. Show some of your own scribbled lists. How can we get ourselves ready for Christmas? Show the children an Advent calendar, with a week of windows already opened, and then

open today's window. The Church calls this time before Christmas 'Advent', which is another way of saying 'coming'. We can use this time to work on something we find hard to do, like sharing our toys, going to bed when we're told to, or remembering to help at home. (Talk over the ideas with the children.) We can do this as a present to give Jesus at Christmas.

Praying

Dear Jesus,
when I open today's window
in my Advent calendar
I remember the present
I am getting ready to give you.
Please help me to do it well. Amen.

Activities

Give each child some modelling clay to make the shape of them doing what they are working at during Advent. Here are some suggestions to help the children think of their own:

• Praying every day
• Helping at home in some way
• Telling the truth
• Sharing without getting cross
• Going to bed at the right time
• Feeding/cleaning out a pet

Next week the children will be making a box to put their model in, and the week after it will be wrapped up so that all the gifts can be part of the offering at Christmas.

PEARL DIVERS

Aim: To learn about John the Baptist and his message.

Starter

Provide each child with a cardboard tube and some pieces of newspaper. They screw up the newspaper and jam it into the tube. Now ask them to look through their tubes at each other, and they will find that they can't unless they pull out the newspaper which is blocking the view.

Teaching

Point out what a waste of time it was screwing up newspaper and blocking the tubes because that stopped us being able to see through them! Today we are going to look at the way our lives sometimes need unblocking so that God's love can get through to us better.

Tell the story of John the Baptist in the form of an interview with him and one of the leaders. Whoever is being John the Baptist could dress up. Arrange the chairs like a chat show and have John coming in and taking charge, starting to interview the leader. The leader answers a few questions and then says something like: 'Hang on, John, the children know all about me already. It's you they want to meet!' Then interview John, asking about his mother and father, his cousin, his time spent in the desert, and his message to the people. John must sound excited about his message, and the need for people to be ready for the kingdom of God. Ask who came to listen to his teaching, and ask why John got angry with the Pharisees and Sadducees. Like a good interviewer, repeat the important answers to make sure the children have picked them up. Finally thank John for coming and all the children can say goodbye to him.

Praying

Lord God,
help us to get ourselves ready
to welcome you
into our lives. Amen.

Activities

Prepare beforehand a large piece of paper with the sky, desert background, and the River Jordan already drawn. While a couple of children paint in these areas (use sponges which cover the space more quickly than brushes), the other children draw, colour and cut out people coming to listen to John the Baptist. John himself will also be needed. The crowds can be stuck on to the picture. There are some outlines of people on the worksheet for the children to copy or use if you prefer.

The second Advent candle is lit today.

GOLD PANNERS

Aim: To see the link between the prophecies and John the Baptist's message.

Starter

Give out road maps and work out the most direct route from one place to another, noting any sections of the route where there may be problems or hold-ups.

Teaching

Show them a picture of a tree chopped down with only the stump still standing. Explain how the

people of Israel had been taken into exile, and must have felt as though their nation was like this tree. Now read the passage from Isaiah and, as it is read, draw a shoot growing from the tree stump. Talk about how the people hearing this prophecy might have felt; the possibility of real hope because of God's faithfulness to them.

Can they give a name to the promised fresh shoot from the stump of Jesse? Help them to see how Jesus was the fulfilment of the prophecy.

Now read Matthew 3:1-12, listening out for another prophecy being fulfilled, linked with the one we have heard. Talk about what the prophecy was and how it was fulfilled. What do they think John meant by making the road ready? They can look at what John encouraged his listeners to do in order to be ready. Did they spot another prophecy? This one is given by John the Baptist. Find it (it's in verses 11-12) and talk about whether it has yet been fulfilled.

Praying

Lord God of Israel, we praise you.
Only you can work miracles.
We will always praise your glorious name.
Let your glory be seen everywhere on earth. Amen.

(From Psalm 71)

Activities

The worksheet helps them to plot the prophecies and their fulfilment, and to think of areas in their own lives which need making ready.

THIRD SUNDAY OF ADVENT

Thought for the day

Great expectations. Jesus fulfils the great statements of prophecy.

Reflection on the readings

Isaiah 35:1-6, 10
Psalm 145:6-10
James 5:7-10
Matthew 11:2-11

John the Baptist's task had been to prepare people for the coming of the Messiah, and that placed him, with all the prophets before him, in the age before the coming of the kingdom. We recall how John had urged people to sort out their lives, stressing the possibility of judgement as the all-seeing God came among his people in person, and it is easy to see how John's enthusiasm had polished his hopes into a specific shape. This is something we are all prone to do.

While it helped the urgency and focus of John's message, the side effect was that when Jesus' ministry started to look different from his expectation John began to wonder if he'd been mistaken. The frustration and suffering of his imprisonment must have added to the undermining negatives.

What Jesus does is hold up the Isaiah prophecy as a checklist. If these signs of the kingdom are indeed happening, then John can trust that the promised Saviour is indeed at work, even if the style of his ministry is different from what he had imagined. It's all to do with our expectations. If we get into the way of fleshing these out completely through our imagination, we may find that we don't recognise the real thing when we see it.

So it is as well to stay flexible, holding on to what we do know for certain and keeping our minds open about the details. This is true for us when we try to imagine God, heaven, or the end of all things. They may look like the paintings and frescoes of the Old Masters, and they may not. We mustn't let our expectations become stunted or narrowed by a particular artist's impression. That is what happened when people expected the astronauts to see God above the clouds and were disappointed. Our great expectations of God will be fulfilled far in excess of anything we might imagine and entirely in keeping with his nature.

Discussion starters

1. Look at the 'checklist' of Isaiah 35:1-6, 10. What kind of kingdom does this suggest, and how does it differ from what John the Baptist was preaching in last Sunday's Gospel passage (Matthew 3:1-12)?

2. How do we sometimes limit God by our narrow expectations?

All-stage talk

Beforehand wrap some objects as presents. Some should be obvious, such as a tennis racket, a balloon and a bottle of wine. Others should be harder to guess from the shape, such as a boxed toy and a book.

Display the wrapped presents, and talk about the way Christmas is getting nearer and we're all getting our presents ready. Perhaps some of us are really hoping for a particular present, even though we know it's the thought that counts and we'll be happy with whatever we get because it means someone has thought of us.

Draw attention to the wrapped presents you have brought in, and pick up the first group of obvious presents, asking people to guess what is inside. Then go on to the second group, discovering that some things are harder to guess – we might look at the parcel and expect something completely different to be inside.

John the Baptist knew that God was coming to his people, and he had done a good job of getting them ready. But exactly how this would happen was like a wrapped present – still hidden from view because it hadn't happened yet. Perhaps John was expecting Jesus to be more of a mighty warrior, judging everyone and destroying those who didn't make the grade.

What *did* Jesus do? We heard about it in the first reading from the prophet Isaiah: he was going around healing the sick, making the deaf hear again, the blind see again and the lame walk again. He was letting the weak and downtrodden know that God was on their side and loved them.

Once Jesus pointed out that he was doing these things, John could see that it really did fit in with the 'shape' he had been expecting, even though it wasn't quite the same, rather like our wrapped-up bottle of red wine which we had perhaps been expecting to be white wine, or sherry. Or like the boxed game that you might have expected to be 'Guess Who' and it turned out to be 'Mr Pop'.

As we wrap our presents, let's remember that God's ways are often hidden and unexpected – he is a God who sometimes takes us by surprise. But the surprises will always be true to his good and loving nature.

All-age ideas

- On banners or posters have the words of Isaiah 35:1-6, 10 celebrated and decorated, so that the very building proclaims them.

- The Isaiah reading contains wonderful poetry. Think how best to bring this out; you could try choral reading, or a combination of reading and music to give the words 'soaking in' time.

Prayer of the Faithful

Celebrant
Knowing that our God loves us and listens,
let us pray to him now.

Reader
Lord, your Church is so full of possibility
and yet so vulnerable;
it is so urgently needed by our world
and yet often so weak;

strengthen each member of the body
and increase our sense of expectation
so that we live with your life.

Silence

Faithful God:
you are the rock we stand on.

Lord, in our constantly changing world,
with its shifting values
and fragile ecological balance,
root us deeply in your unchanging nature
of mercy, goodness, faithfulness and love.

Silence

Faithful God:
you are the rock we stand on.

Lord, we welcome you into our homes,
our streets, and our communities;
where we are blind to your presence,
give us sight;
in the ordinary and the remarkable,
help us to recognise our true and living God.

Silence

Faithful God:
you are the rock we stand on.

Lord, all the needs of your children
are known to you;
with God-given love we bring to mind
those who are suffering physically,
spiritually or emotionally,
that they may find you there beside them
in these dark and painful times.

Silence

Faithful God:
you are the rock we stand on.

Lord, to whom eternity is natural,
help us to realise
that time is not the whole story,
and welcome into your kingdom
those who have lived this life in your company
and have now passed through death;
comfort those of us here
whose hearts are heavy with grieving.

Silence

Faithful God:
you are the rock we stand on.

As we open our hearts to receive Jesus,
we remember Mary's receptive love,
and make our prayer with her:
Hail, Mary . . .

In the silence of our hearts
we pray to our heavenly Father
about our own particular concerns.

Silence

Celebrant
Lord, we ask you to hear these prayers
for the sake of Jesus, our Saviour.
Amen.

TREASURE SEEKERS

Aim: To know that God is more wonderful than we can ever imagine, and to continue getting ready for Christmas.

Starter

Pass the parcel. Inside is a giant balloon, ready to be blown up, with the word 'God' written on it (OHP pens work well). During the game play or sing *Our God is so great* or *Think big*.

Teaching

Tell the children what it says on the balloon, and talk about how small the balloon and the word are at the moment. Is God really small and unimportant like this? No! God is the one who made the world and everything in it. (Start to blow up the balloon.)

Is that all? No! God is the one who knows and loves each of us by name. (Blow up the balloon some more.)

Is that all? What else do we know about the one true God? Collect their suggestions, making the balloon bigger with each one. Add other characteristics yourself:

- He's always ready to listen to us.
- Jesus came to show us how kind and loving he is.
- He helps us when we are sad or ill or frightened.
- He has always been alive and always will be.
- He helps us to be kind and loving and fair.

At each quality, inflate the balloon so that it is huge, and draw attention to how big God's name is now. Our God is more powerful and wonderful and loving and kind than we can ever imagine, and yet he wants to be friends with us! And he's the best friend you could ever hope to have, because he loves you, and is always there for you and will never let you down.

Praying

Our God is so big,
so strong and so mighty,
there's nothing our God cannot do! Amen.

Activities

Using the net below as a guide, cut out the shapes for the boxes from coloured paper. Help the children to assemble the boxes as shown, and place their models from last week inside, talking about what they represent and how their 'present' for Jesus is going. Encourage them in what they are doing.

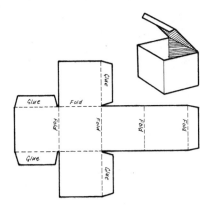

PEARL DIVERS

Aim: For the children to learn to expect and allow God to be himself.

Starter

Sit in a circle. In turn each person goes into the middle and says who they are in a special way. (Or they can go in pairs or threes.) They might dance it, score a pretend goal with it, shout it, sing it, or whisper it, drive or bounce it. We're all different and can enjoy one another's different characters.

Teaching

Sit John the Baptist in prison with his back to everyone. He is discreetly blowing bubbles. The story teller explains that he is thinking as he sits in the prison. Can they see his thought bubbles? Have some of his thoughts written on thought-bubble shapes of card, and have them held up over his head in turn as they are mentioned. For example:

- 'Can Jesus be the one we're waiting for?'
- 'He's making friends with sinners instead of judging them!'
- 'He isn't as strict as I expected.'
- 'Jesus isn't behaving the way I thought he would.'

Now get some of John's friends to visit him, so John can ask them to go to Jesus and find out if he really is the Messiah. The friends agree and walk over to Jesus who is healing a small group of people and chatting to them. They ask their question: 'Are you God's Messiah, the one we're waiting to come and save us, or not?'

At this point ask the children what they think Jesus might say. Then go back to the action, to find out what he actually said: 'Look at what I'm doing.' The people around him say what Jesus has done for them: one was blind and can now see, one was deaf and can now hear, one was lame and can now run and jump, and some have been cheered up by being told how much God loves them.

Hold up a large question mark shape. From the evidence, is Jesus the promised Saviour? Put down the question mark and show a large exclamation mark instead. Yes, he is!

Praying

Lord,
help me
to recognise you today. Amen.

Activities

The sheet enables them to take John the Baptist's question, and link it with Jesus' answer. You will need a stapler and the younger children will need help with the cutting out. For some the tricky cutting could be done beforehand.

GOLD PANNERS

Aim: To recognise that God sometimes takes us by surprise, especially when our idea of him has been too narrow.

Starter

Play twister, where you have to be quite flexible to bend into the right positions. Or try some simple yoga exercises designed to make you flexible and supple.

Teaching

It isn't only our bodies which can be stiff and unbending. Spiritually we also need to be flexible, so we're ready to see God at work in ways we might not expect.

Read the Isaiah passage, making note of the 'marks of the kingdom' in the prophecy. Then go through the list, thinking of how Jesus behaved when he lived on earth many years after Isaiah's prophecy. Tick the things Jesus fulfilled. Now read the Gospel, as far as verse three. Why did John have these doubts, when it was John who had prepared the way for Jesus' coming?

Discuss their ideas, and refer to last week's reading – Matthew 3:12 – to see what kind of Messiah John seems to have been expecting. How might that expectation have caused the doubts to come into his mind? Carry on reading today's Gospel to see how Jesus replied to John.

Praying

My soul glorifies the Lord
and my spirit rejoices
in God my Saviour . . .
for the Mighty One has done
great things for me –
holy is his Name!

(From Mary's song)

Activities

In Advent we are getting ourselves into a state of readiness, and that means being flexible. Some of the group may enjoy putting some flexible exercises to a song about God being greater than we can ever imagine – for example, *Lord Jesus Christ*. The work-sheet also encourages some flexible thinking.

FOURTH SUNDAY OF ADVENT

Thought for the day

Through the willing participation of Mary and Joseph, God is poised to come among his people as their Saviour.

Reflection on the readings

Isaiah 7:10-14
Psalm 23:1-6
Romans 1:1-7
Matthew 1:18-25

Matthew, writing for a Hebrew audience, is keen to show the Jewish people that Jesus is indeed the promised Messiah. He draws attention to Isaiah's prophecy spoken to King Ahaz, and sets out Jesus' credentials. Through Joseph, Jesus is a descendant of King David; through Mary, this son, born to a virgin, fulfils the ancient prophecy and turns out to be 'Immanuel' or 'God with us'.

It is not unusual for prophecies about short-term, immediate events to turn out to have resonances far in excess of their original meaning. One familiar example is the call to St Francis to 'repair my Church, which is in ruins'. It was far more than one stone chapel which was eventually 'repaired'; the whole Church of God became refreshed and invigorated.

The expectant atmosphere of today's readings attunes us to God's way of orchestrating events and working in co-operation with his people. The stage is set, the timing is right, and the focused light of all the hopes and longings of generations is about to shine out in the person of Jesus. Typically, we find God delighting in using the ordinariness of good people so that extraordinary things can be accomplished. Typically, he allows individual people to know their own part in the action exactly as and when they need to know it.

It is because Joseph is expecting God to be God that he is prepared to alter his sensible and considerate plan to make no loud accusations about Mary when divorcing her for assumed unfaithfulness. Whatever that dream was, it made him think again. Perhaps Mary had tried to tell him the truth and he hadn't been able to believe her before. We can only guess at how Mary felt before Joseph changed his mind.

God will still speak to us through our dreams, memories and feelings, if only we take the trouble to notice. They can often be our own personal parables, able to put us in touch with our true selves; enabling us to recognise God's ways forward which we haven't been able to see before.

Discussion starters

1. What methods have you noticed God using to alert people to repentance or to a new and better way of dealing with a difficult situation?

2. How can the transcendent God work in partner-ship with ordinary people? Where have you seen this happening?

All-stage talk

Ask for two volunteers. Stand one on a chair and have the other lie down on the floor. Talk with the volunteers about what they can see from their particular viewpoint. Although nothing else in the church has changed, the descriptions will be different because of where the volunteers are.

You could also suggest that everyone looks at something central, first through one eye and then the other. They can then all notice the change of view even when looking out from the same head!

What our readings today are reminding us is that we need to get into the habit of looking at everything from God's point of view. What we then see may sometimes come as a surprise to us, because we are so used to looking from our own point of view. Take Joseph, for instance. He was in for a surprise. He thought he had worked out the kindest way of dealing with the embarrassing problem of Mary expecting a baby before they were married. He had it all worked out. He'd divorce Mary without a big fuss, so that she needn't be noticed too much.

But through the dream God helped him look at things from another point of view. Joseph saw that Mary's baby was all part of God's plan, and, rather than divorcing her, he had an important job to do – to look after Mary and this very special baby. Joseph must have been a very brave man, as well as a good and kind one. He knew people would think he was stupid; perhaps they would stop being friends with him; his life would never be nice and straightforward again. But he did that brave, good thing because he had seen the situation from God's point of view and was happy to go along with that.

It was the same with Mary. If she had only seen the angel's message from her own point of view she might have refused to go along with God's plan, which was bound to turn her own hopes and dreams upside down. But she saw it from God's point of view – that the people of our earth needed a Saviour; God needed to be born as a human baby so he could rescue humans as an insider. And a baby needed a mum. So she agreed and that made Christmas possible.

All-age ideas

- Use nativity play costumes and dress people up as Joseph and Mary, who can then mime the actions as the Gospel is read.

Prayer of the Faithful

Celebrant
Let us quieten ourselves to notice our God,
here with us now,
who is attentive to our deepest needs.

Reader
Lord, we long for our Church,
in its life and activity,
to be attentive to you,
and ready to go wherever you suggest.
Show us the work of the Church
from your point of view,
and develop our will to co-operate.

Silence

We call on your name, O God:
restore us and revive us.

Lord, we long for your kingdom
to come in our world,
and to flood with truth and love
the disillusion, hopelessness and terror
which traps the human spirit
and chokes its potential joy.

Silence

We call on your name, O God:
restore us and revive us.

Lord, come into the daily relationships
we so easily take for granted,
and enable us to value one another,
delighting in one another's richness,
and responding to one another's needs with love.

Silence

We call on your name, O God:
restore us and revive us.

Lord, you know the need and pain
of those we love and worry about.
As you look after them,
give them the sense of your caring presence
to uphold and sustain them.

Silence

We call on your name, O God:
restore us and revive us.

Lord, for us death can seem so cruel;
give us a better understanding of eternity,
and gather into your kingdom all those
whose earthly journey has come to an end.

Silence

We call on your name, O God:
restore us and revive us.

With Mary,
in whom the promise of the prophets
was fulfilled,
we make our prayer in hope and faith:
Hail, Mary . . .

Upheld by God's peace,
we pray now in silence
for any who specially need our prayers.

Silence

Celebrant
Father, we ask you to accept our prayers
through Jesus Christ, our Saviour.
Amen.

TREASURE SEEKERS

Aim: To see that we can help God.

Starter

Have a selection of jigsaws and other puzzles that the children can work on together, with the leader encouraging everyone to help each other.

Teaching

Draw attention to the way we all helped each other, and how good that was. Talk about what people say when they are asked to help with something. Sometimes they say things like:

'No, I don't want to.'

'No, I'm too busy.'

'No, it's too hard.'

(You could use different toys or puppets to say these things.)

Sometimes when people are asked to help they say things like:

'Yes, I'd love to.'

'Yes, I'll do that for you.'

'Yes, it sounds hard but I'll do my best.'

God needed some help for his plan to save his people. He asked Mary to help him by being Jesus' mum. He asked Joseph to help him by looking after Mary and the baby Jesus. Mary and Joseph could have said, 'No, I don't want to' (and the other refusals). The children can join in, doing the thumbs-down sign each time. But they didn't say that! They said 'Yes!' (thumbs up). So God got the help he needed, and Jesus came into the world at the first Christmas to save us and set us free.

Praying

Dear God,
when you want someone to help,
ask me.
I don't want to say 'No!' *(thumbs down)*
I want to say 'Yes!' *(thumbs up)*
Amen.

Activities

This week we are making the wrapping paper to wrap our present to God. Remind the children of their models, and print some paper with stencils or shapes dipped in paint. Wrap the box which can

then be offered to God on Christmas Day. Encourage the children to keep up their resolution and offer God what they have tried their best to do. On the worksheet there is a picture to colour of Mary and Joseph going into Bethlehem.

PEARL DIVERS

Aim: To learn about the events leading up to Christmas from Joseph's point of view.

Starter

All change. Everyone sits in a circle and is given a number. The leader calls out any two numbers (or throws them on two dice) and these people have to change places. When the leader calls out, 'Calculator!' everyone changes places.

Teaching

In the game we all had to keep changing places. Today we are going to hear about the way Joseph had to cope with some big changes in his life.

Dress two of the children up as Joseph and Mary, and let the others work out who they are. At each 'scene' display a logo, based on the drawings below.

Scene 1: Mary's news

Have Mary and Joseph sitting together talking, and explain how one day Mary, who was going to marry Joseph, met him and told him she was going to have a child – an angel had come to tell her about it and now she was expecting the baby, which would be God's Son.

Scene 2: Help!

Joseph went off on his own and thought about it. He wasn't certain about Mary's story as it sounded so strange. So he decided to divorce her without a big fuss, to make it easier for her.

Scene 3: Sweet dreams

Joseph went home and got into bed. He lay and worried about Mary and the baby, and then he fell asleep. He had a dream in which he felt God was telling him it was fine to marry Mary and look after her and the baby.

Scene 4: Joseph woke up and remembered his dream

Suddenly he wasn't worried any more. Never mind if his friends thought him wrong and stupid – he knew that God really had used Mary to help him in his plan and now God wanted to use him as well. Joseph was needed to work with God in loving Mary and Jesus and looking after them both very carefully. Joseph told God he was happy to do it.

Scene 5: Joseph went to find Mary

He told her that he definitely believed her now, and would like to marry her straightaway!

Praying

Here I am, Lord,
ready to work with you
however you like.
Lead on and I'll follow! Amen.

Activities

On the worksheet there is an activity to help them 'reflect' on today's teaching, using a mirror. They can also create a collage for the children's area in church which shows Joseph and Mary on their way to Bethlehem. Use your own ideas or the outline suggested in the drawing below.

GOLD PANNERS

Aim: To look at the way God enjoys co-operating with us.

Starter

Body shapes. The whole group co-operates to create a shape which the leader calls out. Then they change to another shape. Shape ideas: Make yourselves into a comb/a centipede/a roundabout/a mug/an electric plug.

Teaching

Talk about the way we needed to co-operate to create those amazing shapes out of bodies. God likes to co-operate with his people to bring about all kinds of good; today we are going to look at how Joseph and Mary co-operated with God so that his plan to save us could take place.

Read the Isaiah passage together, and draw attention to the hopes for rescue and the signs which Matthew later picked up as he looked at Jesus' birth. Now read the first part of the Gospel, up to the point that Joseph has decided the most honourable way to act in the circumstances. Ask them to restate this situation in their own language, and record this on a chart. Point out that, for an honourable man of that time, there was not a viable alternative to divorce; the problem for Joseph was whether to make a great fuss of Mary's assumed unfaithfulness and have her publicly stoned, in order to clear his own name, or whether to take the braver step of divorcing her quietly, without making any accusations or voicing his righteous indignation.

Then read the rest of the Gospel, and together try to build up a picture of Joseph going to bed worried by what Mary has told him and the effect of the dream on him.

Praying

Lord Jesus Christ,
you have no body on earth but ours,
no hands but ours,
no feet but ours.
Ours are the eyes through which
your compassion must look out on the world.
Ours are the feet by which
you may still go about doing good.
Ours are the hands with which
you bless people now.
Bless our minds and bodies,
that we may be a blessing to others.

(Based on a prayer of St Teresa of Avila)

Activities

On the worksheet there are some examples of people working in co-operation with God, which can lead into discussion about their own willingness to be available to God's possibilities, both individually and as a church.

CHRISTMAS

CHRISTMAS DAY

Thought for the day

The Word of God is made flesh. In the birth of Jesus we see God expressed in human terms.

Reflection on the readings

Isaiah 52:7-10
Psalm 97:1-6
Hebrews 1:1-6
John 1:1-18

The well-loved reading from Isaiah resounds with hope. It is not wishful thinking, talking about impossible dreams, but rings with utter surety that God has revealed to his attentive prophet, so that the good news can be shared with all the people of Israel. There is a great sense of excitement, like the stirring in a great crowd as word gets round that the famous and adored person they have been waiting for is about to arrive. Today God has arrived in person to live with the people of his creation, sharing their humanity in order to save them.

The writer of Hebrews chooses this to introduce his whole teaching: in the past God had spoken through his prophets, but from the Incarnation onwards we are looking at an entirely new and dynamic experience, as God speaks to us in person, through Jesus, the Son of God.

The introduction to John's Gospel helps us to see the extraordinary depth of the meaning of God's 'Word', flinging us back to the emerging creation from chaos, and forward to the streams of people through the generations who choose to receive the light of God's life to transform them and the world they inhabit. Stretched out across it all is the person of Jesus, expressing God's creative and redeeming love in a way we, as humans, can understand. No darkness can ever extinguish the hope of this light.

Discussion starters

1. Do our own words – as individuals, as a society and as the Church – express God's love? What kind of things do, and what should we aim to change?

2. As you look back over the last year, can you discern Jesus' grace and truth? What are you particularly thankful to God for?

All-stage talk

Begin by getting different people to say, 'Happy Christmas, everyone!' in whatever way they like. A group of friends might like to shout it together; someone might like to stand at the front; others will choose to say it quietly to their neighbour.

Point out how all the 'Happy Christmas!' messages are much appreciated, and they all show the wonderful way we're all different. You don't have to be a particular sort of person to be a Christian. The only sort of person you have to be is yourself! God loves you that way.

Today we've been expressing ourselves when we spoke our Christmas messages, and Christmas is about God expressing himself: Jesus being born as a human baby is God saying to all of us, 'I love you!'

All-age ideas

- Gather the collection in a model manger (made from a box and filled with straw) and use different age groups to do the collecting.

- Ask everyone to bring bells and ring them at the Gloria.

- Gather the children round the crib during the intercessions.

Prayer of the Faithful

Celebrant
As we celebrate the birth of Jesus, the Word of God, let us pray with thankful hearts.

Reader
The bells and lights and presents and decorations
in church and in our homes
express our thanks to you, Lord,
for coming into the world in person.

Silence

On this Christmas Day we want to say:
Thank you, holy God!

The world Jesus was born into
was the world we know,
a world of dangers and risks.
We thank you
for sharing our human weakness
in order to save us.

Silence

On this Christmas Day we want to say:
Thank you, holy God!

Many of us will be celebrating
with our families and friends.
Be with us, Lord, in all the festivities,
and teach us true loving.

Silence

On this Christmas Day we want to say:
Thank you, holy God!

We pray for those who find Christmas
a sad or lonely season;
we pray for those for whom
it brings to the surface
memories, anxieties or dangers.
Through good and difficult times
we ask you to be with us always.

Silence

On this Christmas Day we want to say:
Thank you, holy God!

We pray for those
whose loved ones have died,
and all those who have finished
with earthly celebrations.
May they celebrate with you
and all the angels of heaven.

Silence

On this Christmas Day we want to say:
Thank you, holy God!

Encouraged by Mary's example of love,
we join our prayers with hers:
Hail, Mary . . .

We pray in silence, now,
for our own particular needs and concerns.

Silence

Celebrant
Father, with thanks and joy
we offer these prayers
through Jesus our Saviour.
Amen.

TREASURE SEEKERS, PEARL DIVERS AND GOLD PANNERS

It is important that children, young people and adults worship together for a festival such as Christmas. Involve all age groups in the singing and playing of carols, and in the other ministries of welcoming, serving, collection of gifts and so on. Have nativity toys for the very young to play with, such as knitted Mary, Joseph and Jesus, sheep and shepherds. There are pictures to colour on the Treasure Seekers and Pearl Divers worksheets, but there is no worksheet for Gold Panners. Instead, involve the young people in some of the planning of the service and in decorating the church.

FIRST SUNDAY OF CHRISTMAS: THE HOLY FAMILY

Thought for the day

Jesus, the expression of God's love, lives as a vulnerable boy in the real and dangerous world we all inhabit.

Reflection on the readings

Ecclesiasticus* 3:2-6, 12-14 (* also called Sirach)
Psalm 127:1-5
Colossians 3:12-21
Matthew 2:13-15, 19-23

One of the truths recognised in our readings today is that the work of redemption cannot be done at arm's length. No rescue operation can be carried out successfully without someone being prepared to brave the dangers and go in to share the conditions of those who need rescuing; only by being this close can the rescuer bring the trapped to freedom. It is in the person of Jesus, born into the human condition to live a human life with human temptations and dangers, that the possibility of such a rescue becomes a practical reality.

There is a wonderful sense at this time of the entire created world welcoming God's creative Word, and the special link Jesus has with the rest of us. We share flesh and blood with the incarnate One – God made human. And the side effects of that involvement are itemised clearly in the events following Jesus' birth, as told by Matthew. Although the Christmas cards usually show an idyllic scene of peace and joy, the real and dangerous world we all know is just outside the stable door.

In today's Gospel we find that Jesus has been born into our familiar world of ruthless ambition, cruelty and despair, of rejection and wandering, of isolation and fear. It reminds us that our God does not hold himself remote from our sufferings but is part of them, prepared to share with us the vulnerability of a baby refugee, bundled up in the night and taken off to a strange country in a life and death situation. It is God's willingness to be utterly immanent that means we really can trust him through the searing pain of life as well as its light and comfortable times.

Joseph gives us an inspiring example of committed attentiveness to God's leading, so that God can use his gifts of practical and efficient organisation to keep this child and his mother safe.

Discussion starters

1. From the reading of today's Gospel, what kind of person does Joseph seem to be, and what can we learn from him that might help us in dealing with crises in our own lives?

2. What was the advantage of Jesus being born as a human baby, rather than appearing as an adult to save the world?

All-stage talk

If you have a member of the congregation whose job involves rescue (for example in the fire, ambulance, lifeboat or mountain rescue services), ask if they would be willing to take part in a brief interview before the talk. Talk with them about the kind of dangers they themselves have to accept in order to rescue people, and the way they get alongside the people who need rescuing in order to help them. If you are not having a live interview, talk briefly about these rescuers.

Explain how Jesus is a rescuer, who comes in person to save us and help us. Stand someone on a paper island in the middle of a flood. God doesn't stand a long way off and shout to us. (Stand a long way off and shout to them to get into a boat and sail away.) That's no good, because the person feeling drowned by sadness or guilt or evil can't do what you are shouting even if they wanted to. We can't rescue ourselves; only God can set us free by accepting us, loving us and forgiving us. So instead of being a long way off and telling us what to do, God came in person to rescue us. (Pretend to row over to the person and then rescue them.) That's what happened at Christmas – God came to live among us in the person of Jesus, and he is still with us now. We are all his brothers and sisters.

All-age ideas

• Have the first reading read by a parent who is carrying a young child.

• During the Gospel, have the holy family moving from one place to another, settling down, and then setting off again.

• Have a collection of money or gifts for homeless families or refugees, with some pictures and figures to help people understand the problems experienced.

Prayer of the Faithful

Celebrant
Let us pray to the God who travels with us
in all our celebrations and tragedies,
and understands what it is like to be human.

Reader
As we celebrate Christmas,
when the Word of God became flesh,
we pray for the Church, the Body of Christ.
May we be so filled with God's loving life
that our actions touch the world with hope
which lasts even when
Christmas decorations are put away.

Silence

Thank you, Lord God:
for coming to save us.

As the world is reminded of love and peace
in the words of the carols,
may the reality of a God who loves us so much
transform our social and political thinking,
and energise our plans and negotiations.

Silence

Thank you, Lord God:
for coming to save us.

As Christmas brings together
family members and friends,
and we make contact with those
we seldom meet,
may all our relationships be nourished
with love and forgiveness,
and may we value one another more.

Silence

Thank you, Lord God:
for coming to save us.

We remember all who are forced to escape
from their homes, and live without security;
we think particularly of those with young children
who are homeless or in danger.

Silence

Thank you, Lord God:
for coming to save us.

We pray for those whose earthly journey
has come to an end,
and those who have tended them during their dying;
we pray for those who have died through violence,
and for those who have much to forgive.

Silence

Thank you, Lord God:
for coming to save us.

With Mary,
who mothered the Son of God,
we make our prayer:
Hail, Mary . . .

In silence which God our Father
fills with accepting love,
we name those we know
who are in any particular need.

Silence

Celebrant
Heavenly Father,
we ask you to accept these prayers
for the sake of Jesus, your Son.
Amen.

TREASURE SEEKERS

Aim: To know that Joseph worked with God to keep his family safe.

Starter

Sharks! Scatter some random shapes of newspaper around on the floor to be islands. When the music is playing everyone swims around in the sea enjoying themselves. When the music stops, and the leader calls out, 'Watch out – sharks about!' everyone swims to the safety of an island and stands there until the all-clear, when the music starts again.

Teaching

Talk about how we had to go where it was safe, when we were in danger from the sharks. People who love us look after us to make sure we are safe. We look after those we love (both people and animals) to make sure they are safe. God loves to see us all looking after one another like this, because he loves all of us.

Let the children give some examples of ways people look after them to make sure they are safe, such as marking a yellow line on the station platform to stand behind, belting us up in the car, and helping us to cross the road. When people check that we have warm clothes to go out in, and that we are getting enough sleep, or when they tell us off for doing something dangerous, they are showing their love by looking after us!

God made sure Jesus was as safe as possible in the dangerous world by having Joseph and Mary to look after him. How would they do that? As well as all the usual ways, they had some big dangers to cope with. One night, God told Joseph that King Herod was out looking for Jesus so that he could kill him. So Joseph got up in the middle of the night. He packed up some food and clothes and strapped them on the sleepy donkey. Then he woke Mary up.

'Mary! Wake up! Jesus is in danger. We'll have to leave Bethlehem and go where he will be safe. Come on!'

Mary and Joseph crept around as quietly as they could so that no one would hear them going. They wrapped Jesus up and hoped he wouldn't wake up and cry. They walked through the dark streets, very frightened, and when they left the town they walked on and on through the hills. Jesus woke up and still they walked on, for several days, until at last they got to Egypt, where they knew they were safe. King Herod couldn't come after Jesus there. They only went back home when they heard that King Herod had died.

Praying

God bless my family.
Look after us all.
Help us look after each other.
In life and death
keep us safe for ever. Amen.

Activities

Using upturned bowls and a large cloth, sheet or towel, make a model of the landscape. Using a cut-out picture of Mary, Jesus and Joseph, based on the one on the worksheet, all the children can have a go at taking the family to safety.

PEARL DIVERS

Aim: To get to know the events of Matthew's account of Jesus' birth and the escape into Egypt.

Starter

Shh! Sit in a circle with one person blindfolded in the centre. Someone starts to walk around the circle carrying something noisy, such as a bunch of keys. The person in the centre tries to hear where they are. If they point to the right place, they get to carry the keys and someone else is blindfolded.

Teaching

Tell the escape story from today's Gospel with everyone making the sound effects and miming the actions. Everyone lies asleep, wakes up, yawns, listens, packs secretly, opens and closes the door very carefully, walks through the town without making any noise at all, looks around whenever there's a noise in case it's Herod, and shouts 'Yes!' when they eventually reach Egypt. Show them on a map where Bethlehem is in relation to Egypt, and then trace the return journey, reading from Matthew the reason given for not returning to Bethlehem.

Praying

Lord, keep us safe
as we travel through life.
Help us to love what is good
and hate what is evil. Amen.

Activities

On the sheet there are instructions for making a travelling game, which they can then play. They will need card and a dice for each game.

GOLD PANNERS

Aim: To understand the risk God was prepared to take in coming to save us.

Starter

Rescue! Play this game in which someone needs rescuing from a magic castle. (This is a chair with a length of rope on the floor encircling it.) The only way to break the evil magic is to get the key which fits the lock. (This is a rectangle of card from which a key shape has been cut. The key has been cut into several pieces. When the group has collected all the pieces the completed key should fit the card shape.) Hide the pieces around the building, and pass a dice round the group. When anyone throws a six they can go hunting for a piece of the key.

Teaching

We know that God loves his people and really wants to look after them and save them. But, bearing in mind that we were all created with free will – we are free to choose either good or evil – what are the risks involved if God comes in person to save the world? Make a note of their ideas.

Now read today's Gospel, looking out for the risks and dangers. Make a note of these too. Through Joseph and Mary working with God, the baby is kept safe, at least for the moment. What happened when he grew up? Was the risk worth taking if Jesus was going to end up being put to death? Again, make a note of their ideas.

The risks were worth taking because it meant

that through becoming human and sharing human experiences, Jesus could really help us and save us, even though it meant that he had to suffer death in the process.

Praying

Thank you, Lord Jesus,
for coming to share our human lives.
Dying, you destroyed our death.
Rising, you restored our life.
Lord Jesus, come again in glory.

Activities

On the sheet there is a map which traces the journey taken to Egypt and back to Nazareth, and they can look up the references Matthew uses to show the Jewish readers how Jesus was fulfilling their ancient prophecies. These references will be needed for them to complete a crossword puzzle.

SECOND SUNDAY OF CHRISTMAS

Thought for the day

The grace and truth revealed in Jesus show God's freely given love; through Jesus, God pours out his blessings on us and gives us real freedom.

Reflection on the readings

Ecclesiasticus 24:1-4, 12-16
Psalm 147:12-15, 19-20
Ephesians 1:3-6, 15-18
John 1:1-18

It is an amazing thought that there was never a time for God when he was not yearning for all his creation to be brought into a close, loving relationship as family members. There is the breathtaking cosmic breadth of such a harmony, and at the same time the intimate, personal invitation to each person throughout all time and space. Even as our world was forming, God was longing for you and me and our loved ones to be his own sons and daughters, enjoying his love and responding to it.

The moment of Incarnation, which we celebrate at Christmas, marks a new stage in the journey towards the fulfilment of that longing and out-reach. As Jesus, in the ordinary, messy process of childbirth, emerges into the world of human existence, the possibility is there for our salvation. The Law, given through Moses, was of great value, but with Jesus we have what the Law could never give – God's freely given grace in a totally loving human life, to sort out our sin once and for all.

Mary and Joseph were happy to receive this child into their home and their lives, and the receiving was very costly. There have always been many who consider that receiving Jesus Christ into their lives is too costly and they are not prepared to make that commitment. It is right that we sit down and count the cost before committing ourselves, and it is true that receiving Jesus is likely to be disruptive and is, in worldly terms, complete foolishness.

Paradoxically, receiving Jesus is also the way to such blessings and freedom of spirit that those who have taken the plunge would not have anything any different. Living in that close relationship with the God who is Father, Son and Spirit, allows us into a completely new dimension of living; quite apart from all the many blessings and joys, there is the underlying sense of it being profoundly good and right and true, and the place we were created to live in.

Discussion starters

1. What has or would it cost you to receive Jesus into your daily living, your work, leisure, politics, finances and popularity?

2. Is it worth it?

All-stage talk

Bring something with you to offer as a small gift – a chocolate bar, a sticker, a few flowers or a piece of fruit, perhaps.

Over Christmas we have all been busy giving one another presents. Explain that you have brought something with you to give away today, so that we can understand a bit more about God's Christmas present to us. In Jesus we see God giving himself to set us free from sin and evil because he loves us so much.

Show everyone what your gift is, and ask them to put their hands up if they would like to be considered for it. Choose someone using some random method, such as their name being first in the alphabet, or their birthday coming up this week. When God gives us his present no one has to get left out. Everyone who asks, gets.

Stand a short distance away from the person chosen, and hold out the gift. Can they receive the gift without moving? No, they can't. If we are going to receive a gift we have to change our position a bit. (The person can demonstrate this and receive

the gift.) It's the same with us all receiving God's gift – we are bound to change if we receive Jesus into our daily living.

Just as Joseph and Mary's lives changed when Jesus was born into their family, so our lives will change. As we reach out to receive Jesus, we shall find we are able to reach out to one another in a more loving, positive way; we shall find we are more concerned about justice and mercy being written into our social system; we shall find we are wanting to be more truthful to others and ourselves.

So be prepared – if you don't want to change into a happier, more loving person, freed from guilt and able to be truly yourself, then don't take God up on his offer!

All-age ideas

- At the same time as the collection plate is passed around, have a basket of coloured shapes with the reference to John 3:16 written on them. These are given to everyone, so that they are given a message which they can then decide to receive.

- Just before the Gospel is read, have a single candle carried by a young child ahead of the Bible, or book of readings, into the centre of the congregation.

Prayer of the Faithful

Celebrant
Let us settle ourselves in the stillness of God's peace as we pray.

Reader
Lord, may the Church always be open
to the flood of your love.
Wash away all but what is
constructed out of your love
and built on your foundations.

Silence

O come:
let us adore.

Lord, may our world become sensitised
to hear the whispered voice
of your love;
may we honour your creation
and value one another
as you value us.

Silence

O come:
let us adore.

Lord, may we receive you
into our homes and families,

our shops, schools and places of work;
may we receive you into our conflicts,
our arguments and our expectations.

Silence

O come:
let us adore.

Lord, even as we thank you
for giving us free will,
we pray for those suffering
as a tragic result of wrong choices.
May they experience
your upholding and healing
in body and soul.

Silence

O come:
let us adore.

Lord, may those who are journeying
through death to eternity,
be awakened to the everlasting love
of your Presence.

Silence

O come:
let us adore.

We join our prayers with those of Mary,
whose joy at the Incarnation we share:
Hail, Mary . . .

In the silence of God's attentive love,
we pray our private petitions.

Silence

Celebrant
Father, almighty and ever-present,
we commend our prayers to your mercy,
through Christ our Lord.
Amen.

TREASURE SEEKERS

Aim: To know that Jesus is God saying, 'I love you!'

Starter

Show me you're happy! Sit everyone in a circle. Just using their faces, ask them to show you they're happy / sad / in pain / excited / tired, etc.

Teaching

They were so good at showing those feelings that you could tell what they were thinking inside! Our bodies are very useful for helping us tell people how we feel. How can you show your mum, dad, grandma or baby cousin that you love them? How do they show that they love you?

Jesus is God saying, 'I love you!' No one has ever seen God while they are alive on earth. He can't be seen. But in Jesus, being born as a baby, growing up and walking around as an adult, we can see God's love.

Praying

Thank you, Jesus,
for being born
into our world.
Thank you for showing us
God's love. Amen.

Activities

On the worksheet there is a dot-to-dot picture to complete, so that they can see something clearly which they couldn't see before. Have lots of pieces of Christmas wrapping paper, pieces of ribbon and milk-bottle tops to stick on coloured paper to make the suggested collage.

PEARL DIVERS

Aim: To know that Jesus is sometimes known as the Word of God.

Starter

Have a news session, with the children sitting in a circle and passing round a special stone (or Christmas decoration) so that the one holding it can speak while the others listen. This draws attention to the importance of listening to what is spoken, and helps to focus their attention.

Teaching

Point out that we have all been speaking out, or expressing our thoughts. Then tell them you are going to read them something and you want them to listen out for someone speaking, and what the result was of the word they spoke. Read Genesis 1:1-3. See if they can work out that it was through the word God spoke into the darkness that light first appeared and creation could begin to unfold.

Now read them the first three verses from John. Can they spot the same idea? Show a picture from a Christmas card of the Nativity and ask them a really difficult question to get their brains going: Which person in this picture spoke out, or expressed God's love for us all? The one who did this completely was the baby in the manger – Jesus! So in a way, as St John says, Jesus is the Word of God. He is God speaking out his love to us all.

Make them feel very impressed with themselves because today they have been doing a spot of something called Theology, and they've done it very well!

Praying

Word of the Father,
now in flesh appearing.
O come, let us adore him,
Christ the Lord. Amen.

Activities

Using the guidelines on the sheet and a variety of felt-tips or coloured pencils, they will be writing out the first half of John 1:14 and decorating it to display. There is also a puzzle to help them look at what the word 'word' can mean.

GOLD PANNERS

Aim: To explore the nature of Jesus as the eternal Word.

Starter

One person in the group is given a chart to follow like the one below. This person gives the instructions out so that eventually everyone is arranged on chairs in the way shown on the chart.

Teaching

Discuss the impressive effect of the spoken instructions. Words spoken can bring creative things about. An orchestra or band can play out the ideas in the composer's mind. A book (show some examples) can take you off to other countries or other ages in

your mind, just through the words on the pages. Words have power.

Now read John 1:1-18, checking for meaning as you go along. Link the first three verses with the first few verses of Genesis and help them see the connections. (Pick up on the darkness in which the loving Word brings light; how is that true of both passages?) Draw their thinking together in the last verse: the Son has shown us what God is like. Explain that the Greek word for 'word' (logos) meant any kind of communication, much as we might 'say it with flowers' or describe someone's actions as 'speaking volumes'.

Praying

Word of the Father,
now in flesh appearing.
O come, let us adore him,
Christ the Lord. Amen.

Activities

The worksheet has space to record some of the links between Genesis and John's introduction, and helps them explore the meaning of Jesus as the Word of God.

THE EPIPHANY OF THE LORD

Thought for the day

Jesus, the hope of the nations, is shown to the world.

Reflection on the readings

Isaiah 60:1-6
Psalm 71:1-2, 7-8, 10-13
Ephesians 3:2-3a, 5-6
Matthew 2:1-12

Beginning with one person (Abraham) and developing to embrace one family and eventually one nation, God has painstakingly planted the seed of salvation and nurtured it until the whole earth is involved. Isaiah had sensed that day in terms of a sunrise dawning with the light of day on a world of darkness, with all the hope and joy and relief that a new day can bring after a long, dark night. Probably this was one of the prophecies these magi had read as they studied the signs of the sky and wondered about life's meaning. And perhaps it was then that they felt stirring in them a profound calling to be, in person, those visitors who could symbolise the light dawning on the wider world. Certainly they must have been inspired by a powerful sense of urgency and necessity to make such a journey. And as they travelled, both physically and spiritually, towards Bethlehem, bearing the gifts laid down in those ancient scriptures, perhaps they were drawn by much more than a star. Jesus later proclaimed that anyone who sets out to search always finds.

Paul also knows himself to be commissioned to explain God's nature to the Gentiles. He is overwhelmed by the extraordinary way that the Christ has enabled us to approach the great and awesome God with freedom and confidence – as one of the family. And for all of us who are Gentiles, the feast of the Epiphany is particularly one to celebrate, since it marks the truth that we too are part of God's salvation and can share the light of dawn.

Discussion starters

1. Why did Herod find the prophesied birth threatening, while the magi were excited enough to travel many miles to see this child?

2. The Celtic Christians were very aware that the journey is, in a way, the destination. How is this true?

All-stage talk

Beforehand arrange for a knitter to bring a completed garment to church, together with a ball of wool and needles. Also prepare a large paper cut-out of a similar garment, which is folded up so that the first bit that would be made is the only piece showing. Alternatively use the actual garment, folded up at that point.

Begin by showing everyone the wonderful garment that the knitter has made and asking how long it took to make and who it is for. What did it look like at first, when they started making it? The knitter can show the ball of wool and needles, and do a couple of stitches. Hold up the needles with these stitches and point out that it doesn't look much like a jumper / scarf yet! But the knitter went on working at it, knowing that one day it would be ready.

God knew that one day everything would be ready for Jesus to come into the world, but he, too, took a long time making things ready. He started by calling one person, Abraham. (Show the folded garment, but don't refer to it – it is there to be visual reinforcement of what you are saying.) Over the years God went on to prepare all Abraham's

family. (More of the garment is revealed.) Until over more years that family became one nation. (Reveal some more of the garment.) But God's plan still wasn't finished. He went on to include not one nation but all the nations and everyone in them. (Shake the whole garment out and display it.) Today is called the Epiphany because the word 'epiphany' means 'showing' or 'revealing' or 'manifesting', and when those wise men arrived at Bethlehem with their presents, God was showing or revealing himself not just to Abraham or his family, not just to the whole nation of Israel, but to all the rest of us in the world as well.

Whatever country you come from, whatever you look like and whatever language you speak, God is saying to us today that he is there for you and no one is left out. You don't have to have the right ancestors to know God. You don't have to pass any exams to know God.

We sometimes get so interested in the presents the wise men were bringing to Jesus that we forget what brought them there in the first place. It was God who called these wise men from other nations to be there when Jesus was still a baby, so he could welcome them as well. They were there representing all the nations, so when God welcomed them he was welcoming each of us.

All-age ideas

- Today's Gospel can be acted out, preferably with costumes, as these may well be available from a nativity play. I am not suggesting a full-blown production with hours of rehearsal. All that is needed is a sensitive narrator, and the characters to mime what the narrator says.

- The wise men can take the collection and offer the gifts today. This emphasises their role as representatives of all the nations coming to be welcomed and offer their gifts. A globe can be offered at the same time.

- Have a bowl of burning incense, gold and myrrh arranged among flowers as a display either as people come in or near where they will come to receive communion.

Prayer of the Faithful

Celebrant
We are all companions on a spiritual journey.
As we travel together, let us pray.

Reader
We pray that the worldwide Church
may always be ready
to travel in your way
and in your direction.

Silence

Light of the world:
shine in our darkness.

We pray for the nations
as they live through conflicts
and struggle with identity.
We long for all peoples
to acknowledge the true and living God.

Silence

Light of the world:
shine in our darkness.

We pray for the families and the streets we represent,
asking for a spirit of generous love,
understanding and mutual respect.

Silence

Light of the world:
shine in our darkness.

We pray for all who are finding their way
tedious, lonely or frightening at the moment;
for those who have lost their way
and do not know what to do for the best.

Silence

Light of the world:
shine in our darkness.

We pray for those who have come
to the end of their earthly journey,
and for those who have died unprepared.

Silence

Light of the world:
shine in our darkness.

With Mary, Mother of Jesus,
let us pray:
Hail, Mary . . .

In silence,
as God our Father listens with love,
we name our own particular cares and concerns.

Silence

Celebrant
Heavenly Father,
we ask you to accept these prayers,
through Christ, our Saviour.
Amen.

TREASURE SEEKERS

Aim: To become familiar with the story of the wise men finding Jesus.

Starter

Play 'pass the parcel'. At the different layers have old bus and train tickets. The prize at the end is a star-shaped biscuit.

Teaching

Tell the children that today we are going to hear about a journey. It isn't a bus journey or a car journey or a train journey. This is a camel journey. (All pack your bags and get on your camels.) We are very wise people, but we don't know where we are going. We are looking for a baby king. And we are packing presents for him. (Pack gold, frankincense and myrrh.) Produce a star on a stick as you explain how a special star has started shining in the sky and we are sure it will lead us to the baby king. Lead off behind the star, riding your camels, and pretending to go over high mountains, through water, stopping for the night, and going to sleep and so on. At last you reach the town of Bethlehem (stick up a sign) where you find the baby king with his mum and dad. (Have a large picture, or one of the cribs made before Christmas.) We all get off our camels and give the baby our presents. The baby's name is Jesus and we have found him at last!

Praying

This is a prayer the wise men might have said. We have all been invited to find Jesus as well, so we can say it with them.

Thank you, Jesus,
for inviting me
to come and look for you.
I am glad I have found you! Amen.

Activities

To emphasise that the journey of the wise men was probably a hard one, there is a maze to help the wise men find their way to Bethlehem. The star-making activity will need star templates, and ready-cut card for the younger children.

PEARL DIVERS

Aim: To explore why the wise men made their journey and what they found out.

Starter

Who am I? Fix a picture of an animal or food item on everyone's back. They have to find out who they are by going round asking questions about themselves. The others can only answer yes or no.

Teaching

Point out how in the game they had to search for the right answer, and it was like a journey to find the truth. Sometimes people were helpful in that and sometimes they weren't. Today we are looking at some wise men who set out on a quest.

Have two or three adults meeting up as if they are resting on the journey and chatting together about what the day has been like, what they miss, and what they are hoping to find. It is best to try out the conversation beforehand but without any set words as it will then sound natural.

When the wise men have settled down for the night (or gone to feed the camels), show the children a sheet of paper with these headings on it: Who? What? Why? In the different sections brainstorm ideas about who they were (wise men from the East), what they were doing (following a star to find a baby king of great importance) and why they bothered (they had worked out from the signs that this birth was really important for the human race, and they felt a strong urge to be there and pay their respects). Use the children's words, of course.

Now have the wise men on their way back, talking about how they felt about King Herod, what it was like to see Jesus, and why they are going home by a different route.

Praying

Have some incense, gold and myrrh on display during the teaching. As each is brought to the front pray together:

Gold
The wise men brought gold to Jesus.
Jesus, we bring you the gold of our obedience.
Help us to live as you want us to. Amen.

Frankincense
The wise men brought frankincense to Jesus.
Jesus, we bring you the incense of our worship.
You are God and we worship you. Amen.

Myrrh
The wise men brought myrrh to Jesus.

Jesus, we bring you the myrrh of the world's sadness.
Help us to look after one another better. Amen.

Activities

You will need lots of lining paper or rolls of wallpaper. The best present we can give to Jesus is ourselves. Working in twos, the children draw round each other on the paper, cut themselves out and colour them. On the front write:

Jesus,
the best present
I can give you
is myself!

The cut-outs can be offered with the gifts in church and given back at the end of the service for the children to remember at home.

The worksheet has a sequencing activity to consolidate the teaching, and a look at our own journey to Jesus.

GOLD PANNERS

Aim: To understand how the wise men's visit symbolises all the nations coming to worship God.

Starter

A quest for the truth. As with the younger group, this involves having an identity fixed on your back. You can ask everyone else questions to discover your identity but they can only answer yes or no. Instead of pictures have names of famous people for this group.

Teaching

Read the Matthew passage for today, with different people taking the parts. Point out that the wise men were also involved with a quest for the truth. Use the worksheet to jot down all the things that helped them in their quest and all the things which threatened to make it fail. Also think about what made them set off on such a journey in the first place.

Now look at part of the Isaiah prophecy (Isaiah 60:1-4). How do the wise men fit in with this? Help them to see how they are in a way representing all the nations: God's salvation is not only for the nations of Israel but for the whole world.

Praying

Have a world map spread out on the floor. As you play some quiet music or sing a worship song or a Taizé chant, one by one the members of the group light candles in holders and place them on various parts of the world.

Activities

Make a collage for prayer which can be displayed in church or in the hall. Have a selection of newspaper pictures and stories showing some of the areas of need and evil in our world. Arrange them around a central picture (perhaps from a Christmas card) showing the wise men offering their gifts. Have the words from Isaiah 60:1-4 written on the collage.

THE BAPTISM OF THE LORD

Thought for the day

As Jesus is baptised, the Spirit of God rests visibly on him, marking him out as the One who will save his people.

Reflection on the readings

Isaiah 42:1-4, 6-7
Psalm 28:1-4, 9-10
Acts 10:34-38
Matthew 3:13-17

In this season of Epiphany it is as if the mystery of the Incarnation is gradually being unfolded like a richly patterned carpet. Not that it will ever become totally understood this side of death, but even so, as year by year we examine it and marvel at it, truths of God's working and God's nature will gradually become apparent, and enable us increasingly to understand ourselves and our world. The knowledge of God is the beginning of wisdom.

Gestalt psychology talks of the 'Aha!' moment when fragments of knowledge suddenly form a pattern of fresh understanding in our minds. Peter's experience at Joppa led him to a sudden, new level of realisation about God's purposes: it was all so much bigger and wider than he had understood before. God was not the privately owned treasure of a few, but the glory and hope of the whole of humanity, in all places and all ages.

It must have been a similar 'Aha!' experience for Matthew, when, with his spiritual eyes open, he suddenly linked the moment of Jesus' Baptism with the prophecy from Isaiah. Perhaps you can remember an experience which has been marked with significance for you particularly in the light of subsequent developments? For those who have lived through the subsequent events of Christ's ministry, his death and resurrection, the Baptism of Jesus marks the taking on of the role of that servant described in the book of Isaiah.

It is no mistake that the words of God, heard by Jesus as he comes up out of the water, closely echo the opening words of Isaiah 42. Anyone with a working knowledge of the Isaiah passage would immediately call to mind the rest of the passage, with its hope and its tenderness.

Discussion starters

1. What links are there between the Isaiah passage and the subsequent ministry of Jesus?
2. How does Peter explain what happened at Jesus' Baptism (Acts 10:38)? What is the significance of 'anointing'?

All-stage talk

Ask various children if they know what job they would like to do when they grow up. Ask various adults what they wanted to be when they were children, and whether they did it or not. Ask some of the children if they have seen pictures of their mums and dads when they were babies and toddlers. Do they look anything like that now? Ask some of the mums and dads if they can imagine what their children will be like in twenty years' time.

A week or two ago we were thinking about when Jesus was a baby. Now, suddenly, we're looking at what he was like when he grew up. Here he is at about thirty years old. He's a carpenter, so he's probably quite strongly built. He's heard that his cousin, John (do they remember John?), is washing people in the River Jordan as a sign that God has forgiven their sins. We wash to get our bodies clean. John baptised people to show they were getting their souls clean. They were all getting ready for the Messiah, or Christ.

And now here comes Jesus, wading into the river, and wanting John to baptise him as well! (We know that Jesus is the Christ they were waiting for, but the people didn't know that yet.) John realises who Jesus is, and is shocked that he wants to be baptised. 'It ought to be the other way round!' says John. 'You ought to be baptising me!'

Jesus insists. 'No, it's right for you to baptise me. God's work of putting things right all through the centuries is coming together now in this Baptism.' So John agrees to baptise Jesus. He pushes Jesus down under the water in the river, and when Jesus comes up out of the water, something amazing happens.

It's as if the heavens are opened up, and Jesus sees the Spirit of God coming to him and resting on him. Matthew tells us it looked something like a dove flying down to him. Jesus hears God his

Father speaking to him deep into his being. God is saying that Jesus is indeed his well-loved Son, chosen and marked out for a special life that will save the world.

So that tiny baby, born in the stable, visited by shepherds and wise men, looked after by Joseph and Mary all through his childhood, is now at the start of his important work on earth. His job is to show the world God's love.

All-age ideas

- Use the Rite of Blessing and Sprinkling Holy Water in place of the Penitential Rite.

- Decorate the font today, and have the renewal of baptismal promises displayed beside it. Suggest that people go and visit it after the service or during the week, thinking over their own Baptism as being the start of their Christian ministry.

- Have some floating candles in a shallow tray of water incorporated in an arrangement that people will see as they come up to receive communion.

Prayer of the Faithful

Celebrant
Let us attune our hearts to the God who loves us.

Reader
God of love,
we pray for all those who are newly baptised,
or who have recently found that you are real;
we pray for all in ordained and lay ministries,
and for those sensing a special calling.
Help us all to listen to your guiding.

Silence

In God:
all things work together for good.

God of power,
we pray for those who are in authority
and in positions of influence and responsibility;
may they be earthed in humility,
courageous in integrity,
and mindful of the need to serve.

Silence

In God:
all things work together for good.

God of mercy,
we call to mind those with whom we share
the work and leisure of our life;
we pray for those we treasure

and those we battle with,
and ask you to breathe into all our relationships
the forgiving love which cleanses and heals.

Silence

In God:
all things work together for good.

God of wholeness,
we remember those who are aching today
in body, mind or spirit;
knowing that nothing is unredeemable,
we ask that you will bring good
even out of these barren places.

Silence

In God:
all things work together for good.

God of life,
we pray for those whose earthly lives have ended;
we remember those who have died
violently and tragically, suddenly and unprepared.
We give you thanks for lives well lived
and for happy memories.
May they rest in the eternal peace of heaven.

Silence

In God:
all things work together for good.

Now we join our prayers
with those of Mary, the Mother of Jesus:
Hail, Mary . . .

In the space of silence,
we bring to God our Father
our private petitions.

Silence

Celebrant
In thankfulness for all our blessings
we ask you, Father,
to hear our prayers, through Christ our Lord.
Amen.

TREASURE SEEKERS

Aim: To know that Jesus was baptised in the river Jordan.

Starter

Water play. Protect the floor and have some bowls of water and plastic bowls, funnels and tubes for the children to play with.

Teaching

Talk about all the things we could do with the water. Water is so useful to us because it makes us clean when we're dirty, we can drink it and cook with it, and we can paddle and swim in it too. Show the children some pictures of seas and oceans, rivers and ponds.

We have to be very careful with water because we can't breathe in it. We can drown in it.

That makes water a very good way of explaining what happens at Baptism: we drown to everything evil, and come up with our sins all washed clean away by God.

Talk about any Baptisms in their families that they remember – or even their own.

When Jesus walked into the water in the River Jordan, he asked to be baptised as well. So John poured the water over him, and when he came up out of the water, God's Spirit, like a dove, flew out of heaven and rested on him. God said, 'This is my Son. I love him very much.' When *we* are baptised, God is saying, 'This is my daughter, Eleanor; this is my son, Richard. And I love them very much!'

Praying

Dear God,
I'm glad you love me.
I like being one of your children! Amen.

Activities

Use water added to paint and make some bright pictures to thank God for water. Let the children watch the paint-making, or use blocks of water-colour so they need to keep dipping their brushes in the water to clean them and to make the picture beautiful.

PEARL DIVERS

Aim: To get to know Matthew's account of Jesus' baptism.

Starter

Have a look at some atlases, picture books and travel brochures to find out where the River Jordan is and what it looks like.

Teaching

Wrap a 'camel hair shirt' round someone and stand him in the River Jordan (barefoot on a blue sheet). Can they guess who this is? If not, introduce them to John the Baptist, whom we met a couple of

weeks before Christmas. Remind them that John is using the water as a sign of the people drowning to their old sinful lives and coming up with their sins forgiven by God, so they are clean and ready for when the Messiah comes. The Messiah, or Christ, is God's anointed one who will come and save his people.

Today we hear what happened when Jesus himself came to the River Jordan. He was about thirty years old at the time. (Have someone to be Jesus, walking into the river.) He asks John to baptise him, but John feels it ought to be the other way round. (Why?)

But Jesus persuades him that it is right for him to be baptised with everyone else, so John does it. (They act this out.) As soon as Jesus has been baptised, it's as if the heavens open up, and God's Spirit comes down to rest on him. It looks like a dove flying down to him. And there is a voice from heaven which says, 'This is my Son, whom I love; I am well pleased with him!' Have the words displayed so that everyone can say them together.

Praying

Jesus, I believe and trust
that you are God's Son,
the promised Saviour,
the Christ, the Messiah of God. Amen.

Activities

The worksheet helps them to make the connections between the prophecy in Isaiah and the words spoken at Jesus' Baptism, and there are instructions for making a dove out of salt dough. Here is the salt dough recipe: two cups of flour, one cup of salt, water to mix.

GOLD PANNERS

Aim: To see Jesus gradually being revealed as the fulfilment of God's promises.

Starter

Jigsaw puzzles. These can be done on their own or in pairs, or in a larger group, without the picture to help, so that the understanding of the picture gradually becomes apparent.

Teaching

Start by reading the prophecy from Isaiah, asking them to think of who it reminds them of. (Whoever the prophet was referring to at the time, Jesus certainly saw it as fitting in exactly with his own role.)

Take particular note of the opening verses, and then read Matthew's account of Jesus' Baptism, listening out for any echoes of the Isaiah passage. They are now getting an idea of what it was like for the Jewish people to hear and read Matthew's Gospel – they would pick up on familiar passages from Scripture which would help them to understand the way Jesus fulfilled the old prophecies. They could begin to see God's plan taking shape through history, and everything coming together in Jesus of Nazareth.

Praying

Take my life and let it be
consecrated, Lord, to thee.
Take my moments and my days,
let them flow in endless praise. Amen.

Activities

The worksheet helps them explore Peter's understanding of Jesus' baptism, and their own ideas. There is also a short sketch which can be used in church, or as a way in to discussion about having our spiritual eyes open.

LENT

FIRST SUNDAY OF LENT

Thought for the day

Jesus knows all about temptation; and he can deal with our sin.

Reflection on the readings

Genesis 2:7-9; 3:1-7
Psalm 50:3-6, 12-14, 17
Romans 5:12-19
Matthew 4:1-11

Temptation always has that element of good sense which makes the sin seem appealing and plausible. We can imagine that Eve could be praised for wanting to stretch the limits of her and Adam's potential; wisdom for the human race was arguably a sensible step in promotion terms. The darker side of temptation is that the illusory good sense masks the basic clear fact that doing or saying or thinking this particular thing is simply wrong. In Adam and Eve's case the serpent's suggestion went against God's instructions, and resulted in them choosing to be disobedient. Typically, what initially looks so attractive turns out to cause misery and confusion. The pattern of temptation and sin is a depressing one, and one for which we can all bring regretful and painful examples to mind.

At which point, God's plan for mending and healing springs thankfully into action in the person of Jesus, who is tempted in exactly the same way we are. First, Satan goes for personal well-being and comfort: making stones into bread. When Jesus stands firm on what is really important, rather than self-centred needs, Satan goes for another favourite: self-doubt. He suggests a good and foolproof way for Jesus to test whether or not he really is God's Son. But, if we look at Jesus' answer, we find he is remembering that putting God to the test like this, as the people of Israel had done at Massah in the wilderness, is an insult to God's love and faithfulness.

So Satan, homing in on Jesus' loyalty to his Father and his respect and love for him, suggests a clever and speedy way to please God by claiming all the people and presenting them to the Father, just as he is genuinely hoping to do. There's a big catch here, though. Jesus will need to pay for the privilege by worshipping Satan. Satan has overstepped the mark here, and made it plain who he is, and how

evil the plan is, so the battle is over, at least for the moment.

If we can copy Jesus in clinging on to the real underlying truths during our temptations, they will eventually emerge to be seen as obviously wrong. The danger in temptation is the point when we are being won over by the persuasive attraction and plausibility, so that our hold on what is right and good is temporarily loosened. It is as if we are temporarily 'off balance' and therefore easy to knock down.

Thankfully, Jesus did much more than wade through terrible temptation without sinning. He went on to take on freely the punishing cursed death which results from sin, and so opened the way back into the garden of hope and promise. As we hold on to Jesus in faith, he enables us to exchange lasting death for full and everlasting life.

Discussion starters

1. Can we help one another more to resist temptation or is this always a battle we have to fight on our own?

2. How are Adam and Jesus similar, and how are they different?

All-stage talk

Talk about some of the rules we are given, such as 'Wear your seatbelt', 'Don't lean out of the window of a moving train', 'Don't play on the railway line' or 'Don't keep poisons in old lemonade bottles'. Gather ideas about why they are good, sensible rules which are worth keeping. Point out that they are good rules whether we actually know the reasons or not.

Now ask for some volunteers to stand around as trees in the garden of the story from Genesis. Give the volunteers real or paper fruits to hold. God's rule for Adam and Eve was 'Don't eat fruit from this tree'. Hang this rule round the tree in the centre of the garden. Now God has very good reasons for making this rule, based on his love for Adam and Eve and his concern for them. And since God is God, that rule is the most important thing for Adam and Eve to remember. However tasty the fruit looks, whatever they may be told it will do to help them, they are always to keep hold of God's rule (what was it?), and stick to keeping that. Anything that cuts across God's rule must be wrong.

Ask two people who think they will be able to keep to God's rule without disobeying it. These two are going to be Adam and Eve. Show them how tasty the fruit looks and try to persuade them to try it. Tell them that it will do wonderful things for them, and make them wise like God. When they (hopefully) manage to resist the temptation to do what God's rule told them not to, praise them, and then point out that they managed it this time, but we are always being tempted to be disobedient to God's rule of love, and when it next happens we need to stick close to God, and remember his rule: 'Love God and love one another'.

Adam and Eve in the story stand for all of us who are human. And humans tend not to be very good at resisting temptation. God loves us and understands what it is like to be humans being tempted. We know that because Jesus was tempted during his life on earth. He will give us the strength we need to resist those pressures of temptation, but that doesn't mean it's going to be easy. Resisting temptation is *very hard*, and that's why Jesus told us to pray about it every day of our life: 'Lead us not into temptation but deliver us from evil.' Let's use the strength God offers; we need all the help we can get!

All-age ideas

- The Genesis reading can be accompanied by a group of people miming the action.

- Have different voices to read through the Gospel, either using the *Dramatised Bible* or simply going through the text together and deciding how the meaning and drama can best be brought out.

- Give everyone a cut-out paper shape of a bitten apple, and during the Penitential Rite ask them to hold it and look at it as they bring to mind the times they have gone along with temptations instead of holding on to God's rule of love. The shapes can be collected and placed at the foot of the cross as the words of forgiveness are proclaimed.

Prayer of the Faithful

Celebrant
Our God knows us and the temptations we face. Let us pray to him now.

Reader
As the Church begins this season of Lent
we ask you to remind us of what is important
and what is not;
of where we are wandering away
and what we need to change;
so that by Easter
we will be renewed and strengthened
for your service in the world.

Silence

The Lord is God:
there is no other.

The world's misery and pain
and desperate need of healing
are clear to see and affect us all.
We pray now for this damaged world
with all its weakness, longings and failings,
with all its potential and hope.

Silence

The Lord is God:
there is no other.

Whenever a child is born
we celebrate the creative hope of God.
We pray for all being born this week
and for their families and communities,
that all our children may be loved and cared for,
safe and happy.

Silence

The Lord is God:
there is no other.

We pray for all who suffer through others' sin;
all victims of abuse or oppression or apathy;
all whose adult lives are distorted and misshapen
by early damaging experiences
which need your healing.

Silence

The Lord is God:
there is no other.

We remember those who,
freed from the ageing and pain of their bodies,
can live now with you
in the peace and joy of heaven.

Silence

The Lord is God:
there is no other.

We join our prayers with those of Mary,
whose Son has brought us salvation:
Hail, Mary . . .

In silence now,
we approach our loving Father
with our private petitions.

Silence

Celebrant
Father, accept these prayers,
through Jesus Christ our Lord.
Amen.

TREASURE SEEKERS

Aim: To know the Adam and Eve temptation story.

Starter

Put out chairs all over the room, with a cross on the chair in the middle. Play musical chairs, telling everyone first that they mustn't sit on the chair in the middle, even if it's the only chair left.

Teaching

Talk about how well they managed/how hard they found it to keep the rule during the game. Today we are going to hear about Adam and Eve who had a rule to keep.

Tell the story either from a children's adapted version, in your own words based on the biblical account, or from a suitable Bible translation (see 'How to use this book', page 9). Accompany the words with pictures, either from the book you are using or using the carpet tiles and cut-outs of trees, Adam, Eve and the snake. In this case the children can help by placing the trees and fruit on the background. At the point where they are told not to eat from the tree in the middle of the garden, place a cross on the centre tree.

Praying

Jesus, you want us to be loving each day
and we say, 'OK!'
Jesus, you want us to do as you say
and we say, 'OK!'

Activities

On the activity sheet they can count all the fruit Adam and Eve are allowed to eat, and there are outlines for trees and characters to make into a model. Each child will need a flat piece of card for this, and either green paper or green chopped wool to stick on it. If you prefer, you can make one big communal model.

PEARL DIVERS

Aim: To know about Jesus' temptations in the desert.

Starter

Prepare some coloured pieces of paper and some white pieces with questions on. Stick them on to people with sticky tape. The questions have to team up with the right answers. Here are some suggestions:

What colour is a banana?	Blue
What colour is grass?	Yellow
What colour is the sky?	Black
What colour is coal?	Green

Teaching

Borrow some library books to show the children some pictures of the desert where Jesus went to be on his own with God after he had been baptised. Use a yellow or brown and a blue towel laid on the floor as the background to the story, and sit the children round the edge. Explain that to fast means to go without food, and people sometimes do this when they are praying, especially if they are wanting to find out God's will for them in their life.

After he had been baptised, Jesus went off into the desert to fast and pray. He wanted to make sure he was really listening to God as he didn't want to get it wrong. As you tell the story of the three temptations, place the following objects on the background:

1. A loaf of bread (stone shaped) and a large stone. (Satan was homing in on Jesus' feeling hungry: personal comfort and survival.)

2. A high tower built of bricks and a cut-out question mark. (Satan was picking up on Jesus wondering who he was and what his job would be exactly.)

3. A wrapped present and a bill or invoice. (Satan suggested a way for Jesus to give his Father a present – but it came with a crazy price tag.)

As you tell the story, place beside each set of objects the answers Jesus used:

1. Matthew 4, verse 4
2. Matthew 4, verse 7
3. Matthew 4, verse 10

Praying

Lord Jesus,
when I am tempted to do what is wrong
and unloving and selfish,
make me brave
and keep me strong. Amen.

Activities

On the activity sheet there are instructions for making a temptation wheel. Each child will need a split pin for this. The teaching is also reinforced by a puzzle to match up and look up the temptations and answers, and the children will need access to a Bible for this.

GOLD PANNERS

Aim: To explore the way Jesus is seen as the second Adam.

Starter

Reversals. In pairs, work out a simple sequence of actions both the right way round and in reverse – for example, walking to post a letter; opening a present and being pleased with it; hammering a nail and hitting your thumb; packing a suitcase. These can be written on cards and given out to the pairs who work on them and perform them to the group in the reverse way first, seeing if people can guess from the reversal what the real action is before it is acted out.

Teaching

Today we are going to look at the greatest reversal of all time. Begin with the Genesis reading, encouraging different people to take the speaking parts, but as always being sensitive to readers who lack confidence or fluency. Try to get at the real sin of disobedience to God, and explain that Adam and Eve are the archetypal human beings, blowing it as they succumb to temptation in their weakness. We fail. We mess things up. We cannot put things right by ourselves.

Now read Romans 5, verses 17 and 19. This whole passage is so dense that I suggest you only look at these two verses which focus on the link between Adam and Jesus and the reversal of humanity's disobedience through Jesus' total and loving obedience. Talk about how Jesus showed that obedience, both in his life and his death, and how he did for us what we could never do for ourselves, purely out of love for us.

Finally look at Matthew's account of Jesus' temptations, to see his obedience in action right at the beginning of his ministry.

Praying

O loving wisdom of our God!
when all was sin and shame
a second Adam to the fight
and to the rescue came.
Oh wisest love! that flesh and blood,
which did in Adam fail,
should strive afresh against the foe,
should strive and should prevail.
Praise to the Holiest in the height,
and in the depth be praise;
in all his words most wonderful,
most sure in all his ways.

Activities

On the sheet there is a temptation sketch and some suggestions for recognising temptation and working in God's strength to resist it. There is also an Adam/Jesus factfile to fill in. It is important that they understand the difference between temptation and sin, and that they are made aware of the reality and power of temptation and so the need to wear God's 'armour'.

SECOND SUNDAY OF LENT

Thought for the day

The disciples witness the glory of God revealed in Jesus. It is a glimpse of the glory which will be the great hope for all nations of the world.

Reflection on the readings

Genesis 12:1-4a
Psalm 32
2 Timothy 1:8-10
Matthew 17:1-9

The Genesis passage records the call of Abram to leave his past security and move forward in faith with the God of his making. God promises that through him not just his own immediate descendants but all the nations of the world will be greatly blessed. This is one of those crucial moments in the plan that will bring hope and salvation to the whole human race. Abram responded to that voice of God calling him, and cherished the vision of extensive blessing for the rest of his life.

The Gospel takes us to another moment of vision, on a mountain made holy by God's presence there. Matthew tells us that Jesus has taken three of his disciples with him, and as he is praying, communicating directly with his Father, he becomes transfigured so that Peter, James and John witness the glory of God shining in the human body of Jesus. And into that intimate conversation walk Moses and Elijah, representing the Law and the prophets. To the disciples and to Matthew's original readers, well acquainted with the scriptures, the echoes of Moses' experience on Mount Sinai will have been obvious. It must have seemed almost like a time warp, and perhaps, in a sense, it is, since at such moments of eternity we are as much present with

Moses in the holy cloud, Elijah listening to the still small voice, and Abram hearing God's call and promise, as we are with God speaking through Jesus and drawing together all past and future at a moment of intense reality and depth of love.

No wonder, then, that Simon Peter refers to the subsequent conversation of God and Moses, and wants to build tabernacles so that God's transcendence can become immanent among his people. But Peter has not yet grasped the extraordinary extent of God's immanence which has now gone far beyond tabernacles. As Abram's calling foretold, God was to be in the travelling of the people through their lives; and in the person of Jesus, as the transfigured glory shows, God is personally and intimately among his people in a way never possible before.

The approaching act of self-giving love on the cross, and triumph over death, are going to mean that the personal closeness will be possible far and wide in all places and in all generations and all nations. It is vital that the followers of Jesus understand something of this, and there is urgency in God's voice heard by them, encouraging them to trust the amazing identity of his Son and to hang on to his words. They have been shown God's glory on the top of the mountain so that they will be better able to recognise God's immanence at the bottom, when the cloud of glory has faded.

Discussion starters

1. Do we hit the right balance in our prayer and public worship between intimate friendship and awe in the presence of the almighty God?

2. Do we want to cling on to the 'mountain experiences' rather than accompany the living Jesus down to the demands of life in the valley?

All-stage talk

Bring along a family photograph album with snaps of holidays or celebrations in it, and if possible a camera which takes instant pictures. Also have two cards to hold up, one with a large plus sign on and the other a large minus sign.

If you have an instant camera, begin by taking a picture of some people or the day's flower arrangement. Show the album and talk about the way we all like to snap away to capture the moments when we are on holiday or at a special celebration, or when our children and grandchildren are growing up. We want to hang on to the moment and cherish it for years to come, because we know the moment itself won't last. The children will soon grow up, and we may never have the chance to visit the Eiffel Tower or Southend illuminations ever again!

The 'plus' side of taking pictures like this (encourage everyone's suggestions) may be that we will remember better if we look back at the picture – it may help us see the importance of the occasion, it helps us pass on the family tradition to the next generation, and it lets us enjoy more at our leisure later than we were able to take in at the time.

The 'minus' side may be that we're so busy taking pictures at the time that we aren't able to concentrate properly on the actual moment.

In the Gospel we heard about something amazing which happened on a mountain in Galilee. Three of Jesus' friends – Peter, James and John – saw Jesus shining with God's glory as he prayed. It was one of those times when Peter wanted to reach for the camera (except that cameras hadn't been invented then) so they could hold on to the wonderful moment for ever. Perhaps they had never before felt God quite so close to them! They even heard God's voice. He wasn't saying, 'I hope you're watching carefully and I'm sorry cameras haven't been invented yet or you could have got a pretty dramatic picture here today!' He was helping them understand the real, actual experience they were in, assuring them that Jesus really was God's Son, and wanting them to listen to Jesus in a way they had never listened before.

God doesn't just want Peter, James and John to know – he wants St. Peter's church and St. James's and St. John's and all the other churches to know. He wants all the people in all the world to know who Jesus is, and he wants us all to pay attention to what Jesus says, and really listen to him with our hearts and minds as well as our ears.

All-age ideas

• Have some A4 sheets of paper printed with single words in big letters, such as 'Life', 'Love', 'Joy' and 'Peace'. Print them out in black and again in colour. Make a display with the black words next to the coloured words as a visual way of seeing how God can transform life with shining richness and love.

Prayer of the Faithful

Celebrant
As children together in the family of God,
let us pray now to our Father in heaven.

Reader
Lord, we pray that as Christians
we may listen more attentively
and with greater urgency than ever before
to the words of Jesus;
give us more awareness of your presence with us,
both in our worship and in our daily ministry,
giving us the courage to live out your truth with joy.

Silence

Holy God:
transform us and use us to your glory.

We pray for those who do not know you
or dismiss you as irrelevant to their lives;
we pray for those
who influence and encourage others
in what is evil, destructive or depraved,
and ask for your protection
of all who are vulnerable and in danger.

Silence

Holy God:
transform us and use us to your glory.

We pray for all who are adjusting
to new relationships in the family,
new homes or new work and leisure patterns;
we pray for stronger root growth in you,
so that we are not thrown
by the changes and troubles of everyday life,
knowing the reality of your faithfulness.

Silence

Holy God:
transform us and use us to your glory.

We pray for all who are too exhausted
or overwhelmed by circumstances and pressures
to be able to pray;
surround all those
who are troubled and heavily laden
with the revitalising assurance of your presence,
your understanding and your love.

Silence

Holy God:
transform us and use us to your glory.

We pray that those who have gone through death
may know the brightness of everlasting life
in your company;
may we, with them, come to experience
the glory and joy of heaven.

Silence

Holy God:
transform us and use us to your glory.

As we join our prayers with those of Mary,
may we learn from her responsive love:
Hail, Mary . . .

We pray in silence
for those known to us
who have particular needs.

Silence

Celebrant
Father, your glory fills the world,
and so we entrust our cares to you,
through Christ our Lord.
Amen.

TREASURE SEEKERS

Aim: To think about how wonderful God is.

Starter

Sit in a circle and pass round something natural and beautiful, such as a shell, a flower or a pineapple. Each person says one thing they notice about it. This encourages very careful observation and enjoyment of detail. The leader can draw attention to what a lot of things we managed to notice in this one bit of God's world.

Teaching

Have some quiet, gentle music playing, and ask the children to lie down with their eyes closed as you take them on a lovely journey.

Imagine you find a door in a wall. There is a handle on the door and you open it. On the other side of the door the sun is shining and the sky is blue. There are birds singing. You feel warm and happy. You run in bare feet over the springy grass through the daisies and buttercups, and a bright blue butterfly flies beside you. You can hear the sound of the sea, swishing gently on the sand. Now you can see the water, and you walk over the sand to the edge of the cool water and stand in it, with the water trickling over your feet. A boat is being rowed towards you and inside is someone you know and love and trust. Perhaps it's your mum or dad. Perhaps it's Jesus. They help you into the boat and you sit there safely and happily, looking at the clear water and at the hills in the distance, enjoying the lapping sound of the water against the boat. The boat comes back to the sandy beach, and you climb out and walk back over the soft sand, over the springy green grass with the daisies and butter-cups, till you get back to the door in the wall. You go through the door and close it behind you, feeling all happy and rested. The door has your own name written on it and you can go back there whenever you want.

Tell the children that when the music stops they can open their eyes and sit up, and gradually fade the music out so this is not a jolt for them. If the children want to talk about their journey allow a little time for this; it very much depends on the personality of the child.

Talk about the way God has made us a beautiful place to live in and the way he loves us. With God we can feel safe and happy, because there is absolutely nothing nasty or frightening about God. He is completely good and right and true and fair.

Praying

Go straight into the praying after the teaching, making a beautiful focus for the children using shells or flowers and candles, perhaps with a globe.

Holy, holy, holy Lord,
God of power and might,
heaven and earth
are full of your glory!

Activities

The children will need white candles or white wax crayons to draw pictures with. They then paint with water-based colours over their drawings so that they see clearly what they have already drawn, rather as we have been noticing God's glory in the starter and the teaching. There are also examples of God's glory to colour on the worksheet.

PEARL DIVERS

Aim: To get to know the story of the Transfiguration.

Starter

Eye-witnesses. As the children gather and are talking with the leaders exchanging news, have some events taking place, but without drawing attention to them. For instance, someone might carry two chairs across the room from one side to the other and back again. Someone might wheel a bike through, or walk across with glove puppets or a distinctive hat on. Gather everyone in a circle and see what people have noticed, including the colours and number of objects carried.

Teaching

Explain that we have a special guest today, who was an eye-witness to something that happened about two thousand years ago. Introduce Simon Peter (who could be an import for the occasion, or one of the helpers). If you want to dress him up, use one of the Nativity play costumes, or a striped dressing-gown with tea-towel headdress.

Here is a script to guide you, but it's best if the main ideas are taken on board and the actual words left natural.

Leader   Ah, good morning. You are Simon Peter, I believe.

Peter   Yes, that's right. Nice of you to invite me to your church! Hello, children. Good to meet you!

Leader   Peter, we wanted to ask you about what happened when Jesus took you up that high mountain in Galilee.

Peter   Oh my goodness, I'll never forget that day, and that's for sure. He took three of us, you know – me and James and John – and I remember I got very hot and puffed out on the way up. I wasn't as young and fit as the others!

Leader   What happened when you got to the top?

Peter   Well, we three sat down for a rest and Jesus stood up, praying. He often used to go off on his own to pray, but this time we could see him. He wasn't just going through the words, he was deep in conversation with God. And then it happened.

Leader   What happened?

Peter   Well, although I saw it with my own eyes, it's quite difficult to describe. It was as if he was so much part of God as he prayed that he started to look . . . different.

Leader   Different? How do you mean? Did he start changing shape or something?

Peter   No, his whole face and clothes and everything seemed to be full of light, as if he was shining.

Leader   Perhaps the sun was shining on him?

Peter   Oh no, it wasn't like that. I've seen the sun shining on people lots of times. This lightness was as if it was all part of him. To tell you the truth, I felt a bit frightened. There was God present in all his glory and I was watching it happen! And there's something else.

Leader   What?

Peter   Jesus wasn't on his own.

Leader   Not on his own? What on earth do you mean?

Peter   Well, he wasn't only talking with God; he was talking with two other people – one was Moses. He's our wonderful leader who led us out of Egypt where we were slaves and gave us God's Law. Have you heard of the ten commandments? And the other person was our well-loved prophet Elijah. They were all talking together!

Leader   Are you saying they were ghosts?

Peter No, they didn't seem to be ghosts exactly. It was more that we were outside the usual time and place rules because we were being allowed a peep into God's eternity and his glory.

Leader How amazing! Did you hear anything?

Peter We certainly did! We actually heard God's voice.

Leader How do you mean?

Peter Well, there was this bright cloud which kind of settled on us all, and God was speaking to us from it. Now I can't really tell you what it sounded like. I just know that when we heard God speaking to us it was so powerful that our legs turned to jelly and we fell on the ground – it was all too big for our bodies to cope with, I suppose.

Leader What did the voice say?

Peter It said, 'This is my beloved Son, who I'm well pleased with. Make sure you listen to him.' God was telling us that Jesus had God's authority, and I think we all realised then that he was much more than the wonderful friend and teacher we loved so much.

Leader Well, Peter, what an incredible experience! It's good to talk to someone who was actually there and saw it all. Thank you. Is there anything you'd like to tell us while you're here?

Peter Yes, there is. I'd like to tell you all that God told us and showed us on that mountain: Jesus really is God's Son, he has God's full authority, and you really do need to listen and take notice of what he says. We're talking about more than lifetimes here – we're talking about full life that never ends but lasts for ever.

Leader Thank you, Peter. We're gradually getting to know Jesus here, and we're amazed at the love he has for us. We'll certainly take your advice and listen out to what he says. Goodbye, and thanks again for coming.

Praying

Glory to the Father and to the Son
and to the Holy Spirit,
as it was in the beginning, is now
and shall be for ever. Amen.

Activities

On the activity sheet there are instructions for making

a stand-up model of the Transfiguration and a 'holy mountains' quiz for which the children will need access to a Bible.

GOLD PANNERS

Aim: To see how the Transfiguration links with Abraham, Moses and Elijah.

Starter

Show these pictures (or others of your own) which show only a small section of the complete object, and try to work out what the full pictures are.

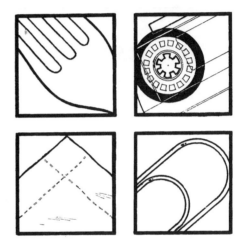

Teaching

Have a speech bubble on which is written God's call and promise to Abram. Look at this first, noticing how Abram is called out of where he is living to go forward in God's company into the unknown, sustained by the promise. Now look at the Gospel reading. In another speech bubble write what the disciples heard God saying, and draw attention to the way Abram's faithful listening enabled much to happen in his life; the disciples' faithful listening will also strengthen and uphold them through the times of suffering ahead.

Why were Moses and Elijah there at the Transfiguration? (They may need you to give a thumbnail sketch of the role of Moses and Elijah.) Help them to see that they represent the authority of the Law and the prophets. See how this links in with the authority of God's words to Abram, and his words on the mountain, declaring to the disciples who Jesus is.

Praying

O worship the Lord in the beauty of holiness;
bow down before him, his glory proclaim;
with gold of obedience and incense of lowliness,
kneel and adore him: the Lord is his name.

Activities

On the sheet there are suggestions to start them off in a Peter, James and John role-play conversation, a mountain-top comparison and some thoughts to get them seeing the value and the dangers of mountain-top experiences.

THIRD SUNDAY OF LENT

Thought for the day

God both knows us completely and loves us completely; meeting us where we are, he provides us with living water, to satisfy all our needs.

Reflection on the readings

Exodus 17:3-7
Psalm 94:1-2, 6-9
Romans 5:1-2, 5-8
John 4:5-42

Whether it's a blind date, a job interview or meeting the future in-laws for the first time, we are likely to take extra care with how we look and behave, wanting to show our best selves in order to give a good impression. That is a kind of game we all play. If we really thought about it we'd realise that it has to do with not trusting these strangers to notice our good qualities unless we underline them a bit with some visuals. We may suspect that if they really knew our ordinary messy selves, before they had got to know and enjoy us better, they may well disapprove or dislike us.

With God it's different. We can't 'dress to impress' because God knows us inside out already. When Jesus had that conversation with the woman at Jacob's well in Samaria she was stunned by the sudden realisation that Jesus knew her; he understood where she was coming from and what was important to her, where she was weak and where she was strong. He understood her potential as well as her mistakes. So it did not feel like invaded privacy because, along with the full knowledge, she sensed full acceptance.

Perhaps you have felt yourself shrivel up in the company of those who seem to judge and condemn, and open out and blossom in the company of those who love and delight in you. In the level, direct gaze of the loving God we can all be reassured that

we are both known and accepted. That accepting love is like living water which our spirits need to survive and thrive and grow.

Out in the wilderness the people of Israel were well aware of their needs, but they were looking backwards nostalgically, rather than trustingly at the living God to supply them. And that too is a very human reaction. We tend to try all kinds of inferior, stagnant or temporary water supplies rather than going directly to the source of living water which never runs dry, is guaranteed pure and wholesome for us, and is exactly what we need at every changing moment of our journey through life.

Discussion starters

1. What kind of sources do we tend to use and rely on rather than God's living water? Why?

2. What does Jesus' conversation with the Samaritan woman teach us about our dealings as Christians with other people?

All-stage talk

You will need some paper cups, one with holes poked in it, a washing-up bowl or bucket and a jug of water.

Remind everyone of the way the people in the desert were very thirsty, and Moses asked God how their thirst could be quenched. He also told God how grumpy everyone was getting – they were so grumpy that Moses began to think they might take their anger out on him physically! God answered by providing water tumbling out of a rock, fresh and pure and delicious. There's nothing more wonderful when you're thirsty than the refreshing sound and taste of water. Now pour some water out and enjoy the sound of it. Invite some thirsty person to drink some from the proper cup. The people wanted to be back in the past, but God wanted to lead them on into the future.

We heard about two more water supplies today. Did anyone notice what they were? One was a well, where a woman had come to collect water, and where Jesus was sitting, feeling thirsty. Perhaps his own thirst reminded him of the people getting grumpy with Moses in the desert, and the way God had given them the flowing, living water they needed.

The other water supply is a bit unusual. Jesus told the woman about some water which would quench her thirst completely, and become a spring of water inside her welling up to give her life that lasts for ever. At first the woman thought this sounded too good to be true! What Jesus was doing was explaining the way God fills our lives, and leads us into the future, satisfying us all the way along, and refreshing us when we are sad and longing for good and right and fair and helpful things to happen in our world. The more we go to God to be filled with his living water of life and love, the more we shall find that we too are becoming sources of love and comfort and fairness and truthfulness for other people.

Let's see what happens when we pour some water into this cup with holes in it. (Station some people around with proper cups.) Pretend this hol(e)y cup is a Christian drinking the living water of life and love from the living, loving God. Can you see how the Christian then pours out that love to other people he or she meets? There's no problem that God will suddenly dry up, because God is living, flowing, for ever. And the other people may well want to become hol(e)y themselves, drinking that eternal supply which they can see is changing us for the better.

So if your life feels rather dry or thirsty or stuck in the past, go to Jesus; keep going to Jesus; and let him fill you up with the living spiritual water that really satisfies. And don't keep it all to yourself – pass it on!

All-age ideas

- Make streamers for the children from green and blue crepe paper, and have them sweeping and twirling like water during one of the hymns.

- Have the Gospel read as a conversation between a man and a woman.

Prayer of the Faithful

Celebrant
Thirsty for God, let us pray to him now,
in the knowledge that he will provide for us
in the way that is best.

Reader
Father, wherever the Church is dry and parched
may the water of your Spirit well up
to refresh and renew,
to bring life and strong new growth.
Lord, make us more aware of our thirst for you,
so that we come to you ready and eager
to receive your living water.

Silence

Living God:
satisfy our thirst.

Father, from the conflicting needs
and agendas of the world
we cry for mercy,
for a deeper understanding of one another
and a greater desire for co-operation and peace.
We pray for sensitivity

in handling delicate negotiations
and the wisdom which respects and listens.

Silence

Living God:
satisfy our thirst.

We pray that in all our relationships
you will make us effective channels
of your love and forgiveness.
Make us awash with your living water
so that our homes and places of work,
our shopping and leisure centres,
our conversations and actions,
are always in touch
with the renewing power of God.

Silence

Living God:
satisfy our thirst.

We stand alongside all those who are suffering,
whether in body, mind or spirit,
and long for your healing and comfort,
your strength for perseverance
and your patience in the dark times;
we long for your living Spirit
to envelop and sustain them.

Silence

Living God:
satisfy our thirst.

We pray for those who have come
to the end of earthly life;
have mercy on them.
May they, placing their faith in the God of life,
share in the light and joy of heaven for ever.

Silence

Living God:
satisfy our thirst.

We make our prayer with Mary,
faithful Mother of Jesus:
Hail, Mary . . .

Now, in silence,
we pray our individual petitions
to our heavenly Father,
who has promised to hear us.

Silence

Celebrant
Christ is among us,
and through him we offer these prayers
to our heavenly Father.
Amen.

TREASURE SEEKERS

Aim: To know that God can supply our needs.

Starter

Give the children little boxes to fill with little things. Either take them outside to do this (if you have a convenient church garden) or scatter suitable objects around the room so that they can go round collecting them.

Teaching

Introduce two or three puppets or character toys who are trying to use things that don't work very well and are disappointing as they keep letting them down. You can have items that are particularly relevant to your group, but here are some general ideas to start your thinking off: a pencil or crayon which keeps breaking, a leaky bucket, gloves with holes in so your hands get cold, a thin plastic knife and fork which snap, and water that tastes horrid.

Jesus is like a good bucket or like a glove/pencil that really works. (Let the puppets try these and be suitably delighted.) Jesus is like good-tasting, clear water which really quenches our thirst. We can trust Jesus to satisfy our deepest needs.

Praying

My lovely God,
thank you for supplying all our needs,
like a fresh, clear spring of water
which never runs dry. Amen.

Activities

On the sheet there are pictures to colour which encourage discussion about the way water can supply different needs, and a 'spot the loving' picture which shows love supplying other needs. The children can also make a water wheel. Prepare for this by cutting a yoghurt or margarine tub as shown below. The children can fix the plastic 'blades' in the slots and thread the wheel on a pencil. When held under a running tap the wheel will turn.

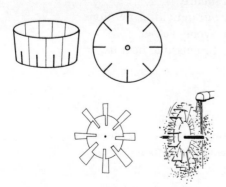

PEARL DIVERS

Aim: To know that Jesus is 'living water'.

Starter

Water from the well. Each team has a bucket of water at one end of the room and an empty washing-up bowl at the other. The teams have to get water from one end of the room to the other, without moving the containers. Each team member is given a small tub and can organise themselves however they wish. (Some may make a human chain, others may run from one end to the other.) If the weather is reasonable, this could be an outside activity.

A quieter, drier alternative starter is to have a water-tasting session, with some bottles of different types of water, their labels hidden, and some cups. The children can tick their favourites.

Teaching

Talk about the freshness of flowing or living water, and show a picture of some women of today collecting water for the family at the local fresh water well. Today we are going to listen in on a conversation which takes place nearly two thousand years ago, by a well in Samaria.

Use two or three women leaders or helpers, dressed in nativity costumes and carrying jars or jugs, to chat the conversation that one of them has had with Jesus. To prepare for this, read the passage through several times and make a note of the main direction of the conversation. Then the woman can tell the story to her friends with them pumping her with questions, and eventually going off to see Jesus for themselves. It is best done informally and unscripted as it then sounds natural, and if someone forgets something one of the others can remind them with a question. Link the need for water to Jesus calling himself 'living water', with the women working out what he meant by this.

Praying

Flow in me, living water of God,
and satisfy my needs.
Flow through me, living water of God,
to bring life and hope to the world.

Activities

On the sheet there are instructions for making a working model of a well. Each child will need a small plastic pot, a drinking straw with a wiggly end, some thin string and some card. There are also discussion starter pictures, showing areas in our world in need of God's living water.

GOLD PANNERS

Aim: To explore the meaning and significance of 'living water'.

Starter

Play hoop-la, using bottles of different spring water. If you don't have any small hoops, cut cross sections from a large plastic bottle. This game is about aiming for water, and how our aim often falls short or wide of the mark.

Teaching

Cut out an arrow from thin card and fix it with a split pin on to the background as shown below.

Read the Exodus passage together, listening out for why the people were grumbling. Which way were they facing? (They were looking back to the *past* in Egypt, rather than seeing that God was with them in the present, leading them into the *future*.) What about Moses? (He was looking at God in the *present*, and helped the people to recognise this too. Now they could look confidently to the *future* in God's company.)

Then look at the Gospel – John 4:5-42. How was the woman still imprisoned by the past? (Her own relationships; society's attitude; religious and national set traditions and expectations.) How is Jesus like clear running water for her? (Look at the cleansing, refreshing and life-giving properties of water and see how these are also spiritual qualities.)

Praying

River, wash over me,
cleanse me and make me new.
Bathe me, refresh me and fill me anew.
River, wash over me. Amen.

Activities

On the activity sheet there are various references to help them unpack the meaning and significance of Jesus as 'living water', and outlets of world and personal needs which they can fill in as prayer concerns.

FOURTH SUNDAY OF LENT

Thought for the day

Jesus gives sight to the man born blind and exposes the blindness of those who claim to see.

Reflection on the readings

1 Samuel 16:1, 6-7, 10-13
Psalm 22
Ephesians 5:8-14
John 9:1-41

We are a very visually orientated species; our sense of sight is highly developed and very reliable. So reliable, in fact, that 'seeing is believing' is a fore-gone conclusion, and visual evidence the proof we are most likely to trust. Visual imagery is scattered through our language; 'I see', we will say on the phone, meaning that we understand, and 'keep an eye on her', or 'look after her', when we mean take care of her. We talk of insight, foresight and hindsight, of vision and perception.

Much of Jesus' teaching was enabling people to 'see' the truth about God and about themselves, and today's Gospel explores this whole issue of what is real blindness and what is real sight. The scene is set by the reading from 1 Samuel, where God's way of looking is contrasted with the usual worldly habit of looking at the outward appearance rather than the heart. Both then and now people are inclined to be impressed or otherwise by appearance, and assume that physical good looks are bound to be an expression of inner goodness. However many novels are written proving this assumption false, we persist in it doggedly.

God, however, is concerned with perceiving the heart of a person, and guides Samuel to anoint the youngest son, still a shepherd boy, to be the future king of Israel. In Ephesians, Paul advises us, too, to find out what pleases the Lord, so that we can live in the light of his sight, and expose all that is contrary to the way of goodness, truth and righteousness. We are to live as spiritually sighted people – children of light.

The man born blind has that openness of vision which allows him to recognise truth, righteousness and goodness when he meets it in the person of Jesus, and experiences it in the healing of his physical sight. He is able to stand his ground with the sceptical Pharisees and challenge their vision, just by seeing the truth clearly. He is therefore in the very best position to learn, and Jesus seeks him out to teach him more about his identity, since he is so ready to receive it. It is almost as if his physical blindness has been transformed into a gift, enabling him to be particularly aware of his need of sight, both physical and spiritual.

The Pharisees, on the other hand, are unaware of their spiritual blindness and do not recognise their need of fresh vision. That places them in a very poor position for learning about truth, because their closed perception acts like shutters, preventing the light of God's love and truth from entering. We are challenged to question our assumptions about where we see and recognise our need for God to light up our lives.

Discussion starters

1. Does the world's habit of looking at the outward appearance rub off on Christians so that even those in the Church do it?

2. In what ways are the sighted Pharisees 'blind' and the blind man sighted?

All-stage talk

Beforehand prepare a message on a piece of paper which will only be visible from the other end of the church through a pair of binoculars. The message is: 'People look at the outward appearance, but the Lord looks at the heart.' Also ask someone with strong glasses if they would mind helping with the talk today.

Ask the person with glasses to come and talk about one or two of the difficulties of poor physical vision; perhaps they wouldn't mind taking off their glasses and saying what they can see without them, contrasting that with their vision when wearing their glasses. So many of us would be forced to live very different lives if we were not helped to see by special lenses, and all that research and developed skill is something to be very thankful for.

Now blindfold a volunteer and ask everyone for ideas about how this lack of vision would make life very difficult. Thankfully there are aids to help those who are blind, and many blind people get really skilled at coping in their lives; but blindness still makes extremely difficult things that sighted people take for granted, and we all need to make sure that we notice the needs, and don't leave our bikes lying on the pavement or anything that might make it dangerous for those who can't see very well.

Today we heard about a man who had been born blind, so he had never seen anything in his whole life. And when Jesus made some mud and put it on his eyes, and told him to wash it off, that man was suddenly able to see for the very first time. (Remove the blindfold from the volunteer as you say this.) Can you imagine how that felt! All the colours and faces and new meaning to the textures he knew from touch alone! It's not a bad idea for us all to spend today looking at everything as if we have just been given our sight – as if we are seeing all the beauty and variety of God's world for the very first time. That will make us freshly thankful to our loving God; and it will help prevent us from being so used to seeing it all that we take God's gift of sight for granted.

Being given your sight is so obviously the work of goodness, and the man born blind is not prepared to go along with what the Pharisees are suggesting – that Jesus is not from God. He hasn't only been given physical sight, but spiritual in-sight as well. And we all need both sorts of sight. Sometimes, like the Pharisees, we think we are seeing everything clearly, so we stop looking.

Ask a volunteer to go to the back of the church and hold up the piece of paper. From the front it just looks like a piece of paper. But if we take the trouble to look at it through binoculars (give the volunteer a pair) you find truths you hadn't noticed before. (Ask them to read out the message they can now see.)

So today we are reminded of the wonder of sight, and encouraged to thank God for all we see. And we are challenged to keep seeking God, keep looking for him, and not shut our spiritual eyes to the light of his truth and goodness.

All-age ideas

- Have a 'still life' collection of glasses, binoculars, telescope, kaleidoscope and various other items designed to help us see clearly, together with a Bible and a cross. Give it a title: 'The blind receive their sight.'

- The Gospel is already written like a script and lends itself particularly well to being acted out.

- At the Penitential Rite, suggest that people close their eyes as they think of any areas of blindness in their outlook or attitudes, their assumptions or priorities, their values or behaviour.
  Our blindness prevents us from seeing your will for us;
  Lord, have mercy,
  Lord, have mercy.
  Our blindness makes us assume we can already see;
  Christ, have mercy,
  Christ, have mercy.
  Our blindness blocks the spread of your kingdom;
  Lord, have mercy,
  Lord, have mercy.

Prayer of the Faithful

Celebrant
Let us open our hearts to God
and pray to him for the Church and for the world.

Reader
Lord, in our blindness we come to you
for insight and perception,
for discernment and vision;
may we focus our gaze on your glory
in constant wonder and praise
until we see with your eyes
and notice with your love.

Silence

Open our eyes:
so that we can see.

Lord, wherever our world is damaged
or communities torn apart
by prejudice, narrow-mindedness,
or the refusal to see injustice or recognise needs,
anoint eyes and hearts to see with honesty
and act with integrity and compassion.

Silence

Open our eyes:
so that we can see.

Lord, help us to see things
from different perspectives,
and from one another's viewpoint,
so that we learn input as well as output,
listening as well as speaking,
the joy of giving as well as the humility of receiving;
may we reverence one another
in all our conversations,
both face to face
and when discussing those who are absent.

Silence

Open our eyes:
so that we can see.

Lord, we pray for all
who are blind and poorly sighted,
that they may be kept safe from danger
and enabled to live full lives;
we ask you to bless
those working to remove cataracts
for the poor in the Third World
and restore their sight.
We pray for those who are spiritually blind;
for those blinded by rage and hurt,
jealousy or complacency.

Silence

Open our eyes:
so that we can see.

Lord, we commend to your safe-keeping for ever
all who have died in faith,
and all who have been working in your service
though they did not know you by name;
as they see you face to face
may their joy fill eternity.

Silence

Open our eyes:
so that we can see.

In our praise we join with Mary and say:
Hail, Mary . . .

We name in silence now
any known to us
with particular needs or burdens.

Silence

Celebrant
Loving Father, we bring you these prayers
through Christ our Lord,
and through him we offer ourselves
to be used in your service.
Amen.

TREASURE SEEKERS

Aim: To praise God for all the things we can see.

Starter

Pass round a 'feelie bag' in which there are two or three things. Each child feels what is inside, and once everyone has had a go, you can share ideas about what is in the bag. Tip the contents out to see how our guesses match up with the reality.

Teaching

Cover several hoops in different colours, laid down on matching coloured paper, and bring an assortment of objects, both natural and manufactured, both tiny and large, and some pictures which the children can sort according to colour, so that you end up with each hoop being a colour display. You could get each child or small group to work on a particular colour. Wind some rainbow colours of ribbon or crepe paper between the hoops.

Admire the displays, and ask everyone to shut their eyes, then open them again. Our eyes give us so much fun; God has made so many lovely things to see, and with our eyes we can see them and enjoy them.

Praying

Red and yellow, green and blue,
we are giving thanks to you!
Orange, purple, pink and grey,
your colours brighten up the day.
Thank you for them all –
my favourite is (*everyone shouts out their favourite*)

Activities

There is a pattern to colour in their favourite colours using mosaic (squares of coloured paper cut from old greetings cards and sorted into colour bowls) and a picture of some red things, some blue things and some green things, so the children will need these colours of crayons.

PEARL DIVERS

Aim: To know about the man born blind being given his sight by Jesus.

Starter

Pass round a 'feelie bag' with a number of different items in. Ask everyone to have a feel of the contents and try to work out what is inside and what colour each is. Once everyone has felt the contents, share ideas about the items and their colours, and then check these by tipping the things out of the bag. Was it possible to tell colours by touch?

Teaching

Beforehand, find a picture of grass and trees and sky, either from a calendar or drawn and coloured. Have a sheet of black paper lying on top of this.

We get so used to seeing that we can't really imagine how hard it must be to see nothing at all. Ask them to shut their eyes to try. They can try walking around with their eyes closed, or taking their shoes on and off, or writing their name on a sheet of paper on the floor. Talk about some of the ways blind people are helped, such as having guide dogs, special computers, special 'touch reading' (Braille) and white sticks. What would they most miss seeing if they were blind?

Today we are hearing about a man who had been born blind. He had never seen the sky or the earth, or the people in his family, until the day Jesus walked into town. For him the world was black darkness both day and night.

When Jesus' disciples saw this man, they asked Jesus whether he or his parents had sinned to cause his blindness. People in those days thought that being blind was a punishment from God. Jesus explained that blindness is nothing to do with

anyone's sin, and that God was going to use this man's blindness to help people see God more clearly. The disciples were puzzled by that, and they watched to see what Jesus was going to do.

Jesus spat on the dusty ground and made some mud. (That might sound revolting to us, but saliva is known to have healing qualities and many people still use it, rather like a dog or cat will lick a wound to make it better. As you explain this, pour a little water on to some earth and mix it into some mud.) Jesus put mud on the man's eyes and told him to go and wash it off in a nearby pool. So the man went off to the pool and washed the mud from his eyes. (Wash your muddy hands and rinse your face in a bowl of clean water.)

As the man wiped the water away from his eyes, he stared around in complete amazement. (Look around at their faces as if it is the first time you have seen them.) For the first time in his life he could see the faces around him. Voices suddenly had faces to go with them, and he could see trees and flowers, the water and the sky. Everything was very bright and so colourful! He blinked to make sure it was real (blink a few times), and the colourful world was still there, as beautiful as ever.

'I can see! I can see! Hey, everyone, I can see!' shouted the man. He ran about touching things and staring at them, shaking his head in amazement at the way it was so easy to walk and run without checking for obstacles. Life seemed suddenly so much easier. He walked home seeing the road and the palm trees, the donkeys and houses, and waving to the neighbours.

'Isn't that the man who was born blind?' said the neighbours to each other. He looked so confident and happy and ordinary that they could hardly believe it was the same person. 'Yes, it's me,' said the man. 'How is it that you can see then?' they asked. 'Well,' said the man, 'this person called Jesus put mud on my eyes and told me to wash it off. And when I did as he said, I could see!'

Praying

Lord, help me to see clearly
with the eyes you have given me.
Help me to see truth and right and goodness.
Help me to notice other people's needs,
and help me to see ways I can be of help.

Activities

On the sheet they can try copying a shape, first with their eyes closed and then with eyes open, and there are two nearly identical pictures of the Gospel story, where they have ten differences to spot. There is also a wordsearch to spot key words from the story.

GOLD PANNERS

Aim: To explore the issue of spiritual sight and blindness.

Starter

Provide a selection of magazines and newspaper supplements, glue and scissors. Write certain characteristics on separate sheets of paper and ask everyone to choose images which seem to go with the characteristics. Here are some ideas: relaxed, ambitious, violent, dangerous, important, stressed.

Teaching

Look at the different collections of images and talk about how we make judgements based on what people look and dress like. Talk about dressing to impress, and the reasons we would choose particular clothes and refuse to wear others. We are constantly being told that our image is very important. Today we hear a rather different message: people look at the outward appearance but God looks at the heart.

Read the passage from 1 Samuel 16, seeing how people were just the same thousands of years ago – still tending to judge from appearances. Then read from Ephesians, which suggests that if we are 'dressed' in God's love it should really show in our attitudes and relationships; that is what walking by the light means. Our behaviour should be consistent with what we claim to believe.

Now read the Gospel, with different voices for the characters and narrator, thinking as you read, 'Who is blind in this story?' Talk about how the blind man is given both physical and spiritual sight, and how the Pharisees are spiritually blind, even though physically sighted.

Praying

God be in my head and in my understanding.
God be in my eyes and in my looking.
God be in my mouth and in my speaking.
God be in my heart and in my thinking.
God be at my end and at my departing.

(Book of Hours, 1514)

Activities

There is a short sketch which explores the way we often make wrong judgements based on appearance, and a look at what is sight and what is blindness, spiritually speaking.

FIFTH SUNDAY OF LENT

Thought for the day

Jesus is the resurrection and the life. He can transform death and despair, in any form, into life and hope.

Reflection on the readings

Ezekiel 37:12-14
Psalm 129
Romans 8:8-11
John 11:1-45

Things don't come much deader than dry scattered bones. It is a powerful image of the totally hopeless, without even a whispered memory of life. Ezekiel the prophet speaks God's unlikely hope to a dislocated and despairing people. In the hands of God there is no abandonment but promise of restoration, inbreathed by the Creator's breath.

Psalm 129 echoes the dazed amazement at the way God proves again and again that with the Lord there is mercy and fullness of redemption. In Romans we find the same realisation worked out in a more cerebral way, celebrating the profound truth, born of real experience, that Spirit-filled life is a completely new and fulfilling life, in comparison with which other life seems like a kind of deadness.

And in today's Gospel reading we hear the whole narrative of Lazarus and his sisters, living through his dying and death, while the Lord of life is elsewhere. It is an evocative story, with Jesus portrayed at his most human, and many layers of meaning packed into the event. Why did Jesus delay? What about those conversations, first with Martha and then with Mary?

John is wanting to tell us deep truths about Jesus' total humanity and divinity; if ever a story revealed the nature of Emmanuel – 'God-with-us' – then this is it. The practical, less emotional Martha is better able to grasp the logic of what it means for the Lord of life to be present, whereas Mary is simply devastated and feels wounded by Jesus' absence which doesn't make sense to her.

We may recognise this terrible sense of loss and distance when in our own lives we feel God ought to be there yet he seems not to be; and Jesus himself knew it on the cross: 'My God, why have you forsaken me?' But it is this raw grief in all its honesty and candour which tears Jesus' heart and shakes him with agonised weeping. With us, too, he is there at such times of raw pain, sharing our searing pain and grief and weeping with us.

Jesus, as the Lord of life, is God's voice speaking right into the darkness of death and drawing out life.

Discussion starters

1. How would the image of bodies raised from their graves help the exiled people Ezekiel was called to speak to?

2. Compare the responses of Martha and Mary and Thomas. What do we learn about the strengths and weaknesses of each?

All-stage talk

You will need an inflatable ball or a balloon, and, if possible, a dummy used for teaching mouth-to-mouth resuscitation. Otherwise, bring along a large baby doll.

Begin by asking everyone to breathe in deeply, hold their breath while you count to twenty and then let their breath out. They will all have noticed how much we need that air. By the end of just twenty seconds we're getting desperate! Most of the time we breathe in and out without even thinking about it. Although it's such a vitally important thing to do, we're designed so that the breathing mostly goes on automatically so we can do lots of other things at the same time. Yet without that breathing we wouldn't be able to do any of those other things because we would be dead. That's how important breath is – it's a matter of life and death.

Ask a volunteer to demonstrate what we have to do if we come across someone whose breathing has stopped. Point out that what is happening when we are doing mouth-to-mouth resuscitation is that we actually do the breathing for the other person. With our living breath we can save someone's life.

Today in the Gospel we have heard an amazing story of Jesus actually bringing someone back to life. It was his friend Lazarus, and when Jesus' voice, as the Lord of life, broke into the place of death, Lazarus heard his name being called and walked out into life again towards that voice.

Jesus calls each of us by name. He calls into the place we are, even if that place is full of darkness and sadness, or if the noise of unimportant things we like wasting our time on nearly drowns his voice, or if we're running as fast as we can away from God's way of living. Wherever we are, Jesus keeps calling because he wants to bring us out into new life. He knows his breath in us will transform our time in this life, and beyond that into the time after our physical death. As Jesus breathes his life into us it will make such a difference to us that we'll wish we'd gone for it ages ago!

Ask someone to blow up the ball or balloon, and as they do so point out what a difference it is making

to have that breath inside. Once they are filled with our breath they have a whole new dimension – they're much more useful and they're much more their true selves. It's the same with us. When we let God breathe his life into us every minute of every day, we become much more our true selves, our life has a whole new dimension, and we are of more use to God in caring for the world he loves.

All-age ideas

- Have the Gospel read through by a group, with people taking the different parts, so that the different conversations in the story are brought out.

- Ask some of the creative people in the congregation to make a poster or banner about God's power to renew us, using the 'dry bones into living people' image.

Prayer of the Faithful

Celebrant
As the people of the living God,
let us join together in our prayers
for the Church and for the world.

Reader
Holy God, breathe your life into the Church;
breathe holiness and deepening faith,
breathe energy, inspired teaching and fervent praise;
unblock the channels and make us more receptive
to your gentleness and your power.

Silence

Breathe into us:
so that we live in you.

Holy God, breathe your life into the universe;
breathe caring, honesty and compassion,
breathe right values and good stewardship,
peace and reconciliation, vision and hope.

Silence

Breathe into us:
so that we live in you.

Holy God, breathe your life
into our homes and places of work;
breathe increased patience and understanding,
and the courage to live the Christian life,
when to do so brings ridicule or demands sacrifice.

Silence

Breathe into us:
so that we live in you.

Holy God, breathe your life into those who suffer;
breathe comfort and wholeness,

forgiveness and new confidence,
breathe peace of mind
and the knowledge of your love.

Silence

Breathe into us:
so that we live in you.

Holy God, breathe your life into the dead and dying;
breathe courage for the journey
and the realisation that you can be trusted.
Breathe life that lasts for ever.

Silence

Breathe into us:
so that we live in you.

We join our prayers with those of Mary,
the Mother of our Saviour:
Hail, Mary . . .

Trustingly we pray in silence
to our loving Lord,
who considers each one of us special.

Silence

Celebrant
Father, we thank you for your constant love,
and offer these prayers
for the sake of your Son, Jesus.
Amen.

TREASURE SEEKERS

Aim: To know that God gives life and hope.

Starter

Inflatable toys to blow up and then play with.

Teaching

Get all the children breathing in and out while they
hold their ribs, so they can feel the air going in and
out. Talk about the way we breathed air into the
inflatable toys so that we were able to play with
them. Just as our bodies need air, so our spirits
need God's Spirit. God gives us life and God gives
us hope.

Now spread carpet tiles, bath towels or a sheet
on the floor, and use the pictures below to make
larger cut-outs from thin card. Gather the children
around the edge and move the figures as you tell
the story of Lazarus being brought back to life
again.

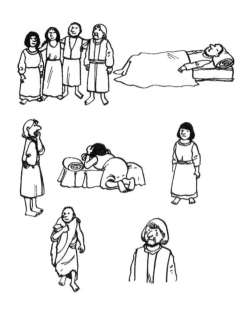

Praying

God be in my head and in my thinking.
  (hold head with both hands)
God be in my hands and in my doing.
  (hold out hands)
God be in my heart and in my loving. Amen.
  (hands on heart, then arms and hands stretched out)

Activities

On the sheet there are some pictures of people and
animals in very tricky situations. The children can
draw in something that brings them hope. Also the
Lazarus story can be made into a book to take
home and read. The children will need coloured
mounting paper already cut to size, a hole punch
and a length of wool, or a stapler.

PEARL DIVERS

Aim: To know that Jesus is the resurrection and the
life.

Starter

Play musical statues. Choose some appropriate
music to play during the dancing, such as *Dem
bones*, *Every minute of every day* or *The race*.

Teaching

Beforehand draw a large picture of a person and
cut it up into pieces to match the number of people
in the group. Give each person a piece of the
puzzle and invite them a few at a time to add their
section to complete the picture. When the picture is
finished tell the children how God is able to put
together again people who feel broken up by sadness

or bad things that have happened to them. Even when everything seems hopeless, God can breathe in hope. There is nothing he can't use somehow, even the worst things.

Now get everyone involved in telling the story of Lazarus, most as the crowd of friends who are sad when he dies and amazed and happy when Jesus brings him back to life again. Either narrate the story in your own words, or use this script:

Jesus had some friends called Lazarus, Martha and Mary. He often stopped off at their house for a meal, and sometimes he'd stay with them. One day Lazarus got very ill. His sisters looked after him and gave him cool drinks, and mopped his hot head, and did everything they could to make him better, but Lazarus got worse and worse. Martha and Mary wished their friend Jesus was around to help, but Jesus was away in Jerusalem. Then a very sad thing happened. Lazarus got so ill that he died. Mary and Martha cried, and all their friends and neighbours were sad as well and tried to comfort them. 'At least he isn't in pain any more,' they said. That was true of course, but Mary and Martha just knew they loved their brother and wanted to have him back living with them again and for everything to be normal and ordinary.

Four days later Jesus returned with his disciples and Martha went out to meet him as soon as she heard he was on his way. When she saw him she burst out, 'If you had been here, Jesus, my brother wouldn't have died!' Then she stopped and thought a moment. Perhaps there was still hope even though Lazarus was dead. 'In fact,' she went on, 'I'm sure that even now God will give you anything you ask.' Jesus looked at Martha and saw her sadness, her love for her brother, and he saw that she really wanted to believe that Jesus was the Christ, the Son of God.

Then Martha ran back to the house and told Mary that Jesus was there. Mary went out, still crying, and met Jesus. She couldn't understand why this had happened when Jesus wasn't there to help and she said so to Jesus. Jesus looked at her and saw the ache of sadness in her heart. He saw her not understanding how a good God could let such terrible things happen. And Jesus sobbed and sobbed at the sadness of it all. They cried together. At last Jesus said, 'Where did you bury him?' Martha and all their friends had joined them now and they all said, 'Come and see.' They all walked until they came to the tomb where Lazarus had been laid. Some of the crowd realised how much Jesus loved his friend Lazarus. Other people couldn't understand why Jesus hadn't stopped his friend from dying.

Jesus gave the order for the stone that sealed up the tomb to be rolled away. Jesus looked up to heaven and prayed to his Father, thanking him for hearing his prayer and longing for the people to believe and understand. Then he called out loudly, 'Lazarus, come out!'

Everyone watched the tomb and heard the power of life in Jesus' voice. It was reaching right into death. And then there was a shuffling noise, and there was Lazarus, still wrapped up in his death clothes, but pulling them off and smiling as he walked out of the tomb, completely better and completely alive! Everyone gasped and took a step back in amazement, and then crowded round Lazarus, hugging him, some of them crying again – but this time for joy! That day many more people came to believe that Jesus was the Messiah they had been waiting for. He really was the Lord of life.

Praying

Lord Jesus, bring us all to life
by the power of your love.
Bring us all to live
in the life of your kingdom. Amen.

Activities

On the sheet there are instructions for making a jigsaw puzzle which reinforces today's teaching, and a wordsearch that includes the keywords and characters from the Lazarus story.

GOLD PANNERS

Aim: To explore the ways in which Jesus is the resurrection and the life.

Starter

Use a paper kit for constructing a skeleton, or make a simplified home-grown one from thin card, following the illustration below.

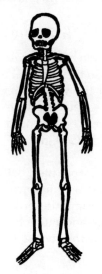

Teaching

First explain that the people of Israel were living in exile, and felt there was no hope for them when Ezekiel had his vision of people being raised from their graves. Then read the Old Testament passage. What would this image have said to the people, bearing in mind where they were coming from? Bring out the message of hope and God's capacity for transforming even the deadest situation.

What about the dead situations in our world and in our own life? Write some of these down on paper and then read the story of Lazarus. Several people can take part in this reading, or it could be acted out. What has it to say about some of the situations you wrote down? What does it tell us about Jesus and who he is?

Praying

Out of the depths have I called to you, O Lord:
Lord, hear my voice.
If you, Lord, should note what we do wrong:
who then, O Lord, could stand?
But there is forgiveness with you:
so that you shall be revered.
I wait for the Lord, my soul waits for him:
and in his word is my hope. Amen.

(From Psalm 130)

Activities

On the sheet there are various pictures used by the prophets to explain God's message which can be matched with the meanings. These can be used as discussion starters for opening up their receptiveness to the different ways God speaks to us. There is space for them to explore and note the ideas that come from reading the story of Lazarus, from various different viewpoints.

HOLY WEEK

PALM (PASSION) SUNDAY

Thought for the day

Jesus rides into Jerusalem cheered by the crowds. Days later, crowds will be clamouring for his death.

Reflection on the readings

Liturgy of the Palms:
Matthew 21:1-11

Liturgy of the Passion:
Isaiah 50:4-7
Psalm 21:8-9, 17-20, 23-24
Philippians 2:6-11
Matthew 26:14-27:66 or Matthew 27:11-54

Today we begin the heightened drama of the walk through a week known as holy. Since Christmas we have traced the life of Jesus through his birth, childhood, Baptism and preparation in the wilderness, and touched on the main areas of his ministry; and now we come to that final week of his earthly life. All the Gospel writers move into noticeably greater detail in their narratives, with these events taking up a sizeable proportion of each Gospel. The words and events are carefully and thoroughly recorded, in keeping with the intense significance of these days which focus all of life before them and all that has happened since.

Quite deliberately, the readings and liturgy take us on a roller-coaster of spiritual experience. We stand with the ecstatic crowds waving palm branches and celebrating the entry into Jerusalem, the holy city, by Jesus the Messiah. There is great hope and expectation that final things are drawing to accomplishment. We are poignantly aware that Jesus is both acknowledging the crowd's excitement at his kingship and also trying to show them something of the true nature of his kingship which has nothing to do with temporal power and wealth or narrow nationalism.

And then we are gripped by the detailed seriousness of all that led up to the crucifixion, like a profound family memory indelibly written on hearts and handed down with great care and reverence from generation to generation. We both cry out against what is happening and also know it to be necessary and inevitable. We both balk at the way people could treat Jesus, the Lord of life, and also know that we do it ourselves every day. We recognise the utter failure and futility of it all and

also know it to be the strangest and most complete victory for the entire world.

Discussion starters

1. What particular details did you notice in this reading of the crucifixion?

2. Why did Jesus choose not to call on all the angels to be at his disposal? (Matthew 26:53-54)

All-stage talk

Have the London Underground map printed out on the weekly sheet, or have some larger versions available to show everyone.

Look at the plan and talk about the way it is simple sign language to help us make sense of a huge complicated network of rails and tunnels criss-crossing under the streets. The whole thing is so enormous to understand that we need this simple map.

But when we travel on the underground it only works because, as well as the simple map in our hand or on the station wall, the real massive tracks are laid in all those dark tunnels, and the electrical power is surging through all the thick cables, and the tilers have been busy fixing tiles on the station walls, and the computers are busy checking where each train is so that they don't bump into one another, and those moving stairs, the escalators, are well oiled and running smoothly. Although all this doesn't show up on our plan of coloured lines and blobs, we only have to look at it and we know that all the real stuff is right there.

In a way the cross shape is like one of those plans. Draw people's attention to the crosses they can see around them in church. It is only a simple shape, and we can all make it ourselves by placing one index finger across the other. (Do that now.) When people say 'fingers crossed' what do they do? (Ask some people to show this.) Today it usually means hoping we'll be lucky, but a long time ago it was people making the sign of the cross as they prayed about something they were worried about. (We could go back to using the sign that way!)

Now if the shape of the cross is like the underground train plan, what is all the real, deep stuff that the cross reminds us of? Ask everyone to find or make a cross and look at it, as you tell them about the deeper meaning: God loves the world so much that he was willing to give up everything, and come and live with us in person as Jesus. That loving led him to a cross where he gave up his life for us, taking all the selfishness and sin on himself, and stretching out his arms in welcome and forgiveness, because he so longs for us to be free.

All-age ideas

- The reading of the Passion can be sung by the choir, or dramatised using different voices, with the whole congregation joining in the crowd's words.

- A drama group could prepare a short mime to bring out the meaning of the crucifixion. Rather than having set movements to follow, give them some familiar religious keywords to pray about, unpack and express, such as *Saviour, Redemption* or *Justification*.

Prayer of the Faithful

Celebrant
As we recall the extent of God's love for us,
let us pray.

Reader
Father, if we as the Church
are truly to be the body of Christ,
then let us stand at the foot of the cross
and learn what it means to love
and keep on loving;
to serve and keep on serving.

Silence

God our Father:
let your will be done in us.

If the world is ever to see real hope,
then purify and transform our lives
and stretch out our arms in loving forgiveness,
with no exceptions and no small print,
so that we shine as lights in the darkness.

Silence

God our Father:
let your will be done in us.

If our work places and neighbourhoods and homes
are to display and respond to your values,
then make us more fervent in prayer,
more courageous in self-discipline
and, above all, more loving in reaching out to them.

Silence

God our Father:
let your will be done in us.

If the terrible suffering of extreme poverty,
injustice and oppression
is to be addressed realistically,
then take away our greed and complacency
and our assumptions
about appropriate living standards,
and teach us sacrificial self-giving
of time, energy and resources.

Silence

God our Father:
let your will be done in us.

Father, through the life-giving death of Jesus,
may the dying turn to you
and know your merciful love;
may the grieving be comforted,
and may we all one day share
with those who have died
the eternal joy of your heaven.

Silence

God our Father:
let your will be done in us.

With Mary, the bearer of God's Son,
we make our prayer:
Hail, Mary . . .

Knowing that God our Father
hears the cry of his children,
we pray in silence for our own needs and cares.

Silence

Celebrant
Merciful Father,
we know that you hold all life in your hand;
please hear our prayers,
through Jesus our Redeemer.
Amen.

TREASURE SEEKERS

Aim: To welcome Jesus, the king on a donkey.

Starter

If your church has a Palm Sunday procession, then the children will be joining in with this. Provide them with palms to wave, and ask for one of the hymns to be one the children can cope with, such as *Hosanna, hosanna!* or *Rejoice in the Lord always*. If the church doesn't organise a procession, there might be a special one for the children.

Teaching

Tell the children the story of Jesus coming into Jerusalem on a donkey, either using your own words based on a careful reading of the Bible text, or one of the versions available for young children. As you tell the story, get the children to join in with all the actions, such as miming the untying of the donkey and leading it to Jesus, the waving of palm branches and laying coats on the road, and shouting 'Hooray for Jesus!'

Praying

Clip, clop, clip, clop!
Hosanna! Hosanna!
Hooray for Jesus,
the king on a donkey!
Hosanna! Hosanna!
Clip, clop, clip, clop!

Activities

Use the pattern on the sheet to make palm branches from green paper. There is also a road drawn on the sheet and a donkey to cut out and lead along the road into Jerusalem. Children will need assistance with the cutting. For very young children have the donkey already cut out.

PEARL DIVERS

Aim: To look at why Jesus came riding into Jerusalem on a donkey.

Starter

If your church has a Palm Sunday procession the children will be joining in with this. Provide them with palms to wave. Otherwise, have a procession with all the children and young people, making it lively and joyful with taped music, singing, dancing and percussion instruments.

Teaching

With the children's help go over the events of Jesus' life from his birth in Bethlehem and childhood in Nazareth in a country which was ruled over by the Romans. Mention Jesus' Baptism and his time of testing out in the wild country on his own. Mention his job as a carpenter and his ministry, bringing out that he healed those who were ill, or unable to walk or hear or speak or see, as well as telling the people about the way God loved them. He talked about the kingdom of God, or the kingdom of heaven. This wasn't so much a place as a way of living – the loving way of living. As the events are mentioned, draw or write them along a time line.

The people wanted to make Jesus their king, but the kind of king they had in mind would lead them to fight the Romans and throw them out of their country. Was this the kind of king Jesus was?

Tell the story of the entry into Jerusalem, first practising these sound effects, which can be used during the story:

- Donkey – 'hee-haw!' and tongue clicking for a 'clip, clop' noise
- Jesus – 'Hosanna to the son of David!'

- Jerusalem – 'Holy city of peace' (whispered)
- Palms – rub palms of hands together to sound like the wind in the trees
- Crowd – 'Jesus! Jesus! Jesus!' in a chant

Praying

You laid aside your majesty,
gave up everything for me,
suffered at the hands of those you had created.
You took all my guilt and shame
when you died and rose again,
now today you reign
in heaven and earth exalted.

(From a song by Noel Richards
© Copyright 1985 Kingsway's Thankyou Music)

Activities

Following the instructions on the sheet, the children can make palm crosses. The other activities encourage them to see both the rejoicing as Jesus comes into Jerusalem and also the seriousness and sadness of Palm Sunday as he rides towards the cross.

GOLD PANNERS

Aim: To look at Jesus as both hero and failure in the world's eyes.

Starter

Join in the Palm Sunday procession if there is one. Otherwise, join in a procession with the younger children, with branches and possibly even a donkey.

Teaching

Begin by reading the passage from Matthew 21. Look at a palm cross and unwind it so they can see it as a palm leaf, which reminds us of how the people reacted when Jesus rode into Jerusalem on a donkey. Why were they giving him this hero's welcome? Make a note of their ideas on a sheet of paper; these may include such things as:

- They loved Jesus because he had been making people well.
- Jesus looked as if he really was the Messiah they were waiting for.
- They wanted a leader who would help them throw the Romans out.
- Jesus made them think about life in a more exciting way.

Now look at the passage from Philippians 2. Fold the palm leaf into the shape of a cross. What are our palm crosses reminding us now? The people were expecting Jesus to be powerful in the world's way, but instead he was a Servant King, and the kingdom is in people's hearts, not in a particular country. The triumphant procession into Jerusalem was going to lead Jesus straight on towards the cross – no longer a hero, but a complete failure. And yet it was his complete obedience even in this suffering and failure, with most people refusing to understand his mission, which actually turned it all into a fantastic victory, setting us free in a way nothing else could.

Praying

Give thanks to the Lord, for he is good;
his love endures for ever.
In my anguish I cried to the Lord,
and he answered by setting me free.
The Lord is with me; I will not be afraid.
Give thanks to the Lord, for he is good;
his love endures for ever. Amen.

(From Psalm 117)

Activities

The activity sheet encourages them to look at the way Jesus turns accepted values of power and patterns of kingship upside down. They will also be looking at crowd behaviour, and how Jesus tried to teach them through the nature of his entry into Jerusalem, addressing some of their real and false hopes and expectations.

GOOD FRIDAY

CHILDREN ON GOOD FRIDAY

Many churches organise separate worship and teaching for children on Good Friday. It is important that they are enabled to be part of this time, and Easter cannot really be celebrated with meaning unless we have also stood at the foot of the cross.

Whether you are planning to create a children's 'way of the cross' in and around the church, a prayer trail, craft activity, or dramatic presentation of the events, bear in mind that young children need to have the whole story, including the Resurrection, rather than being sent home with the pain and suffering of Jesus and no mention of Easter. We

also need to be sensitive about dwelling on the horror of the Crucifixion, and it may be necessary to split the children into age groups for part of the time, even if you have very small numbers in each group. Hot cross buns with a drink can be part of the event, and they need to come away with some sense of the amazing love of God.

EASTER

EASTER DAY

Thought for the day

It is true. Jesus is alive for all time. The Lord of life cannot be held by death. God's victory over sin and death means that new life for us is a reality.

Reflection on the readings

Acts 10:34-43
Psalm 117:1-2, 16-17, 22-23
Colossians 3:1-4
John 20:1-9

Just as in the story of creation, God rests on the Sabbath, when his great, creative work is complete, so now there has been a Sabbath of rest following the completion of this great re-creative work of salvation. In Jesus' last cry on the cross, 'It is finished!', there was the sense of accomplishment and completion, and now, in the dark of early morning on Sunday, the tomb is no place to stay and linger.

It is wonderfully human that all the accounts of the resurrection are slightly different; just as in any life-changing, dynamic event, people's accounts of the details are fused with their attempts to interpret and grasp the significance of what has happened. What is clear beyond all doubt is that somehow they began to understand the extraordinary truth – that Jesus had died but was no longer dead, in the human sense of the word. He was totally alive, but not in the merely human way – like Lazarus, for instance – where it would only be a matter of time before death came again.

Jesus, having gone into death with the power of life, and with his selfless love untarnished, could not be held there, but broke out into a new kind of life which is never going to end. Compared with this life, death is shadowy and powerless; it is temporary suffering and a journey of darkness which leads into unending daylight.

Peter and the other disciples can tell it from first-hand experience. They have actually seen Jesus fully alive, and have even eaten and drunk with him. Not that they were any different from the rest of us in finding it all impossible at first to imagine and believe; Jesus had been preparing them for this, but they still didn't really expect it to happen. After all, full life like this, after that very definite and horrific death through crucifixion, is simply impossible. Isn't it?

Like a catapult that has been pulled and stretched right back in one direction, the force of a sudden change of direction is very vigorous. Having been through the bewildered acceptance of Jesus' death and having lived a couple of days with numbing absence, the truth shoots them into a passion for telling everyone the amazing news, once they are equipped with the Holy Spirit's anointing. It is those who are witnesses to what God has done in their lives who tell the good news of the Gospel for real. And that is what convinces others of a truth which has the power to transform their entire life, both in time and after death.

Discussion starters

1. Look at the different reactions of those who were at the tomb. What convinced them that the Resurrection was a real event?

2. How is Jesus' resurrection life different from before he died?

All-stage talk

Bring along a few fresh eggs in a carton, and a chocolate egg.

Begin by reminding everyone that we are here for an exciting celebration. Draw attention to all the flowers, and the cleaning that has been going on, and the Paschal Candle or other special Easter decorations and symbols. What is it we're celebrating? That Jesus had died on the cross and is now alive – alive for ever!

Introduce the chocolate egg. For some reason we've been seeing a lot of these at Easter. No doubt some people gave some away. No doubt some ate one before breakfast! What have they got to do with Jesus? Why do we all like to give one another eggs at Easter time?

One reason is that people were giving one another eggs around the time of Easter long before they had heard about Jesus. This is springtime, and eggs are all part of the spring, with its promise of new life.

New life! That's interesting – we've been hearing about the new life that Jesus gives us. When people came to our country and told us about Jesus, they thought the egg was a very good way of explaining the Gospel, so they kept it.

How does an egg help us to understand the Easter story? Show everyone the carton of ordinary eggs, and hold one up on its own. What is it? (An egg.) What comes out of a fertilised egg like this? (A chicken.) Yes, it's a new life – in this case a chicken. An egg is the way new creatures come into being. And Easter is about Jesus being alive in a new way and making it possible for all of us to be given new life.

What does the inside of an egg look like? (It's got yellow yolk and some thick runny stuff which is white when it's cooked.) What are some favourite ways of eating an egg? (Gather suggestions.) So what is inside the shell turns into something quite different. Jesus' life now, as from the first Easter Day, is different. For a start, he's never going to die again; his new life isn't a life that runs out.

Now break one of the eggs. When we enjoy eating an egg the shell needs to be broken; otherwise we wouldn't be able to get at the white and the yolk. When a chick is ready to live in the big wide world it has to crack the eggshell before it can climb out. What does that tell us? Sometimes we want to hang on to things just as they are. We don't always want to change, even if change in our lives is for the best.

Will we let our shells be broken ready for the new life Jesus wants us to have? God is calling us out of our shells into a whole new, different way of living. It is the loving way of living, trusting in God with our heart and soul and mind and strength, and loving one another. That may mean that some of our habits and fears may, like shells, have to be broken before we can live freely in the loving way. The good news of Easter is that Jesus has already broken through death and sin, so if we hold on to him, he can bring us through the shell breaking and out into the light and space of day – a daylight which lasts for ever.

All-age ideas

- If part of the children's worship on Good Friday has involved art and craft work, such as banners or posters or Easter gardens, these can be used to decorate the church today.

- Make a celebration arch of flowers at the entrance of the church, either by attaching oasis in chicken wire around the doorway, or actually constructing an archway using three ladders, lashed together and fastened securely. Weave plenty of greenery in and out of the ladder rungs to hide the main structure, and then decorate with flowers and ribbons.

- Bells may be rung in a burst of praise, together with the organ or music group at the beginning of the Gloria.

- Rather than a traditional Easter garden, consider a cross made of wire and deadwood, which has flowers in oasis fixed into it.

Prayer of the Faithful

Celebrant
As we celebrate the new life of Resurrection,
let us pray to the one true God,
who brings us all to life.

Reader
Lord God, we pray that the Church
may proclaim with joy your message of hope
for the world;
may our lives, as well as our worship,
testify to the truth of the Resurrection;
broaden our vision of what is possible
through new life in you.

Silence

Life-giving God:
transform our lives.

Lord God, we pray for the world we inhabit;
for those who lead, and take important decisions,
and for those who follow or are coerced,
or who have no voice.
We pray for mercy and justice,
compassion and integrity.
We pray for protection against evil
and strengthening of goodness.

Silence

Life-giving God:
transform our lives.

Lord God, we pray for all babies,
and those as yet unborn,
that they may be born into a world
of love and acceptance.
We pray, too, for those who provide foster care,
and for all children at risk.
We pray for all parents and those who support them.
We pray for the newly baptised
and recently confirmed;
for a deeper commitment to supporting one another
as we grow in faith.

Silence

Life-giving God:
transform our lives.

Lord God, we pray for those who cannot think,
for the pain or anguish which engulfs them;
for all whose lives are troubled and insecure;
for those who have little energy left to rejoice.
Bring healing,
and the resources to cope with suffering,
and give us the grace
to carry one another's burdens in love.

Silence

Life-giving God:
transform our lives.

We make our prayer with Mary,
who knew the cost of loving:
Hail, Mary . . .

In the silence of God's accepting love,
we pray our individual petitions.

Silence

Celebrant
In silence we praise you, Father,
for your abundant blessings,
and ask you to hear these prayers
for the sake of Jesus Christ.
Amen.

TREASURE SEEKERS, PEARL DIVERS AND GOLD PANNERS

If possible, it is recommended that the children and young people are in church with the other age groups today. Use and adapt some of the all-age ideas, and involve the young people in some of the music and in the cleaning and decorating of the church.

TREASURE SEEKERS

Aim: To enjoy celebrating that Jesus is alive.

Starter

Have an Easter egg hunt, preferably outside if this is safe and practical.

Teaching

Using a blackboard and chalks, draw the story as you tell it. Please don't be put off and think you won't be able to do it as you can't draw! Young children will be fascinated by the story being drawn, however simple the drawing, and will be quite happy to imagine the bits your drawing leaves out. So do try it!

Start with the green hill outside the city of Jerusalem with the three crosses on it, and tell the children that this is where Jesus had been killed on Good Friday. Now draw in a garden with a cave, and tell the children how Jesus' friends sadly took his body down from the cross and put it in a cave. They rolled a huge heavy stone across the front of the cave to shut it. (Draw in the stone.) The next day was the day when everyone rested. Then on Sunday (which is the same day as today), when it was very early and not even light yet, some of Jesus' friends came to the garden. They wanted to put some sweet-smelling ointment on Jesus' body. (Draw them in at the cave.)

They had been wondering who they could get to move the heavy stone for them, but they were in for a big surprise. When they got to the cave they found that the stone had been rolled away! (Rub it out and draw it in at the side of the cave.) Sitting on the stone was an angel, all full of light. (Draw in the angel.) The angel told them that Jesus wasn't dead any more but had risen from the dead and was alive! The women were very surprised. (Make O shapes for their mouths.) Then suddenly they realised that Jesus was standing there, right next to them! (Draw him in.) The women were very happy to see Jesus. (Change their mouths into smiles.) They went back to tell Jesus' other friends that he was alive, not just for now, but for ever. (Change their legs to be running.)

Praying

Jesus, you died for me
  (arms out like a cross)
Jesus, you came to life for me!
  (arms up)
Jesus, you are alive for ever and ever and ever!
  (clap, clap, clap during the 'evers'.)

Activities

On the sheet they can follow the footsteps of the women to find where they have gone, and draw in the flowers in the garden. They can also decorate a hard-boiled egg with felt-tip pens or paints.

PEARL DIVERS

Aim: To teach them about the first Easter.

Starter

Have an Easter egg hunt, preferably outside if this is safe and practical.

Teaching

Invite a man from the congregation into the group this week to be Peter, and interview him about who he is, and what had happened on Friday. Then ask him what happened on the next Sunday morning. Here are some questions to give you an idea:

- Good morning! What's your name?
- Now you're a friend of this Jesus, aren't you?
- I've heard that last Friday he was put to death by the Romans. Is that right?
- I expect you were there with him through it all, being such a good friend?
- Well, what happened on Sunday morning? We've heard a lot of confusing reports!

- Is it possible that someone could have stolen Jesus' body?
- Now hang on a minute. You're saying that Jesus is alive again for ever. That must mean that he'll still be just as alive in about two thousand years' time! Is that right?
- Well, thank you, Peter, for coming this morning to tell us this amazing news. We'll be looking out for Jesus. It's really good to know he's still alive!

Praying

Christ has died. *(arms out)*
Christ has risen. *(arms up)*
Christ will come again! *(kneel on one knee, arms down, palms up)*

Activities

Give the children a large letter (at least A4 size) to colour and decorate. When they get back into church these letters can be held up or fixed up on the wall or laid on the floor to make the message: JESUS IS RISEN!

GOLD PANNERS

Aim: To celebrate the good news of Easter.

Starter

A time of praise, with everyone playing instruments or singing and dancing to recorded music suitable for this age group.

Teaching

Read both the John and the Matthew account of the Resurrection noticing the similarities and the differences, and looking for the central truth in both accounts. Talk about how the different characters might have felt, and why they behaved as they did. Then read the section of Peter's speech in Acts and link this with the accounts they have just read.

Praying

To God be the glory! great things he has done;
so loved he the world that he gave us his Son;
who yielded his life, an atonement for sin,
and opened the life-gate that all may go in.

Activities

Paint posters to express the meaning of Easter. These can be brought into church and displayed there, or used on the church notice boards. The group can work individually or in pairs and threes.

The sheet has space for them to plan and design their work, and there is a wordsearch for them to make and swap.

SECOND SUNDAY OF EASTER

Thought for the day

Through the risen Jesus we have a living hope which will never spoil or fade.

Reflection on the readings

Acts 2:42-47
Psalm 117:2-4, 13-15, 22-24
1 Peter 1:3-9
John 20:19-31

In these Easter readings we have a rather intriguing perspective, since we hear first from the post-Holy Spirit days and then go back to the events close to the Resurrection in the Gospel reading. It has the effect of sharpening our senses, making us more aware of the changes in this group of disciples.

Peter has a new-found confidence and enthusiasm, as we see in the reading from 1 Peter, where he encourages those having to endure very real and terrifying suffering for their faith. Only someone who had also suffered would be able to make such assertions with any credibility, and Peter speaks from the heart. He knows what it feels like to be scared of standing up for what you believe in; he knows what it feels like to fail miserably after good intentions, when you try to do things in your own strength. And he also knows that even the most timid of us can cope with anything when we are living the risen life in the power of Jesus Christ.

The Gospel shoots us back to a very anxious group of people, terrified of the Jewish authorities even though they are (apart from Thomas at this stage) actually convinced that Jesus is alive. Although they know he is risen, they have not yet accessed the power of that risen life, and have at present the boldness of mashed potato.

What Jesus does is to reassure them by his visible and tangible presence. There is a wonderful sense of normality in his greeting. When someone we love has died, and our life seems thrown up in the air and is falling slowly in pieces around us, what we crave is for things to be back to normal again.

Jesus understands this, and provides his friends with the reassuring presence they need. Then he breathes into them, as Adam was breathed into at the creation. This breath is what gives the disciples the power of new life, and with it comes the conferring of authority, whose hidden side is responsibility. Like Jesus they are sent out, as the word 'apostle' proclaims, to tell the good news with confidence in the living spirit of Jesus.

Thomas was also scared. He was scared, like many of us, of being taken for a ride – of belief being only wish-fulfilment. Thomas was going to stick to an honest recognition of where he stood until he had definite proof. When he is offered it, he finds he no longer needs it; the sight of Jesus is quite enough. Suddenly prophetic, Jesus acknowledges the faith of all those, including us, who do not have the benefit of visual and tactile sightings of Jesus, and yet are still able to believe in him and share his risen life.

Discussion starters

1. How do you think you might have felt if you had been there that evening when Jesus appeared in the room? Does Jesus appear among us today?

2. Is there any way we can be sure that someone is speaking with God-given authority, rather than personal aggrandisement?

All-stage talk

Ask for one volunteer who is brave and one who is more scared and timid. Tell the timid one that you are asking them to fall backwards. You promise them they won't come to any harm (but you don't say you will catch them). Suggest that they watch the brave volunteer to try it first, so they can see what happens. Now ask the brave volunteer to fall backwards, and make sure you catch them, or arrange to have someone strong to catch them.

Now ask if the timid person is able to try it, now that they have seen that it is safe. If they are, let them try it, making certain they are safely caught!

Sometimes it is very hard to know whether we can trust something or not unless we have seen it in action. Perhaps we have bought a tape recorder, or a jigsaw puzzle at a boot sale or a jumble sale, and it looks fine, and we are assured that it's in good working order. But when we get home we find the tape recorder chews up our favourite tape, and the jigsaw puzzle has two or three pieces missing.

It's all very disappointing to be let down like that. And the longer we live, and the more we are let down by things or by people, the more disappointed we get, and the more determined we are not to trust anyone or anything in case we are

let down again. Thomas was a bit like that. He had probably been badly let down by people during his life. Like lots of us, it made him scared to trust good news. We and Thomas would love good news to be true, but we'd rather not trust it at all than trust it and risk being let down.

Now Jesus himself knows that he is alive, and will stay alive for ever. He knows it would be quite safe for us to believe this, because he knows it's true! He hopes very much that we will be able to believe, because he knows it will make such a wonderful difference to our lives – we'll be able to live in a new kind of freedom, and become more and more our real selves.

So what does he do about it? In our Gospel reading today we heard how Jesus came into the room, joining his friends as they were praying, so that they knew he was there. And Jesus still does that, nearly two thousand years later. He is here now, with us, his friends. Whenever we gather in Jesus' name, he joins us. When we live on the lookout for him, we'll find we start noticing him more and more. We won't see him with our eyes, but we'll feel his love and peace, and suddenly know he is there.

All-age ideas

• Try this short sketch to alert people to the way we don't see what we aren't expecting, or what doesn't seem relevant.

Phil and Robert are waiting with their coats on at a bus stop. Both have briefcases. Robert is reading his newspaper. Phil is checking his watch.

Phil Excuse me, but has the 7:42 gone yet? The 25A?

Robert The 25A? I wouldn't know. I'm waiting for the 26. That's the bus I catch.

Phil Well, how long have you been waiting?

Robert Oh, since 7:40. But it isn't due till 7:50, and it's always late.

Phil Is the 7:42 ever late? *(Checks watch.)*

Robert I wouldn't know. I wait for the 26, you see.

Phil Well, have any other buses come since you've been waiting?

Robert Oh yes, there's been a few others, I think.

Phil What numbers were they?

Robert I wouldn't know. I wait for the 26 you see. That's the bus I catch.

Phil   Oh. Thanks. *(Folds arms in resignation and looks the other way.)*

Phil   Hey there's a bus coming . . . It's the 25A! So I haven't missed it! *(Checks watch.)* And it's only two minutes late. *(Sticks out arm to stop it.)*

Robert   The 26 is due at 7:50, you know. That's the bus I catch.

Prayer of the Faithful

Celebrant
As we gather here
with God's presence in the midst of us,
let us pray.

Reader
We bring to you, Lord,
the Church in all its richness and all its need;
all its diversity and all its division.
Give us a fresh understanding
of what it means to live in you;
may all of us celebrate the reality
of your presence among us,
filling us with new life and new hope.

Silence

Lord in your presence:
we lift our hearts to you.

We bring to you, Lord,
all those areas of our lives and our world
where there is confusion and bewilderment;
help us to go beyond our doubts and insecurity,
and to experience the joy of Christ's peace.

Silence

Lord in your presence:
we lift our hearts to you.

We bring to you, Lord,
our homes and families,
and all the joys and sorrows
of our relationships.
We ask you to be with us
in all we say and do.

Silence

Lord in your presence:
we lift our hearts to you.

We bring to you, Lord,
those whom life has damaged,
and all who find it difficult to trust in you;
give them refreshment and hope,
comfort, healing and inner serenity.

Silence

Lord in your presence:
we lift our hearts to you.

We bring to you, Lord,
those who approach death with great fear
and those who die unprepared to meet you.
Have mercy on us all,
forgive us all that is past
and gather us into your everlasting kingdom
of peace and joy.

Silence

Lord in your presence:
we lift our hearts to you.

Remembering Mary's dedication and love,
we make our prayer with her:
Hail, Mary . . .

Knowing that God loves us personally
and with full understanding,
we make our private petitions
to him in silence.

Silence

Celebrant
Father, coming together with thanks and praise
to worship you,
we ask you to accept these prayers
for the sake of Jesus Christ.
Amen.

TREASURE SEEKERS

Aim: To know we can sometimes trust what we can't see.

Starter

With the very young play a 'peep-bo' game. With the older children play 'hunt the trainer', telling the children first that there is a trainer somewhere in the room, even though they can't see it yet.

Teaching

Was the trainer there all the time? Yes it was, even though we couldn't see it. We can't see the air all around us but we know it's there because we are alive, breathing the air in and out of our bodies. We can't see Jesus, but we know he is here with us and he can see us.

Jesus can hear us, too, so we can talk to him. Who has some good news to tell Jesus and the rest of us? Have a time of sharing the children's news, in Jesus' company. Jesus loves us, so we can trust him with the things that make us sad as well as the happy things. Have a time of telling Jesus about some of the things that make us sad. After each one lead the children to ask for Jesus' help, either to comfort the person or animal, or simply to be there with them and bring some good thing out of a bad time.

What shall we sing to Jesus? All sing a favourite song (it doesn't have to be a hymn), singing our best, just for Jesus, who is listening, and loves to be with us.

Praying

Who cares if I can't see you?
(shrug shoulders with hands open)
I certainly know that you're here!
(nod)
Who cares if I can't touch you?
(shrug shoulders with hands open)
I certainly know that you're here!
(nod)
You love me.
(hands on heart)
You listen to me.
(touch ears)
You see me
(point to eyes)
and you talk to me.
(fingers to mouth then out from it)
So who cares if I can't see you?
(shrug shoulders with hands open)
I certainly know you're here!
(nod)

Activities

The children will need a piece of white candle each. On the sheet they can draw Jesus in wax in the picture of the Treasure Seekers in their group, and then with a light watercolour wash, paint over the picture so that Jesus can be seen. Protect the children's clothing before they start.

PEARL DIVERS

Aim: To know what it was that convinced Thomas and the others that Jesus was alive.

Starter

Place a few objects in a 'feelie bag'. Show the bag and point out that at the moment we can't tell what is in it. Now pass it around the circle. Each person has a feel and tries to identify the contents, but must not say anything. When everyone has had a go, each person in turn has a chance to name one thing they think is in the bag. Empty the contents so that everyone can see whether they were right.

Teaching

Would they have believed you if you had said there was a toothbrush in the bag? What about an elephant? Why are we more likely to believe some things than others? We use our common sense and our experience. We know that an elephant wouldn't fit inside this bag, but a toothbrush would. Today we are going to hear about someone who found it very hard to believe that Jesus really was alive. In fact he said this . . . (have John 20:25b written in a large speech bubble). The person's name was Thomas, and he was one of Jesus' disciples and loyal friends.

Now here is our first question: 'How likely do you think Thomas thought it was for him to be able to see and touch Jesus' wounds?' (Have a temperature chart headed, 'Thomas thought it was . . .' with these markings on it: impossible, very unlikely indeed, most unlikely, unlikely, possible, likely, very likely, dead certain.

Different children can come and point to the level they think. (There isn't a right or wrong answer, but it gets them thinking!)

Next: 'Thomas wished it could be true, because he loved Jesus and missed him.' (Place this heading over the first with blutack.) Again, let various children come and point to the level they think.

Sometimes we believe things because we want them to be true. Who believes that (West Ham) will win their next game? Thomas didn't want to pretend to believe. He didn't want to kid himself. If it was really true that his friend Jesus was alive, then he would believe it and be very happy. If it wasn't, he'd rather face up to that. Perhaps some of you feel like that, or know someone in your family like it.

A week after the disciples had told Thomas that they had seen Jesus alive, and he had said (verse 25b), Thomas went with the other disciples to pray and eat together. Suddenly, there was Jesus standing with them, large as life and obviously completely alive! 'Hello!' he said. 'Peace be with you!'

Now for our next question: 'Jesus will ignore Thomas because Thomas hadn't believed that he was alive.' How likely is that? (Use the chart again.) Well, we are told that what happened was this. Jesus went straight across to Thomas, and said, 'Put your finger here. See my hands. Reach out your hand and put it into my side. Stop doubting and believe.' (Have this written large on another speech bubble.) So what will Thomas do now, do you think?

Last question: 'Thomas will only believe when he has touched Jesus' wounds to make certain it's true.' How likely is that? (Use the chart for their ideas.) Well, in fact Thomas found he didn't need to do all that. Just knowing Jesus was there was enough for him, and this time, instead of saying (verse 25b), he said, 'My Lord and my God!' (Another speech bubble.) Jesus was very glad that Thomas now knew he was alive, and would be alive for ever. And he thought of all the people who would still believe even though they couldn't actually see him. I'm looking at some of those people now! Is there anyone here who knows that Jesus is alive, even though they haven't seen him? Well, Jesus was talking about you in that room nearly two thousand years ago. And this is what he said: 'Blessed are those who have not seen and yet have believed.' (Last speech bubble.) That's us!

Praying

With my eyes I may not be able to see you, Jesus, but I know you are real and I know you are here. With my hands I may not be able to touch you, Jesus, but my heart feels your love, your peace and your strength.

Activities

Following the instructions on the sheet, the children can make a kite which can fly in the invisible wind. Each child will need a plastic bag and some wool or thin string, and various decorative stickers.

GOLD PANNERS

Aim: To explore the way different people come to faith.

Starter

I know what this is, it's a . . . Pass around the group an ordinary object such as a sieve. Each person mimes a different way of using it. (For instance, someone might use it as a tennis racquet, someone else as a hat, and someone else as a ladle. The uses can be as ridiculous as they like.)

Teaching

We are all different, and we all have different ways of doing things, as we have just seen! Today we are going to look at the different ways people were convinced that Jesus was alive again, and the different ways people find they come to faith today; there isn't just one way that is valid.

Have a sheet with the heading, 'Why I believe Jesus is alive', and find the resurrection accounts so that people can refer to them. Go through some of the characters we were looking at last week, and as you mention them work together as a group to put into their words what seems to have clinched it for them (for example, Mary: 'I met him in the garden and he talked to me by name.') Look at Mary Magdalene, the other women, the guards, Peter and John in this way.

Now write up Thomas' name, and read together today's Gospel. Why might Thomas not have been with the others on the first occasion? (We don't know, but it helps to imagine round the story.) Why might he have made sure he was there exactly a week later? What might he have been hoping? What might he have been dreading? What finally convinced Thomas? (Write this up with the others.)

Now look at all the reasons on the chart. Are there any reasons that are possible for us? (Believing what someone we trust has told us; meeting Jesus when we're together with other believers; meeting Jesus on our own when we are upset or in great need.) Point out that overwhelmingly it seems to be contact with the living person of Jesus that really convinces people, rather than argument and physical proof, though these certainly help to prepare us for believing. Add to the chart other reasons they have met (or known in their own experience) for people coming to a real faith (such as learning about Jesus at church, seeing Christian behaviour in their family and their upbringing, seeing the effects of unchristian behaviour in society).

Look again at the way Jesus recognises where Thomas is, and talks to him through it. That's what Jesus will always do. If we genuinely want to know the truth, he will help us to see it, starting from where we are and using our past experiences, both good and bad, in bringing us to faith along a path we can understand and manage to follow.

Praying

My Lord and my God!
My Lord and my God!

Activities

The sheet helps to reinforce the teaching and the discussion about ways to faith, including our own, and there is a maze game to make. They will each need some card and a marble for this.

THIRD SUNDAY OF EASTER

Thought for the day

Jesus explains the scriptures and is recognised in the breaking of bread.

Reflection on the readings

Acts 2:14a, 22-28
Psalm 15:1-2, 5, 7-11
1 Peter 1:17-21
Luke 24:13-35

In the first reading, Peter talks of the great joy that he has for, despite the awfulness and horror of the death inflicted on Jesus, it was impossible for anything, even the depths of Hades, to hold him. Peter recalls the words of Psalm 15, our Psalm for today, which celebrates that wonderful sense of trust in the God who will free us from our chains, even the chains of death; and in his letter, Peter writes of the cost of our freeing, which points to such an extraordinary love that it draws out love in us both towards God and towards one another.

We are then taken back to that period of numb misery after the crucifixion, when all hope seemed dead for ever. We are on a road, with two grieving and confused disciples of Jesus, walking away from Jerusalem towards the town of Emmaus where they lived. Why was it that Jesus drew alongside these particular people, we may wonder. Perhaps his heart went out to them as a shepherd might look at his sheep who are in pain and lost and don't understand. Certainly Cleophas, who presumably shared this detailed account with Luke, recognises the low point their faith had reached and doesn't try to hide that.

Jesus walks along in the same direction they are going, leading them patiently and carefully to see the hints and clues in the scriptures which point to the necessity for the Messiah to suffer and die before being glorified. When they near their home, Jesus gives them the option of taking his words thus far and no further. He never forces his company on us. But the disciples can't bear to part from him now, and as he breaks bread they suddenly realise who he is, at which moment he no longer needs to be visible to them. They rush straight back, seven or eight miles, to Jerusalem, in their utter joy and excitement.

With us, too, Jesus draws alongside and helps us understand the words of scripture. He gives us the option of walking with him no further. And

whenever we invite him to stay, he comes in and shares bread with us. Whenever we meet together and break bread in Jesus' name, Jesus is there in person among us, and very often that presence is almost tangible as we sense his love and his peace.

Discussion starters

1. What guidelines about evangelisation can we learn from the way Jesus helps the two disciples from Emmaus?

2. How can we help newcomers, visitors and ourselves to recognise Jesus in the breaking of bread?

All-stage talk

Bring in some kind of game or piece of equipment which needs putting together and setting up properly before it can be used. This could be anything from a computer to a folding bed – it all depends on what is available and the interest area of the group. It needs to have a set of instructions to go with it.

Begin by introducing your item of equipment. We are continuing to look at the resurrection stories, when one person after another is astonished by amazing events. The congregation may well be astonished to see one of these brought into church for the sermon! Pretend that you are having a real problem with this thing because you don't understand it at all. You don't understand how to get it to work.

Have a primed helper who comes up at this stage and shows you the instruction leaflet. They tell you that if you read that it will tell you how the thing works and how to use it. Be surprised, but set to reading some of the instructions, without relating them to the equipment. They don't make much sense to you, and you get fed up. It's no good – you don't understand and it doesn't make sense.

Explain that this is rather like the way the two disciples felt as they walked sadly back home on the very first Easter Day. They didn't understand anything any more. They had great hopes about Jesus, but now he was dead, so their hopes were dead as well. They had heard about the women saying they had seen Jesus alive early that morning, but that didn't make any sense to them either. How on earth could someone be dead as dead and now be alive? It couldn't possibly be true!

Just then, as we read in today's Gospel, someone joined them and asked what they were so sad about. And when they told him, he started to show them how it actually did make a lot of sense. (Break off as the helper comes and offers to take you through the instructions and sort the equipment out. Accept their help and marvel as gradually, step by step, it starts to come together, and eventually works. Be excited about this and thank the helper. Then come back to the Emmaus story.)

Well, it certainly helps to have someone who really understands to help you when you are in a muddle! That's how those disciples felt when the stranger explained that it was all there in the scriptures (pick up a Bible) about the promised Messiah having to suffer and die before there could be new life. When they reached their home they invited the helpful stranger in to stay with them, and when their guest took the bread and blessed and broke it (mime this) . . . what do you think they suddenly realised?

It was Jesus!

And that is still what Jesus does. He walks along with us where we are walking. He helps us understand about God through the words of scripture (pick up the Bible again), he helps us make sense of life and its problems (stand beside the working piece of equipment), and (move to the altar) he makes himself known to us in the breaking of bread.

All-age ideas

- Have the Gospel mimed as it is narrated, using the centre aisle as the road and the sanctuary as the house, so that the breaking of bread is mimed at the altar. Have Jesus wearing an alb so that the links are there with the breaking of the bread in the Eucharist.

- Have a display of Bible reading notes and various Bibles suitable for different age groups, so as to encourage people to get to know the scriptures better and deepen their understanding.

Prayer of the Faithful

Celebrant
As we gather to hear the word of God
and to break bread in the presence of Jesus,
let us pray.

Reader
Walk with us, Lord, on our journey of faith,
both as individuals and as the Church of God;
open up to us the truths
you long for us to understand,
and inspire all who teach and encourage.
Equip us all to pass on the good news of Easter.

Silence

Lord God:
abide with us.

Walk with us, Lord, down the streets
of our cities, towns and villages,
drive with us down the motorways
and fly with us down the air corridors.

Meet all those who are curious, searching,
or moving in the wrong direction.
Let your presence be sought
and recognised in all the world.

Silence

Lord God:
abide with us.

Walk with us, Lord, in our life journeys,
guiding, teaching and correcting us,
as we learn the lessons of loving
in our homes, our work and our communities.

Silence

Lord God:
abide with us.

Walk with us, Lord,
through the times of suffering and pain,
alerting us to one another's needs
and providing for us
in whatever ways are best for us.
Help us to trust you through the dark times;
breathe new life and hope
into those who are close to despair.

Silence

Lord God:
abide with us.

Walk with us, Lord, through the valley of death;
may our love and prayers support those
who walk that journey today.
Draw close to them and welcome them
into the joy of heaven.

Silence

Lord God:
abide with us.

May we learn from the humility of Mary
as we pray with her to the God of heaven:
Hail, Mary . . .

Confident in God's welcoming love,
we pray in silence, now,
for our individual needs.

Silence

Celebrant
Father, in silence, we adore you,
and open ourselves to your healing love.
Accept us, and our prayers, dear Father,
for the sake of Jesus, the Christ.
Amen.

TREASURE SEEKERS

Aim: To know that the risen Jesus walks beside us through life.

Starter

Play with various puzzle games such as jigsaws and shape puzzles. Or play Kim's game, where you set out a number of different objects on a tray and let everyone look at them for a while. Then cover the tray and see how many things they can remember. The children are having to work things out, and experience that this isn't always easy.

Teaching

Set up a length of lining paper on which you have drawn Jerusalem at one end (with the green hill, the crosses and the cave in the garden) and the little town of Emmaus at the other end. Draw a winding road going between the two places. Use this as you recap on the events leading up to the Resurrection and also for today's teaching.

Remind the children that on the first Easter Day – Easter is the day we all have Easter eggs – Jesus came to life. He had died on the cross on the Friday and his friends had put his body in the cave and fixed a great big stone like a door to shut the cave. And early on the Sunday morning, when the women came to the garden, what did they find? They found the stone rolled away and Jesus' dead body wasn't in the cave because he wasn't dead any more – he was alive! Alive so that he would never die again. (They will be able to help you with the story. It will be interesting to discover which details they remember best!)

Today we are going to hear about two friends of Jesus who lived about seven miles from Jerusalem. On that same day they were walking home. (Have two toys to walk along the road, starting at Jerusalem.) They were very sad because their dear friend Jesus had died. Just then another traveller caught them up and they all said hello. The stranger said to them, 'Why are you both looking so sad?'

'Haven't you heard?' they said, 'We're sad because Jesus is dead. He was so kind and good, and he told us good stories to teach us about God, and he made people better, and we hoped he would be the leader of our country. But he was put to death on a cross, even though he hadn't done anything wrong at all. Some women said they saw him alive this morning but we don't know whether to believe their story. It's all a big puzzle, and we don't understand it at all.'

As the three of them walked along, the stranger talked. He helped them to understand the things they were puzzling over. He helped them understand that Jesus had said he would have to go through pain and death, but that he would come through that to be alive again. The two friends started to feel a bit happier and a bit more hopeful.

Just then they got near their town. The stranger began to wave goodbye. 'Oh, don't go!' said the friends. 'Come in and have something to eat with us.' So he did. At the meal, the stranger took some bread and thanked God for it. Then he broke it . . . and suddenly the two friends knew exactly who the stranger was! (Can the children guess?) Yes, it was Jesus, and he really was alive!

Praying

Walk with me, Jesus,
today and every day.
I want to walk with you, Jesus,
right through my life! Amen.

Activities

On the sheet there is the road for the children to make the two friends walk down with Jesus. To make the friends stand up, stick them on card as shown. Then they can tell the story again, and to their parents in the week.

PEARL DIVERS

Aim: To know what happened on the road to Emmaus and the effect it had on the two disciples.

Starter

AA road map. Sit the children in a circle and label them (only verbally) in order, so that everyone is called one of three or four local roads. If you wish, you can include 'Emmaus Road'. When you call out a particular road name, those with that name have to change places. If you call 'AA road map!' everyone changes places.

Teaching

Ideally you may want to take the children out on a short walk as part of today's teaching, provided this is safe and practical, and there are sufficient adult helpers. If you can take them out, plan a route where you can move from Jerusalem to Emmaus and back; for instance, if Jerusalem is in the church hall, Emmaus might be the church porch. If an outside journey is not practical, then make your Jerusalem and Emmaus within the teaching area, but as far from each other as possible. Gather the children in Jerusalem.

Since Easter we have been looking at how Jesus' friends discovered that he wasn't dead any more, but very much alive. Today's story takes place along a road – the road between Jerusalem and Emmaus. Luke was told this story by someone called Cleophas, who remembered all the details for ever afterwards, because he and his wife or friend – we don't know which – had never been so surprised as they were that day. We are going to walk where these two friends of Jesus walked, and find out what happened.

Explain that the two disciples were very sad that day because Jesus was dead and they missed him. They were also very confused and disappointed, because they had great hopes for Jesus being a national leader; they'd even thought he was the promised Messiah, but presumed they must have got it all wrong. They started off for home, which was seven miles from Jerusalem.

At this point gather everyone up and walk slowly along as you tell the next part of the story. Have one of the leaders who has been absent up till now join the group. This person takes up the story, from the point where Jesus joins them, and explains how the stranger helped the disciples to understand some of the prophecies from the scriptures which suggested that the Messiah would actually have to suffer and die in order to save his people, but that he would rise again.

By this time you will be approaching Emmaus. The first leader takes over the story, about the disciples inviting the stranger in, when he is making as if to go on, and the group goes into the Emmaus 'home'. The leaders produce some bread as they talk about the disciples having a meal together with the stranger. The second leader takes the bread and begins to break it while telling the children what the stranger did. The disciples suddenly realise who this stranger is – they recognise that he is Jesus, fully alive! During the excitement of this discovery, and the children guessing, the second leader discreetly leaves, and then the first leader tells how Jesus vanished once the disciples have realised who he is. They are really happy and decide to go straight back all the way to Jerusalem. (How far was it?) So everyone runs back to Jerusalem to tell the disciples there that they now know Jesus is alive – they've just met him!

Praying

The children can say this prayer as they walk along, perhaps with everyone walking round in a circle as at a skating rink. The leader can be one of the children.

Leader	Walk with me, Jesus.
All	Walk with me, Jesus.
Leader	Show me the way.
All	Show me the way.
Leader	Walk with me, Jesus.
All	Walk with me, Jesus.
Leader	Every day.
All	Every day.

Activities

On the sheet the teaching is reinforced with a puzzle path, and the children are encouraged to think about areas in their lives where they specially want to ask Jesus to walk with them and their friends.

GOLD PANNERS

Aim: To explore the Emmaus story and its relevance to our own journeys.

Starter

Pairs of shoes. Cut out a number of different sized pairs of feet and mix them up. The group have to get them into pairs again, either with everyone being given a foot and trying to find the partner, or with all the feet displayed with letters and numbers around the room, so that the aim is to match number and letter correctly without actually touching any.

Teaching

Today we are looking at a fourteen to sixteen mile walk, which took a lot longer going than coming back.

Read the passage from Luke together, with different people taking the speaking parts. Make a note of *who* is in the story, *where* it happened, *when* it happened and *what* took place. Sometimes it helps us to get down to practical details like this, and we notice things we may otherwise overlook. Suggest it as a useful way for them to think through their reading of the Bible at home. Also look at possible *why*s. Why did Jesus appear to his disciples like this soon after the Resurrection? Was it for his benefit or theirs? What did he want them to understand about his risen life?

Praying

You have shown me the path of life;
your presence will fill me with joy.

Activities

On the sheet there is space to record some of their ideas and keep track of the discussion, and they can also match the prophecies about Jesus to the New Testament references, so that they have some idea of the way Jesus was fulfilling what was spoken about him.

FOURTH SUNDAY OF EASTER

Thought for the day

Jesus, the Good Shepherd, has come so that we may have life in rich abundance.

Reflection on the readings

Acts 2:14, 36-41
Psalm 22:1-6
1 Peter 2:20-28
John 10:1-10

Our first reading takes us into the middle of a crowd of people who are listening, devastated, to Peter, as he speaks powerfully about who Jesus is, and the terrible truth begins to dawn on them that they have all been instrumental in annihilating the Messiah, the hope of the nations. Yet Peter is not proclaiming God's imminent judgement but his fulsome mercy and offer of forgiveness. Somehow this God of limitless love is able to take anything and transform it; we can know this for certain because in Jesus he has taken death itself – and a cursed death – and turned it into the Resurrection, with new and lasting life.

It is always easy in life to fall back into old habits and mind-sets where we are entitled to moan and protest about any hardship or punitive treatment we don't consider we deserve. Peter, in the reading from 1 Peter, takes issue with that way of thinking. Suppose we turned it on its head, taking Christ as our example? Suppose we were able to consider all those unjustified sufferings not simply as painful (which they certainly are, of course) but also as a kind of privilege to be taken to God for transforming, rather like raw diamonds which we might take to be expertly cut and polished.

Could we then treat those insults and unkindnesses towards us with more grace and reverence – as raw hope in the making, perhaps? And as we wrestled to live out God's foolishness like this, could it be that we would actually be involved in a huge and vital strengthening of the whole body of Christ, worked out in each of our individual battles, whenever joyful self-giving triumphed over self, and unlimited loving over presumed rights?

The possibility sets alarm bells ringing in us, as we recognise the risk of exposure and vulnerability involved in such complete self-giving. Are we prepared to trust God that much? Isn't it all too much to expect?

Today's Gospel shows us a God who is not out to get us, to steal from us or put us down. He is not in the business of destructive behaviour; he is not wanting to wear us down with guilt or demand of us more than we can possibly give. Jesus chooses the image of a shepherd whom the sheep sense they can trust, and who will only use his power to provide wisely and faithfully for those in his care. In that care they are free to come and go, living out their lives doing what sheep do without panic or confusion.

What does that mean for us? We too are like sheep in the way we tend to panic and scatter, the way we are so vulnerable to following wrong values, empty and unsatisfying lifestyles, and unprincipled and irresponsible leaders. We desperately need the Good Shepherd, but need so much coaxing before we realise it. I sometimes wonder if the angels of heaven are standing around like the spectators at sheepdog trials, willing those sheep to go where they need to and cheering when they finally get the message!

Yet in the keeping of the Good Shepherd we are set free to live out our lives more truly as ourselves than ever before.

Discussion starters

1. How does the picture of the church community in Acts compare with our own church community? What are the similarities and differences?

2. Do we sometimes treat God as if he were out to destroy or condemn instead of save?

All-stage talk

Using chairs, build a circular sheepfold, with a gap for the entrance. Ask for some volunteer sheep to go inside. Explain that this is what a sheepfold was like in Jesus' day, except that it was made of stones, not chairs. Is there a door? No, there isn't. That's because the shepherd himself was the door. Ask a volunteer shepherd to come and be the door of the sheepfold. (You could even give the shepherd a stick or crook from the Nativity costumes, and a shepherd's sling.) Why is this living door likely to be a good safe one for the sheep? Because the shepherd would hear any dangers, such as wolves, or bears, or sheep stealers, and take action to protect the sheep, using his staff or sling. (The shepherd can pretend to frighten off a dangerous wolf.)

Another thing about sheep is that they get very frightened by lots of things, but when they hear the voice of the shepherd at the door they know they can trust him, and they feel safe. They will even follow him when he calls them and leads them off to some good juicy grass. (The sheep can try this.) And then they will follow the shepherd back home at the end of the day. (They do this.)

Now why are we getting a lesson in sheep farming this morning? What has all this got to do with Jesus? Or us?

In the Gospel today we hear Jesus telling the people that he is the sheep-door. (And you know what that means, now.) He told them all about the sheep being safe when the shepherd is the door, and the sheep knowing the shepherd's voice and following him. (You know about that too.) But the people didn't have a clue why Jesus was talking to them about sheep and shepherds. So they asked him to explain.

Jesus said he was trying to tell them something important about God. (Can anyone think what it was?) He was telling the people that they were a bit like sheep and Jesus was like the good shepherd who lies down in the doorway to keep the sheep safe. He was saying that God looks after us and defends us with his life because he loves us so much. He hates the thought of us coming to harm, and fights off evil. We can trust God's voice when he calls us, and follow him without any fear because we know God is always faithful and good and loving.

So whenever you are scared to face a bad problem, or bad ideas and temptations keep coming at you, stand there in the sheepfold behind Jesus, the sheep-door, and you will be safe. And whenever you are muddled about whether to do something or not, or whether to be selfish or not, listen out for the quiet calling of the Good Shepherd (you won't hear it with your ears, but you will know it in yourself) and follow him into the way that is right and good and kind and loving.

All-age ideas

- Include some model or toy sheep and lambs, or a shepherd's crook in one of the flower arrangements, which could make use of wild meadow flowers and grasses.

- Consider making a parish photograph album, scrap book or a video which aims to capture something of the real Christian identity of your church community, based on the portrait of the Early Church given to us in Acts. This may well be a year-long or an ongoing project, and could include prayers and excerpts from special service sheets, as well as pictures.

Prayer of the Faithful

Celebrant
The Lord is our shepherd,
and we are the sheep of his pasture.
Let us bring to him our cares and concerns
for the Church and for the world.

Reader
Good Shepherd of the sheep,
we pray for the Church;
for all congregations, for pastors
and all who minister in word and sacrament;
we pray particularly for bishops
in their shepherding of the world Church.
We pray for clear guidance and direction
in those issues which disturb us,
asking not that you lead us the easy way
but the way that is right and good.

Silence

The Lord is my shepherd:
there is nothing I shall want.

Good Shepherd of the sheep,
we pray for the world we inhabit –
the world we have inherited
and will pass on to successive generations.
Teach us to look after it carefully and wisely,
to share its gifts more fairly,
and work together to ease its sufferings.
Turn the hearts of those
who are excited by evil things
and encourage the timid to speak out
for what is wholesome and good.

Silence

The Lord is my shepherd:
there is nothing I shall want.

Good Shepherd of the sheep,
we pray for our places of work,
our colleagues, friends and neighbours,
and the members of our families.
We ask not for popularity at all costs,
but the grace to do your will
and to be your witnesses
to what it means to live lovingly,
both when this is easy and also when it hurts.

Silence

The Lord is my shepherd:
there is nothing I shall want.

Good Shepherd of the sheep,
we pray for the weak and vulnerable,
for those who must live
depending on others for every need,
and for those who are bullied,
or constantly despised.
We pray for a greater reverence, one for another,
for a greater willingness
to uphold and encourage one another;
we pray for healing and wholeness.

Silence

The Lord is my shepherd:
there is nothing I shall want.

Good Shepherd of the sheep,
we pray for those who have died;
we pray for those who ache
with sorrow at their going;
we commend them all into your unfailing care
which lasts throughout this life
and on into eternity.

Silence

The Lord is my shepherd:
there is nothing I shall want.

We make our prayer with Mary,
who was so open to God's will:
Hail, Mary . . .

In a time of silence
we share with God our Father
our personal burdens, joys and sorrows.

Silence

Celebrant
Father, we bring you our cares and concerns,
and ask you to hear these prayers
through Jesus Christ.
Amen.

TREASURE SEEKERS

Aim: To know that Jesus is like a good shepherd who loves his sheep and lambs.

Starter

Have hidden around enough toy lambs and sheep (or pictures of them) for each child to find one. Lay down a mat which can be a sheep pen and tell the children that there are lots of sheep all over the hillside which need bringing home for the night. Send the children off to collect one sheep each and put them safely in the sheepfold.

Teaching

Praise them for being such good shepherds when they brought in all the sheep, and talk with them about why sheep need to be safely looked after at night if there are wolves and foxes and bears around. (They may have pets which need putting away at night for the same reason.)

Talk about the way shepherds are people who look after sheep. How do we look after our pets? Bring out the need to care for them every day and night, and not just when we feel like it.

Show them a picture of Jesus as the Good Shepherd and explain that Jesus looks after us like a good shepherd looks after his sheep – so we are like Jesus' lambs, and he is our shepherd, taking great care of us all the time. He gives us sleep when we are tired, food and drink when we are hungry and thirsty, and other lambs to play with.

Praying

Dear Jesus, you are my shepherd
and I am one of your lambs.
Thank you for loving me
and looking after me. Amen.

Activities

The children can make a sheep mask to wear, based on the shape drawn on the sheet. They will also need some glue and chopped white wool. There is a picture to which the children can add other sheep and lambs, either by drawing, or by sticking on pre-cut shapes.

PEARL DIVERS

Aim: To look at what Jesus meant by saying he was the Good Shepherd, and the sheep door.

Starter

Give everyone a paper sheep to cut out and write their name on, and stick them all on a pre-painted hilly background with a shepherd standing in the middle.

Teaching

Display the sheep picture and start writing the words to go underneath it, one by one: *The Lord is my shepherd.* As you write the first word the children repeat it, catching hold of the thumb of their left hand. With the second word they catch hold of their index finger and so on. Soon they will have learnt the whole sentence. Now point out that each of the sheep on the picture has a particular name. If we are all those sheep, who do they think the shepherd is? It's Jesus. Jesus called himself the Good Shepherd because he looks after his sheep (that's us). Go through the sentence again, hanging on to your ring fingers as you emphasise that the Lord is *my* shepherd – and that means John's, Abigail's, Thomas's and Ali's shepherd.

We all need food and drink, shelter and sleep, of course, but we are not just bodies, so it is not just our bodies that need feeding and looking after. Our spirit is the real us that lives in our body, and that part of us is what goes on living in heaven after our body has died.

When Jesus said he was like a shepherd to us, he was talking about looking after those spirits of ours. (Place a jagged sign called 'Sin' on the floor.) Jesus knows that bad and wrong ideas come to us sometimes in life, like attacking wolves, and he says he will fight off those evils to keep our bodies and spirits safe, if only we will let him. (Place a cross to 'cross out' the sin.)

(Place a compass on the floor.) Our spirits need guiding and teaching, and Jesus will whisper into our hearts the sense of what is right and wrong, so that we know, and can choose the best direction to go in.

(Place a phone on the floor.) Our spirits need friendship, and Jesus gives us that, too. We can talk with him about anything, anywhere, and be sure that he is interested, and has time to listen to us. And he gives us the company and friendship of other Christians to help us as well, which is very important.

Praying

The Lord is my shepherd;
I have everything I need.
He gives me rest in green pastures.
He leads me to calm water.
He gives me new strength.
For the good of his name,
he leads me on paths that are right.
Even if I walk through the dark valley of death,
I will not be afraid because you are with me.
Your rod and your staff comfort me.

(From Psalm 22)

Activities

On the activity sheet there are instructions for making today's prayer into a stand-up card in the shape of a sheep. The children can either use the shape drawn on the sheet or you can make thin card templates from this beforehand, and they can draw round these on to coloured card. There is also a code to crack for which they will need to refer to a Bible.

GOLD PANNERS

Aim: To look at what God's shepherding involves.

Starter

Animals. First go round the group with each person choosing an animal and doing some appropriate action as they say what they are. Now someone starts by saying and doing their own animal and then naming another from the group. The next person round takes on this identity, copying the original action. They name another animal which the next person round has to take on, and so on. It needs to be played quite fast and is a fairly ridiculous game!

Teaching

Today we are going to be thinking about one particular animal: the sheep. There were a lot of sheep around where Jesus lived and that is no doubt why he used them and their shepherds as teaching aids. Read together the Gospel for today, stopping after verse 6. Jesus has only been talking about sheep, hasn't he? No wonder they don't understand! What else might he be talking about? Record their ideas.

Now go on to read Jesus' plain speaking and go over it systematically so that we don't take it for granted: how is Jesus the door for the sheep? Who are the sheep? How do sheep behave if they are always scared? How do they behave when they feel safe? What about *us* – how do people behave when they feel threatened and insecure? How do they behave when they know they are safe, accepted and loved? Help them to see that with Jesus as our shepherd we are set free to live out our lives as our true selves. He provides for us and is there for us, but he won't overpower or try to dominate. When we talk about giving ourselves to God, it doesn't mean that we are giving up our character and personality – only the selfishness and sin which chain and snarl us up so we can't move freely.

Praying

The Lord is my shepherd:
there is nothing I shall want.
Fresh and green are the pastures
where he gives me repose.
Near restful waters he leads me
to revive my drooping spirit.
He guides me along the right path,
he is true to his name.
If I should walk in the valley of darkness,
no evil would I fear.
You are there with your crook and your staff;
with these you give me comfort.

(From Psalm 22)

Activities

On the worksheet they are encouraged to see what God is and is not, as the Good Shepherd, and there are situations given for them to pray about, where people are in great need of good shepherding. Provide some card and art materials so that they can make a prayer requests board for the church with a background of sheep on the hillside and the text: 'The Lord is my shepherd.'

FIFTH SUNDAY OF EASTER

Thought for the day

Jesus is the Way, the Truth and the Life, through whom we can come into the presence of God for ever.

Reflection on the readings

Acts 6:1-7
Psalm 32:1-2, 4-5, 18-19
1 Peter 2:4-9
John 14:1-12

Rocks are solid things, which makes them very strong as foundations but exceedingly painful and obstinate to kick. They do not give. This makes the rocky image given to us by Peter, himself nick-named 'the rock', such a splendid one for helping us visualise the utter faithfulness and solid assurance of Jesus. Being built up on such a foundation is an exciting prospect for the household of faith. And the building depends on those living stones in every generation which continue to be added to the great living temple of worship and praise. Like stones we are to be strong in our faith, a faith that is not merely existing but fully and dynamically alive. What a Church it can be, when it is firmly set on the foundation of Christ and built through his power alone with the offered lives and gifts and sufferings and struggles of millions and millions of ordinary human beings!

The Church exists as an extension of Christ's ministry as 'one who serves'. In the reading from the Acts of the Apostles, we see a special ministry of service emerge from the rough and tumble of everyday church life. The Apostles laid their hands on seven chosen men who were to undertake prac- tical service in the church community. They were the first deacons, a word which means 'servant'.

We may feel we have much in common with Philip, as he tries so hard to understand what Jesus is saying, but is thinking on a completely different plane, unable to put the signs and clues together and come up with a meaningful answer. It took the death and resurrection of Jesus for things to suddenly start making sense to the disciples, and that is still true for us today. Still it is the death and resurrection of Jesus which enable everything else to make sense.

In the light of Jesus' death and resurrection we can grasp that he really is the Way, the Truth and the Life. It is through believing in this Jesus, who gave up his life in total self-giving love for us, and lived out for us in human terms the loving nature of almighty God, that we too can die to sin and be brought into a new life relationship with God which is valid both in time and eternity. So the Way is not a code of behaviour but a relationship with a person. And that is as basic to our human experience and need as the child/parent bonding which is also present from birth, rather than the codes of behaviour which are only later acquired.

It is a living, personal relationship that Jesus offers and hopes for us to accept. The relationship will never end, but will continue getting deeper and more satisfying, and continue developing and strength- ening us in our faith, throughout our entire life.

Discussion starters

1. Why are we sometimes more inclined to go for a code of rules than a personal relationship with the living God?

2. Are there practical ways in which we can give greater witness as a 'serving' community?

All-stage talk

Ask two or three experts to come and explain the way they do whatever it is they are good at. (The actual areas of expertise depend on the interests of your congregation, but try and choose people from representative age and interest groups. The skill should be capable of being demonstrated in front of everyone, so it could be ironing, juggling, dribbling a football, doing a cartwheel or skipping, for example.)

First ask each one to explain it to you, placing them out of sight of everyone as they do so. Share with the group how it all sounds incredibly complicated, and difficult to follow, even though it is obviously expert advice. That's rather how it is with the Old Testament Law – everyone respects it highly and it's very good advice for living, but somehow we never seem to manage to follow the instructions or get the hang of them. They help us to know how to live a good life, but they don't change us so that we are able to do it. Some of the prophets had told everyone that one day it would be different. People wouldn't need those instructions any more, because they would already know, in their hearts, how to behave properly.

Let's find out if we can understand our experts any better if we can actually see them doing these clever things. (Invite them to demonstrate, one by one.) Ah, that's much clearer! We may not be able to do it ourselves, yet, but at least we have their example in front of us, to learn from and copy. (Someone might like to try copying one of the skills.)

When Jesus came, it was like being able to see God's way of living – in person. 'So that's what it means to love God and love one another!' people thought. 'So that's what God's love for us is like!' And even though we may not yet be able to do it very well, at least we have a wonderful example to learn from and copy.

If we're still full of bitterness about something that happened to us long ago, we can look at Jesus and copy his forgiving. If we're looking down on someone because they aren't as clever or rich as us, we can look at Jesus and copy his way of enjoying people and accepting them for what they are. If we are always worrying about clothes and possessions, we can look at Jesus and copy his simple way of living, and spend our energy cultivating the treasures that we can take with us to heaven. So Jesus is like a living 'Way' – he's a walking, talking Way to live.

In fact that's what Jesus called himself in our Gospel today; he said, 'I am the Way, the Truth and the Life'. With Jesus we go one better than having his example to copy – since the Resurrection we can have his life living in us! That would be rather like our experts being able to fill us with all that makes them able to do those clever things. Imagine what a skilled parish we would be if that were possible! We'd all be expert ironers, football dribblers, jugglers and cartwheelers! Well, I have to tell you that we can't do that. As humans we have to pass on our skills the hard way, by teaching and learning. But with Jesus it's different. He really can live in our lives, enabling us to love God and one another. All we need to do is invite him into our personal lives and our church, and be prepared to be gradually transformed.

All-age ideas

• On a wall or pillar display a very large speech bubble made of paper, on which is written: Lord Jesus, receive my spirit!

• Incorporate rocks and stones and a builder's trowel in one of the flower arrangements today.

Prayer of the Faithful

Celebrant
As living stones,
let us pray for the building up of God's Church,
and for the world God loves.

Reader
Living God, build us up by the power of your Spirit
into a spiritual temple
where you are glorified day after day,
in all our praise and worship,
and in our love for one another.

Silence

You are my strong rock:
my strong rock and my shelter.

Living God, sharpen our consciences
to sense your direction
and protect us from all that draws us away from you.
Guide our leaders in the way of truth
and realign us all to the values
which are built on you.

Silence

You are my strong rock:
my strong rock and my shelter.

Living God, may the Way which Jesus shows us
be the Way we live out our daily lives
around the table, in the daylight and the dark,
in the misunderstandings, the tensions and the rush,
in the eye contact,
the conversations and the growing.

Silence

You are my strong rock:
my strong rock and my shelter.

Living God, we lay before you now
those who are travelling through a time
of pain or anguish, tragedy or conflict
which is hard to bear.
We stand alongside them in their suffering,
and ask that you give them
your transforming, healing love.

Silence

You are my strong rock:
my strong rock and my shelter.

Living God, we remember those who have died
and pray for them now.
Lead them out of their pain
into the light of eternity,
and keep us all in the Way that leads us
to share that everlasting life with you.

Silence

You are my strong rock:
my strong rock and my shelter.

Mindful of Mary's quiet
and prayerful acceptance of God's will,
we join our prayers with hers:
Hail, Mary . . .

As our loving Father listens in love,
we pray our own petitions
in silence and stillness.

Silence

Celebrant
Merciful Father,
we ask you to accept our prayers
for the sake of Christ, our Lord.
Amen.

TREASURE SEEKERS

Aim: To know that Jesus is like a road that leads us to heaven.

Starter

Gather a collection of vehicles to play with – model cars and lorries, and a sit-and-ride or two. Have a time of car play, either all over the floor, or on a road mat if you have one.

Teaching

Take the children to look at a road, either looking through a window, or going outside (in which case ensure that the children are holding hands with adults or some of the older children, and are well supervised). Talk about what the road looks like, and where it is going. Then come back inside.

Roads are very useful things. You can drive along a road easily without bumping into trees or falling into the sea, because the road is a clear way. A road will take you straight to the shops, or the park, or to church. It stops you getting lost in the mountains if you keep on the clear roadway.

Jesus said he was like a clear roadway that we can travel on to heaven. The Jesus road is clear and strong. If we travel the Jesus Way through life, then, like the best roads, it will take us safely home, at the end of our life here, to live with God for ever in heaven.

Mark a road with chairs, and all walk along it, repeating the prayer in time to the marching.

Praying

Left, right, left, right,
Jesus you're the Way!
Left, right, left, right,
we'll walk your Way today!

Activities

On the sheet they can try drawing roads from one place to another, and there is a 'Jesus knows the way!' badge to colour. It can then be stuck on to pre-cut thin card, and attached to their clothes with a piece of double-sided sticky tape.

PEARL DIVERS

Aim: To explore what it means to look at Jesus as the Way, the Truth and the Life.

Starter

Set up a narrow way to walk along. (It might be a thin strip of card, or two skipping ropes, laid on the floor.) Everyone can try walking along it without falling off and being caught by all the alligators (those who are not walking along the thin road!). If they are caught by an alligator (touching is quite enough) they are out. Alligators are not allowed to get them while they are on the road.

Teaching

Bring along some newspaper pictures and headlines which tell of war and sad things, and introduce them, one by one, before dotting them around on the floor in the centre of the circle. Talk with them about there being so many sad and bad and dangerous things in this life, as well as all that is lovely and good. It is important for us on our Christian journey to know that this is true. There are lots of things to tempt us into doing wrong and unkind and selfish things. It is not easy to walk through life doing what is right.

Read together what Jesus says about all this: 'Don't let your hearts be troubled. Trust in God and trust in me . . . You know the way to the place where I am going.' Thomas said to Jesus, 'Lord, we don't know where you are going. So how can we know the way?'

Now take a length of string and wind it on a safe way between all the pictures and headlines, right across the circle, as someone reads the next sentence: 'Jesus answered, "I am the Way. And I am the Truth and the Life. The only way to the Father is through me."' Explain that Jesus was saying that he is like the safe path through a minefield; his close friendship with us all through our life is like a clear road for us to walk along to heaven. Give out separate words of 'I am the Way, the Truth and the Life' to different children and let them lay these words in order along the winding string 'road'. Then everyone can say them together.

Praying

Jesus, I know that you are the Way,
the Truth and the Life.
Let me walk safely each day
through all the troubles and temptations
by walking your Way
which leads me to heaven. Amen.

Activities

Today's teaching is reinforced and developed in the activity sheet with situations to think about which will help them see where the Jesus Way lies, and there is a compass to make to sense Jesus' directing in each situation. If you want to, you could adapt this and give each child a real compass to stick on the centre – that depends on your numbers and your budget!

GOLD PANNERS

Aim: To see Jesus as the Way, the Truth and the Life, and as the cornerstone on which we are being built up into a spiritual temple.

Starter

Using some road maps, give each couple of people a destination and a place to set out from. They have to work out the best route to take. Share their recommendations.

Teaching

Point out that although they may never have been somewhere, it is still quite easy to get there, providing you know the way. That's why the AA make all these maps! They recognise that if we didn't know the way, we'd all get hopelessly lost and they'd have to keep coming out to rescue stranded motorists. Today we find Jesus talking to his friends, who are very worried about the future. They know that their leader is in great danger, and they don't really know what is going to happen, or how they are going to be able to cope. It's like lots of us feel at some points in our life. There is confusion, anxiety, and insecurity about the future, and how we will cope.

We are going to find out what Jesus has to offer to anyone in that situation. Read together John 14:1-6. Draw out the lovely reassurance that Jesus gives, and the way he understands how the disciples are feeling, and doesn't tell them to pull themselves together, but gives them a promise that he is going to provide for them personally. Their relationship with him will be like a clear road to walk along which will bring them safely through every danger to heaven.

Now read on to verse 10. Philip (and perhaps the others as well) still doesn't understand that Jesus is the way we are able to see God. We wouldn't be able, as humans, to cope with seeing the full glory of God without it being acted out in a human life – which is why Jesus was born as a human baby.

Look at the living stones passage from 1 Peter, to see how the image here is of Jesus being like a strong cornerstone, or foundation stone, on which we are all being built, as the Church of God. Again, the picture reminds us of the fact that Jesus is totally reliable, totally faithful, and in him we can find real life, not just the temporary excitements or pleasures that sin offers, but deep, lasting life, in which we are strong and know a security and inner peace which is very satisfying.

Praying

You, Lord, are my rock and my stronghold;
lead me and guide me
for the honour of your name.
Set me free from the net
that has been hidden to catch me;
for you are my refuge.
Into your hand I commit my spirit. Amen.

(From Psalm 30)

Activities

The worksheet includes a role-play of a road being made, which helps them to explore further what it means for Jesus to be the Way, and also the solid bedrock of our life. There are also examples of other people who have walked the Jesus Way and found it safe and strong.

SIXTH SUNDAY OF EASTER

Thought for the day

The Spirit of truth, given to us, enables us to discern the living, risen Christ.

Reflection on the readings

Acts 8:5-8, 14-17
Psalm 65:1-7, 16, 20
1 Peter 3:15-18
John 14:15-21

What God chose to do through the Incarnation was to draw close to his beloved people in such a way that they could see what this mystery we call God was like, in human terms of reference. That had to include a demonstration of what love means even in the face of total cursing and rejection, and God went ahead and showed that, too, in the death of Jesus. It had to include a demonstration of how this power of creative life is even stronger than death – which is, in human terms, annihilation and destruction. So God went ahead and did it. It's called the Resurrection.

In our continued reading of Peter's letter, we are advised to hold on, literally for dear life, to this Christ, who is God's dependable love, and brings us through all suffering with the dynamism of resurrection life.

The reading from John's Gospel unpacks that for us a bit. What do people look like who are living Christ's risen life? How would we know one if we saw one? John states Jesus' words with a straightforward bluntness that does not let us hide behind high-sounding and noble ideals: it is the way we live obediently to the commands of love that sets us apart and proves that we are followers of the way of Christ. Well-intentioned, but never getting round to it, is not part of the deal. Neither are excuses, cop-out clauses or allowable exceptions. It is quite clear from today's Gospel reading that if we really love, we will live that love out, not in a fair-weather friendship, but in a sacrificial way that often chafes and hurts, and leads us in ways we may not have taken by the comfort choice.

And what is the point of choosing such a path? What is in it for us? Jesus promises that, through the gift of the Spirit of Truth, we will become intimate friends with the almighty and merciful God, and will increasingly be honoured with discerning his presence, not as a memory or a hope, but as a real experience of the living person who brought us into being, redeemed us and loves us for ever.

Discussion starters

1. Do we sometimes expect God to answer our prayers by making us immune from suffering? How does the reading from 1 Peter help us see our relationship with God incorporating suffering?

2. Philip went to a Samaritan town and proclaimed the Christ to them. How can we proclaim the Christ to the people of our time and place?

All-stage talk

Start by displaying a fairly simple equation, such as $2x+3=x+10$, or $y(5+2)=21$, or $x+4=6$ (difficulty depends on your group), perhaps on a blackboard. Provide chalk, and ask someone mathematical to take us through the stages of solving the mystery of this unknown value of x or y.

When we tried to solve our x mystery, we worked it out, step by step, gradually getting a clearer idea of what x meant, until, in the end, it was quite clear to us (or some of us!).

That's rather like the way we can look at the beauty and order of our world, and all the physics and chemistry of it, and all the variety and colour and shape in it, and begin to work our way towards discovering what God is like. We can work out that he must be clever and thoughtful, and imaginative and faithful, for instance.

But with Jesus coming, and showing us exactly what God is like, it's more like this.

Set up the same equation as before, using solid shapes, like building blocks. Each x is a bag, filled with the correct number of blocks. We could still work out what x is, but if the bag is opened, we can actually see what it is. (Do this.)

With Jesus' life there in front of us through reading the Gospels, and through living in his company every day, we can have a very clear idea of what God is like. We can see that he is forgiving and totally honest and good, that he is responsible and stands up for what is right, whatever happens to him and however much people sneer. We can see that he looks for the good in people and doesn't condemn them or give up on them. We can see that his love has been proved stronger than death.

If we put our faith in that God, whom Jesus has revealed to us in a new and clear way, and if we claim to love him, then we will have to start doing what he says. Who finds it easy to be obedient? Most of us find it very hard. We don't want to do what we are told; we want to do what we like!

Jesus says that the way you can tell if someone really does believe in him and love him, is by whether they are obedient to him, and obey what he says. That means listening to God and saying yes to him, whether it's what we want to do or not.

That is a *very hard* thing to learn, but it's worth learning, because being friends with Jesus is the best and happiest thing that could ever happen to us.

All-age ideas

- Have a group of dancers (these can be mixed ages and gender) to work on expressing in movement the truth that we are brought through the waters of death into new life, and given the guiding Spirit of Truth to lead us onwards. They could use waving silver and blue cloth or streamers to represent the flood water as they pass through. They need to make it clear that they are turning their backs on the old life, and going willingly into this 'drowning', from which they emerge, with the Spirit to hold their hands and guide them, first to an attitude of praise and worship, and then out, through the congregation. Suitable music would be something like *Amazing grace*.

- If you have an OHP, make up an acetate which has in the centre: 'Our God is . . .', and invite people to tell you characteristics about God that they know to be true. Write the suggestions up and then invite everyone, in their own time and order, to read out these truths – Our God is faithful, our God is forgiving . . . – so that there is a general noise of praising God for who he is. As the voices die away, finish by a single voice saying just the centre words: 'Our God is. Amen.'

Prayer of the Faithful

Celebrant
As we gather in the company of the living God, let us pray.

Reader
Lord of life,
we pray that the Church
may be alive with your risen life,
refreshed and revived by the breath of your Spirit,
purified and refined like gold and silver,
so that we truly offer the possibility
of saving love to the searching world.

Silence

You are the one true God:
and we worship you.

Lord of life,
we pray that in all meetings and conferences
where important decisions are taken,
hearts may be turned to honour what is just and true,
compassionate and constructive.
We pray that in all areas

where there is corruption, deceit or distrust,
consciences may be sensitised afresh
to know what is right
and strive towards it.

Silence

You are the one true God:
and we worship you.

Lord of life,
we pray for the streets
and places of work we represent.
May they be places where the truth of your being
is proclaimed daily by the way we live
and handle the everyday situations,
through your leading.
May our words and actions
speak of your faithful love,
your graciousness and your purity.

Silence

You are the one true God:
and we worship you.

Lord of life,
we pray for all who feel out of their depth,
all who are drowning in their pain,
sorrow or guilt.
Set them free, O God, and save them,
support them to a place of safety
and fix their feet on the solid rock of your love.

Silence

You are the one true God:
and we worship you.

Lord of life,
we pray for those who have died;
may they now see you as you really are.
We ask for mercy and forgiveness,
and commend them to your keeping for ever.

Silence

You are the one true God:
and we worship you.

We pray with Mary
who, in wonder and trust,
accepted the impossible:
Hail, Mary . . .

In silence we bring the individual names
of any who have hurt us,
or those we love,
to the healing power of God.

Silence

Celebrant
Father of mercy,
look compassionately on your children
and hear us as we pray, through Christ.
Amen.

TREASURE SEEKERS

Aim: To know that we can go on getting to know God more and more till we are old.

Starter

Bring along some clothes belonging to people of different ages to be sorted in order. They should range from baby clothes and nappies to walking sticks and warm sensible slippers, taking in some fashionable items for teenagers and smart office clothing along the way. Have some fun deciding which age would wear them, and end with them in a line, from youngest to oldest.

Teaching

Those clothes told us a story. They told us that we don't stay the same as when we are born. We get older and bigger and grow up. As we grow up we learn all sorts of things. Like what, for instance? Share their ideas of what they think we learn. As we grow we also get better at doing things, like moving about, talking, singing, eating tidily and dressing ourselves. What would they like to be able to do which they can't quite manage yet?

Another important thing we do as we grow up is to make friends. We get to know people and we like them. We get to know them a bit more and like them even better. Friendship grows like we do, as we spend time with our friends and talk, and play together. Friendship grows as we help one another, too.

It's just the same with our friend, Jesus. First of all we don't know him very well. People tell us about him and we think he sounds nice. But we make friends with him by spending time with him and talking and playing with him. Bit by bit we get to know Jesus better, and find that we love him more and more. Even now, the leaders are still getting to know him. Think of some elderly Christians they know at church, or invite one or two along. Even these people are still finding they're getting to know Jesus and love him more.

So as you grow, and grow out of your clothes, right through until you are so old that your hair is white and you need a stick to walk with, you and Jesus can go on being friends, and he'll show you more and more of what he is like, all through your life.

Praying

When I was a baby,
  (*crouch down small*)
I know you loved me, Jesus.
Now I am as tall as this,
  (*stand at normal height*)
I know you as my friend.
When I am as tall as this, or this, or this, or this,
  (*measure with hand at levels above head*)
or even when I walk like this,
  (*pretend to walk with stick as an old person*)
we'll still be best of friends.

Activities

On the sheet there are people to put in order of age. Then they can count the friends of Jesus, so they realise that they all are his friends, whatever the age. There is also an illustration of a height chart to make. Each child will need a pre-cut length of paper which has the heights marked on it, and the words: 'Jesus' friends grow'. The children decorate the chart with paints or stickers.

PEARL DIVERS

Aim: To see obedience as a mark of love.

Starter

Square bashing. First teach the children how to stand to attention, to stand at ease, to about-turn right and left, and to march. Then line them up like an army and be a sergeant major, taking them through their paces.

Teaching

Explain how, in the army (or navy or air force), everyone has to obey orders, and drill like that helps the soldiers get used to doing what they are told straight away. It just wouldn't work, where there are guns and explosives around, to have people who were not disciplined; obedience is a matter of life or death.

Most of us find it hard to be obedient – we would rather do what we want than what we are told! But Jesus can't use us as his soldiers in the battle against evil unless we are trained to obey him, like good soldiers obey their commanders. Jesus told his followers this: 'If you love me, you will do the things I command. The one who knows my commands and obeys them is the one who loves me.'

Jesus isn't getting hold of us in a half-Nelson and saying, 'Now listen you, obey me or else!' He would never, ever want to force us to do anything.

He respects us too much for that. But he *is* saying, 'OK, you say that you love me and trust me as your Lord. If you really meant that, you would be doing what I told you, out of love and respect for me. If you just go on pleasing yourself, and doing what you want all the time, it shows that you don't really love me at all.' He's right, and we can't get away from it. If we do mean it when we say we love and trust Jesus, then we'll have to get in training to be more obedient.

Praying

(To be said while marching on the spot.)

I love to be with you, Jesus,
so I'm going to do as you say,
I'll show that I love you and want to be like you
by doing your will TODAY.

(End by jumping to attention.)

Activities

On the sheet there are instructions for making an arm-band badge which says 'God's soldier in training'. The children will each need a strip of material (cut from an old sheet or shirt, perhaps) long enough to tie round their upper arm. There are also examples of ways God can use our obedience.

GOLD PANNERS

Aim: To look at the consequences of loving obedience to God.

Starter

Borrow for today either a remote control car or train, or a few computerised games. Try these out together.

Teaching

When you were playing just now, you were in control of the action. Whatever order you gave was obeyed immediately, so you could use the car or hero in the way you needed to. Suppose they'd been able to argue with you, or ignore you or simply refuse to do what you said? You couldn't have used them as effectively. The mission you wanted to accomplish couldn't have happened.

God has plans for his world, and he would love to use us in helping accomplish great things, but he can only do that if we are willing to be under his command, obeying what he says.

Read the Gospel for today, and notice how our obedience is not forced, but seen as a sign of our love – if we obey his commands it shows that we really love Jesus; if we don't, it shows we don't

really love and trust him at all. We need to look at ourselves and check that out.

Notice, too, what Jesus says will happen once our lives, in tune with our voices, show our love for him. We are promised three things:

1. At Jesus' request, God the Father will give us a helper – the Spirit of Truth – to be with us for ever.
2. The Father will love us, as he loves the Son.
3. Jesus will show himself to us, even though in the world's eyes he is invisible.

Now read the passages from 1 Peter 3 and from Acts, looking out for evidence of those three promised things.

Praying

Here I am, Lord – body, heart and soul.
Grant that, with your love,
I may be big enough to reach the world,
and small enough to be at one with you.

(A prayer of Mother Teresa)

Activities

The worksheet helps them to look at different areas of their life where they can check how far their living is obedient to Jesus' commands, and where it needs changing. There are questions to think about concerning our obedience and our willingness to be used, and some 'job advertisements' to apply for, which encourage commitment to Jesus' values.

THE ASCENSION OF THE LORD

Thought for the day

Having bought back our freedom with the giving of his life, Jesus enters into the full glory to which he is entitled.

Reflection on the readings

Acts 1:1-11
Psalm 46:2-3, 6-9
Ephesians 1:17-23
Matthew 28:16-20

The Ascension marks the end of Jesus' appearances on earth and his physical, historical ministry. It is also a beginning, because this moving away from the confining qualities of time and place means that Jesus will be present always and everywhere. It also means that the humanity of Jesus is now within the nature of the wholeness of God. Our God has scarred hands and feet, and knows what it is like to be severely tempted, acclaimed and despised.

In a way, it is at the Ascension that the value of all the risk and suffering involved in the Incarnation becomes apparent. The saving victim takes his rightful place in the glory of heaven, and only that can enable God's Holy Spirit to be poured out in wave upon wave of loving power that stretches to all peoples in all generations.

Amazingly our own parish, our own congregation, is part of this glorious celebration with its far-reaching effects. Each of us, living squashed into a particular time frame lasting merely a lifetime, can be drenched in the power of that Spirit, and caught up in the energising nature of it.

As we celebrate the Ascension we, like the disciples, are expectant with joy at the prospect of the gifts God has in store, and yet still mulling over the breathtaking events of Easter. It is like being in the still centre, in the eye of the storm.

Discussion starters

1. Why were the disciples returning with great joy, even though Jesus had left them?

2. Why do you think Jesus made sure that his final leave-taking was definite, and actually witnessed by the disciples?

All-stage talk

Imagine staging a Mexican wave, which runs through the whole church. Point out how it could only work well because all of us as individuals would work together as a unit of energy.

Remind everyone of the events leading up to today, giving them a whistle-stop tour of Jesus' life, death, Resurrection and post-Resurrection appearances. Explain how the disciples needed that time to get used to Jesus being alive and around, though not always visible or physically present.

Now they were ready for the next stage in the plan. Jesus leads them out of the city and he gives them his blessing, telling them to hang around Jerusalem without rushing off to do their own bit of mission work. (Enthusiasm is wonderful but it can sometimes make us race off to start before we've got everything we need.) The disciples have got to wait because God is going to send the Holy Spirit to empower them and equip them for the work they will be doing. It will make it possible for the news of God's love to spread out through the world like our Mexican wave.

When Jesus had finished giving the disciples their instructions and his encouragement, we are told that the disciples watched him being taken into heaven, until a cloud hid him from their sight. Those are the only practical details we have, so we don't know exactly how it happened. But we do know that the disciples were in no doubt about where Jesus had gone, and they were full of joy and excitement as they made their way back to the city to wait for the Holy Spirit, as Jesus had told them to.

A lot of years have gone by since Jesus ascended into heaven – nearly two thousand years. But that isn't much if you aren't stuck in time as we are, and God isn't stuck in time. He's prepared to wait to give us humans the chance to turn to him in our lives, and we don't know the date when Jesus will return. We do know that in God's good time he will come back, and everyone will see his glory together, both the living and those who have finished the earthly part of their life.

In the meantime, we have been given the Holy Spirit, so that God can be with us in person every moment of our life, helping us and guiding our choices, steering us safely through temptations, and teaching us more and more about our amazing God. All he waits for is to be invited.

All-age ideas

• Any artwork or writing that the children have done on what the Ascension is about can be displayed around the building.

• Have a beautiful helium balloon at the ready. Write on it an Ascension message that the children would like to send. After the service two representative children can let the balloon float away.

Prayer of the Faithful

Celebrant
As we celebrate together, let us pray together.

Reader
God of love, as we celebrate this festival
of Jesus' entry into heaven as Saviour and Lord,
we pray for unity in the Church
and reconciliation and renewed vision.

Silence

Both heaven and earth:
are full of God's glory.

As we recall the shout of praise in heaven
as the Lamb of God appears,
we pray for all who are hailed as heroes
and given great honour on earth;
for all who worship anyone or anything
other than the true God.

Silence

Both heaven and earth:
are full of God's glory.

We pray for all farewells and homecomings
among our families and in our community,
and for all who have lost touch with loved ones
and long for reunion.

Silence

Both heaven and earth:
are full of God's glory.

We pray for those who are full of tears,
and cannot imagine being happy again;
we pray for the hardened and callous,
whose inner hurts have never yet been healed.
We pray for wholeness and comfort and new life.

Silence

Both heaven and earth:
are full of God's glory.

We commend to your eternal love
those we remember who have died,
and we pray too for those
who miss their physical presence.

Silence

Both heaven and earth:
are full of God's glory.

We make our prayer with Mary,
who, in joy, poured out her thanks and praise:
Hail, Mary . . .

God our Father loves us;
in silence we pray
our personal petitions to him now.

Silence

Celebrant
Father, trusting in your great love for us,
we bring you these prayers
through Jesus Christ our Lord.
Amen.

TREASURE SEEKERS, PEARL DIVERS AND GOLD PANNERS

It is likely that Ascension Day services for schools will not need a separate programme for children and young people. However, in the books for TREASURE SEEKERS and PEARL DIVERS I have included a drawing and colouring activity for today.

SEVENTH SUNDAY OF EASTER

Thought for the day

God's glory is often revealed in the context of suffering and failure in the world's eyes.

Reflection on the readings

Acts 1:12-14
Psalm 26:1, 4, 7-8
1 Peter 4:13-16
John 17:1-11

When Jesus prays to be glorified he is looking straight into the face of a cursed death. At first it shakes us that this imminent time of suffering and apparent failure, of disappointed rejection and dashed hopes should be what God deems glory. But of course it speaks of what is at the very heart of our faith, that our God is a Servant King, and his kingdom is one of humility and love, rather than success and popularity. Power and glory are emotive words which often conjure up images of military strength and empire-building, but God's power and glory are of a very different kind.

In today's Gospel we see Jesus at prayer, his will and total direction aligned with that of the Father, ready to be the human person in whom God's glory will be perfectly shown through the outpouring of love on the cross. In an extraordinary paradox, the nails of rejection and ultimate insult are allowed to fasten his body into the classic position of welcome and acceptance, arms outstretched. His written accusation means that he is even given his authentic title to die under, mocked and despised. And this is glory. This is what shows the length to which perfect loving goes, for the innocent One to take on all the sins of the world, accept their pain without complaint or retaliation, and offer them for transforming into freedom and new life at the cost of everything.

In the light of this it begins to make sense that Peter can encourage the early Christians, undergoing severe persecution for their faith, with the thought that to suffer in this way, in Christ's way, is the earth where glory flowers. To undergo suffering beautifully, by the grace of God, is to have the Spirit of God in all his glory resting upon us, and the privilege of witnessing to God's strength and capacity to transform and redeem anything.

We are nearing the end of this season of Easter, as the disciples were nearing the end of their earthly understanding of who Jesus was. Having gone through death and accomplished his work on earth, Jesus' risen life will take him out of the world, in one sense, but only in order to be right in the centre of faithful lives across the world and the centuries. Just as the angels at the tomb had asked the disciples why they were looking for Jesus in the place of death, when he was alive, so now, as Jesus is hidden from their sight and returns to heaven, the angels ask why the disciples are peering up into heaven.

We can all get far too bogged down in the technical details, which don't actually matter that much. What does matter is that Jesus hasn't gone away and left us, but is going to be with us and in us as we make ourselves increasingly available for his loving service.

Discussion starters

1. What do you think the disciples had to learn about Jesus, between the Resurrection and the Ascension?

2. Is our society so frightened by suffering, and so bent on avoiding it, that we can no longer appreciate the way it can show us God's glory?

All-stage talk

Before the talk, use the short sketch in the all-age ideas section.

Begin by talking about saying goodbye. The kind of goodbye it is depends on how well we know each other, whether we love or hate each other, and whether we are saying goodbye for a short time, a long time or for ever. Today in our first reading we were with the disciples as Jesus said goodbye to them. Since Easter we have been looking at various times when he had been meeting up with them after the Resurrection. Sometimes he had met them when they were all together, sometimes on their own. They would suddenly recognise him, or he would suddenly be there among them, and the disciples had begun to get used to Jesus being with them even when they couldn't see him with their eyes.

Now, here they are, all together with Jesus, and this is going to be their last goodbye to him as a person whom they see with their eyes, because he is going back to heaven. He tells them two things: (show a picture of rushing wind and flames) that they are going to be given power when the Holy Spirit comes upon them, and (show a picture of an empty speech bubble) that they are going to tell lots of people all over the world about the Jesus they know and love so well.

Then we are told that he was lifted up, while they watched, and a cloud took him from their sight so that they couldn't see him any more. So they stood there, peering up into the sky, rather like you do when you've just let a balloon go, and you watch and watch until you can't see it any more. What happened next?

They realised that two people, dressed in white, were standing next to them. 'Why are you standing here looking up into the sky?' they asked. They told the disciples that one day Jesus would come in the same way they had seen him go. But what they wanted them to know was that there wasn't any point in hanging around in that one place for a glimpse of Jesus, because he had gone on to the next phase, where he would be with all his friends, including us, all the time, not in a way that we can see, but in new ways. Just as real, just as much alive, but in a form which makes him free to be in all kinds of different countries and places and dates and times all at once!

What he said to the disciples that day, he says to us as well: we will be given power when the Holy Spirit comes upon us (show the first picture again) and we are going to tell lots of people about the Jesus we know and love (show the second picture).

All-age ideas

• *A goodbye sketch.* This works with either a number of different pairs of people, of different ages and gender, or one pair who keep changing style and props. They simply walk on, say goodbye (it can be a wordy or a one-word goodbye) and walk off, but in several different roles. Here are some suggestions:

1. A mother and her son at his first day at school.

2. Lovers at a station.

3. Host and unwelcome visitor who has overstayed his welcome.

4. Two friends after school.

5. Daughter with well-loved elderly parent in hospital or nursing home.

• Incorporate some horse chestnut blossom in one of the flower arrangements. It is traditionally known as the candle tree, in flower to celebrate the Ascension.

Prayer of the Faithful

Celebrant
As the Church of God,
let us be still, and pray together.

Reader
God of glory,
may your light shine in our church community
as you work among us
and bless us with your presence;
with gratitude for the gifts you have given us,
we ask you to bless our various ministries.

Silence

Holy God:
may we live with your life in us.

God of glory,
may the whole world come to know you
and give you honour and praise.
Encourage us all to stand up to the devil,
when he prowls,
firm in our faith,
and strengthened with your power.

Silence

Holy God:
may we live with your life in us.

God of glory,
may our homes, schools, shops, offices and factories
become places where your glory
is seen and experienced
in the ordinary things and the everyday routines.
Fill us to overflowing with ongoing thankfulness
both in the sunlight and in the storm.

Silence

Holy God:
may we live with your life in us.

God of glory,
with your special affection
for the discarded and marginalised,
the weak and the vulnerable,
we pray for all those
who find life an exhausting struggle
or who long for some respite from pain or depression.
Support them in their troubles,
bring healing and reassurance,
and touch them with the gentleness of your peace.

Silence

Holy God:
may we live with your life in us.

God of glory,
teach us to understand death
in the context of your eternity,
so that our fears are calmed as we approach it.
Welcome with merciful love
those who have recently died
and shelter their loved ones, too,
in the shadow of your wings.

Silence

Holy God:
may we live with your life in us.

Mary's example teaches us
the power of loving response;

with her we make our prayer:
Hail, Mary . . .

In silence, now,
we pour out to God our Father
any needs and burdens known to us personally.

Silence

Celebrant
Father Almighty, take us by the hand
and lead us in your ways of peace and love;
we ask you to hear our prayers,
for the sake of Jesus Christ.
Amen.

TREASURE SEEKERS

Aim: To know that Jesus went back into heaven.

Starter

Guess who's coming through the door. Introduce a number of different toys and then bundle them all behind a 'door'. The leader says, 'Guess who's coming through the door', and the children all shout out who they think it is. Vary the length of time they shout, before making one of the toys walk through the door. Repeat until all the toys are outside. Sometimes a toy can go back behind the door again and come out for a second time.

Teaching

What a lot of coming and going there was in that game! Remind the children that since Easter (which will seem a very long time ago) when we remembered Jesus coming to life again, we've had stories of him coming and going, meeting his friends. Sometimes they could see Jesus and sometimes they couldn't.

It went on like that for about the same time as from Easter Day to now. Jesus' friends were starting to understand that Jesus could still be with them, even if they couldn't see him.

One day Jesus was with them all outside. It was time for Jesus to say goodbye to his friends and go back to heaven. 'Don't worry,' he said, 'I won't leave you on your own. I will ask my Father and he will send you the Holy Spirit to give you strength and comfort. It means that I shall be with you all the time, wherever you go.' Then, as they watched, Jesus was lifted up from the ground and a cloud hid him from them. They knew they would not see him again in the same way, but they knew he would be with them, loving them and looking after them.

Like those friends of Jesus, we can't see him with

our eyes, but we know he is just as real and alive now as he was then. And when we ask him to be near us and help us he is right there, straight away.

Praying

Jesus, you were born as a baby
 (rock baby in arms)
you worked as a carpenter, sawing the wood.
 (saw wood)
You died on a cross and you rose again.
 (arms out, then jump and clap hands)
You are loving and kind and good.
 (put up fingers, counting to three)
In heaven and on earth your glory shines.
 (point up and down,
 then trace big circle with fingers stretched out)
You are loving and kind and good.
 (count on fingers again)

Activities

On the sheet there is a picture of the Ascension for the children to add to and colour, or they can complete the picture as a mosaic. For this, pre-cut pieces of different colours from old greetings cards, and place the different colours in separate tubs. The children stick on the bits with glue sticks.

PEARL DIVERS

Aim: To see the Ascension in the context of the Resurrection and the coming of the Holy Spirit.

Starter

Cut several series of pictures from comic strips and fix them in groups on the walls, in random order. The children walk around the room on their own or with a friend or two, sorting the pictures into the right sequence. You can then take each group of pictures down in turn and put them in the correct order so everyone can check it against their own ideas.

Teaching

Using one of the sets of pictures, get the children to explain why one picture couldn't possibly come before another. We have been picking up the clues based on what we know – a cat can't get wet before it has fallen into the water; a rocket cannot be in a thousand pieces before it has exploded. Today we

are going to look at the order of events after Jesus' death, and see why they had to be in that order.

First there had to be the cross. (Place a cross on the floor at one end of the room.) It was through dying for us that Jesus set us free. This is how he saved the world with love. (Unwind a ball of string, starting at the cross, and taking it across the floor to a message which says, 'Jesus is alive!') Being the Lord of Life, death simply could not hold him prisoner for long, so the next thing for Jesus the Son of God had to be the Resurrection on Easter Day. (Unwind the string further, and place some broken bread on a plate on the floor.) Jesus needed his friends to know that he really was alive, so he appeared to them at different times, and often it was when he broke the bread that they recognised him. (Unwind the string a bit more, and place down a cut-out cloud.)

Once the disciples had begun to realise that Jesus could be with them without having to be seen all the time, they were ready for the next stage. Jesus had promised his disciples that he was on his way back to the Father, but that he wouldn't leave them on their own. Once he had returned to heaven they would be able to receive the power of the Holy Spirit. Jesus first had to go in glory back into heaven, so that (unwind more string to a picture of tongues of flames) the disciples could receive that power of the Holy Spirit.

Praying

Jesus, you are our Lord and Saviour,
reigning in the glory of heaven!
You were sent to love us to freedom
and you did it!
Glory to you for ever.

Activities

On the sheet there is a picture of the Ascension for them to complete, and a wordsearch to help reinforce the Easter season vocabulary. They can also create their own picture(s) of how they imagine it might have been in heaven as Jesus appeared, with all the angels cheering and praising God for the great victory.

GOLD PANNERS

Aim: To explore the nature of Jesus' glory both on the cross and in heaven.

Starter

Make some rubbings of various coins, from different countries, a heads and a tails rubbing for each coin.

Teaching

The two sides of a coin both belong equally to the coin, but show us completely different faces of it, and today we are going to look at something which at first sight seems like two different things, but which is actually two sides of the same coin.

First read the account in Acts of the Ascension. Place on the floor a large cross cut out of dark coloured sugar paper, and chalks to record ideas on it, and also a large sun shape with zigzag edges cut out of sunny coloured sugar paper, and crayons to record ideas. Explain that one of the things we are looking at is the cross of Christ, and the other is Christ in glory, having ascended into heaven as a hero. Ask the group to write on the two shapes any words or phrases which come to mind about these two things.

Share what has been suggested in each case, and you will find that they are much more closely linked than you might expect. Read together John 17:1-11, and relate it to your findings recorded on the cross and glory symbols. The Ascension brings us to a place where heaven and earth meet and overlap for a while (overlap the two symbols).

Then read the passage from 1 Peter 4, and listen out for any overlapping of the cross and the glory in that.

Praying

O what a mystery,
meekness and majesty.
Bow down and worship –
this is your God.

(From a song by Graham Kendrick
© Copyright 1986 Kingsway's Thankyou Music.)

Activities

To express something of this mystery, suggest they create a picture which shows the Ascension from two angles at once – from the earthly and the heavenly viewpoint. They can use symbols and colours, and make the dividing line clear, or mingle the two 'plains'. On the sheet there is space to plan and keep track of ideas, and also some drawings which can be viewed in several different ways.

PENTECOST

Thought for the day

With great power the Spirit of God is poured out on the expectant disciples.

Reflection on the readings

Acts 2:1-11
Psalm 103:1, 24, 29-31
1 Corinthians 12:3-7, 12-13
John 20:19-23

The coming of the Holy Spirit on God's people at Pentecost is directly the result of the victory won over sin and death on Good Friday, which became obvious with the Resurrection on Easter Day. Since Easter we have been tracing the growing understanding of what all that meant, and where it might lead, rather like a potential smouldering fire that has suddenly burst into flames. The disciples had already experienced the risen Christ appearing among them and filling them with peace and happiness, reassurance and enlightenment. Now, on the day which celebrated the giving of the ancient law, the new, fulfilled law is seeringly burnt into their hearts; Jesus comes not so much among them, as right within them, in a breathtaking way which is, in answer to his prayer, allowing them to be truly at one with him as he is one with the Father. From now on, the group of followers are collectively the Body of Christ, breathing the breath of his life, which is the life of God.

That power is immediately noticeable. The Jewish tradition was familiar with spirit-filled ecstatic prophecy, and many recognised that these people were proclaiming the wonderful works of God which had just been revealed to them with a new vitality and heightened perception. But it was even more than that. It is the day when the new Israel is born. For from now on the bright revelation of God's reality, power and mercy, sown in the promise to Abraham and his family and spreading to the chosen nation who were called to be God's light, will be available to the whole world; all believers will be part of that holy nation, filled with the life of the living God.

Pentecost was only the beginning. It was not only to those first disciples that God came intimately and completely in the Holy Spirit. There is plenty of it left for us! Freshly and vigorously in our times, too, God is prepared to make his dwelling with expectant believers of any tradition and any age, culture or personality. It is a terrible myth that the Holy Spirit is only for some, that any are shut off from that inner God-given life. The truth is simple: anyone at all who prays expectantly and longingly for the real, living God to come upon them in power will receive the gift that God longs to give. Let's not get too worked up about the 'how'; that is God's agenda, and we can trust that it will always be in the time and way which is best for each asking person.

What we do need to return to is deep, passionate longing for God, more than anything or anyone else. And God will come and breathe his life into us all, and the effects will show.

Discussion starters

1. Think of how we prepare for important exams, interviews or the birth of children. How does this compare with the seriousness we give to seeking the Holy Spirit of God in our lives?

2. We all know there are areas in our church which do not breathe with God's life – yet. What can we do to change that?

All-stage talk

Bring along an electrical appliance and, if necessary, an extension lead. Alternatively, have a torch or game powered by batteries, and keep the batteries separate at first.

Refresh everyone's memory of today's dynamic event, with the disciples praying and waiting on God, and the early morning experience of his power coming to them like a rushing wind, or flames, searching out each one of them and touching them with the touch of God.

It quite overwhelmed them, and left them fired up with excitement at what God is capable of doing in people. They were bursting to tell everyone else about it, and wanted everyone to share this sense of God actually living in them. It was quite different from knowing about God; it was even different from walking about in the company of Jesus. This was like being flowed through with new life that set them living, talking and working in a new way.

Show the electrical appliance you have brought. Explain what this thing is capable of doing, but point out that at the moment it can't do any of those things. It has everything in place to work in that lively way, but something is missing at the moment – it isn't linked up to the power supply. Would it help if the appliance knew exactly how electricity works? Not really. However much is known about electrical circuits and the power grid, that won't bring this appliance to life. What it needs is this. (Plug the appliance into the power supply and switch on.)

Now the thing springs into life, and all kinds of potential are activated. That's what it's like having

God's Spirit living in us and flowing through us. It makes that much difference! Just think what our world could be like if we were all full of the power of God's Spirit. Just think what a difference it would make in the world if all those in churches today all over the world asked God, seriously and openly, for a fresh outpouring of the Holy Spirit!

So often we are like well-finished appliances or games, knowing all about God's power, but not wanting to have the power switched on in us, just in case. Just in case what? Our God is the true, living God of love and compassion and mercy. Which means that any power he sends to touch us and affect us, will be only and entirely good for us. God is longing for his Church to be 'live' with the active power of his Spirit; we may be in good working order, but we also need to have the power, so that we actually 'work'!

All-age ideas

- This is a day to bring out those flame-coloured banners, flags and streamers.

- Lots of flame and white colours in the flower arrangements, with the swirling sense of movement and power.

Prayer of the Faithful

Celebrant
As the body of Christ,
in the power of the Spirit,
let us pray.

Reader
For a fresh outpouring of the Holy Spirit
on the people of God
all over the world,
and in all worship traditions.
For a readiness to be changed and made new;
for a softening of the ground of our hearts
to receive without fear.

Silence

With our whole selves we pray:
come, Holy Spirit of God.

For all the peoples of the earth
to know you and honour your name.
For the healing of the nations
and a new thirst for righteousness and purity
at every level and in every aspect of society.
For a dissatisfaction with the pursuit of pleasure
and all that distracts us from our true calling.

Silence

With our whole selves we pray:
come, Holy Spirit of God.

For the grace and power to live out our faith
in the real and challenging world,
among those we meet and eat with,
whose lives we share,
without compromising that calling
to be the body of Christ,
living God's integrity and purity,
forgiveness and love.

Silence

With our whole selves we pray:
come, Holy Spirit of God.

For those whose lives feel empty or cheated,
or filled with pain, or worry or guilt.
For all whose hopes and dreams are in tatters;
all who are in any way imprisoned.

Silence

With our whole selves we pray:
come, Holy Spirit of God.

For those who walk the dark journey of death
and all who have come through it
into your presence;
for mourners distressed by regrets
or angry with God at their loss.

Silence

With our whole selves we pray:
come, Holy Spirit of God.

We pray with Mary,
Mother of the Church:
Hail, Mary . . .

Together in silence,
we name those known to us
who need our prayers.

Silence

Celebrant
Father, in grateful thanks
for all your blessings in our lives,
we relinquish our wills to yours,
and ask you to accept these prayers
through Christ our Lord.
Amen.

TREASURE SEEKERS

Aim: To celebrate the birthday of the Church.

Starter

Play with balloons, enjoying the way they float about
in the air.

Teaching

Bring in a birthday cake with two candles on, each
candle standing for a thousand years. Explain that
today is the Church's birthday. 'Church' doesn't
really mean the building, but the people inside. It
means a group of Christians who are filled with
God's love. That first happened at Pentecost, nearly
two thousand years ago, when God's Holy Spirit
was poured into the followers of Jesus, until they
were filled with his love. So that's how old the
Church is – nearly two thousand years old! Sing
'Happy birthday to you' to 'dear Church', and
while the cake is being cut up, try the finger rhyme
which reminds us that the Church is really the
people inside, filled with God's love. (And all of us
here are part of that Church.)

Here's the church, **1**

here's the steeple, **2**

open the doors
3

and here's all the people
4

Praying

We are the Church
and you are our God.
You fill us with love every day.
We are the Church
and you are our God.
We're a body of people who pray.

Activities

Today's sheet can be decorated and made into a
Pentecost birthday hat, which the children can wear
into church. They can also have another game,
dancing and jumping about to some recorded
praise songs. Every time the music stops, call out a
name, and everyone prays for that person in the
group. (Thank you, God, for Jessica. Fill her with
your love.) Make sure every person is prayed for.

PEARL DIVERS

Aim: To know the Pentecost story.

Starter

Using red, orange and yellow crepe paper, cut strips and bunch some of these strips together to make cheerleader streamers, like this:

Teaching

First practise making a collective sound of wind, not by blowing, but breathing out with mouths open. Try it quietly at first, and then much more loudly. We are going to hear about the day when God breathed his life and power into his people.

First go round noisily shutting windows and doors, and turning keys in locks, as you tell the children how the disciples were gathered as usual to pray. Just over a week ago they had seen Jesus taken up into heaven, and had been told to wait in Jerusalem for the coming of the Holy Spirit. They had no idea what that meant, or what to expect, but Jesus had told them to wait expectantly, so that is what they would do.

Now play some quiet music. Suggest we all sit waiting for God, as those disciples did that morning, waiting for God to give us the gift of his Spirit.

Suddenly there was a sound, like this (all start the quiet out-breathing), rather like wind, coming from the sky and getting closer. It was the sound of God, breathing his Holy Spirit into his loyal friends. The sound got louder (all breathe out more loudly), until the whole house they were in seemed surrounded by the living, moving presence of almighty God. (Everyone picks up their streamers and shakers, stands up and whirls them round about as you tell the next part of the story.) Now it was as if tongues of flame flickered out from the breath of God and found each person, resting on them very gently. (The streamers are brought gently down to rest on the floor between the children.)

The disciples were all filled with God's Holy Spirit, and they started praising God and shouting out their love for him. They didn't care what anyone else thought of them, their love for God bubbled up inside them and all they wanted to do

was thank him and tell him their love. They lifted their hands and all started talking at once. (Put on a tape so they can all dance and sing their hearts out to their God, waving their streamers.)

Quite a crowd had gathered outside the house, wondering what was going on so early in the morning. Still full of God's Spirit, the disciples ran out to share the good news. That's what the Church, including us, has been called to do ever since – to be filled with God's living Spirit, and in our excitement and joy, run out to share the good news with all the people we meet.

Praying

Breathe on me, too, Lord God almighty,
as you breathed on the disciples that day.
Touch me with your fire
and set me ablaze with your love!

Activities

Have some red, orange and yellow pieces of tissue, out of which the children can cut flame shapes to stick on the headband and make a hat of flame. There are also flame shapes on the sheet with space for them to write on the message of God's love they want people to know. They can colour these, cut them out and give them to people.

GOLD PANNERS

Aim: To know that the Holy Spirit can also come today.

Starter

If there is a suitable place, start today by building and lighting a small bonfire. If not, have a metal tray and give everyone a nightlight each, which they can light and place on the tray. Gather round the fire or the candle flames and watch them for a minute or two in silence.

Teaching

We can't save ourselves, however hard we try, but Jesus did the saving for us. How? (Show a cross.) By dying on the cross, Jesus took all our sin on himself. It was only after his death and Resurrection, and once he had returned to heaven, that the Holy Spirit of God could come pouring out in all its fullness on those who believe in Jesus as their Saviour.

Now, sitting round the fire or the candles, read the passage from Acts, imagining this group of Jesus' followers waiting expectantly and obediently.

When they rushed out in their joy and excitement at what God was doing, and saw it all as a great fulfilment of the prophets' longing, it was the first day of the Church rushing out to tell others the amazing good news of God's love, powerfully present in his people. It is still going on today. In every generation, people who are expectant and obedient, believing in Jesus as their Saviour, can experience that same anointing of the Holy Spirit of almighty God. They don't just know about it, they know it for real, and that is what makes them excited about what God is doing, and what makes them want to rush out and spread the good news.

Praying

Breathe on me, Breath of God,
fill me with life anew,
that I may love what thou dost love
and do what thou wouldst do.
Breathe on me, Breath of God,
till I am wholly thine,
until this earthly part of me
glows with thy fire divine.

Activities

On the sheet there is a picture of the Pentecost experience with questions to help them think through the meaning of it, both for the disciples and for themselves. There are also descriptions of other outpourings of the Spirit in the lives of people through the ages since Pentecost.

FEASTS OF THE LORD

TRINITY SUNDAY

Thought for the day

The mystery of God – Creator, Redeemer and Sanctifier all at once – is beyond our human understanding, yet closer to us than breathing.

Reflection on the readings

Exodus 34:4-6, 8-9
Daniel 3:52-56
2 Corinthians 13:11-13
John 3:16-18

There are some things which we sense, but which start slithering out of our grasp as we try to pin them down in words. Some deep relationships are like this, and some intense experiences. It is also true of the nature of God. Whenever we attempt to explain what we mean by the Trinity we are bound to end up falling short of the truth, and inadequately picturing what is simply so deep and vast that it is beyond the power of human understanding.

If we take the image of a young baby being suckled, we can see that here the baby has a wonderful sense of what being loved, cared for and nurtured is all about. Yet all it can do is gurgle its understanding, and is probably more likely to express that knowledge by falling asleep, trusting and satisfied.

That is rather how it is with us. To understand the nature of God, and what the Trinity really means, is in one sense always beyond our scope as humans. God is never going to be quantifiable in human terms because he far surpasses what it means to be human. But in another sense we are able to understand his nature as we experience relationship with him and feel his love, nurturing and committed care. All our attempts to express that are rather like a baby's gurglings, or a contented and trusting tranquillity which shows in our lives.

Jesus' words to Nicodemus give us a glimpse of God as he is in himself, a God of unimaginable love. On account of his love we are given his Son, not only to know him but to share his life, that is, to have eternal life.

Discussion starters

1. If the God we worship has been revealed to us as community in unity, and we pray for God's kingdom to come on earth 'in the way it happens in heaven', what does that suggest about the way the Church should be operating?

2. Why are we baptised in the name of the Father, Son and Holy Spirit, rather than the one true God?

All-stage talk

Produce a jacket or sweater of a young child's size, and invite a much larger volunteer to get into it. (It should be obvious that they won't be able to, even though they try.) Agree that it is impossible to get Ben into Justin's jacket – he's simply too big to fit!

Sometimes we expect God to be able to fit into our human-sized minds. We start to think about God, and say things like, 'But how can he possibly be able to hear us all praying at once?' when what we really mean is that we know humans couldn't do that, so it must be impossible for God as well. Or we say, 'God *must* have had a beginning sometime, because *everything* does!'

When we do this we are holding out a small human shape (hold out the little jacket) and expecting God to climb into it. And of course he doesn't fit, because being God is much bigger and deeper and wider than being a human being. God is so great that he is always going to be full of wonderful mystery for us, however much we learn about him. As humans we cannot hold his nature and understand it, any more than this small jacket will hold a big boy like Ben.

So does that mean that we can't really know God? Not at all! Invite Ben and Justin to come up and shake hands, and say hello to each other. You could have Ben asking Justin some questions, so that everyone can see that both boys are able to have a conversation.

Just because God is God and you are human doesn't mean you can't be good friends. There are lots of people here today who talk with God every day (it's called praying) and know that he is the person they love and trust best in their whole life.

We have been given a lifetime to get to know God really well and live as his friends. Sometimes we waste that time, and sometimes we suddenly realise that nothing else is quite so important. Sometimes we don't bother to tell other people about our loving God, or we let our behaviour tell them that we don't think he is worth very much at all. And other times we feel such love for our God that we can't wait to let other people know about him. And then our loving behaviour tells them as well as our words.

Our God is wonderful and all-knowing. He is the maker of our universe and of us all, he is the one who came as Jesus to die for love of us and save us, and he is present with his people, living in us as the Holy Spirit. How could we possibly ever expect to completely understand a God as amazing as that!

God being so great that he is full of holy mystery should make us excited, not frustrated. Let's enjoy being friends with the God who is so amazing that no human can ever explain what he is really like! And let's lavish our worship on him; any god smaller, or knowable, wouldn't be worth worshipping anyway.

All-age ideas

- Have a length of lining paper on which are drawn several outlines of a Celtic expression of the Trinity, shown below. Provide green crayons and invite some people (they do not have to be children – adults would benefit from it just as much) to come and draw round the lines continuously, following their path of inter-relatedness so that they sense, rather than understand, the harmonious community of the One God. This could be done during the singing of *St Patrick's breastplate (I bind unto myself today)*.

- In the flower arrangements use evergreen for eternity, shamrock and clover leaves, and three colours blending in and out of one another to make a unified whole.

Prayer of the Faithful

Celebrant
Called by the great God we worship,
let us pray fervently for the Church
and for the world.

Reader
We bring before you, O God,
the needs of the Church,
in its weakness and its potential;
revive and refresh us, teach and direct us,
inspire all who preach, teach
and gossip the good news,
and uphold all who suffer for their faith in any way.

Silence

God of mystery and compassion:
you know us and you love us.

We bring before you, O God,
the particular problems of our age and our culture;
renew in us a commitment
to community and mutual trust,
give a sense of value to all
who despise others and themselves;
protect the vulnerable and sensitise the hearts
of all who have become anaesthetised
by images of violence.

Silence

God of mystery and compassion:
you know us and you love us.

We bring before you, O God,
the nurturing of our children and young people,
in homes and parenting, schools and teaching,
in the expectations, pressures and dangers,
in the hopes and possibilities for good.

Silence

God of mystery and compassion:
you know us and you love us.

We bring before you, O God,
the hungry and malnourished,
the greedy and complacent;
those who are ill and those who care for them;
the unhappy and those who comfort them;
all who are undergoing surgery or painful treatment,
and all who have no one to turn to.

Silence

God of mystery and compassion:
you know us and you love us.

We bring before you, O God,
those who have died in faith
and will now see you face to face;
those for whom death speaks of fear or annihilation,
and those who are unprepared to meet you.

Silence

God of mystery and compassion:
you know us and you love us.

With Mary, who, in loving obedience,
made herself available to God's will,
let us make our prayer:
Hail, Mary . . .

Together in silence,
we name those known to us
who need our prayers.

Silence

Celebrant
Father Almighty,
in the Spirit we pray,
and ask you to hear our prayers
through Jesus Christ our Lord.
Amen.

TREASURE SEEKERS

Aim: To know that God is the greatest.

Starter

Play with sand and buckets, spades and pots, or with water, filling and emptying, and discovering that big amounts won't fit in small containers.

Teaching

Use examples from the starter activity to show how we can't fit big amounts into small containers. Our God is much greater and more wonderful than we can imagine, so it's not surprising that all he is won't fit into our little human minds!

But even though we cannot ever understand all that God is, we can certainly be best friends with him, and snuggle up in his loving, and know that he loves us and cares for us. It's all a bit like this.

There was once a puppy called Pete. He was very soft to stroke, very wriggly and he ran about a lot, and liked eating. Best of all he liked eating rabbit-flavoured crunchy biscuits, but he wasn't allowed many of those in case he got fat. Pete belonged to Oliver, who thought he was the best puppy in the world. Pete thought Oliver was the best boy in the world. They loved each other. Sometimes they played with a ball. Oliver threw the ball and Pete went racing after it, with his ears flying out behind him. He could catch the ball while it was still in the air! Then he would hang on to the ball so Oliver couldn't get it back, wagging his tail because it was such fun. But if Oliver started to walk away, Pete came racing over and dropped the ball at his feet, waiting for Oliver to throw it again.

Every day Oliver disappeared for a while. He didn't really disappear, of course; he just went to nursery school for the morning. Pete was puzzled and sad whenever Oliver disappeared, and he was happy and waggy as soon as Oliver came back. Because he was a dog, Pete couldn't understand things like people going to nursery school, and, however long Pete lives, he will never be able to understand things like that, any more than we will ever be able to understand everything about God.

But what Pete did know very well indeed was that he loved Oliver and Oliver loved him, and they both enjoyed being together. Whenever they played and laughed together, whenever Oliver fed him (especially rabbit-flavoured crunchy biscuits!) and whenever Pete fell asleep on Oliver's feet, he knew that he was loved and owned by someone very special, just as we know we are owned and loved by a wonderful God.

Praying

Our God is so BIG, so strong and so mighty,
there's nothing that he cannot do!
The rivers are his, the mountains are his,
the stars are his handiwork too!
Our God is so BIG, so strong and so mighty,
there's nothing that he cannot do!

Activities

On the sheet there is a pattern which the children can trace round and round to get a feel of how God is unending, and they can look at and colour the pictures to see the different aspects of God.

PEARL DIVERS

Aim: To start exploring how God is one God, yet community.

Starter

Play a game where teams are involved. Depending on your group this could be a ball game, or a party team game, such as 'flip the kipper' (each team member waving a newspaper fish along a course using sheets of newspaper).

Teaching

In a large bowl have a jug full of water, and a small cup. Tell everyone we are going to stage an experiment today. We are going to see if all the water in the jug will fit into the cup. Try this and discover that it won't. Why not? There was too much water for the little cup to cope with all at once.

Ask them to imagine that the little cup is a human mind, and all the water, not just in a jug, but in all the seas and oceans and rivers and clouds, is like God. There is far more to God than we, with our little cup-sized human minds, can possibly cope with or understand. But then, if God was just another little cup like us, why on earth would we worship him? We worship God because he is the source, or beginning and the end of all things, because he is the great power behind all life and existence, and because he is the one true God, altogether too great and full of mystery for us to ever understand.

The amazing thing is that this God, full of mystery, has got time for us! He actually knows everything about each person in this room, each person in church, each person in this town and this country, and each person in every country of the whole world. Not just those alive now, but all the ones who have ever lived and who will ever live. And that's pretty impressive. And what's more, he was willing to come and live among us as a human person, called Jesus, and through the Holy Spirit he is alive in human people of every time and place, when they put their trust in him.

We find ourselves saying, 'But how can God be One God when we talk about him as the Father, Jesus and the Holy Spirit? Isn't that three, rather than one?' Well, no, it isn't three Gods, it's all One God, but it is three persons united and co-operating in the one God, which we call TRI (=3) + UNITY (=1) = TRINITY. Yes, it's impossible for us to understand. That doesn't mean it can't be true, though; it means that God is truly the greatest, and far greater than a human mind.

Praying

Holy God, greater than our knowing,
we worship you.
Holy God, more than we can understand,
we worship you.
Holy God, knowing all things,
yet loving each of us,
we worship you.

Activities

Traditionally, the Trinity colour is white. Stick white wool on to the Celtic Trinity pattern on the sheet, to help everyone sense the way God is three in unity and co-operation, without beginning or end. There are also examples of things they are trying to understand and others they may understand some day but would never be able to fully explain.

GOLD PANNERS

Aim: To look at how we came to see the One God as Trinity.

Starter

Give everyone sketching materials and ask them to draw the same object but from all kinds of different angles and viewpoints.

Teaching

Since today we celebrate the mystery and beauty of the Trinity, we are going to look at how people have come to see God in this way. Point out that the term 'Trinity' does not appear anywhere in the Bible, but there are lots of hints and clues in scripture which have led us to this way of describing God. First of all, what does the word 'Trinity' mean?

Show two signs, one saying 'Tri' and the other 'Unity'. Talk together about what each of these means. 'Tri' is quite straightforwardly 'three': the Father who is Creator, the Son who is Jesus the Redeemer, and the Holy Spirit who is the living Breath of God. 'Unity' has the sense of several being united in a kind of team effort, of a group being of one mind, of co-operation and intertwining of ideas and gifts. Put the two sections together so that they overlap and form the word 'Trinity', which combines all you have been talking about.

Now fix three small circles of paper on the floor to outline a triangle. In the Trinity the three persons are both distinct and bound up in one being. Sometimes through the history of the Church some Christians have thought of them as so completely distinct (move the circles far apart) that the sense of unity is lost; others have thought of them as so closely bound (move the circles on top of one another) that the sense of community is lost. The truth is that for our great, loving God of mystery and wonder, the 'Tri' and the 'Unity' are both possible.

Now look through the following references together, looking out for the presence of Creator, Word (Jesus' title) and Spirit, to see how they speak of this mystery which is God, so great that our human minds can't expect to be able to 'nail it down'.

Genesis 1:1-3
John 1:1-4
Matthew 28:18-20
Romans 8:3-4
Ephesians 3:14-19

Praying

Holy, holy, holy! Lord God almighty!
May the grace of our Lord Jesus Christ
and the love of God
and the fellowship of the Holy Spirit
be with us all evermore. Amen.

Activities

On the sheet there is space to link the references to our understanding of God, and they can try to express something of the Trinity nature of God in art forms such as wire sculpture, mobiles or collage.

CORPUS CHRISTI

Thought for the day

Jesus Christ is the living bread; as we feed on him we share his life.

Reflection on the readings

Deuteronomy 8:2-3, 14-16
Psalm 147
1 Corinthians 10:16-17
John 6:51-58

Today is set apart as a time to celebrate and reflect on the mystery of the body and blood of Christ, shared among the people of God. The Last Supper itself is, of course, remembered particularly on Maundy Thursday, but that is in the context of all the other events of Holy Week, so it is important that we have another occasion to marvel and meditate, as we thank God for the sacramental feeding which keeps us spiritually alive.

The first reading takes us back to the feeding of the people of Israel during their time in the desert, when their needs were provided, so that in the wild and inhospitable landscape they did not thirst or go hungry. Water was provided from the hardest rock, and manna fed them daily. The word 'manna' means 'what is it?', and all of us who share the sacramental feeding at the Eucharist are likewise aware that there is mystery about this spiritual food. We do not make our children wait to receive its blessing until they have graduated in theology, but recognise that in a sense we none of us fully understand with our minds; we are simply required to trust God in love and receive his feeding.

Physical feeding is an urgent need for our survival, and we demand it by our crying even as tiny babies. That early suckling establishes a deep emotional bond between being fed and being loved. Spiritual feeding by our loving God is very similar. In coming to receive the sacrament, we approach God with our raw need, knowing our utter dependence on his love for our survival and nurture. This is the feeding of salvation, only possible through the death and resurrection of the incarnate Christ, who meets our need and feeds us with nothing short of his very self, hidden in the form of bread and wine.

As we share this living bread, we are built up not just as individuals but as a community, bound together and united in the common life of the God we worship. This is life which is not interrupted by our physical dying, but lasts for the whole of eternity.

Discussion starters

1. How does God feed us?

2. How can we best prepare ourselves to receive the body of Christ?

All-stage talk

Bring along some examples of junk food, such as crisps and sweets and various snacks. Talk about how many of us enjoy eating this kind of thing, and read out some of the ingredients. Although we like eating them, they have very little real food value, and if we tried to live entirely on junk food our health would soon suffer.

For our bodies to grow and repair and be kept in good working order, we need good, wholesome feeding at regular intervals. Give some examples of 'real' meals, and ask others for examples of their favourites. We can feel the difference when we are properly nourished; we have more energy, and we don't find ourselves needing so many snacks between meals.

Sadly, there are many living today in areas of drought and war who are not able to give their children adequate feeding, and must watch them growing weak from lack of nourishment. Good feeding is a shared responsibility, and we cannot pray, 'Give us this day our daily bread' with any real meaning unless we are doing all we can to right the injustices and wrongs which make for terrible hunger and the suffering of starvation.

Our need for spiritual feeding is just as urgent and vital. In our world we are offered lots of spiritual junk food, and many try to survive on this. The sentimental and tinselled religion of Christmas and the themed chocolate eggs and cards with baby rabbits and lambs at Easter are the only spiritual feeding many are getting. Other things, like human relationships, music and art, football and shopping, may be good in their own way but make poor value substitutes when they are used as spiritual food.

What God offers us is *real* food – feeding which will nourish and sustain us in our life with all that we have to face in the way of problems and sorrows, joys and challenges. This feeding provides for our deep spiritual needs so that we can journey through life well fed, with spiritual energy and inner resources to deal with the problems. This feeding is nothing less than being fed with Christ, who loved us so much he was ready to die for us. As we share the bread and wine, we are nourished with his life and love and forgiveness and hope. That is real feeding.

All-age ideas

- Make a flower arrangement around a loaf of bread and a carafe of wine, with some grapes and wheat amongst the flowers.

- Read the last two paragraphs from Donald Nicholl's book, *The testing of hearts*.

Prayer of the Faithful

Celebrant
Gathered as the Body of Christ,
let us pray together to our heavenly Father.

Reader
We pray for all who celebrate
the Eucharistic mysteries,
all who administer the sacrament
of the body and blood of Christ,
and all who receive it, day by day,
week by week and year by year.
Through the loving nature of this feeding
may we all grow in holiness
and bring your life to all we meet.

Silence

In our need:
we come to you.

We pray that all who know
their hunger and thirst for real feeding
may find the spiritual nourishment they crave,
and receive new and satisfying life
through Christ our Lord.
We pray that the world may know God's love for it.

Silence

In our need:
we come to you.

We pray for the spiritual feeding of our families,
and our parish family, through word and sacrament;
may we daily draw closer to the God who loves us,
and our lives become increasingly filled with his life
as we feed on him.

Silence

In our need:
we come to you.

We pray for those who, through frailty or illness,
receive the sacrament in their homes or in hospital;
for all who are malnourished or starving,
whether physically, emotionally or spiritually.

Silence

In our need:
we come to you.

We pray for those who have died,
that in your mercy they may be brought
into the eternal joy of heaven.

Silence

In our need:
we come to you.

We make our prayers with Mary,
who brought the living bread into the world:
Hail, Mary . . .

Let us be still in the presence of God
and bring to him the needs and concerns
that weigh on our hearts.

Silence

Celebrant
Heavenly Father,
you nourish us by the body and blood of Jesus,
so that we can share the life of heaven,
both now and at the end of time.
Hear our prayers and provide for us all.
Amen.

TREASURE SEEKERS, PEARL DIVERS AND GOLD PANNERS

It is likely that Corpus Christi services for schools will not need a separate programme for children and young people. However, in the books for TREASURE SEEKERS and PEARL DIVERS I have included worksheets for children in church today.

ORDINARY TIME

SECOND SUNDAY OF THE YEAR

Thought for the day

Jesus is recognised and pointed out by John to be God's chosen one.

Reflection on the readings

Isaiah 49:3, 5-6
Psalm 39:2, 4, 7-10
1 Corinthians 1:1-3
John 1:29-34

Today, as we continue to think of Christ being shown, or revealed, to the world, there is another of the 'servant' readings from Isaiah. Set apart before birth, the servant has been brought into being to gather up Israel and bring her back into a right relationship with God, not through a dynamically successful campaign which the world might recognise and expect, but actually through worldly foolishness – failure, suffering and rejection.

Not only that, but as the plan unfolds it spills out of its original boundaries to include the possibility of salvation for the entire world. Gradually the prophet is starting to understand the scale of God's intended action.

We pick up echoes of the Gospel pictures of Jesus in that reading from Isaiah: the pre-natal cherishing, the light for the world, the redeemer. They are echoes that the people of Israel would have noticed, and they reveal Jesus as the One who fulfils the Old Testament writings in a most remarkable way.

John wants to tell everyone about it. It says a lot about John that he was able to direct his own disciples to Jesus. Probably with hindsight, the Gospel writer has John describing Jesus as 'God's Passover Lamb', with all the significance of sacrifice and the way to freedom which that suggests. Though he had been preparing them for this, it could still have been a moment to indulge the human instinct to be possessive, critical and defensive, yet in John we rather sense excitement and great enthusiasm.

In John's Gospel the emphasis is not so much on Jesus going out to find his disciples as them going to find him, and bringing one another along. We are aware of the attraction of this itinerant teacher and holy man, with his remarkable gift of discernment and wisdom. Can this really be the promised and long-awaited Messiah? It will only be time spent in Jesus' company that will enable these followers to decide about the truth of Jesus' identity.

And, as Paul writes in his letter to the church in Corinth, the same is true for all those who seek Jesus, whatever time or place they live in. As we spend time in Jesus' company we will find that it shows, and then others, spending time with us, may recognise the truth that Christ is living in us.

Discussion starters

1. What can we learn about evangelising from today's Gospel?

2. How does John's way of narrating Jesus' Baptism differ from Matthew's? What do both accounts agree about?

All-stage talk

Start by hiding some treasure while a volunteer 'seeker' covers their eyes. Everyone else needs to know where it is hidden. Now set the treasure-seeker off to search, with everyone else guiding them by calling out whether they are colder or hotter. With all this help it shouldn't take too long for the seeker to find.

Lots of people are truth-seekers. They want to find out the truth about life and about God and about the reason we are here. These are the deep questions that humans have always asked, and it is important that we ask them. Questions are good things; never stop asking them, just because you're grown up. Grown-ups need to learn from the children here – children are very good at asking important questions!

When we are seeking for the truth about God, it helps if there are people who have already found him, who are happy to tell us when we're getting nearer or drifting further away. John the Baptist is one of those who is calling out to us, 'Warmer! You're getting warmer . . . you're boiling hot!' That's what he was doing to his disciples when Jesus came by. 'Look!' he said. 'That's the one I was telling you about – this is the one you've been waiting for! This is the Son of God!'

Think about whether you ever help other people find the truth about God. Think about whether other people help you, and how they do it. And if you don't think you've been doing much helping, today's readings are giving you some ideas as to how to start:

- telling people what you have noticed and found out about God;

- mentioning that he's worth spending time with;

- suggesting that they come with you to find out more;

- and introducing them to God by the way you live.

All-age ideas

• Have a display of different Bible reading schemes for people to browse through and order after the service.

Prayer of the Faithful

Celebrant
Let us voice our cares and concerns,
knowing that God is listening to us.

Reader
Lord God, make yourself known
to the people who come into our churches,
or who pass by and sometimes wonder,
but have not yet come in;
make us better bearers of your life
to those who need you
but have never met you.

Silence

True and living God:
we want to know you more.

Lord God, the world lurches from crisis to crisis,
and there is much misleading and misdirecting;
help us recover the natural sense
of what is right and just, honest and good,
so that our hearts are inclined
to hear the voice of your leading and respond to it.

Silence

True and living God:
we want to know you more.

Lord God, help us to take more seriously
our responsibility of helping one another
forward into faith, as brothers and sisters;
we pray for those in our own families
whom we would love to bring to know you,
and for those who have drifted away.

Silence

True and living God:
we want to know you more.

Lord God, there are some who are going through
very distressing, painful and worrying times.
We stand alongside them now,
and ask for them your comfort, reassurance,
healing and peace of mind.

Silence

True and living God:
we want to know you more.

Lord God, even as we pray now,
there are those journeying through death.

We pray for them, for all who have recently died,
and for all those left without their loved ones,
grieving, or numbed with shock.

Silence

True and living God:
we want to know you more.

Mary opened her life
to the loving power of God;
we now join our prayers with hers:
Hail, Mary . . .

In the silence of God's stillness,
we name any we know
who especially need our prayer.

Silence

Celebrant
God our Father,
you know us better than we know ourselves;
we ask you to hear our prayers
through Jesus Christ, your Son.
Amen.

TREASURE SEEKERS

Aim: To know that we can tell others about Jesus.

Starter

Sit in a circle and play 'pass the smile'. You smile to the person next to you, and they smile to the next person until the smile has gone all round the circle. With very young children you can pass a big smiley face around the circle; with older ones you could also try a short message, such as 'God loves you! Pass it on', which they can whisper to each other.

Teaching

First tell a story about the way some good news is passed on from one person to the next. Use simple puppets (wooden spoons and spatulas with faces drawn on and paper clothes stuck on with blutack).

Justin was excited. That morning the postman had delivered an airmail letter from his Uncle Kent and Auntie Betty. They lived in California, in the USA, and Justin had never seen them. Every birthday they sent him a birthday card and an American present, and every Christmas they sent a Christmas card, an American Advent calendar, an American Christmas present, and a photograph of them and their family sitting smiling in front of their Christmas tree. They had a large black dog called Corby.

Although he had never seen them, Justin felt he knew and loved Uncle Kent and Auntie Betty already. He knew that Uncle Kent liked gardening and making bird tables out of wood. He knew that Auntie Betty made big chocolate cakes which you ate with ice cream. And he knew that they both loved getting the drawings and paintings he often sent them, and that they kept a photo of Justin on the fridge in their kitchen.

In this airmail letter Uncle Kent and Auntie Betty said that they were able to come to England, and stay with Justin and his family. So that's why Justin and his mum and dad were so excited!

They would all be driving to the airport to meet them. 'How will I know who they are?' asked Justin. Dad got out the latest Christmas photo. 'We'll take this with us and that will help you recognise them,' he said.

When they got to the airport they stood at the barrier while lots of people walked towards them, pushing trolleys piled high with bags and cases. Justin kept looking at the photo and then at all the people. Suddenly he spotted them. Auntie Betty looked just like the sort of person who would bake chocolate cakes and serve them with ice cream. Uncle Kent looked just like the sort of person who would enjoy making wooden bird tables. And from their smiles as they saw Justin, he knew they were just the sort of people to like his drawings, and keep his photo on their fridge because their smiles told Justin that Uncle Kent and Auntie Betty really knew and loved him. 'Hi, you guys!' shouted Auntie Betty, and Uncle Kent wheeled their trolley towards them as fast as he could, with a big grin all over his face.

It was a lovely visit. Justin liked the way Auntie Betty and Uncle Kent spoke, and were interested in everything. He couldn't wait to have his best friend round to meet them. As soon as he could, he told Imogen about them.

'Auntie Betty and Uncle Kent are here from America,' said Justin.

'What are they like?' asked Imogen.

'Come round and see!' said Justin.

So Imogen came round to see, and by the end of the afternoon she, Justin and Auntie Betty had made a big chocolate cake, which they all ate – with ice cream.

'How about you help me make a wooden bird table tomorrow?' said Uncle Kent.

Justin and Imogen looked at one another. 'You bet!' they said.

Praying

Jesus, we haven't seen you
but we know you love us.
We want to get to know you
and enjoy your company. Amen.

Activities

On the sheet they can think about how Jesus shows that he loves them, and how they can tell their friends about Jesus.

PEARL DIVERS

Aim: To get to know the story of John the Baptist showing us that Jesus is the Chosen One of God.

Starter

Divide the children into pairs, giving each pair one half of an old Christmas card. One of the pair goes looking for the hidden piece of the picture and when they have seen it, they leave it where it is and go and sit down at one end of the room, saying nothing. Meanwhile the others are sitting at the other end of the room, following their partner with their eyes. At a given signal, once everyone is back, the group with one half of the picture go to the hidden part, collect it and join their partner. The first pair with the completed picture wins.

Teaching

Talk about how their partners had shown them exactly where to find what they wanted, so they were able to go straight to it, without wasting any time. Today we are going to find out how some people were helped by their friends to find someone they were looking for.

Using the carpet tiles method, let the children help to build up a picture of a road, some houses and trees (palm and sycamore), lake and distant hills. We are in Galilee about two thousand years ago. Go through the account in John's Gospel, with cut-out pictures of John the Baptist and Jesus. You can base these on the pictures below.

Talk with the children about the way we always want our friends to share any good news, and that's what happened when John the Baptist showed us Jesus.

Praying

Jesus, I want my friend . . .
to meet you and find out how good it is
to live in your company. Amen.

Activities

On the sheet there is a friendship quiz, and instructions for making a friendship chain to help them pray for their friends.

GOLD PANNERS

Aim: To explore why the disciples thought Jesus was the Messiah.

Starter

Giant Mastermind. Fix up three chairs as shown below, with three pieces of coloured card hung round the back, so only the person behind the chairs can see the colours. In front of the chairs have a length of lining paper marked out as shown. People use crayons or marker pens to record their guess as to the colour and position of the hidden colours. The person behind the chairs responds by placing a tick for every correct colour and for every correct position. Eventually they should be able to work out the exact hidden pattern using reasoning and deduction.

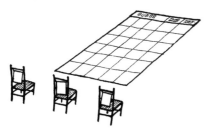

GUESS			Right colour	Right place
●	●	●	✓✓	✓
●	●	●	✓✓✓	✓
		●		

Teaching

Draw their attention to the way we had to work out the answer to that puzzle by going on the information we were given, linked with a 'hunch' that our idea was right, and a little help from our friends. That's what the first disciples had to do.

As they read John's Gospel, they can look out for the puzzle they were trying to solve (Who's this?),

and notice how they did it. Record their observations. What information do we already have about the Messiah? Read the passage from Isaiah, and again record their observations. (One day God's anointed One – the Messiah – would come in person to save them and set them free. It wouldn't be just for the people of Israel but for the whole world.) Who gave them other hints and clues? (John the Baptist; Jesus' conversation.)

Praying

O most merciful Redeemer,
friend and brother,
may I know you more clearly,
love you more dearly,
and follow you more nearly
day by day. Amen.

(The prayer of Richard of Chichester)

Activities

On the sheet there is a short sketch in which a group of people talk over their first encounter with Jesus and what impressed them about him. There is also space for them to record their own remembered 'first impressions' of Jesus, and how they have changed, or been added to, as they have grown older.

THIRD SUNDAY OF THE YEAR

Thought for the day

The prophecies of Isaiah are fulfilled in a new and lasting way in Jesus of Nazareth.

Reflection on the readings

Isaiah 8:23-9:3
Psalm 26:1, 4, 13-14
1 Corinthians 1:10-13, 17
Matthew 4:12-23

At the time when Isaiah of Jerusalem spoke of the great light of hope appearing in the darkness, and the yoke of oppression finally being shattered to bring people freedom, the people of Israel were threatened with a takeover bid and exile by Assyria, if they did not sort their values and reconcile themselves to their God. All their dreams as a nation could be wiped away if they were taken captive, under the yokes of their conquerors, away from their own beloved land, their city and their temple. (And eventually, through the Babylonians, this did happen.)

Any of us who have watched our hopes and dreams crash in pieces around us will have some idea of how such an experience takes us on a journey through questioning, self-doubt, anger, guilt, reassessment and eventually, hopefully, into a new maturity born of acceptance, greater self-knowledge, forgiveness and the value of encountering human suffering.

In their collective experience, the people are given hope, both in the short term (Jerusalem was indeed saved from the Assyrian threat) and, as we now can see, in the long term, since Jesus startlingly clearly fulfils the prophet's words as he treads the ground of Galilee, preaching, teaching and healing. The liberation he proclaims is not tied to one generation whose threatened oppression is averted, but, as Paul emphasises in his letter to the church in Corinth, it also applies to every person sensing the liberating power of God's forgiving love which can set them free to live life to the full.

Discussion starters

1. Find Zebulun and Naphtali on a map. Are there any areas of land (either geographical or spiritual) where we need to invite Jesus to walk?

2. What good news do the people need him to preach there?

All-stage talk

Out of strong card (or a wooden broom handle) make a demonstration yoke to show, on a brave volunteer, how conquerors used to subdue their captives. When you release the volunteer captive, talk to them about how good it feels to be free of the yoke.

Explain how in our first reading today we heard from a man called Isaiah. He was a prophet – someone who clearly speaks out God's words to the people. At the time, the people he was speaking to were being threatened by another country. It looked as if Assyria might well come and yoke the people up as captives, and take them far away from their own homes and their temple and their country, to live in exile in the country of their conquerors.

Isaiah showed the people that if they went on turning away from him by treating the poor unfairly, and spoiling themselves while others starved, then God would not save them from this attack. They were already 'yoked' up as slaves to their greed and selfishness, and their worries about the Assyrians.

Through Isaiah the prophet, God spoke to his people. He told them that he loved them, and that

he longed for them to sort their lives out and trust him again. God would then be able to look after them and keep them and their holy city of Jerusalem safe. It would be like their yokes being broken in pieces, so they would be completely free.

Show the demonstration yoke again on another volunteer. Do any of us wear invisible yokes and need to be set free? We may be wearing yokes of selfishness, or resentment; we may be always wishing for things we can't have. We may still feel guilty about something we did. We may need healing of some emotional damage which is holding us back from living freely.

Jesus came so that we could be set free from all these yokes. He's an expert 'yoke shatterer'! He's the kind of light that makes all the darkness in our lives and minds and hearts disappear. If we let him in to walk around our own lives, as well as the lake of Galilee, he will set us free from all those yokes that hold us captive. And then we'll be able to walk through life with a new spring in our step, full of hope.

All-age ideas

• Gather as mixed a group as possible to work on this mime about Jesus setting captives free. First have the line of captives, wearing card yokes and roped together, walking dejectedly up the aisle, sometimes flinching as if from a captor's whip. At the front of the church stands the Christ figure with arms outstretched, both in welcome to the captives and also in the shape of a cross. As the others approach they stretch out their hands towards the human cross, and begin to line themselves up against its shape. As they do this the Christ figure unties their yoke and sets them free. Eventually the captives are helping each other until all are free. Then all stretch out their arms (this time because they want to, and not because the yoke makes them) towards one another and the whole congregation.

• Have a light arrangement, rather than a flower arrangement, using lots of different containers and candles, perhaps in conjunction with a mirror.

• Use this prayer of penitence:

All Father, forgive us, for we have sinned.
A   Into the darkness of our selfishness
All shine with the light of love.
B   Into the darkness of our thoughtlessness
All shine with the light of love.
A   Into the darkness of our unkindness
All shine with the light of love.
B   Into the darkness of our greed
All shine with the light of love.
         Father, forgive us, for we have sinned.

Prayer of the Faithful

Celebrant
Let us pray to the loving God we have seen in Jesus.

Reader
We pray that the light of God
will shine in the Church throughout the world,
to set us free from prejudice,
small-mindedness and hypocrisy.
As members of the Body of Christ
may we move freely through the power of God
wherever we are called to go,
available and active in God's service.

Silence

Lord God of power:
set us free to live.

We pray that our world may be lit
by this light in the darkness
to bring freedom and hope
wherever there is oppression,
recognition and respect where there is none,
and in all conflicts
positive ways forward.

Silence

Lord God of power:
set us free to live.

We pray that in our homes, our workplaces
and our neighbourhoods
the light of godly loving may soften harsh edges,
encourage mutual caring,
and heal dysfunctional or damaging relationships.

Silence

Lord God of power:
set us free to live.

We pray that all those
whose lives are fettered by the past,
by rejection, guilt, pain or anxiety,
may be set free and encouraged to live to the full.

Silence

Lord God of power:
set us free to live.

We pray for those who have died,
and those who miss them
and are finding it very hard to cope with their loss.
We pray for all those who have no one to help them
through that last journey.

Silence

Lord God of power:
set us free to live.

We join our prayers with those of Mary,
who ministered to her Son:
Hail, Mary . . .

We pray for our own needs and concerns
in silence to God our Father.

Silence

Celebrant
Father,
rejoicing in the richness of your love,
we ask you to accept these prayers,
for the sake of Jesus Christ.
Amen.

TREASURE SEEKERS

Aim: To know that God wants us all to be safe, free
and happy.

Starter

Have a selection of toys which encourage co-opera-
tive play, such as a farm, train set and building
blocks. Leaders and children play together, setting
up a non-threatening environment for successful
interaction and contentment.

Teaching

Use a few toys as 'puppets' to act out a situation in
which one is not letting the others play happily.
This toy's behaviour is stopping the others from
being free. First time through ask the children to
spot what is happening and offer solutions to the
problem. Listen carefully to all the ideas, even the
extremely impractical and decidedly unchristian
ones! Help them to see it as a problem to solve,
rather than as a downer on a particular person.
Now have an action replay, and this time have one
of the other toys explain to the one behaving badly
that they can't play their game if the buildings
keep getting knocked over or taken away. The toy
listens and says s/he would like to play as well.
They let him/her have some bricks to knock down,
so everyone is set free to play as they like to.

All of us sometimes make life difficult for other
people. Perhaps we feel grumpy so we start being
nasty to someone else. Perhaps we want something
someone else has so we take it away from them. We
are all learning how to live in the loving way that
Jesus shows us. God sets us free so we can set one
another free.

Praying

Lord Jesus,
thank you for setting us free.
Help us to let others be free as well. Amen.

Activities

Using the sheet the children can make a moving picture to reinforce today's teaching. They will each need some card and string. Vary the amount of preparation already done by leaders according to the age and skills of each child in the group.

PEARL DIVERS

Aim: To see that Isaiah's prophecy is fulfilled in Jesus.

Starter

Use this puzzle which contains two solutions at once:

CLUES

1. The capital city of Judea.
2. We listen with these.
3. A prophet from Jerusalem.
4. It will come, but hasn't yet.
5. What God can do for all captives.
6. Who fulfilled Isaiah's words? (The answer is already there, but we might not have understood it before.)

SOLUTION

```
          6.
1.    J E R U S A L E M
2.    E A R S
3.  I S A I A H
4.  F U T U R E
5.    S E T   F R E E
```

Teaching

Use a length of string as a time line to help the children understand the time scale. Have today's date hung at one end, Abraham at the other, Jesus in the middle. Then hang Isaiah's name about two-thirds of the way along from Abraham to Jesus.

Explain that a prophet is someone who speaks out God's Word. Sometimes, but not always, this will mean telling people about things which are going to happen. Isaiah was a prophet who spoke out God's Word in Jerusalem about 740 years before Jesus was born. He told the people of Israel

about the fair and good way of living that God expected from his people, and looked forward to a time when God's light would shine out all over our world which is so often darkened with evil and unfairness. (Collect suggestions about some of the evil and unjust things that happen.)

Read the section of Isaiah's prophecy which is today's reading, and then find on a map the places mentioned. Now for a question: Who do they know about who did walk about Galilee bringing light into people's lives? Jesus did! Read the passage from Matthew and see if they can spot the bit from Isaiah.

Praying

Thank you, Lord, for using Isaiah
to help us recognise Jesus
as your Son.
Thank you for making it possible
for us all to be free. Amen.

Activities

On the worksheet there is a message which only looks right if you look at it from the right angle, to help them explore the idea of looking at things in different ways to get to the deeper meaning. There are also instructions for making a spinner which only makes the complete colour when it is spun round so that all the separate colours merge together.

GOLD PANNERS

Aim: To look at the situation Isaiah was in, and see how prophecy has more than one level.

Starter

Have some small pieces of scraper-board for them to scratch pictures in. These can either be bought, or home-made using coloured wax crayons rubbed thickly on to paper and covered with a layer of black wax crayon or waterproof ink.

Teaching

Using an enlarged version of the map below, or an atlas of the Bible, show how Judah was placed, so that they can see why the Assyrians (and later the Babylonians) wanted to conquer it. It would be useful, for trade and communications, to have control of it. Have a brainstorm and record ideas of how the people may have felt with Assyrian power so close.

Find Jerusalem and explain how Isaiah had been sent to speak out God's words to the people there. He is disturbed by all the social injustice, and lack of honesty and integrity in the way people are living, and can see that a people which is rejecting God's values of love, justice and mercy is likely to be overtaken by Assyria. Isaiah urges the people to turn back to God and trust him to save them.

Now read today's passage from Isaiah. Remembering how the people were feeling, what would they have made of this? Help them to pick up on the sense of hope and reassurance.

Read the passage from Matthew, listening out for similarities (place names, language). What is Matthew trying to tell us by the way he quotes the Isaiah reading? (Jesus must be the light and the yoke-breaker we've been waiting for.)

So Isaiah's prophecy meant more than one layer of truth. There is both the immediate hope in a nasty situation and a more universal meaning which can help people of all races, social grouping, financial state and in each age. That is often true of prophecy; it can, like our scratch-pictures, have several different layers, some of which only become clear later on.

Praying

Use this version of the Nunc Dimittis – or Simeon's song (Luke 2:29-32):

Lord, now let your servant go in peace:
your word has been fulfilled.
My own eyes have seen the salvation:
which you have prepared in the sight of every people.
A light to reveal you to the nations:
and the glory of your people Israel.

Activities

Using thin card, and the instructions on the worksheet, make a 3D model of the word 'prophecy'. There is also space for thinking about different social injustices in our own world to which Isaiah may well have drawn our attention in the eighth century before Christ.

FOURTH SUNDAY OF THE YEAR

Thought for the day

Happy are the poor in spirit, who are aware of their need of God.

Reflection on the readings

Zephaniah 2:3; 3:12-13
Psalm 145
1 Corinthians 1:26-31
Matthew 5:1-12

The messages with which we are all daily bombarded from the media advise us to seek personal comfort and success, as a priority. Today's readings cut right across this and turn worldly thinking on its head. Zephaniah the prophet speaks out God's urgent concern for his people's direction, knowing that their ultimate hope of fulfilment lies in seeking God and his ways of integrity and humility. Though many will choose to opt out of this, eventually suffering God's anger as a result, the faithful remnant will be able to live in tranquillity and safety.

Paul, in his letter to the Christians in Corinth, points out the way God so often seems to choose the weak, foolish and marginalised to work through, rather than the strong, wealthy and powerful. It is then all the clearer that the graciousness of goodness and courage, integrity and wisdom are indeed God-given; our very weaknesses help direct people towards God, the source of all goodness. It also makes clear to us that, since God is the source of all holiness, we can enjoy noticing evidence of it in our own lives without getting boastful, since we recognise that the glory and praise belong not to us but to the God who has been developing that holiness in us.

When Jesus taught the crowds in the words we know as the Beatitudes, he was trying to overturn their materialistic values and free up their rusted expectations. Overwhelmingly, the recognition of our dependence on God and our desperate need for his grace and love in our lives is what counts to make us blessed, rather than natural gifts, skills, wealth or power. God longs to work with us, but can only do so if we acknowledge his authority and lordship. We are back to Zephaniah's message and the necessity to seek first the kingdom of God and his righteousness, focusing on that as a priority from which everything else takes its right position and direction.

Discussion starters

1. Is it possible to kid ourselves that we are seeking God when in fact we are self-seeking?

2. In what ways do the poor in spirit become rich?

All-stage talk

You will need a jug of water, a tumbler and a bowl. Have these hidden (not too well!) in different places around the church.

Begin by reminding everyone of the words of the prophet Zephaniah, telling us to seek or search for the Lord in our lives. If we are going to search for something, it helps to know what we are looking for, and the prophet suggests seeking God's ways, like truth and humility. Hidden around the church are three things to be found. We'll ask three people to seek them, and, to make it easier, we'll tell them what they are looking for. (Tell one to look for each item. While they are looking, ask everyone to notice how they search.)

When the volunteers return with the objects, collect observations about how they searched, with their eyes looking around, with concentration and attention on the task, listening out for helpful clues from the congregation. That's how we are to seek for God, giving the job our full attention and concentration, and listening out for helpful clues from one another and from the Bible and other books. That way we will be sure to find him and get to know more about what God is really like.

As we get to know God better we shall start to realise that we need that godly love very badly. It's as if we are empty tumblers coming to be filled up with God's life and love. (Ask one of the volunteers to hold the empty tumbler as you pour water into it.) We can pass that love on to the world (pour the tumbler of water into the large bowl) and the more of us there are doing that, the more full of God's love the world will be.

But sometimes we don't realise we need filling with God's love; that's like putting our hand over the top of the tumbler when God offers to fill us and saying, 'No, thanks, I'm full already.' We block ourselves off from receiving God's gifts to us if we think we don't need them. That's why Jesus said in today's Gospel, 'How happy are the poor in spirit' – those who know their need of God. As soon as we know our need of God, we shall come to him in our emptiness, without our hands in the way (the volunteer removes his hand), and God can fill us up with goodness and love, truth and wisdom, courage and strength (fill the tumbler up again as you speak), not just for our good, but the good of the whole world.

All-age ideas

• Use the following alternative to the Penitential Rite:
We have failed to seek you with our whole heart;
Lord, have mercy
Lord, have mercy.
We have failed to recognise how much we need you;
Christ, have mercy
Christ, have mercy.
We come to you now in our emptiness and need;
Lord, have mercy
Lord, have mercy.

• Have some very small, simple arrangements of wild flowers with the Beatitudes printed beside them.

Prayer of the Faithful

Celebrant
Let us settle ourselves to stillness as we pray.

Reader
Lord, we ask not for ease and comfort
but the disturbing power of your truth
and the challenge of your committed love,
so that as a Church we may be prepared
to move at your bidding and act on your will.

Silence

In our need:
we cry to you, O God.

Lord, we ask not for the riches to fall in our favour
but for right sharing
and just distribution of resources.
We ask not to be cocooned against reality
but strengthened to work for peace and justice
and trained to discern what is right and good.

Silence

In our need:
we cry to you, O God.

Lord, we ask not so much to receive
as for the grace to give with generosity
and to recover the joy of living simply,
contentedly and open to your guiding.

Silence

In our need:
we cry to you, O God.

Lord, we stand alongside all
with great needs, hurts and troubles;
we ask you to lay your hands
on those we mention now by name
in the silence of our hearts.

Silence

In our need:
we cry to you, O God.

Lord, we commend to your mercy
and loving kindness
those who have reached the end of their earthly life
and step into the realm of your eternity.
May they be surrounded with your joy for ever.

Silence

In our need:
we cry to you, O God.

We pray with Mary,
so full of God's grace:
Hail, Mary . . .

As God's stillness fills our hearts,
we pray for our own cares and concerns.

Silence

Celebrant
Father, we lay before you these prayers,
and ask you to accept them
for the sake of Jesus, your Son.
Amen.

TREASURE SEEKERS

Aim: To know that we are dependent on God for everything.

Starter

Have hidden around the room some different fruits, and a fruit bowl. Play some music, during which the children dance and jump about. When the music stops you call out, 'Fruit bowl!' and they find it and bring it to you. Then whenever the music stops a different fruit is called and has to be found and brought, until everything is found and the fruit bowl is full.

Teaching

Thank them all for their help in gathering the fruit, and enjoy looking together at the shape and colour of them. Everyone can say what their favourite fruit is. (Pass an orange round the circle so that only the person holding the orange is allowed to speak.)

All these good things to eat come from things God has made – including the fire to cook them. God has made us a lovely place to live on (it's planet earth) and he has made it so that there is good food to eat and people to play with and look after us. God gives us life, and all we need in life.

Praying

Thank you for the big round earth,
    (trace big circle in air with both hands)
thank you for the sky,
    (look up)
thank you for our food and drink,
    (pretend to eat and drink)
and trees that grow so high.
    (squat down, arm out to show tiny plant, and gradually stand up on to tiptoes, reaching arm up)
Your love is all around me,
    (turn around with arms out)
in front and behind.
    (point in front and behind)
I trust in you, my Father,
    (grip one hand with the other)
you are wonderfully kind!
    (arms up)

Activities

Have lots of pictures of God's provision (such as landscapes, fruit, flowers, animals and people) from magazines, calendars and greetings cards, and some sheets of coloured paper, so the children can choose pictures to stick on and make a group scrapbook to say 'Thank you' to God. There is space on the sheet for them to stick a picture or two, and a big 'Thank you' to colour in.

PEARL DIVERS

Aim: To know that we are to seek God first and all the rest of life will then fall into place.

Starter

Do a jigsaw puzzle together.

Teaching

Point out that we could only make sense of the picture on the jigsaw when we had our pieces in the right order. Before that it was just a muddle of bits and pieces. Today we are going to look at how that is also true in the picture of life.

Have a large sheet of paper on which you have already drawn and coloured in large letters the word 'God'. Don't show the children this side of the paper. Write the word 'Life' in bubble letters on the clean side of the large sheet of paper, and then cut it up into several pieces. Lay the pieces down randomly on the floor, face down, so that the coloured sections of the word 'God' are showing. Who gives us life? God does. What does he want for us? He wants for us to seek him and find him so that our whole life will make sense. If we seek God, all the rest will fall into place.

Have a couple of people to help put the puzzle together so that the word 'God' is clear, and stick sellotape along the cut edges to fix them. When you turn it over, 'Life' has also taken shape and hangs together.

Have the following words from Zephaniah written up so everyone can say them together: 'Seek the Lord all you, the humble of the earth, who obey his commands.'

Praying

You are our God, and we love you.
It was you who gave us life
and all the good things on earth.
It is you who guides us and keeps us;
it is you we need and you we trust.

Activities

On the sheet the children are introduced to the Beatitudes and will need access to a Bible to check the references and puzzles.

GOLD PANNERS

Aim: To look at the Beatitudes and their meaning.

Starter

Have an Ordnance Survey map (any area) and give out map references which they have to find to discover the route from one place to another.

Teaching

Read the passage from Zephaniah, noticing that it is the humble, seeking God, who will be saved in the end, rather than the self-seeking and powerful. The passage from Corinthians reinforces this, recognising that the followers of Christ are often the weak and unremarkable, except that in Christ they end up doing remarkable things.

Now look at Jesus' teaching in today's Gospel, using a version which is accessible to them. *The Message* (Eugene Peterson) helps explain the meaning; *Into the Light* and *The Youth Bible* have clear language. Draw out the importance of recognising our need of God, of hungering and thirsting for him, and wanting to put God first in our lives. It all turns selfishness and self-seeking on its head, and sets us on a giving rather than a getting way of life.

Praying

Lord our God,
help us to love you with all our hearts,
to seek after you and find you,
to long for what you long for
and rejoice at what gives you joy.

Activities

On the sheet the Beatitudes are looked at in terms of their implications for us and our life choices. They can also get the sense of re-aligning our lives to God by placing a magnet under the paper where it says 'God's way' and placing a paper clip fixed to 'My life' on top of the paper so that it settles firmly on the magnet.

FIFTH SUNDAY OF THE YEAR

Thought for the day

We are commissioned to live so that we shine like lights which direct others on to God, the source of Light.

Reflection on the readings

Isaiah 58:7-10
Psalm 111:4-9
1 Corinthians 2:1-5
Matthew 5:13-16

Salt and light can both make a great difference. Apart from its wonderful preserving and disinfecting qualities, a pinch of salt brings out the full flavour of other ingredients; light allows everyone in the room to see the shape and texture of all kinds of different objects which were hidden by darkness. And we as Christians are called to be salt and light to the world. We are called to live so that our way of living brings out in other people their full flavour, or potential; we are called to live in a way that helps people see where they are going, in the room, or context, of eternity.

We have all met people whose attitude and behaviour towards us makes us shrivel up inside, and others in whose company we feel accepted and acceptable, and therefore free to be our true selves. It is loving reverence for one another that makes the difference, and the Gospels are full of incidents where people noticed this in their encounters with Jesus.

If we behave as the salt of the earth, we will be content to make ourselves available so that others feel free to become more truly themselves, and we shall recognise the need to be there, but not to overwhelm! Too heavy a dose of salt kills off the flavour. If we behave as the light of the world we shall once again be in the role of enablers: we are at the service of the world, quietly enabling it to see more clearly. And again, we recognise the need to provide illumination, but not to blind or dazzle. Dazzling performances of ostentatious 'religion', such as those we heard about in the Isaiah reading, are not at all what God has in mind for his people, either then or now. What God wants is for the people in our world to be so impressed with the light we shine around that they want to find out where we get it from. Our shining is to set others off on their way to discover God for themselves.

Of course, we can only behave as salt and light if we are the genuine article, and are prepared to work co-operatively with God. That is where it is so helpful to have our faith 'earthed' in practical living. As Christians we all need to have our feet on the ground; we need to be engaged in the messy, hard work of caring, challenging injustice and offering practical help and support. Only then will our praises mean something, and our worship glorify God.

Discussion starters

1. What do the qualities and usefulness of salt tell us about our calling as Christians?

2. How can we be effective light in the world?

All-stage talk

You will need a large saucepan, a pack of spaghetti, a jar of Italian sauce and a large carton of salt, a jug, a teacup and a tablespoon. You will also need a table lamp and a bright spotlight.

Produce the first set of items, setting them out and talking about cooking pasta. Invite a good cook from the congregation to supervise! Explain that the best cookery books say that pasta can't be seasoned after it's cooked, so we need to add the salt to the cooking water. Pick up the salt, and wonder aloud how much salt to use. A jugful? Get the cook to explain what would happen if you put in that much salt. A teacupful? Still too much! A tablespoonful? Still too much. If we use that much all we will taste will be the salt, and the whole idea of salt is that it isn't really noticed but brings out the flavour of the other ingredients.

That's what we are called to do as Christians: not to take over and dominate or possess people, or want to control them, but in humility to make ourselves available and useful in helping to give other people the freedom and the confidence to be themselves. That may mean more listening and less speaking; it may mean being less concerned about being thought important and more concerned about other people's needs being recognised. It is the way of quiet, loving service.

Now flash the spotlight around so that it goes in people's eyes (but don't overdo this!). Explain that Jesus also calls us to be light. That doesn't mean trying to blind people with our natural brilliance, or trying subtly to impress others, so that we're more like disco lights, designed for a flashy effect. The kind of light we are called to be is a much more practical sort, rather like a table lamp, perhaps, which simply helps people to see better, so they don't bump into things and hurt themselves, and so they can get on with living more effectively.

Salt and light are just simple things, but they are things which can make a great difference. As Christians we are called to be like that – just our ordinary selves, but through our faith in God, able to make a difference.

All-age ideas

• Have a salt mill and a table lamp included in one of the flower arrangements today.

• Read the Isaiah passage chorally, with a group of men, women and children.

• Include actions with this penitential meditation:
  We have used our words selfishly. (*touch lips*)
  We are sorry. Lord, have mercy.
  We have used our hands selfishly.
    (*look at open hands*)
  We are sorry. Christ, have mercy.
  We have used our minds to think selfishly.
    (*touch heads*)
  We are sorry. Lord, have mercy.

Prayer of the Faithful

Celebrant
Let us pray to the God who has drawn us here today, who loves us, and loves our world.

Reader
We pray that there may be a revival of longing
for your kingdom to come,
and a renewed commitment to working for it;
for a desire to live out our faith and worship
in our daily lives this week.

Silence

Come, Holy Spirit:
set our hearts on fire.

We pray that all who have authority and power
in our nation and our world
may use it for good,
upholding and instigating what is right and fair,
and listening to the needs of those they represent.
May we recognise our responsibility
to support and stand up for God's values.

Silence

Come, Holy Spirit:
set our hearts on fire.

We pray that within our homes and communities
there may be a new awareness
of one another's gifts and needs,
more sensitivity and respect in our relationships;
may we reverence one another as fellow beings,
born of your creative love.

Silence

Come, Holy Spirit:
set our hearts on fire.

We pray for all who are oppressed,
downtrodden or despised;
we pray for those who will not eat today
and all who live in the degrading circumstances
of poverty and powerlessness;
we pray for a heart to put injustices right
and strive for a fair sharing of resources.

Silence

Come, Holy Spirit:
set our hearts on fire.

We pray for those whose life expectancy is short,
for the babies and children who have died
while we have been praying;
for all who have come to the end of their earthly life
and made that last journey through death;
thank you for your welcoming mercy
and the promise of eternal life.

Silence

Come, Holy Spirit:
set our hearts on fire.

Joining with Mary,
who brought the Light into the world,
we make our prayer:
Hail, Mary . . .

In silence now,
we make our personal petitions to God,
who is always ready to hear us.

Silence

Celebrant
Father, God of love,
increase our love for one another,
and hear us as we pray,
for the sake of Jesus Christ.
Amen.

TREASURE SEEKERS

Aim: To know what salt does and think about being like it.

Starter

A little makes a difference. Have a very quiet bell and give this to one of the children. Explain that whenever Suzie rings the bell, everyone freezes. Then get everyone moving and dancing around. Let each of the children have a turn at ringing the bell. It's only a little sound but look at what a difference it makes when it is used!

Teaching

Sit everyone in a circle and have a plate of plain crisps and a salt cellar in the middle of the circle. Explain that sometimes even little things can make a big difference – like our little bell in the game. Salt is like that. Spill a few grains (no more!) into everyone's hand to look at. The bits of salt aren't very big and we can't smell them, but we can certainly taste them. (If they want to, they can taste the salt in their hand.) What does the taste remind them of? We only need a little salt to flavour and bring out the taste of our food. For instance, a little salt on plain crisps helps us taste the nice potato flavour. They can all eat a crisp to notice this. Enjoy the eating of these together.

What would happen if we covered our food with salt? It would be bad for us, and we wouldn't taste anything except salt! So the job of salt is to bring out the good taste of other things.

Guess what Jesus said once – he said God wants us as his friends to be like salt! This is what he meant. Even if there aren't many of us, and even if we aren't very big, we can still make a big difference to the world, and help it to be a kinder, fairer and more loving place. The little bits of salt on the crisps help us to taste the real potato, and God wants us to be so loving and friendly to people that they feel happy and free. Instead of going around making people frightened, or making life hard work for them, God wants us to help people, and let them know we care about them.

Praying

Dear Jesus,
I would like to be like salt
and help people
to enjoy being themselves. Amen.

Activities

On the activity sheet there are some little things to search for, and some pictures of Jesus' friends being salt. There is also a label to colour which they can stick on to their salt mill at home.

PEARL DIVERS

Aim: To look at how we can be salt and light in the world.

Starter

Together scatter tables and chairs around the room and then make the area as dark as possible. Every-one walks around, trying not to bump into any objects or people. Now switch on a light, or have a few torches available, so everyone can see where they are going.

Teaching

Talk about how useful light is, as it helps us see so that we don't bump into things. It helps us to see where we are going. Now read them the section from today's Gospel about light and salt, with parts of each displayed on sheets labelled 'Salt' and 'Light' as the words are read. Explain how light and salt are both things which allow good things to happen. Salt allows the full flavour of something to come out, and light allows people to see clearly so that they don't bump into things and hurt themselves.

So how can we be salt and light?

On the 'Salt' and 'Light' sheets, write down their suggestions. How can we behave so that people feel confident and happy in our company? How can we help to bring God's light into a frightening or wrong situation?

Praying

Help us, Lord,
to be salt in the world,
bringing out the best in people
by our love and respect for them.
And help us to be light in the world,
shining with your truth and goodness. Amen.

Activities

On the activity sheet there are suggestions for ways of being salt and light in different situations, and a puzzle which looks at the things God wants us to get involved with, which are spelt out in the Isaiah reading. There are instructions for making a doily so the 'salt' message is made clear. Have some crisps to put out on plates lined with the doilies. The children can hand these round after the service.

GOLD PANNERS

Aim: To look at the way Christians are called to be salt and light, and the practical implications of this.

Starter

Bring along some mirrors and torches and in small groups experiment to get the light shining all over the place by using the mirrors. Help them to see that this is only possible when the mirrors are turned to reflect the light.

Teaching

When you have lots of reflectors they will pass on the light outwards, and anyone wanting to find out more about where the real light is has only to line themselves up with a mirror and look in that direction. It's the same with us as Christians – if we are shining with Christ's light, then other people will notice, and if they want to find where we are getting our light from, they only have to face the direction our lives are facing.

Read together the Gospel passage for today, listening out for this teaching.

What else did Jesus say we were to be like? Salt. In this instance, Jesus talks about the seasoning quality of salt; just a tiny amount is enough to make all the difference to a dish by bringing out the best flavour in the other ingredients. And that means that we as Christians are to be the kind of people who bring the best out in others, enabling them to feel valued and respected. Salt and light are very practical things. The problem is that the people are not being salt and light in their world. They may be good at talking about godly living but they aren't actually living it out. God wants to see some action, both in their lives and ours.

On a sheet have the headings taken from Isaiah (free the oppressed, share food with the hungry, etc.) and collect suggestions for ways we are and ways we could be doing these things in our world, as individuals, as a church community and in society.

Praying

Lord God,
let us not just hear and talk about
being salt and light;
help us to *be* salt and light
so that we make a difference. Amen.

Activities

On the activity sheet there is space to record some ideas for action, following today's teaching, and there is the outline for a role-play to bring out the way we all prefer to talk about things rather than actually getting our hands dirty.

SIXTH SUNDAY OF THE YEAR

Thought for the day

To live God's way is to choose the way of life.

Reflection on the readings

Ecclesiasticus 15:15-20
Psalm 118:1-2, 4-5, 17-18, 33-34
1 Corinthians 2:6-10
Matthew 5:17-37

Jesus always insisted that he had not come to abolish the Law but to fulfil it. One of the challenging ways he does this is to take the ten commandments and work through them, pointing out not just the letter but the spirit of the law. Today we have an excerpt from this teaching in the Gospel reading, and by the time Jesus has finished preaching it is clear that the way of love is a demanding commitment, involving one's whole attitude and outlook as well as one's actual behaviour. The ten commandments are a kind of shorthand for this; they are the broad brush-strokes or guidelines, but not the whole picture. The danger is that people can feel they have completely fulfilled the law when they have

simply taken care about the 'brush-stroke' examples; they can feel virtuous about not committing murder, for example, while their attitude to others continues to be destructive and patronising. With the law of love, expounded by Jesus, these attitudes are also considered 'murderous'.

Life is full of choices. Many times each day we have to decide whether to choose the way of life or the way of death, and unless we have taken time to decide what main direction we want to walk in, we can become hopelessly confused. That is why it is good to use today and the reading from the Old Testament as a challenge: what direction do we really want to face?

If we make such a decision calmly and in our right mind, rather than waiting until we are in the grip of some temptation, then we are far more likely to have the courage to stand up for what we know in our hearts to be right.

As the community of Christ, we all need to be facing the 'Godwards' direction of life, using godly love as the compass. Then all the greater and lesser decisions to be made in our individual lives, and in our society and in the Church itself, can be worked out in line with these principles. Recognised mistakes are far healthier and easier to put right than unrecognised hypocrisy.

Discussion starters

1. How do rules help, and in what sense are guidelines sometimes more useful?

2. Why is it that when we have chosen to face life we still want to behave as if we are facing the other way?

All-stage talk

Begin by drawing attention to the direction everyone is facing in church. Obviously this will vary according to your architecture and the age of the building. The architecture reflects a focus and a general direction which the planners thought of most importance. Perhaps if you were all about to start planning from scratch, you might arrange things slightly differently!

Once you have established the general seating focus, move to another part of the church, such as the baptistry. If people are going to continue facing you, they will all have to turn round. That is because at the moment the important thing going on is you speaking, and that takes over in importance from the general focus of the building.

Now move somewhere else so that everyone has to turn round again. Today we heard Jesus teaching about the Law, which is summed up in the ten commandments. Have these displayed on card, or on an OHP, or walk to the part of the church where they are written on the wall. They are good rules to live by and our whole law system is still based on them. But with all rules there is a problem. Jesus wanted his followers (and that includes us) to remember that the really important thing is to stay focused on God in everything we do.

Perhaps you haven't ever killed someone. But the spirit of the law means more than that, just as our focus is more than just sitting facing the front. It also means making sure we haven't got unkind or destructive thoughts about people, that we're not making people feel stupid or useless, that we aren't putting other people down or running them down behind their backs, because those things are in the destructive spirit of hate, which is the opposite of God's law of love. As you mention each of these, move around the building so people have to move their 'attitudes' to see you.

What we need to do is keep our eyes fixed on Jesus, and whatever we are doing we can think to ourselves, 'Does this thing I'm doing or saying or thinking make Jesus happy? Is it a loving thing to do or think or say?'

And if it is, carry on. If it isn't, stop and change direction.

All-age ideas

• Have two people standing in different places in the church, calling out the following contrasting attitudes alternately:

I want!

What do you need?

Me first!

Let's share!

Why should I?

I'll help!

I believe in freedom so I can do whatever I like!

If we think of one another we can all be free!

You've got to look after number one. Never mind anyone else.

Love God – and love your neighbour as yourself.

This is the way of death.

This is the way of life.

• Fix to the floor four footprints with the letters L, I, F and E on them, so that people can read them as they come in.

Prayer of the Faithful

Celebrant
Gathered together in one spirit,
let us pray to our God.

Reader
Father, wherever our attention
has wandered from your calling,
wherever we have fallen short of your will for us,
and failed to keep the spirit of your law of love,
forgive us and transform us,
so that we walk again
the path that leads to life.

Silence

Show us the way of life:
and help us to walk in it.

Wherever the Church is asked
to give leadership on sensitive issues;
whenever the current
world expectations of behaviour
need to be challenged in the light of God's love,
give us the wisdom and guidance we need.

Silence

Show us the way of life:
and help us to walk in it.

Wherever our homes are lacking
in love and mutual respect,
wherever destructive relationships
cause distress and heartache,
and wherever people are made to feel
they don't matter,
give a new realisation of your ways
and your hopes for us
so that your kingdom may come
and your will be done.

Silence

Show us the way of life:
and help us to walk in it.

Wherever there is illness, unhappiness,
injustice or fear;
wherever people feel frustrated,
imprisoned or trapped;
give us a greater sense of loving community,
a heart to put right whatever we can,
and the willingness to stand
alongside one another in our sorrows.

Silence

Show us the way of life:
and help us to walk in it.

Wherever earthly lives have come to an end,
and people are grieving the loss of their loved ones,
fill these places with the eternal peace
of your presence
and prepare us all through our lives on this earth
for everlasting life with you in heaven.

Silence

Show us the way of life:
and help us to walk in it.

We make our prayer with Mary,
who loved God with all her mind and heart:
Hail, Mary . . .

In this silence,
we approach our loving Father
with our private petitions.

Silence

Celebrant
Father, we ask you to hear our prayers,
for the love of Jesus, your Son.
Amen.

TREASURE SEEKERS

Aim: To know that God's way is the way of love.

Starter

Using some cut-out paper arrow signs, two of the children go with a leader to lay a trail. The others then go off in pairs to follow the trail, so that eventually everyone should end up at the same place. Make sure the children are supervised very carefully, and that the trail is within sight of a leader all the time. (Or use the Gold Panners group to work with the Treasure Seekers on this.)

Teaching

We followed the way Zac and Phoebe led us because we followed the arrows they left. Today we are going to find out what God's way is, so that we can follow that in our lives.
    Ask them to follow these instructions:

- Walk quickly
- Creep quietly
- Clap loudly
- Sit silently
- Smile happily
- Frown crossly

    Praise everyone for following the instructions so well. Jesus tells us that to follow him we are to live lovingly. All get up and hold hands in a circle as you talk about ways to live lovingly when we are at home/at playgroup/visiting grandparents and so on. Talk about how to live lovingly with different people (such as people who are sad/have got a headache/want to play with your toys.) Then walk

round, still holding hands, singing these words to the tune of *Frère Jacques*.

Follow Jesus, follow Jesus
walk his way, walk his way,
loving one another, loving one another
every day, every day.

Praying

Lead on, Jesus, I will follow!
I want to live your way,
loving you and loving other people. Amen.

Activities

On the activity sheet there are other trails to follow, and a signpost to make which helps them remember that Jesus' way is the way of love. They will each need a short stick (about 6 centimetres long) and some glue.

PEARL DIVERS

Aim: To see that the ten commandments (God's way) are choosing life rather than death.

Starter

Scissors, stone, paper. In pairs everyone counts, 'One, two, three, GO!' and then chooses to show paper, stone or scissors to their partner. Paper is an open hand, stone a clenched fist and scissors two fingers opening and closing.

- Paper wins over stone (because it wraps it up).
- Stone wins over scissors (because it can smash them).
- Scissors wins over paper (because it can cut it).

Teaching

In that game we kept making choices, but we had no way of knowing whether they were going to be good choices or not. In the Old Testament God gave his people some rules to help them make good choices about the way to live.
    Lay out ten objects to stand for the commandments, so they are easier to remember. Here are some suggestions, but choose whatever you think would work best for the children.

1. A figure 1, cut out of card. (Worship only the one true God and no other.)

2. An empty picture frame. (Don't make and worship pictures or models of God.)

3. A name tag. (Don't use God's name disrespect-fully.)

4. A 'closed' shop sign. (Honour the Sabbath and keep it holy, resting from work on it.)

5. A photograph of a family. (Honour your father and your mother.)

6. A toy gun or sword. (Do not kill.)

7. A purse. (Do not steal.)

8. Wedding rings. (Don't steal other people's partners; be faithful in your relationships.)

9. Tape – video or sound. (Don't accuse people falsely or tell lies about them.)

10. Leaflets which advertise coveted items. (Don't keep wanting to have what other people have got.)

Go through the commandments in order, showing the objects and discussing the meaning as you go along. Then repeat them round the group, so everyone can use the visual clues to help them remember.

Praying

Whenever we turn away from you,
turn us back to face you,
so that we can live a lifetime
of love and truth. Amen.

Activities

Using the pattern on the activity sheet the children can make a 'chooser' with the suggested Bible references on it. There is also a scrambled roads puzzle to sort out so that they have to choose the best and safest route.

GOLD PANNERS

Aim: To see how Jesus fulfils the Law.

Starter

Getting the whole picture. Cut up a large poster or picture into nine squares, and number the backs of the pieces. Arrange them upside down, but in the right order. Work out a quiz based on the ideas below but adapted to suit your group. Each time a question is answered correctly a piece of the picture is turned over, until eventually the whole picture is revealed.

Ideas for quiz questions:

Who won the last cup final?

Who scored?

Who were they playing?

What was the score?

Who was in goal?

What colours did . . . . . . play in?

Who is . . . . . .'s manager?

What was the score at half-time?

Where was the match played?

or:

What's their latest release?

What are their names?

How old are they?

Name two of their hits.

What are the lyrics of . . . . . . ?

Who sings?

Who plays . . . . . . ?

What does . . . . . . like to eat?

Where do they come from?

Teaching

Gradually, as we had more information, we got the whole picture. It was rather like that for the Jewish people, because they had gradually understood more and more about who God was and what he was like. When Jesus came and lived among them, he built on all that knowledge and experience, and showed them the whole picture by his life, death and resurrection.

Read the Matthew passage to see where the people were coming from, and compare Jesus' teaching with the commandments concerned. How was it the same and how did it take the law and fill it with more complete meaning? There is space on the activity sheet to record ideas, or you may prefer to use a flipchart or large sheet of paper and copy the activity sheet format on to this.

Praying

Saviour, breathe forgiveness o'er us,
all our weakness thou dost know.
Thou didst tread this earth before us,
thou didst feel its keenest woe.
Lone and dreary, faint and weary,
through the desert thou didst go.

Spirit of our God, descending,
fill our hearts with heavenly joy.
Love with every passion blending,
pleasure that can never cloy.
Thus provided, pardoned, guided,
nothing can our peace destroy.

Activities

On the sheet there are some examples of Celtic knotwork to copy using string, craft glue and coloured paper or card. There is also space to explore the ideas arising from Jesus' teaching, suggesting that a 'murderous' or destructive attitude can be just as deadly as actual murder.

SEVENTH SUNDAY OF THE YEAR

Thought for the day

We are called to be holy; to be perfect in our generous loving, because that is what God our Father is like.

Reflection on the readings

Leviticus 19:1-2, 17-18
Psalm 102:1-4, 8, 10, 12-13
1 Corinthians 3:16-23
Matthew 5:38-48

When those who were adopted as young children meet up with their birth parents, it is often startling and amusing to find that they share some mannerism which must have been inherited but had seemed more like a personal habit. When Jesus talks about our calling to be perfect in such things as generous loving, he gives as his reason the fact that God our Father is perfect. We, as God's children, need to share his characteristics – his 'mannerisms' – an example of which is a tendency to generosity of spirit which is lavish to the point of extravagance.

We are to be like 'chips off the old block', so that the way we live and behave demonstrates to everyone our spiritual parentage. This is not so much learned behaviour, in the way that one might act out a part in a drama production, but more like the natural result of being God's children. When we wake up each morning allowing that to happen, and giving the living God access to our minds, emotions and bodies, then God's natural characteristic of generous loving will start to show through without our having to contort ourselves to achieve it.

Jesus is trying to get us to examine not only our actions but also our motives and our attitudes. We are to think at all times not 'What can I gain out of this?' but 'What can I give away and how can I serve here?' The worldly perception of perfection is measured by a completely different set of success criteria. The ever-present danger is that even Christians soak up the worldly values of success and start applying them to spiritual matters. That leads into the legalistic and judgemental zones which Jesus so deplored. God's way is as happy to use our failures as our strengths, our muddles and mistakes as much as our slick, poised control.

God's way has us viewing cancelled trains and traffic jams, undeserved criticism and demanding phone calls as unscheduled opportunities for learning and possibly serving. It is our God-filled attitude to them that unclenches the tight jaw and relaxes the facial muscles! It may also be what enables us to express our concerns calmly and sort out a workable alternative without being churned up inside with resentment and hidden rage. God's way of generous loving is not only the best way to live; it is also the way God designed us to be, and the way in which we are most fulfilled and most effective.

Discussion starters

1. Is Jesus' teaching unworkable? Or is it simply more challenging than we would like to take on seriously?

2. How does our society's concern with self-value and self-assertion fit in with our Christian faith, and where does it clash?

All-stage talk

Bring along a rubber stamp and ink pad, making sure it isn't permanent ink. Begin by putting the stamp on a number of volunteers. Talk about the way we sometimes get stamped at theme parks or discos to show that we have a right to be there because we have paid our entrance fee.

When we are baptised we have the sign of Jesus Christ marked on our foreheads. (What is that sign? It's the cross.) It's as if we've got God's stamp on us. (You could get everyone to trace a cross on their foreheads with their thumb to feel it freshly.) We are marked out as his children, whether we are one-day-old children, twenty-three-year-old children or ninety-seven-year-old children, and we have been freely given the right to belong in God's kingdom, which is a kingdom full of love and peace and joy, patience and kindness, goodness, gentleness and self-control.

As well as us belonging in God's kingdom, God's kingdom now belongs in us! As we've got God's stamp on us we will be wanting to behave like him, and he will help us to do that. Our behaviour will then be a visible sign to other people that we really do belong to God as his children. When they see us being honest and kind and patient and joyful, loving and working for peace and justice, they will be able to say, 'That must be a child of God – look how generous he is, even when he isn't going to gain anything by it!' And, 'That must be a child of God – look how loving she is with those difficult people!'

The whole point is this: we don't work to behave nicely so that God will love us. We don't need to do that, and we can't ever earn his love anyway. God simply loves us! He thinks we're really special, and he always wants the best for us.

When we love him back, and let him work in us, we will find we are beginning to behave more like our God. The closer we get to God, the more generous loving we will find ourselves doing. Instead of looking out for what we can get all the time, we'll find we're looking out eagerly for ways we can give instead! Instead of making sure we are doing whatever *we* want, we'll find we are looking to check if other people are OK. And that is actually a much happier and more fulfilling way to live.

All-age ideas

- Print out in large letters: 'Love your friends, hate your enemies!' with a line crossing through the second part and the alteration written in: 'Love your enemies too!'

- Express God's extravagant generosity by having some lavish flower arrangements with garlands and cascades.

Prayer of the Faithful

Celebrant
God has chosen to call us here
and we have chosen to come.
Let us pray to him now.

Reader
Lord, we want to pray for stronger faith
and the courage to live up to our calling;
for the grace to act always
with the generosity of spirit you show to us,
until the whole Church models the wisdom
which the world counts as foolishness.

Silence

Holy God:
we commit ourselves to your service.

Lord, we want to pray
about all the unresolved conflicts in our world.
We ask you to give us your desire for peace,
your spirit of discernment,
your understanding of unspoken needs,
and your capacity for forgiveness.

Silence

Holy God:
we commit ourselves to your service.

Lord, we want to pray
for the homes and families we represent,
and for all with whom we live and work.

Help us to recognise the opportunities
for generous, loving service
and take away any destructive possessiveness
or self-interest.

Silence

Holy God:
we commit ourselves to your service.

Lord, we pray for peace of mind and spirit
in all those who are distressed or enveloped in pain.
May they know the reality of your inner healing,
and may even the worst situations
become places of growth and new life.

Silence

Holy God:
we commit ourselves to your service.

Lord, we pray for those approaching death
with fear, resentment and anger,
and for all who counsel the dying and the bereaved.
We pray that those who have died will know
the joy of everlasting life with you.

Silence

Holy God:
we commit ourselves to your service.

With Mary, who was full of grace,
we make our prayer:
Hail, Mary . . .

As God's stillness fills our hearts,
we pray for any needs known to us personally.

Silence

Celebrant
We rededicate ourselves
to your love, Father,
and ask you to hear our prayers,
through Jesus Christ.
Amen.

TREASURE SEEKERS

Aim: To know that God wants us to love one another as he loves us.

Starter

Bring along lots of cartons and boxes and place them all over the room. Tell the children we are going to build a high tower, and let them help by collecting boxes and bringing them over to add to the tower.

Teaching

Show the children the comedy trick of having your own hands behind your back while your partner's arms pretend to be yours. Try talking and gesticulating, and try to eat or drink something! Enjoy the silliness of it, and then get everyone to look at the way we train our own arms to look after all our needs. Suppose your nose itches – what happens? One of your arms stretches out to exactly the right itchy place and scratches it better for you. Suppose you want to eat a biscuit? One of your arms gets hold of the biscuit and holds it for you, bringing it up to your mouth every time you want to take a bite.

It isn't just our arms we use. If we want to get across the room to see out of the window, we get our legs to take us over there. We don't have to wait for them while they finish what they are doing, or just sit and watch a bit more television. They do what we want straightaway. That's because we love ourselves, and do our best to make sure we are comfortable.

God's idea for us is that we should love one another like that. That means noticing what other people are needing and going to help them. Let's try it.

Suppose Mum is trying to carry lots of bags out of the supermarket. (Act this out with real bags from the local store.) Get the children to suggest ways they could do some practical loving. Suppose it's time for the cat to be fed and her bowl is empty. (Have a bowl and some dry cat food.) The children can suggest how to do the loving. Suppose Dad is feeling very fed up because his team has lost an important match. (Mime this.) How can they do the loving?

Teach the children this 'love your neighbour as yourself' code to help them remember:

• Look (*make hands into binoculars and look around*)

• Think (*put finger to head thoughtfully*)

• Do (*stretch out hands*)

Praying

The more love we give,
the more love there is!
Help us to spread your love around
so there's lots and lots and lots! Amen.

Activities

On the sheet there is a picture to which the children can add lots of apples, lots of flowers and lots of sunshine and raindrops. There is also a picture to spot the loving going on, and the needs which are not being noticed by the people in the drawing.

PEARL DIVERS

Aim: To know we are called to be loving and generous-hearted, like God.

Starter

Pass the ball. Stand in a circle with a ball – a large blow-up beach ball is good to use. If the children don't already know each other's names, go round saying these first. Then whoever has the ball says, 'Here you are, Laura', and throws the ball to her. Tell the children to make sure that everyone has the ball thrown specially to them, so that no one is left out.

Teaching

Talk about the fun of giving presents to people, both the wrapped-up sort we enjoy giving at Christmas and birthdays, and the little everyday presents like smiles and hugs, a crisp from our packet, a sweet from our bag, or our help with a job. Whenever we give in this loving way, we are being like God because he does it all the time. He loves giving us good things to enjoy and use. Using the carpet tiles as a background, add some pictures of the presents God gives, like sun and rain, fruiting trees, animals, people.

Now show a chart with ten faces on it, arranged in two groups of five. Explain how instead of loving one another, we tend to only love those we feel are 'on our side' by being in our family, our gang, or our country. And this is what happens: an eye for an eye, a tooth for a tooth. (Keep blacking out eyes and teeth in a tit-for-tat way, till all the faces end up blind and toothless.) Now let's listen to the teaching Jesus gave. Read Matthew 5:43-45, and across the picture of the faces write: 'Love your enemies'.

Praying

Jesus, this loving you talk about
is HUGE!
I know I don't always want to do it
but I can see it's a good idea.
Please help me to be better at it. Amen.

Activities

On the sheet there are instructions for making warm fuzzies to give away to people. The children will need wool for this. If you don't have any spare balls of wool, you can usually find some in charity shops quite cheaply. There are also instructions for making love stretch, using a pair of scissors and the chart provided.

GOLD PANNERS

Aim: To explore the implications of our call to holiness.

Starter

Friend or foe? Have a number of qualities written on cards which can be sorted into the 'friend' or 'foe' pile. Ideas for the cards:

- Lets you down all the time
- Lends you their kit when you have forgotten yours
- Mistreats someone you love
- Accuses you so you get the blame unjustly
- Puts you down in front of other people
- You can trust them to keep a secret
- Makes you pay for everything and never offers to help
- Cheers you up when you're feeling down
- Winds you up constantly
- Waits for you if you're late out
- Keeps your place in the queue
- Understands when you don't agree about something

Teaching

Read together Matthew 5:38-48. Begin by clearing up a common misunderstanding about Christians and enemies. There are always some people we get on really well with, and others we dislike. It is natural to feel hostile to anyone who treats you or your loved ones badly. God knows about all this. He knows we have both friends and enemies, and he doesn't want us to pretend about our true feelings – it's much healthier to take them out and look at them so that we are aware of what's going on inside us. Jesus is teaching us how to deal with our enemies, and our feelings.

We are not told to *like* our enemies, but to treat them with love. That means being absolutely fair and honest with them, however dishonest they are with us. It means treating them with respect and consideration, however much they insult and scorn us. That way we will be showing them the kind of behaviour we consider right, and we won't have been dragged down into behaving as badly as they are.

What Jesus doesn't mean is for us to lie down like doormats for people to walk over! If an enemy is bullying us, for instance, the loving way to treat them is not to suffer it all in an agony of silence and fear, but to tell them that they are behaving badly, and let someone in authority know, so that the situation can be properly dealt with. That is kinder to them than letting them carry on bullying without being checked.

We also need to look at our own behaviour. Are we sometimes behaving as enemies to people in our own families, for instance? Are there people we despise, or treat badly, or refuse to help?

Being holy means behaving in a godly way to everyone, without taking some for granted, or drawing a line round a particular group we give ourselves permission to hate.

Praying

Give me understanding, Lord,
that I may keep your law of love
with my whole life and energy and will.
I pray now for those I dislike
and find it hard to get on with.
Teach me how to treat them with love. Amen.

Activities

On the sheet there is a form for them to fill in which will actually benefit someone else. And there are instructions for playing a competitive game (such as the game of life, or snakes and ladders) with someone else's gain as our priority for a change.

EIGHTH SUNDAY OF THE YEAR

Thought for the day

God is creative and good; seeking his rule, as our priority, will mean that everything else falls into place.

Reflection on the readings

Isaiah 49:14-15
Psalm 61:2-3, 6-9
1 Corinthians 4:1-5
Matthew 6:24-34

As soon as we become aware of the fact that we are individuals, living in somewhere called 'place', the natural human reaction is to start wondering about it. Why are we here? Who are we? How are we here? These are universal, important questions, and enable us to become fully ourselves.

In the reading from Isaiah we see that, in some sense, the parental longing and care for children are the human reflection of the divine love which fashioned us.

Today's readings celebrate the overarching and undergirding love and care of our God. Jesus shows a wonderfully childlike and relaxed assurance about this, which he longs for us to know and share. So much of our time is spent anxiously worrying about things over which we have no control, and it is not God's will that we should go through life harassed and agitated like this. We can learn much from young children here. Toddlers are so good at accepting the way they drop off to sleep in one place and wake up somewhere completely different, while we in the meantime have vacuumed and washed up, fixed them into the car seats, driven through the roadworks and emerged at the supermarket. The sleeping child trusts that the parent will be looking after them. Humans take time to learn to distrust.

Jesus is recommending that we relearn that trust in our Parent God as soon as possible, so we can live freely, basking in the faithful love that will never let us down. It is this security which enables us to meet and cope with all the inevitable stresses and strains of living, because our roots are firmly fixed in what is greater and more profound than anything else.

If that is in place, the rest becomes manageable and less threatening. And once we are feeling our survival unthreatened, we are able and willing to take risks, and accept disappointments and pain without being overwhelmed by them. Eventually, all things will be accomplished and transformed.

Discussion starters

1. How is God's creative nature still apparent today?

2. What is the difference between loving concern for people and the kind of anxious living Jesus recommends we reject?

All-stage talk

Beforehand prepare some large speech bubbles from thin card, with the typical worries of those in the congregation written clearly on them. Here are some suggestions:

• My hair's going grey/thin on top!
• What can I wear?
• Weetabix or cocopops or toast?
• Suppose they don't like me?
• Brut or Denim – and how much of it?
• I'm the wrong shape!

Ask some volunteers to hold these worries up high. They're the kind of things we all waste our time and energy worrying about. Jesus was sad to see

people worrying their lives away, and he wanted them to be free of this constant worrying. Point out that the volunteers will start to get aching arms if they have to go on holding the worries up for too long.

In our Gospel reading today Matthew tells us that Jesus says to us, 'Put all those worries down – they're heavy to carry and are making your arms ache.' Let the volunteers put the worries down, and talk about what a relief it is to have our worries sorted out.

Jesus wants us to know that although life is bound to be full of difficult and uncomfortable times as well as easy and happy times, we don't need to worry about it as well as live through it! That makes it twice as bad for us. The way to be free of worry is not to be massively rich or refuse to grow up, or bury your head in the sand and pretend not to see the problems. The way to be free of worrying yourself sick is to trust that your Parent God loves you, likes you, and is well able to help you cope with everything you'll face in your life.

Jesus suggests we live one day at a time, instead of worrying about things that might never happen, or which are bound to happen, and God will bring us safely through it all to heaven, where we will be safe with God for ever.

All-age ideas

• To celebrate the way God looks after us as a loving parent, have a display of photographs showing young children being fed, washed, cared for and played with; young children simply being absorbed and happy in what they're doing. Mount them all on the wall or on a display board and have various scriptures written out among the pictures. Here are some possible texts to use: Matthew 6:9, Genesis 1:27, Genesis 1:31, 1 Corinthians 3:16.

• Have some banners or posters illustrating God's creative love displayed on banners or the wall, and flower arrangements that include fruit and vegetables.

Prayer of the Faithful

Celebrant
Let us pray to the God who knows us so well and understands our needs.

Reader
Lord, in all the daily concerns of parish life, and in the great issues facing the whole Church, may we never lose sight of your priorities but see everything through the eyes of compassion, with honesty and integrity.

Silence

Lord of creation:
let your kingdom come!

Lord, in the local issues of this community,
and in the difficulties and dilemmas
on the world stage,
may we look for the face of Christ
and fix our attention on his underlying values
of love, justice and mercy.

Silence

Lord of creation:
let your kingdom come!

Lord, in all the minor squabbles
and major rifts of family life,
may we know the assurance of your promise
to be with us always,
and your power to transform and renew.

Silence

Lord of creation:
let your kingdom come!

Lord, in the shock of sudden illness and pain,
and in the wearing endurance
of long-term weakness,
give your peace and tranquillity,
your healing and hope.

Silence

Lord of creation:
let your kingdom come!

Lord, through the journey of death
and in the grieving of those who mourn,
gather us up into the everlasting arms of love
and comfort us,
and bring us to life in all its fullness.

Silence

Lord of creation:
let your kingdom come!

We pray with Mary
who was full of peace and trust:
Hail, Mary . . .

In the silence of God's attentive love,
we pray our private petitions.

Silence

Celebrant
Father, in confidence we pray,
and ask you to accept these prayers,
through Jesus Christ.
Amen.

TREASURE SEEKERS

Aim: To know that God made the world and looks after us.

Starter

Using either a real baby and parent or a baby doll, have someone talking about looking after a new baby, bathing and feeding, and showing some of the normal baby equipment like rattles and shampoo, nappies and bibs.

Teaching

Talk over the loving care parents give their babies, bringing in the way they may help look after any baby brothers and sisters. Explain that God loves and looks after us like that, noticing what we need, comforting us when we are sad, and sorting us out when we get into a mess. Just as we can help our parents in the care of our brothers and sisters, so we can work with God in helping to look after one another, because we are all brothers and sisters in God's family.

Look at some pictures of God's world to see what a beautiful place God has given us to live in. We can help look after the world as well as the people who live in it.

Praying

Thank you, God,
for making us such a lovely world to live in.
Help us to look after it
and the other people who live here. Amen.

Activities

Using a paper plate each and some salt dough (two cups of flour, one cup of salt, and water to mix) the children can make a model animal and put it in a suitable landscape, following the instructions below. There is also a dot-to-dot puzzle on the worksheet. Add to the dots provided or delete some according to the age and ability of the children in your group.

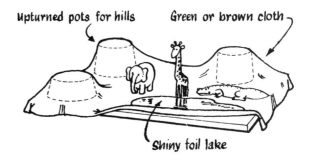

PEARL DIVERS

Aim: To see God's love in his creation.

Starter

Use modelling clay to make something they are glad God has made. These can all be gathered on to a tray covered in green and blue paper.

Teaching

Prepare cut-outs of each creation day's work, which can be stuck on to a blank sheet of paper in order while the Genesis passage is being read. Use these ideas or design your own.

1. A plain sheet of black paper.
2. Sky blue paper to cover half of the top of the black paper. (You'll need to keep some of the 'sky' black.)
3. Shiny blue paper across the bottom part.
4. Brown land shape in the blue sea. Trees with fruit, flowers and grass.
5. Sun in the blue half of sky, moon and stars in the black side.
6. Birds and fish.
7. Animals and humans.
8. The title: 'God saw that it was very good.'

Have some music playing as a background, someone to read the creation story, and someone else to get on with the developing picture, so the narrative is not interrupted but interpreted as it goes along, and the children experience with several senses at once.

Our creative, loving God has given us all this. Isn't it beautiful! If God takes all this care over everything he makes, then we can be sure he will take great care of us, too. We don't need to waste our time worrying and being anxious, because our God is the powerful creative God who brought our whole universe into being and our planet into life.

Praying

Throw a ball which is designed to look like the earth, as you sing:

You've got the whole world in your hand,
you've got the whole wide world in your hand,
you've got the whole world in your hand,
you've got the whole world in your hand.

Activities

Have smaller versions of the large collage so the children can each make their own creation picture following the order given on the sheet. Arrange each set of items, ready cut, in different boxes so the children can work their way along, picking up one item from each box.

GOLD PANNERS

Aim: To look at priorities in life in the light of Jesus' teaching.

Starter

First things first. Give each person in the group a piece of card to hold, on which is written a possible priority. Holding their cards, they arrange themselves in order of priority according to the situation you give them. Priorities might include:

- Buying food before the shop closes
- Getting outside before a newly discovered bomb explodes
- Finishing the crossword puzzle
- Getting an early night
- Washing your hair
- Praying
- Doing your homework
- Getting to work on time
- Reading the Bible

Teaching

First read the passage from Matthew 6. What is the priority that Jesus suggests is best? Jesus is reassuring his listeners that they really can trust God completely. What kind of God is he? What is he like?

Look now at the creation narrative in Genesis, searching in it for hints and clues about God's nature, and write down all the ideas. These can be placed around the outside of the creation picture on the sheet.

Praying

Oh give thanks to the Lord,
for he is good,
for his steadfast love endures for ever. Amen.

(From Psalm 135)

Activities

There are places on the sheet for them to discuss and name some of the usual worries they have. Take some of these out and look at them, working out together which ones are not worth wasting our energies on, and which need to be properly addressed. They can pray together and for one another, about some of the worries raised.

NINTH SUNDAY OF THE YEAR

Thought for the day

Wise listeners build their lives up on the strong rock of the word of God.

Reflection on the readings

Deuteronomy 11:18, 26-28
Psalm 30:2-4, 17, 25
Romans 3:21-25, 28
Matthew 7:21-27

Those whose homes are built in an area of clay or sand will be familiar with the extra insurance required. Prolonged dry spells following heavy rain are notorious for causing ominous cracks. In such areas underpinning is a common sight – manufactured rock foundations out of reinforced concrete. Jesus' example still holds today: lives built on rock foundations last without ending in ruin.

There was plenty of rock in the landscape of the psalmists, who would often use the reassuring security and permanence of it to describe God and, by extension, God's law – the words of God. Rather as we might stick revision facts to the bathroom mirror, or leave scribbled notes about swimming kit by the front door, the hearers of Deuteronomy are advised to strap reminders of the Law everywhere, so that it becomes really soaked into their everyday life. It is all aimed at turning hearers into doers, at getting that Law turned into a holy people.

Of course, it was no easier for the people of Israel to keep up their practice of God's Law than it is for us to keep up our violin or German-speaking practice without a weekly lesson. We all need the constant nagging nudge which the strapped-on law boxes were designed to provide. But besides being strapped on to the outside of us, they really need strapping to our hearts. And that is what the Holy Spirit can do for us, setting our hearts on fire with such love for our God that we long to spend ourselves in pleasing him and working for the coming of the kingdom. Yes, it is certainly wise to build on the words of God, but wisdom is itself one of the gifts that grows out of love – love for the One who has freely given us the freedom we could never achieve by ourselves.

Discussion starters

1. What does it mean to 'do the will of my Father', rather than saying only, 'Lord, Lord!'?

2. What could be a practical present-day equivalent of the Deuteronomy advice for reminders that we are God's people?

All-stage talk

Set up some young children and an adult or two to build with Lego, building blocks or a variety of cartons. Draw attention to the building they are involved with and explain that today we have heard Jesus advising us on a wise building policy in our lives. We are also concerned that we do as much as possible to ensure that our faith is passed on faithfully to our young children, and their children yet to come. Having them building here in front of us will serve as a memory jogger to remind us both of our life building, and our responsibility to the young ones entrusted to our care.

The passage from Deuteronomy goes on to talk about passing on our faith. We are not to expect our children to pick up the faith all by themselves – we are to talk to them about it in all kinds of situations, so that they get to realise that it is relevant and valuable, of great importance for the whole of life. What does that mean in practice?

- It means that our children will not see God as the firm, secure rock he is unless they see the adults around them trusting that rock and building their lives on it. They need to see adults living their faith, every day of the week.

- It means that if our children see the adults in their Christian community saying they believe in God, coming to church and behaving in ways which are selfish, prejudiced, unforgiving or without loving respect for everyone, they may get the impression that God is not strong rock at all, but sand; that he is not to be taken seriously. Heaven forbid that we should lead any of our little ones astray by the inconsistency of our life.

- It means that we need to get over our embarrassment in talking about God, and chat about him with our children as we would talk about all the other things that are important and excite us.

- It means that we need to start praying aloud with our children, and praying daily with them, so they learn what it is to talk over everything with the loving God, sharing both the lovely times and the sad ones with him. We need to get back the habit of thanking God – aloud – for our food before we eat. Our homes need to become places where it is natural to pray. How else will our children learn to pray naturally?

Of course, this is not going to be easy, especially if we live in a community where only part of the family are believers. But that makes our church community particularly important. Children can cope with the fact that one of their parents believes and one doesn't. It is the hypocrisy of conflicting words and behaviour that confuses them. All our families need the support of the whole Christian community in the precious work of parenting. We are all part of that, whether we have young children ourselves or not.

So let us watch how we build. When we hear Jesus' words, let's really start acting on them, changing our behaviour and our habits to sing out those words in all we do. And then we shall be taking seriously our charge to nurture our little ones, and pass on to them faithfully the Gospel that sets us free to live abundantly, even through storms and floods.

All-age ideas

* In one of the flower arrangements incorporate bricks, a trowel and a spirit level.

Prayer of the Faithful

Celebrant
As the community of God's people,
let us focus our attention and still our bodies to pray.

Reader
Father, we have heard your words
and your challenge
to build our lives wisely on the bedrock of faith;
may all of us who profess to be Christians
act on what we have heard.
Bless and inspire all who preach and teach the faith
and make our worship pure and holy
and acceptable to you.

Silence

Lord God of wisdom:
you give us the word of life.

Father, we are conscious of the double standards
and inconsistencies in our world,
and ask for hearts to be opened to hear you
and recognise the wisdom of your law of love.
We ask you to strengthen
and encourage each attempt
to govern with your principles,
and deal justly with your sense of mercy.

Silence

Lord God of wisdom:
you give us the word of life.

Father, we want to take more seriously
our community commitment to our children.
Show us what needs to be started,

developed or changed
in our attitudes to one another,
and in the way we help one another's faith to grow.

Silence

Lord God of wisdom:
you give us the word of life.

Father, the needs and concerns of all who suffer
are our concern, through love.
May we strive to address
the imprisoning poverty and hunger
of much of our world,
and involve ourselves
in the comfort, help and healing
we ask of you.

Silence

Lord God of wisdom:
you give us the word of life.

Father, we commend to your love and mercy
those who have died to this earthly life.
We thank you for lives well lived and love shared.
Bring them, and us in our turn, safely to heaven.

Silence

Lord God of wisdom:
you give us the word of life.

We pray with Mary,
whose faith was based on firm foundations:
Hail, Mary . . .

In silence,
we make our private petitions to God,
who always hears our prayers in faith.

Silence

Celebrant
Loving Father,
we ask you to accept these prayers
for the sake of Jesus, your Son.
Amen.

TREASURE SEEKERS

Aim: To know that Jesus is like strong rock to build on.

Starter

Bring along plenty of construction toys, such as Duplo, blocks or simply lots of boxes and cartons, and work with the children to build.

Teaching

Jesus was once talking to his friends and he told them this: 'All the things I teach you to do are very important, and will help you live a good life. Wise people will listen to what I teach them *(cup hand to ear as you say this)* and then do it *(open hands up)*. Foolish people will hear what I tell them *(cup hand to ear)* and yet do nothing about it *(fold arms)*.'

Explain that you are going to tell them all something, and they can choose whether to listen *(cup hand to ear)* and then do what you say *(open hands)* or just listen *(cup hand to ear)* and do nothing about it *(fold arms)*. Tell them that you have some sweets in a tin. Only children who put their hands up will be given one. They can now choose whether to put their hands up or not. Then give out sweets to those with their hands up.

It is wise and sensible to do what Jesus tells us, because he loves us and knows what is best for us all. But lots of people are not very wise. They hear what Jesus says, and yet do nothing about it. Jesus said, 'If you listen to what I tell you *(cup hand to ear)* and do what I have said *(open hands up)* you will be as sensible and wise as a person building on a good strong rock. If you listen to what I tell you *(cup hand to ear)* and yet do nothing about it *(fold arms)* you will be as silly and foolish as a person building on wobbly, moving sand!'

Let's see what happens if we build on rock (which is strong, like this floor). Build up on this and see how firm the house is. Let's see what happens if we build on wobbly, moving sand. Have a floppy surface such as an old pillow, or rumpled blanket and pretend that is sand, because it is wobbly and moves about a bit, like sand. Even if you carefully manage to keep your building together while you are building, as soon as the pillow or blanket is jogged the whole building collapses. (Do this as you speak.)

So if we are going to build up good strong lives, let's not be foolish, listening to what Jesus says *(cup hands to ears)* and doing nothing about it *(fold arms)*. Let's make sure we are wise, listening to what Jesus tells us *(cup hands to ears)* and doing what he says *(open hands)*.

Praying

Jesus, I don't want to be foolish,
hearing what you tell me
 (cup hand to ear)
but not doing anything about it.
 (fold arms)
Jesus, I want to be wise,
hearing what you tell me
 (cup hand to ear)
and doing it in my life.
 (open hands)

Activities

Each child will need a strip of thin card so they can stick their house models on to it and stand them up. Also on the sheet, a picture with some people doing what Jesus said, and some not, helps them notice the godly way of living and the contrasting selfish way.

PEARL DIVERS

Aim: To think about the need to change words into a way of life.

Starter

Divide the group into teams and have a set of instructions for each team. Each team is given their first instruction which they rush off and do, bringing back the answer before you give them the next instruction. The first team to complete all their instructions wins. Here are some suggestions for the instructions; you will need to vary them according to the size and age of the teams and the practicalities of your meeting area.

- Bring a list of signatures of everyone in the team.
- Make a thumb-print pattern using everyone's thumbs.
- Collect six different coloured pieces of wool from around the room.
- How far from the wall do you stretch if you all lie end to end?
- Stand in order of height/hair length.
- Bring the total number of fingers and toes in the team.

Teaching

Draw attention to the way they needed to do two things in that game:

1. To listen carefully to what they were told.

2. To carry out the instructions.

Praise them for doing that really well, working with each other and helping one another. That's very much what Jesus was teaching – how to listen carefully and then put what we hear into action!

Anyone who goes to dancing, or sports training, or is learning to play a musical instrument will know that the way to do it is to listen to what your teacher or trainer says, and then do your practice. As you put into practice what you have been taught, you find yourself getting better and better. When you listen, and then don't get round to practising, you don't make nearly as much progress.

Jesus is our trainer and teacher, who tells us all about living. One day he was getting rather fed up with people coming to listen to him and saying they were his followers, even though they weren't changing their lives at all. And this is what he said to them: 'Not everyone who says that I am his Lord will enter the kingdom of heaven. The only people who will enter the kingdom of heaven are those who *do* the things that my Father in heaven wants.' It just isn't enough to say that we are followers of Jesus – if we really mean that, we will make sure we put into practice what he tells us.

Then Jesus told one of his stories to help the people understand what he was saying. He said that the people who hear what he says and then act on it are like wise builders, who build their house on proper foundations of solid rock. (Build a brick house on a firm but well-protected surface as you speak.) Those who hear what Jesus tells them and yet do nothing about it are as foolish as builders who build their house on sand. (Build another house on a tray of dry sand.)

What is so wise about building on rock? When the storms of life pour down it will still stay standing. (Pour water over the house on rock.) When the storms of life pour down on a house built on sand, it's a different story completely. (Pour water over the sand so that the house built on it collapses.)

So the wise thing for us to do is not just to hear what Jesus says, or even to hear and say, 'Oh yes, I'm a follower of Jesus – he's my Lord!' The wise thing is actually to do something about what he tells us – to start putting his teaching into action so that our lives and behaviour are like strong houses built on strong foundations.

Praying

Lord Jesus, I want to be a real follower of yours.
I don't just want to say it,
I want to do it as well.
Please help me to put what you tell me
into practice this week. Amen.

Activities

On the sheet there are Deuteronomy-style reminders to make and strap on to themselves with bracelets and headbands, and fridge magnets and mirror messages to fix around the house. The children will need a blob of blutack each, or a small piece of magnetic strip (available from craft shops).

GOLD PANNERS

Aim: To explore what it means to build our lives on the rock of God's teaching.

Starter

Beforehand make a simple picture of a house, cut from coloured paper. At the same time cut enough identical pieces for each couple of people in the group to make up the same picture. (You might have background pieces of green and blue, a different green hill, the main house shape, different coloured window and door shapes.) The pieces will need to be put together in the right order and position if they are to look exactly like the original.

First show the original to everyone for twenty or thirty seconds, and then cover it up while they all make their own pictures. Then show the original again to check who got it exactly right.

Teaching

They probably noticed in that activity that they had to concentrate carefully during the viewing time so as to pick up and store as much vital information as possible. Then, building on that, they were able to get close to the right picture. Today we are looking at something Jesus said to some of those who came to listen to him. They claimed to be his followers but in fact their lives showed no attempt to carry out God's teaching. Jesus always hated any kind of hypocrisy – or saying one thing and doing another. Being full of truth and integrity himself, he was disturbed by people thinking God could be fooled by what they might say. God matches up what we say with what we do, and he can easily tell if we are pretending.

Read Matthew 7:21-27. If we really listen to what Jesus tells us – listen with our heart and will as well as our ears – we shall be wanting to use what we have heard in the building of our lives. If, on the other hand, we assume those words are not really meant for us, and have no intention of acting on them, we shall be throwing away all that Jesus offers, and end up building our lives on things that give way on us and let us down, instead of the solid rock which we can always rely on.

But there is a problem. Being human we can genuinely want to build on the right foundations, and mean it at the time we say that we believe in God and want to be his followers. Then often we find ourselves getting carried away living in the same old bad habits, and pleasing ourselves yet again. In the Old Testament the people had found the same problem. They had tried all kinds of ways to remind themselves of God's Law so that they would remember how to live his way. Read the Deuteronomy 11 passage to see how seriously they tried.

To some extent it worked, but then the reminders themselves would start to become more important to people than what they were there for! With the coming of Jesus, and the filling of our lives with the Holy Spirit of God, there was a drastic and exciting change to this state of affairs. Paul talks about it in today's passage from Romans: we know we can't manage it on our own, but through God's freely given grace, won for us by Jesus, the impossible becomes possible. Read Romans 3:21-25, 28.

Not only can we listen to Jesus' words, and make the decision to build on that strong foundation, but God will also be there with us in the work of building.

Praying

O God, the strength of all who put their trust in you,
we know that, being human,
we can do no good thing without you.
We ask you to give us your gift of grace
so that we can live lives that are pleasing to you.
Amen.

Activities

On the sheet there is a building plan to fill in, to help them put into practice God's teaching in their everyday lives. These can be decorated, cut out and placed in envelopes to be offered and blessed in church, before being given back after the service so they can be used in daily living.

TENTH SUNDAY OF THE YEAR

Thought for the day

Jesus' life of healing and compassion acts out God's desire for mercy rather than empty sacrifice.

Reflection on the readings

Hosea 6:3-6
Psalm 49:1, 8, 12-15
Romans 4:18-25
Matthew 9:9-13

Last week we were looking at the dangers of giving empty lip-service to Christ, yet not being prepared to put his teaching into practice in our lives. Today we look at another danger – of going through the motions of following God, but without our hearts being in it, and without any real acknowledgement of the sacrificial cost involved.

What was basically wrong in the story of Matthew's calling? At one level we can accept that the religious leaders are justified in pointing out to Jesus that he is associating with those whose lives appear to have deliberately rejected God's values. Surely these people are a disgrace to the name of the chosen nation of Israel? How are they a light to the rest of the world? The speakers know that they themselves have deliberately chosen to keep the sacred law, and follow all the teachings to the letter. They know they are doing their bit to uphold the values of a chosen people set apart for God. So far, so understandable. If we are honest, how would we feel if Jesus came and spent more time with the gang smashing into our church and spray-painting it, than with us in our specially prepared Bible studies?

The crunch comes with the attitude of the religious leaders to what Jesus is doing with these 'sinners'. Had they been genuinely seeking to uphold God's values of mercy and justice, they would have had an openness which looked curiously at what Jesus was doing and tried to understand it. They would have noticed the gradual change in the 'sinners' and suddenly realised with excitement and delight that, although Jesus was acting unexpectedly, he was actually helping these people to healing and wholeness. They would then have been there rejoicing with Matthew and the others, and nothing could have given Jesus greater joy.

As it is, they disassociate themselves from the healing work of God; they are, in a sense, selling their true birthright for a bowl of broth. Jesus listens to their complaints, and we can imagine his heart aching at their blindness. He gives them a clue as to what he is doing, by talking about sick people and doctors. They must have reacted to that, not with sudden insight and joy but with supercilious self-righteousness which told Jesus they knew better; these people were evil, not sick, and if he was really a religious teacher he would know they should be avoided and rejected for the purity of the nation. Such an attitude was an appalling insult to the God of mercy and compassion, and brought out Jesus' passionate response: 'Go and learn what this text means . . . and start getting your priorities right!' The whole point of Jesus coming was to do this work of loving sinners into a right relationship with the God of their making.

The story is a sobering one. What had begun as well-intentioned ways of lavishing true worship on the living God had become distorted into worship of empty systems and rituals, to the extent that, when faced with the genuine active presence of God, it was not even recognised. We need to come back, constantly, to the heart of worship, to the feet of God, and listen intently to what he is saying, so that our worship expresses our loving service to the loving God.

Discussion starters

1. How does ritual of any kind (or absence of it), originally a genuine expression of worship, sometimes turn into an empty shell, and how can we avoid it happening?

2. What assumptions does Jesus question in the call of Matthew?

All-stage talk

Beforehand work with one or two people who don't mind acting. They are going to say 'Hello' to one another in various different ways that mean:

- I was really hoping I wouldn't meet this person here.
- I have no respect for this person whatsoever.
- This person is of no interest to me at all.
- This person has a swimming pool and I'd like to be invited round, so I'll suck up to them.
- I'm really glad to see this person.
- I respect and love this person very much.

Begin the talk by getting the actors to say 'Hello' to one another in each different way, and each time follow their greeting with the interpretation, read like a label.

We all show what we think of each other by the greeting we offer one another. (Incidentally, does the way we offer the Sign of Peace tell the other person that they are really valued, or are we looking at someone more our type or more interesting while we greet some people?)

Today we have come to meet together as Christians for a reason. Why have we come here? We haven't come just to see our family or friends (though that is always nice to do!) and we haven't come just to play with the Noah's ark, or to get out of mowing the grass. We have come to greet our God in worship and to greet one another in his name. What kind of 'Hello' are we giving to God by our worship?

Perhaps we are hoping that we won't actually meet God here, in case he asks of us something we don't want to give. We glance in his direction, but don't want to make eye contact, so to speak. Today we are reminded that to worship God beautifully we need to COME TO GOD HONESTLY, JUST AS WE ARE. (Display this.)

Perhaps we nod in his direction, but have really got our thoughts on the people coming for dinner and whether the bathroom should be white or pale green. Or we are thinking more of the piece of chewing gum under the seat in front of us, or the behaviour of the young, or the middle-aged or the elderly, or how many candles need replacing. Today we are reminded that to worship God beautifully we need to GIVE GOD OUR FULL ATTENTION. (Have that written up.)

Perhaps we are here thinking God will notice and tick off our names for good attendance, so that when we die we will have a pre-booked place in heaven. We intend to join in with all the hymns and prayers in church, but for the rest of the week we plan to carry on with the real life in the real world, where Christian values are not actually practical. Today we are reminded that to worship God beautifully we need to KNOW THAT GOD IS NOT FOOLED, and MATCH UP OUR WORDS WITH OUR LIFE (or WALK THE TALK).

Our God is the God of compassion and healing. He does not want our empty words, dry habit worship or closed-up prejudice. He does not want pretence or hypocrisy. God loves us and delights in his people coming to meet with him in worship, Sunday by Sunday. Wherever we are in our spiritual journey he can work with us, and he will never turn anyone away who is genuinely seeking. But whether we greet him in worship with our faces scratched and bruised, as we lie sprawled in the dust of life, or whether we greet him as we stop for breath from running away from him, or whether we greet him timidly but bravely, what we must do is greet him honestly, openly and expectantly.

Suggest that, not out loud but in the silence of their hearts, everyone says their own 'Hello' to God, honestly, openly and expectantly.

All-age ideas

- Draw up a short list of the people you would like to invite to your house. Draw up a second list of the sort of people you would not like to have in your house. Now think of reasons why those on the second list should be added to the first list.

Prayer of the Faithful

Celebrant
Come, let us return to the Lord who loves us, and pray to him now.

Reader
God of truth,
we pray that your Church may be led
into the way of truth

and an ever-deepening understanding
of your nature and your will.
We pray for our leaders and teachers and pastors;
we pray for right priorities
and a softening of the ground of our hearts.

Silence

Come:
let us return to the Lord.

God of power,
we pray for those with authority,
influence and power in our world;
for all who are easily led,
often against their conscience;
we pray for a re-aligning of right values
and a reawakening of mutual respect and trust.

Silence

Come:
let us return to the Lord.

God of loving kindness,
watch over our homes and families,
our friends and neighbours;
we pray too for those who wish us harm
and those we find it difficult to love;
we pray for more of you in all our relationships.

Silence

Come:
let us return to the Lord.

God of mercy and compassion,
we bring to you all those who, through illness,
accident, age, abuse or human weakness,
are suffering as we gather here.
Gather them up in your love
and give your healing, your strength and courage,
your hope and wholeness.
We make ourselves available
as channels of your love.

Silence

Come:
let us return to the Lord.

God of eternity,
in whom there is no beginning or end,
welcome into your presence those who have died,
and give comfort to those
who miss their earthly company.
Give us all a greater understanding
of the new life you offer.

Silence

Come:
let us return to the Lord.

We pray with Mary,
Mother of Mercy:
Hail, Mary . . .

Trusting in God's loving mercy,
we pray in silence
for our own cares and concerns.

Silence

Celebrant
Father of mercy,
we rejoice at your welcoming forgiveness,
and ask you to accept our prayers
through Jesus Christ.
Amen.

TREASURE SEEKERS

Aim: To know that Jesus made people better.

Starter

Sit in a circle and pass round a teddy with bandage on him. Each person holding the teddy can share with the others about a time they were poorly, or what it is like to be poorly.

Teaching

Hold up a picture (from a children's Bible) of Jesus healing someone which is covered up by a piece of card. Explain that before Jesus came, people couldn't see what God was like. But when Jesus came to live on earth (uncover the picture) they could see that God was very kind, because Jesus was always very kind. What is he doing in this picture? He is making someone better. Jesus hated to see people suffering and being poorly, and often he would make them better. Today we are going to hear about a child who was very ill at the time Jesus was living on earth.

Unroll a bed mat (this can be a blanket) and explain that this is the kind of bed that people slept on in those days. The child was feeling very, very ill, and her mummy put her to bed. (Have one of the children to lie on the bed.) Just like you, when you are ill, her mummy and daddy probably stroked her face, wiped her hot head with nice, cool water, and gave her water to drink. (Do these things as you speak.) Her daddy and mummy were worried about their daughter, because instead of getting better, as usually happens, she got more and more ill.

Then they heard from a friend that Jesus was walking to their town. They had heard that Jesus was very kind, and that he could make people better, and they badly wanted their daughter better, because they loved her so much. But before Jesus got to the town, their daughter died, and everyone was very sad. 'Well,' said the girl's daddy, 'I'm still going to ask him to come!', and he got up and ran out of the house towards Jesus. 'Jesus!' he said, 'my daughter has just died! But if you come and touch her with your hand I'm sure she will live again!'

Jesus felt very sorry for this man and his family. He wanted to help them, and said that of course he would come. When they got to the house everyone was crying and making a lot of noise. Jesus told them to go away. 'The child is not dead,' he said. 'She is only asleep.' The people laughed at that, but they went out and left Jesus with the little girl and her mummy and daddy. He went to where she was lying and held her hand. The little girl started to open her eyes! She looked at Jesus and smiled. She looked at her mummy and daddy and smiled. Then she got up from her bed mat. 'Thank you, Jesus!' she said. 'I feel better than I have for ages!' And they all hugged one another and cried again – but this time because they were so happy.

Praying

Jesus, you are kind; Jesus, you are loving.
You made people happy and you made people well.
Jesus, you are kind; Jesus, you are loving –
so God is kind and loving, I can tell.

Activities

On the sheet there is a picture of a child, ill in bed, and they can draw in the things that might make them feel better. They can also colour, cut out and put in the right order the pictures of today's story. Provide them with strips of coloured paper to stick the pictures on to, then fold the strip of paper to make a zigzag book.

PEARL DIVERS

Aim: To know about our calling to show mercy in our lives and be real in our worship.

Starter

Lying. Sit in a circle. The first person mimes an action (such as brushing their teeth) and everyone else joins in the mime. The person next to them says, 'What are you doing?' to which the first person lies, 'I'm blowing my nose' (or anything else that they aren't actually miming), and everyone says, 'I'm blowing my nose', while they continue to mime brushing their teeth. Then it's the next person's turn to start a mime.

Teaching

In that game they were saying one thing and doing another. That's just fine in a game, but today we're looking at what can happen if people say one thing when they're talking to God, but do something quite different in their lives.

Tell the children to put both thumbs up each time they think something sounds good, and down if they think it sounds bad.

It all started with Jesus making some friends. (This is a thumbs up.) These friends led bad lives, cheating people of money, and working for the Romans. (Thumbs down.) One of these friends was called Matthew, and Jesus called Matthew to follow him and be one of his disciples. (Thumbs up.) Matthew was very pleased to be asked (thumbs up) and threw a party for all his friends to celebrate. (Thumbs up.) There was lots to eat and drink (thumbs up), and Jesus and his friends were really enjoying themselves. (Thumbs up.)

The Pharisees, who were the religious leaders, saw Jesus enjoying himself with these bad people and they were angry. (Thumbs down.) They went up to Jesus' followers to complain. (Thumbs down.) 'What does Jesus think he's doing, spending his time with these kinds of people?' they said. 'They are bad people, and it isn't right for a religious teacher to waste his time with bad people. He should have nothing to do with them!' (Thumbs down.)

Jesus heard what they were saying and came over to talk with them. (Thumbs up.) He wanted them to understand that God loves all people, whether they are bad or good. (Thumbs up.) He wanted them to see that he was giving these people the love and healing they needed. (Thumbs up.) So he decided to give the Pharisees a clue. He said to them: 'Healthy people don't need a doctor. Only the sick need a doctor.' He hoped this would help them see that what he was doing was good, not bad; that it was not against God's way, but was exactly what God would want. (Thumbs up.)

But the Pharisees did not understand. (Thumbs down.) Although in their worship they said they loved God (one thumb up) here they were being angry at Jesus for showing the love of God to these people who needed it (other thumb down). They were saying good things to God in their worship (one thumb up), but thinking bad things about God in their lives (other thumb down).

Jesus told them to go and sort out what was really important to God – saying you love him but not showing love to other people (thumbs down) or saying you love him and showing that by loving those he has made (thumbs up).

Praying

I want to worship the real, living God.
And I want my worship to be
not just an empty shell
but real.

Activities

On the sheet there are instructions for using a hard-boiled egg to reinforce today's teaching. Each child will need a hard-boiled egg, salt, pepper and mayonnaise, a spoon and a clean empty yoghurt pot. There is also a picture of Jesus at Matthew's party for them to add the Pharisees and colour.

GOLD PANNERS

Aim: To explore the contrast between Jesus showing God's mercy and compassion, and the Pharisees' empty ritual and hypocrisy.

Starter

Which is the truth? On separate pieces of card, write out a number of words with various possible meanings. Read out all three possible definitions. They have to decide which one sounds most likely. Here are some examples to give you the idea:

BELLBIND: (a) a bell rope; (b) a bandage; (c) a weed

PAINTER: (a) a rope on a boat; (b) an artist's overall; (c) a pain killer

BASTE: (a) to cover paper with glue; (b) to pour liquid over cooking food; (c) to sing in a low voice

IRE: (a) happiness; (b) misery; (c) anger

DAMASK: (a) a kind of fabric; (b) a pale colour; (c) a kind of deer

LYRE: (a) someone who does not tell the truth; (b) a stringed instrument; (c) a wind instrument

Teaching

Ring a bell. In that game we were trying to work out which meaning rang true. God is concerned that our worship rings true, that what happens in our weekly services expresses the loving way we have been trying to live during the rest of the week. Look together at what God had said about this through the prophet Hosea, reading Hosea 6:3 and 6.

Explain how the Pharisees had become so enthusiastic about doing all the rituals of worship that these details had become far more important to them than the real work of giving honour and reverent worship to the loving God. Read the first part of today's Gospel, and stop at the end of verse 10. What do they think about Jesus' behaviour here? Was he right to be associating with people like this, or should he be avoiding them?

Now read verse 11. How would they answer this question from the Pharisees? Why do they think Jesus eats with tax collectors and 'sinners'?

Finally read about the way Jesus responds to them, in verses 12-13, picking up on the quotation from the prophet Hosea and comparing it with their own ideas.

Praying

I'm coming back to the heart of worship
and it's all about you, all about you, Jesus.
I'm sorry, Lord, for the thing I've made it
when it's all about you, it's all about you, Jesus.

(From a song by Matt Redman
© Copyright 1997 Kingsway's Thankyou Music.)

Activities

On the sheet there is a role-play to try, based on the Gospel reading, to bring out the feelings and attitudes behind the Pharisees' questions and Jesus' response to them, and there is space to plan a prayer vigil for the church on a matter of real social concern which they want to see addressed.

ELEVENTH SUNDAY OF THE YEAR

Thought for the day

Jesus sends his ambassadors out to proclaim God's kingdom and bring hope and peace of mind to the harassed and lost in every age.

Reflection on the readings

Exodus 19:2-6
Psalm 99:2-3, 5
Romans 5:6-11
Matthew 9:36-10:8

Stand on any railway station at rush hour and you see the harassed and tense faces all around. Perhaps that is an unfair place to pick, but it is noticeable that the stress and conflicting demands and expectations, and the relativism of our society, which places huge pressures on individual choice of action, combine to make 'peace of mind' a yearned-for impossibility for many. Today's readings speak quite a lot about hope, and being at peace with God and oneself.

In the passage from Exodus we find the people of Israel being given the hope of becoming the treasured possession of God, of being a kingdom of priests and a holy nation, if they are prepared, as a whole community, to work with their God rather than against him. We hear their confident response: 'We will do everything the Lord has commanded.' What poignant reading this must have made for those in exile, with the scattered trail of sin and rebellion behind them. What poignant reading it makes for us as we think back to promises confidently made and subsequent failures!

The wonderful thing about Christianity is that it speaks hope, not to a non-existent strong people who can save themselves, but to the reality of a well-intentioned and blundering race who know that saving themselves is not one of the things that humans can do.

In the reading from Matthew we feel Jesus' fondness and longing for the people, whom he describes as harassed and disturbed, agitated and without peace. He urges his disciples to join him in praying earnestly for more workers in the harvest, knowing that God will be dependent on human co-operation and availability to accomplish the healing and gathering in. That is just as true for us today as it was then, and we need to take Jesus' urgency to heart. True religion is being at peace with God, and the absence of that peace is obvious in our society.

Immediately after this, the twelve are sent out, in the role of ambassadors, to proclaim the kingdom of God and accompany the news with signs of healing. All the detailed instructions they are given point to a loving commitment which is total and without ambition, personal gain or personal comforts. That still needs to be our attitude, as the Church, so that our motives are transparent and uncluttered by sub-agendas or empire-building. We are called simply to love people into the kingdom, where they can know the joy and hope of being at peace with God.

Hope is an intriguing word. It is a mixture of desire for something and expectation of getting it. If either of those is missing, it isn't hope, and if either is overbalanced, there is no peace. But when you have both in balance, hope makes you very happy and contented in the present, as well as in the fulfilment. Paul addresses this phenomenon in his letter to the Romans. We are justified by faith, or provided with an 'honorary pass' to God's presence through Jesus' self-giving death, rather than trying hopelessly to earn it. It is this which gives us freely the illusive peace we all crave.

This is not just for the good times but for the grim ones as well. The kind of love that was ready to die for us when we were God's enemies, in effect, is hardly going to let us down now that we have been reconciled to God. We can be assured that our loving God will provide everything we need in the way of support and comfort during the worst sufferings life may throw at us. In fact, it is his love in us that enables us to grow and develop through such times.

Discussion starters

1. Is it foolish to talk about rejoicing and suffering in the same breath?

2. How would you interpret Jesus' instructions to the twelve for workers in the harvest today?

All-stage talk

Ask everyone to place their hand flat on their tummy. This is often the place where we can tell if we are anxious or stressed, because it feels 'uptight'. When we are at peace, and not tensed-up, this place is where we feel calm and relaxed, and contented. (In fact, one way of calming yourself down is to do what you are doing now, and breathe slowly in and out a few times.)

Recently we have been looking at what religion *isn't*. We've found that it isn't telling God he is Lord of our life and then behaving as if he is not important. And it isn't going through the motions of worshipping him without showing his love and compassion to other people.

Today we are looking at what religion *is*. It is all about being at peace with God. Ask for two people who are really good friends to come to the front, and talk to them about what it feels like to be with each other. How does being together make them feel? Do they feel worried about how the other friend will treat them? Would they trust their friend with a secret?

Best friends are good news. You are contented and happy to be with them, and are not worried all the time that you might say the wrong thing and offend them, or that they may start being nasty to you, so you need to be ready to hit them back if necessary. You know you can trust them with your secrets, and they won't laugh at you or think you are stupid. Even going through bad experiences isn't as bad if you are both in it together, because you know you will help one another along.

Well, that's what being at peace with God is like, and it has the spin-off effect of making us deeply happy and calm inside – a feeling that, whatever happens, all will be well. We heard today how Jesus wanted everyone to know this sense of calm assurance and peace and joy in their lives. He knew there were lots and lots of people going around worried and lost, with no peace inside them because they were not at peace with God. And he sent his disciples off to tell them that the kingdom of God was coming very soon, and soon they would be able to have that closeness with God which would give them peace.

Between the two 'best friends' put up a very large piece of cardboard with the word 'Sin' on it. Sin shuts us off from God and from one another. It makes us think of God as our enemy instead of our friend.

We know that Jesus went on to die for love of us all, which knocked that block of sin away between us and God. (Knock the cardboard away.) So now we can all know that lovely closeness to God which gives us real peace and hope, not just when everything is going well for us, but also through the times of suffering.

All-age ideas

• Try this sketch to draw attention to the right attitude of those sent out to proclaim the good news of the Gospel of Peace.

Make a 'Take 1' clapper-board using card and a split pin. An assistant shows 'Take 1'. They will also need a carton full of the various items to be given out.

A new recruit is being prepared for a mission by a couple of people holding clipboards and ticking off items as they are given out. (Their lines can also be on the clipboard.)

Tony OK. We've got the necessary info and equipment for you ready now. Let's see . . . ah yes, overnight bag, complete with nightwear, toiletries (mouthwash included) and towel; mosquito net, insect repellent (this is the one with the unclogging nozzle), and lightweight complete Bible (with matching magnifying glass).

Margaret Yes, and here's your fully comprehensive insurance policy (it includes return of body to country of origin, if necessary), travellers' cheques, ID card, small change in each currency in case of emergencies, first aid kit and manual, visa card and PIN number – that's sealed, of course.

Tony Now you'll need these letters of introduction, all on headed notepaper, naturally, and our emergency number should you have any difficulties. Oh, and rations . . . dehydrated lasagne and chips, cranberry ice cream, and

plenty of soya mince to keep you going if you're not offered anything better.

Margaret Right, there you are! And good luck!

Assistant Cut! (She comes on with the 'Take 2' clapper-board.) Take two!

Tony I say, you've got an awful lot of stuff there – it looks as if you're more interested in keeping yourself safe and comfortable at all costs than telling them the good news. How about getting rid of some of it? (Takes bag away.) Better to travel light, I think. Then they'll be able to see that you don't mind too much about personal comforts, and you'll have your hands free for healing and comforting other people instead of being weighed down with your own possessions all the time.

Margaret All this paperwork is a bit OTT, don't you think? You're supposed to be ready to go wherever God leads you, and if you've planned every detail of your life already how are you going to stay available? (Takes the paperwork.)

Tony Ah, that's better – there's only one thing you really need, you know, and it's this. (Places a simple cross round neck.)

Both So go in peace, to love and serve the Lord!

Missionary In the name of Christ. Amen!

• By the entrance door place the following notice: 'Labourers needed for the harvest – attractive rates. No charge for equipment or training – corresponding salary.'

Prayer of the Faithful

Celebrant
Let us join in praying together with all God's people to the Lord of the harvest.

Reader
Heavenly Father, we thank you for the gift of life, and above all for your love in dying for us who so often act as your enemies.
Break down any barriers which prevent us from being at peace with you, and fill your Church with love for all who do not yet know your peace.

Silence

You, O Lord:
you are our hope and joy.

Father, we thank you for the diversity
and richness of our world,
for the natural goodness of many,
and the innocence of the very young.
We pray for all victims
of our world's mistakes and evils,
and ask your guidance and courage
for our leaders and advisers.

Silence

You, O Lord:
you are our hope and joy.

Father, we thank you for the joy
of our families and friendships,
and the opportunities provided in our homes
for learning what real loving is all about.
We pray for those we love and worry about,
and those who love and worry about us,
commending one another to your keeping.

Silence

You, O Lord:
you are our hope and joy.

Father, we thank you for all the medical research
that has brought healing
and quality of life to so many.
We pray for all who work in our hospitals,
hospices and clinics,
and for all the patients in their care.
We pray for all who are harassed and worried,
and long for the peace of mind that eludes them.

Silence

You, O Lord:
you are our hope and joy.

Father, we thank you
for all who have lived your praise
and worked for the coming of your kingdom.
Receive into the joy of heaven
all who have died in faith,
whose strong hope in the eternal God
is not disappointed, but fulfilled.

Silence

You, O Lord:
you are our hope and joy.

Father, we thank you for all
who sense your calling and respond to it with joy.
We pray for still more workers in your harvest,
to gather in many to share the joy of your peace.

You, O Lord:
you are our hope and joy.

We pray with Mary,
whose gift to the world was the Good Shepherd:
Hail, Mary . . .

In a time of silence,
we share with God our Father
our personal burdens, joys and sorrows.

Silence

Celebrant
Father, we ask you to hear these prayers,
through Jesus Christ,
our Saviour and our brother.
Amen.

TREASURE SEEKERS

Aim: To know that Jesus chose twelve followers to teach, and to work with him.

Starter

As the children arrive, give them a piece of paper with their name written on it, which they can decorate. Then they all hold their names as they jump about to some music. When the music stops choose a name, and that child comes to stick their label on a poster titled 'We are the Treasure Seekers'. Continue until everyone has been chosen, and the names are all stuck on the poster.

Teaching

Count to twelve with various things – leaves, stones, toys and crayons, for example. Then try counting to twelve together, using fingers of both hands and stamping each foot.

When Jesus was living on our earth he often taught crowds and crowds of people. They would all come out in the sunshine to the beach or the hills, and sit down to listen to what Jesus said. There were mums and dads, babies, toddlers, teenagers, uncles and aunties, grandmas and grandads. Jesus enjoyed teaching all the people and showing them God's love.

He didn't just talk to the crowds. He also chose some people to be his followers, so he could spend time with them and train them ready for when he had gone back to heaven. Can you guess how many people he chose? It was one, two, three, four, five, six, seven, eight, nine, ten, eleven, twelve! As you all count, place on the floor twelve paper shapes of people, based on the pictures below. They were all in Jesus' gang – they were like a class and Jesus was their teacher. As they walked along or sat around the fire in the evening eating their supper, Jesus would talk to them, and answer their questions. They were called *disciples*.

One day Jesus sent his one, two, three, four, five, six, seven, eight, nine, ten, eleven, twelve disciples out to try teaching the people in all the towns and villages round about, and making people better. They would be doing the kind of work Jesus usually did. Did he send them out with posh shoes? (Put a pair down.) No! Did he send them out with lots of spare clothes in a bag? (Put a bag down.) No! Did he send them out with lots of money to spend? (Put down a purse and cheque book.) No! He sent them out just as they were, with his blessing, and his prayers and his love.

Praying

Jesus chose
1 2 3 4 5 6 7 8 9 10 11 12 disciples
and told them all about God's love.
They told others, who told others, who told others
who told ME! So I know, too!
Thank you, Jesus.

Activities

If you have a set of Russian dolls, bring these along to show the children how the news gets passed on from person to person. Use a person shape cut from polystyrene so that the children can print twelve disciples in their places on the sheet. Make sure you protect clothing during the painting process.

PEARL DIVERS

Aim: To know the names of the disciples and why they were sent out at this stage.

Starter

Harvesters. Cut out lots of 'wheat', or scatter lots of long grass stalks all around the room. The idea is to see who can gather up most stalks between the starting and finishing whistle.

Teaching

They have just been gathering in the harvest, and, as with the real harvest, it's an urgent business, because you have to work hard to get all the harvest in before the winter storms begin. Where Jesus lived, in the area around Galilee, there were fields where the workers raced to get the harvest in each year. That's why Jesus used the harvest to explain the work his followers needed to be trained to do.

He could see that lots and lots of people were anxious and unhappy and discontented in their lives, and he wanted them all to know the happiness and hope of living at peace with God. They were a bit like all the wheat, ready and waiting to be gathered in to God's love. So Jesus said to his disciples, 'There are many people to harvest, but there are only a few workers to help harvest them. God owns the harvest. Pray to him that he will send more workers to help gather his harvest.' (Can they think of any harvest-workers they know who are spending their time gathering people into God's love?)

At that time Jesus had his little band of disciples, who he was training up for the job. (Lay twelve cards with their names on face down on the floor. On this side only the initial letter is written.) With a mixture of knowledge and guesswork, see how many correct ones they can uncover. Put these in one line and turn over the others, one at a time, with everyone saying the name, before turning it over again. Now try to remember what this group of names was. Carry on until they have managed to name all the disciples, and all the names are face up. Then read through the whole list, in whatever order you point to them. (This discourages some from going too fast for the others.)

Jesus sent these disciples out to all the surrounding villages and towns to tell people that the kingdom of God was very near, and to heal any who were ill. This was good training for when Jesus had returned to heaven, and it also meant the disciples were working as a team with Jesus. They were sent out without lots of personal comforts, or extra clothes, or heavy luggage, and were told not to take any food or money with them, but accept the food and shelter they were given, whatever it was like. That way the people would see that there was nothing in it for them, and they were doing it just out of love.

And that's how we need to live, when we are working with Jesus in God's harvest.

Praying

Dear Jesus, here I am, signing on.
I'd like to be a worker in your harvest.
I understand that the only pay
is the joy of knowing
that we are doing your will.
Use me, Lord!

Activities

Have twelve balloons so that the children can draw faces on them with acetate pens (protect clothing!) and fix name labels to them which they have copied from the sheet. These are in coded form to be worked out. There are also pictures of workers in the harvest, and suggestions of ways they, too, can join the team.

GOLD PANNERS

Aim: To look at the sending-out of the twelve and its relevance for contemporary mission.

Starter

String up a length of washing line with pegs on it. Have a chart with everyone's name on, and let each person have a go at collecting the pegs one-handed. The aim is to hold as many pegs as possible in that one hand. This score can be entered against the names. The prize for the winner? A peg.

Teaching

First, read the passage from Exodus. Explain how Moses went back to his people with these words, how the people agreed to do what the Lord had said, but then didn't do what they said they would do. Talk about the problems that humans have of being unable to pull ourselves up by our own bootlaces. We can't save ourselves, but now Jesus has done for us what we could never do ourselves.

Read Romans 5:6-11 to see how Paul explains this.

Go over with them the fact that Jesus needed to train a small team of people to carry on the work of spreading this good news, so that everyone in the world can benefit from it, and live their lives in a state of inner peace instead of turmoil and being harassed all the time. How many disciples (students) did he choose? Twelve. Do we know their names? Collect as many as they know and supply the rest. Today we are going to read about the time when Jesus sent these twelve out on mission.

Read today's Gospel (Matthew 9:36-10:8). Talk together about how they were to go first to the 'lost sheep of Israel' (link this with the Exodus reading), and how having few possessions and living simply they could act out the message of trusting in God. The principle of living simply – so that you are available to 'travel light' wherever God calls you, and have more time for people – still holds true today. The Church is still called to go out, without lots of wealth or power, and preach the good news and bring God's wholeness to people.

Does the church do this well, partly, or hardly at all?

Praying

This is a prayer of Saint Francis.

Lord, make me an instrument of your peace.
Where there is hatred let me sow love;
where there is injury, pardon;
where there is despair, hope;
and where there is sadness, joy.
Divine Master, grant that I may seek
not so much to be consoled as to console,
to be understood, as to understand,
to be loved, as to love.
For it is in giving that we receive,
it is in pardoning that we are pardoned,
and in dying that we are born to eternal life.

Activities

On the sheet there is some information about Saint Francis, who was particularly struck by today's Gospel, and they are encouraged to question some of our assumptions about possessions and lifestyle.

TWELFTH SUNDAY OF THE YEAR

Thought for the day

When we are willing to take up our cross with Jesus we will also know his risen life.

Reflection on the readings

Jeremiah 20:10-13
Psalm 68:8-10, 14, 17, 33-35
Romans 5:12-15
Matthew 10:26-33

There is a fundamental paradox in the Christian faith which sounds like nonsense and yet turns out to be true when you try it. Today's readings paste it up large so that we cannot avoid it, however much we might like to. It is the claim that through death you gain life. In fact, it goes even further: unless you take on death you cannot know life. How on earth can this really be true?

We all know that our strong life-force, or libido, works constantly for our survival. Our brains use vast quantities of energy in supporting life systems and keeping us alive. There are all kinds of emergency strategies that kick in when anything threatens our survival, and the body is so good at managing these that it all goes on without us noticing, most of the time, and while we are occupied in other ways. Had it not been so, the human race could not have continued for as long as it has, nor succeeded in a fraction of its remarkable achievements.

There is much value today placed on self-confidence and self-assurance, in an effort to help people become their true selves without being so vulnerable to abuse or pressure from others. Self-assertiveness is the quality to prize, and any deliberate giving-up of one's rights is viewed with suspicion and often considered weak and wrong. How does this fit in with Jesus' teaching that whoever declares themselves for Christ to others will be declared by Christ to his Father: those who don't, won't be?

We cannot get away from the fact that this is a hard teaching to accept. It requires a drastic and complete change of values and direction in life. It can hurt. It is very costly. Jesus wants his potential followers to understand the full implications of commitment. So why would any normal person want to 'lose' their life like this by choice?

Jesus' answer has been experienced and found to be true by many people in each generation. Just as the result of Jesus' total self-giving in death was new, resurrection life, so the result of us giving up our natural self-centredness is a new sense of life in which we find we are more free to be ourselves than if we had slaved over it. It is the answer of a God who loves and cherishes us.

It is like the difference between a tissue-paper flower and an alpine meadow in spring. The kind of fulfilling life we think we are going to gain by accumulating wealth and prestige at other people's expense, over-indulging our tastes, and feverishly totting up as many experiences as possible in case we lose out on anything, turns out to be disappointing and never as satisfying as we had hoped; there is always something else we really must have or try. In comparison, the way of Jesus, in which everything will be made known, gives an inner sense of rightness, calm and integrity, which is very richly fulfilling and enables others to become their true selves as well.

Discussion starters

1. Jesus says that what we hear from him in whispers, we are to proclaim from the housetops. What practical ways are there of doing this?

2. Jesus talks as if our Christian faith will be obvious to people. Is it? Or do we prefer to say what people want to hear, in case we upset them?

All-stage talk

Bring along a kitchen knife, a pen or pencil, a can of paint spray and a £10 or £20 note. You will also need two signs, one saying 'Good' and the other 'Evil'.

Begin by observing that lots of things we handle every day can be used either for good or for evil. Ask for two volunteers to hold the signs, some distance apart, and go through each of the objects in turn, gathering from different people how each can be used. Take the objects to the appropriate notice for each suggestion.

Now ask a person to stand up. It's not only *things* which can be used for good or for evil; it's people as well. Stand the person beside the 'Evil' sign. In what ways can a person use themselves for evil? (Collect suggestions from people of all ages.) Stand the person by the 'Good' sign. In what ways can a person use themselves for good? (Collect suggestions.)

In our readings today we heard about how the false prophet Hananiah used his voice to encourage God's people to believe lies, and how Jeremiah wanted to use his voice differently – to build up God's people. We need to try and use our voices to encourage one another and help one another. We need to use our voices to tell out the truth, to proclaim from the housetops, but not to use the voices God has given to spread unkind gossip, or lies, or to be rude and unkind.

It is not just with our voices that we can proclaim the Gospel. What about our hands? Our minds? Our maleness or our femaleness? Our feet? Our ears? Suggest that during this week they make a point of checking how they are using all the parts of their body, and seeing if they offer all those parts of themselves to God for good.

All-age ideas

- Have little posies of flowers scattered in various corners of the church. At one point, perhaps during a hymn, the children can be sent off to find these 'little acts of kindness', and everyone can say together, 'No act of kindness, however small, goes unnoticed by the God of love.'

- Display the objects used in the all-stage talk with the 'Good' and 'Evil' signs and a large question mark shape in the middle, so that people are reminded as they go out of church. This could be on display for people to see next week as well, so they can check up on their week's focus and keep the teaching in mind.

Prayer of the Faithful

Celebrant
Let us focus our bodies, minds, hearts and wills as we pray to the God of all creation.

Reader
Holy God, you are the focus of our love and worship, because you alone are the Lord who has made us and rescued us.
May we not return to the slavery of sin but live in your freedom, serving you with joy, in thankfulness for all you have done for us.

Silence

Heal us, Lord:
and use us to your glory.

Holy God, though the world may often reject you, you never fail to believe in us all and love us with tenderness.
We pray for all areas of conflict, deceit, mismanagement and greed, and for all who are drawn into the chaos of evil.

Silence

Heal us, Lord:
and use us to your glory.

Holy God, our daily lives provide such rich ground for acts of loving kindness,

self-discipline and courage.
Remind us of the opportunities, and strengthen us to use them.

Silence

Heal us, Lord:
and use us to your glory.

Holy God, we thank you for all who lovingly look after those in nursing homes, hospitals, nurseries and prisons, and we pray for all who need such care and rely on others' help.

Silence

Heal us, Lord:
and use us to your glory.

Holy God, we call to mind those who have recently died and thank you for each act of goodness in their lives.
Have mercy on them and forgive their failings, so that they may share the joy of heaven for ever.

Silence

Heal us, Lord:
and use us to your glory.

Even when her Son was on the cross, Mary put her trust in him.
With her we pray:
Hail, Mary . . .

Knowing that God loves us with full understanding, we make our private petitions to him in silence.

Silence

Celebrant
Merciful Father, protect us during this week and through all our lives, and hear these prayers for the sake of Jesus Christ.
Amen.

TREASURE SEEKERS

Aim: To know that we can use our bodies for good.

Starter

Draw some signs on separate pieces of card: eyes, ears, hands, mouth, feet and a whole body outline. When the whole body sign is shown, everyone dances around to some music. Whenever the music stops, one of the other signs is shown and everyone holds that bit of their body until the music starts again.

Teaching

Tell the children how God has made us with these lovely bodies that can do all sorts of things. Place the signs from the starter activity on the floor, face down, and uncover them one by one, as you talk together about all the things these parts of us can do. They can demonstrate some of them, too. Focus on all the positives, so that you are celebrating the way we can work in God's team for good.

Praying

Thank you, God, for this body of mine.
It can shout and help and play.
I like to use this body of mine
to show your love each day. Amen.

Activities

On the sheet there is a picture of a person to which the children can add various parts by drawing them, or you could cut out the appropriate parts beforehand and the children can stick them on.

PEARL DIVERS

Aim: To learn about the difference between being slaves to sin and being free to do what is right out of thankful love.

Starter

Yes, your majesty! One of the leaders puts on a crown and robe, and holds a sceptre. (This can be a cracker hat, a curtain and a ruler.) She sits on her 'throne' and all the others are her slaves. She tells them what she wants done and everybody does it, first bowing down and saying, 'Yes, your majesty!' She might want to be fanned cool, given a can of drink, have it opened . . . and tested for poison, picked up, put down, or have a book brought and read and put away, or be scratched with a back-scratcher.

Teaching

Collect together some pictures from library books which show slaves building the pyramids, or rowing galleys, making bricks or harvesting sugar cane. When you are a slave someone pays money for you and then owns you, as if you are a bicycle or a TV. (You could act this out with one of the leaders being the buyer, and one of the children a person for sale.) As a slave you have to do what your owner tells you to do, and you don't belong to yourself any more. No one wants to be a slave, and even if you are lucky enough to have a kind owner, it's still hard to be owned like a thing, instead of being a free person, and slaves are often unhappy. It is not right for humans to be bought and owned like this.

Pin up a heading 'Slaves to sin'. When we are slaves to sin it is as if we are owned by sin, and spend our lives doing what our selfishness tells us to do. Give some examples of this, read by different children from speech bubbles of card:

- You want that big bit of cake, so take it quickly before anyone else can have it.
- He's better than you at swimming – go and get in his way so he comes in last.
- Don't bother to clear up – you want to go on playing.
- Pretend you didn't break that door; then someone else can get the blame.

If we keep doing all these things, whenever we want to please ourselves, we are just like slaves to sin. There are grown-ups who started like this as children and are still like it. But that way doesn't make us happy. We pretend to other people that we like living like this, but really it makes us feel horrid inside and we start not to like ourselves very much. If that's how it is, then we need some help to put things right, so we can be happy and free again.

Over the 'Slaves to sin' sign put up a long piece of paper with the word 'Jesus' written downwards on it, so that you have made a cross, with 'Jesus' crossing out the 'Slaves to sin'. As you do this, explain how Jesus is the one we need to help us, and what he can do is set us free from being slaves to sin! When we decide to follow Jesus, and let his life fill our living, we don't have to live like slaves any more. We are free to work with other people instead of against them all the time. We are free to see that being kind and thoughtful and honest *feels* good because it *is* good. We find that it's more fun to help other people and make them feel better, instead of making them feel sad and frightened.

Now, if we do something selfish, we find we want to put it right quickly and get on with enjoying life again. It's great to be free, instead of being a slave!

Praying

We pray for all people who are slaves to sin,
whether they are children or grown-ups.
We want them all to know you, Jesus,
and we want you to set them free,
so they can live good lives and be happy.

Activities

On the sheet there are instructions for making a slavery chain. The children will need a packet of paper chain strips, or you can make your own from strips of coloured paper and glue. Before they are glued into a chain, the different examples of sin are written on to the links. When the chains are long enough to wear, the children can hang them around their necks, breaking them apart as they pray for Jesus to set free those people who are slaves to sin.

GOLD PANNERS

Aim: To look at what it means to put God first in our lives.

Starter

Prepare fourteen sheets of paper as shown below, and arrange them in the right grid but the wrong order. They have to rearrange the letters by sliding the sheets, one move at a time, like those interlocking tiles puzzles. If it gets too frustrating they can cheat and simply arrange them by the number guide so that they end up with the correct message.

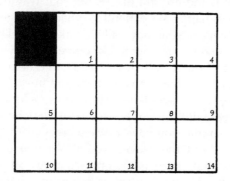

Teaching

Talk about how difficult it can be to get things in the right order of importance in our lives, and how getting the wrong order in life can be a messy business (like opening your bottle of ketchup before shaking it). More seriously, wars can cause a vast number of people to suffer, all because greed or power is a top priority rather than co-operation and sharing.

Read Matthew 10:26-33, to discover what Jesus has to say about what is important, and which things we should take most seriously. Notice how for God all our details – even the number of hairs on our head! – are very important because to him we are so precious. That's why he was willing to go through anything for us, even a tortured death. If Jesus is worth following at all, he is worth following

closely, and to do that we really do need to put him first in our lives.

Look at the passage from Romans 5 to see how following Jesus through death to sin into resurrection life we will be dead to some things and alive to others. Some things will no longer have their hold of importance (like what?), and others will become more and more important to us (like what?).

Praying

True and living God,
I want to put you first in my life
so that all the rest can follow.
I want everything I think and do and say
to express what I know to be true:
that you are the living God
in whom I live and move and have my being.

Activities

On the sheet there is an interview with someone who has taken up caving, so that they can see how taking up some things seriously affects the way you organise your life. This then opens up the practical implications of being a follower of Christ.

THIRTEENTH SUNDAY OF THE YEAR

Thought for the day

As Christ's people we are no longer slaves to sin, but available for righteousness.

Reflection on the readings

2 Kings 4:8-11, 14-16
Psalm 88:2-3, 16-19
Romans 6:3-4, 8-11
Matthew 10:37-42

Some people are unfortunate enough to suffer from vertigo, and find that when they are perched anywhere high there is a terrible urge to throw themselves off into that space beneath them. They have to back away from the edge for fear of plunging to their death. It is as if the space commands them and they have to fight against it. Sin is like that. It pulls us strongly towards our death, and we have a real battle to fight against that urge to go along with its pressurising command. Even while we know that sin is bound to be damaging to us, to those we love, and to our world, our wills and emotions can still drag us over the edge into behaviour which leads to death. As Paul says, it is like being a slave to a tyrannical master, obeying its commands and feeling 'owned' by it. It can seem impossibly difficult to imagine how we could ever break free.

Holding on to Christ, through the cross where that grip of sin has been broken for us, leads us into a completely different place. Sin will still attempt to pull us over, but the power of Christ living in us enables us to back away from the edge as free agents, rather than slaves. It is as if, rather than being drawn to look down into the strangely enticing death-fall all the time, we can enjoy the loftiness of the breath-taking view without fear.

It is interesting that Paul talks of sin earning death, which implies hard, wearying work. That is true: living enslaved to sin drains us of energy and wears us down. In contrast, righteous living is not a heavy duty, but a loving, happy response to a personal free gift.

In today's Gospel we are reminded that anyone responding to one of God's people will actually be responding to their God. This suggests that our behaviour as freed slaves will be obvious to those around us, since we will be behaving differently. Our attitude and outlook will be open and available to good, rather than knotted up with fear and self-absorbed in our own wants and demands. We will be more ready to speak out God's words rather than pandering to what we think people will want to hear, so that we are popular. But it is important to realise that this change is a natural result of responding to God's love, and not an unhealed determined effort in which we remain slaves.

Discussion starters

1. If we think of ourselves as dead to sin and alive to God, how will we react in times of temptation, and when we are despised or ridiculed for our faith?

2. Obviously God wants us to love the people in our families, so how can we expect them to take second place to God in our lives, especially if they themselves are not believers? (Clue: think of a hosepipe fixed on to the water supply, compared to a water butt. How many buckets could get filled in each case?)

All-stage talk

Today we have heard in the reading from Romans that we are to think of ourselves as dead to sin and alive to God through Christ Jesus. What does that mean?

Well, perhaps a few sleeping lions can help. Ask for a few volunteers to play 'sleeping lions', while you and some others try to get them to move. They have to remain as still as they possibly can. Point out that they have to think of themselves as 'asleep' to all those temptations to move which are going on around them. That is rather like us thinking of ourselves being dead to sin. We have to remind ourselves that sin is something which no longer concerns us or has any hold on us.

Ask a few people to say what noises there are in their home at night – any creaks or tickings or chimes. Then draw people's attention to the way we have no difficulty sleeping through these noises, because we know we don't have to worry about them. Some parents will have found that if it isn't your turn to get up and feed the baby you're quite likely to sleep through the crying. You are 'dead' to that sound because you know it isn't anything to do with you. And we are told that we are to think of ourselves as dead to sin.

But it isn't just being dead to sin – it's also being alive to God. What does that mean? Perhaps some people who like chocolate can help us here. Choose a few volunteers and tell them to stand with their backs to you and the congregation. When they think they can detect the presence of chocolate, tell them to raise their hand. Now, as you talk about the way we can always hear what we want to hear, start to open a bar of chocolate, and even though there isn't much sound, and they have their backs to you, it probably won't be very long before they notice, either by hearing or smelling, or both.

That's like us being 'alive' to God. We are going to live as dead to sin, but expectant and interested as far as God is concerned. We will be so tuned in to God that we notice his still, small voice, recognise him in all we see and in those we meet, and live with our hearts and ears and wills turned in his direction all through every day, whatever is going on around us.

All-age ideas

• While the choir or congregation are singing a hymn related to the Cross, have two people at the front of the church holding upright a large wooden cross. In the first verse, three people walk slowly up to the front and kneel at the foot of the cross. In the next verse one of these people is given the cross and carries it, with some difficulty, around the church. By the next verse they come back to the front and return the cross to those who were holding it. They now stand with these people while the cross is given to the next person during the following verses. With the last verse all five are standing facing the cross, holding it with both hands. They all carry the cross high down the centre aisle.

Prayer of the Faithful

Celebrant
Let us pray to our heavenly Father,
who is familiar with our world
and understands our humanity.

Reader
Lord of all, wherever Christians are ridiculed
or persecuted for their faith,
we ask your courage and inner strength;
wherever we are called to be your witnesses,
we ask for the grace to communicate your love.
Wherever love for you has grown cold
we ask to fan the flames again.

Silence

In Christ we can be dead to sin:
and alive to God.

Lord, wherever the human spirit
is ground down by oppression,
and wherever our silence allows injustice
and corruption to flourish,
we ask for deeper compassion and commitment;
we ask for our kingdoms to become your kingdoms,
and the desires of your heart to be ours.

Silence

In Christ we can be dead to sin:
and alive to God.

Lord of all, wherever families are struggling
to stay together,
and wherever there are ongoing arguments
and family feuds,
we ask your anointing for tranquillity and harmony.
Wherever children are unwanted and unloved,
neglected or in danger,
we ask your protection and help.

Silence

In Christ we can be dead to sin:
and alive to God.

Lord, wherever bodies, minds or spirits
are wracked with pain,
or too weak or exhausted to pray,
we ask the bathing love of your presence,
and the practical caring
of hands working in your name.
Wherever there are doubts and the battle is strong,
we ask your empowering and clear guidance.

Silence

In Christ we can be dead to sin:
and alive to God.

Lord of all,
wherever the dying are anxious and afraid,
we ask your peace;
wherever the faithful have passed
from this life into eternity,
we commend them to your unchanging
and everlasting love.

Silence

In Christ we can be dead to sin:
and alive to God.

As we join our prayers with those of Mary,
may we learn from her responsive love:
Hail, Mary . . .

Together in silence,
we name those known to us
who need our prayers.

Silence

Celebrant
Almighty God,
accept the prayers we bring you here,
for the sake of Jesus Christ.
Amen.

TREASURE SEEKERS

Aim: To be introduced to the idea of taking up something hard, and sometimes painful, out of love.

Starter

Play the singing game 'The princess slept for one hundred years', which includes the handsome prince cutting the forest with his sword in order to reach the beautiful princess.

Teaching

Tell the children this story, either reading it to them or preferably memorising the main points and telling it with your own character.

In Africa there was a village, and in the village there lived a girl called Eunice and her three brothers and her mother. Her father had to work in a big town a long way off, so he was not often at home. Every day Eunice and her little brothers went out with their mother, and all the other mothers, to fetch the water, because in their village there were no taps to get their water from. They walked quite a long way out of the village, until they came to a place where the water bubbled up out of the ground. The children played in the water while the mothers lifted down their heavy pots from their heads and filled them with water. Then the water pots were lifted high on to the heads of all the mothers, who were very strong, and everyone walked (more slowly, this time) back to the village, with enough water for the day.

One morning Eunice woke up to find that her mother was very ill. She was hot and shivery, and could not get up. One of the older women in the village came in to sit with her, but the family still needed the water to be fetched. Who could do that? Eunice thought to herself, 'I will get the water today for my mother.'

So she went down with her brothers and the other mothers, carrying the bucket, and when they got to the place where the water bubbled up out of the ground, she filled the bucket up to the brim. It was very heavy to carry, but Eunice kept thinking of her mother at home, and how happy she would be to have the water collected for the day, and somehow that made it easier to keep going. Some of Eunice's friends were playing together and they called out to her, 'Hey, Eunice, put that bucket down and come and play with us!' Eunice loved playing with her friends, but she knew that today it was more important to get the water home to give her mother a drink, and save her worrying. So she called back, 'Not today, I can't. I have the water to carry home.'

It seemed a very long walk back to the village, but at last Eunice reached the house, and carried the water inside. Her mother was lying there, weak and ill, but when she looked up and saw Eunice with the bucket full of water for the day, she smiled, and whispered, 'Well done, my child. God bless you for your kind heart!' Eunice ran and gave her a drink, and wiped her mother's head with some cool water. Suddenly it didn't matter that the bucket had been so heavy to carry, or that her muscles ached. She had carried it out of love.

Praying

Dear Jesus,
you gave up everything for us
because you love us.
Help us to do loving things
for one another
even if they are hard work. Amen.

Activities

On the sheet there is a week's chart for them to fill in when they do something kind for someone else, and there are some pictures of ideas to help them. It would also be nice for the group to do something kind and thoughtful, such as gathering up the litter outside (or inside!) or preparing a song to sing for the rest of the congregation in church.

PEARL DIVERS

Aim: To look at what it means to take up our cross and follow Jesus.

Starter

Follow my leader. The children can take it in turns to be leader, standing in front of everybody and doing various actions that are copied by the group.

Teaching

Show a number of crosses – one that hangs up, one on a neck chain, and a standing one, for instance, and gather from the children the reasons we Christians have a cross in our church and often in our home, and round our necks as well. What happened on a cross that we want to remember? Why is that so important to us? Draw out the fact that Jesus on the cross shows us that he was willing to die out of love for us, so that we could be freed to live as God planned for us, in close friendship with him.

When Jesus was teaching his disciples, he wanted them to know that following him would not always be easy. When we follow someone, we do what they have done. Jesus was willing to give up his life out of love for us. So true followers of Jesus will be the same. They will be so full of love for other people that they will be willing to give up their own selfishness. And that is what the shape of a cross is: a capital I crossed out. (Draw this for them as you say it.) Followers of Jesus do not put themselves first all the time; they think of the needs of other people. They don't push other people around or want everything their own way. Instead, because they love God and other people, they are happier working together with one another.

Jesus does not try and pretend that this will be easy, because he knows we all want to have our own way all the time, and if we are in the middle of a programme we really like, we don't want to stop and help someone else, or change channels so someone else in the family can watch their favourite film. It takes a long time to learn to cross out our selfishness, but the more we do it, Jesus says, the happier people we will become, and it will make God very happy, too.

Praying

Jesus, I know I am sometimes selfish.
   (draw a capital 'I')
Please help me to follow you closely,
crossing out the selfishness
   (cross through the 'I')
and living more lovingly. Amen.
   (look at the shape you have made)

Activities

On the sheet they can draw their own large 'I' and then cross it out, as they say the prayer. There is also a coded puzzle to solve which leads them to Matthew 10:39, and some examples of different areas of possible selfishness to look at.

GOLD PANNERS

Aim: To look at how we can offer ourselves either to sin for evil or to God for righteousness.

Starter

Sit in a circle and pass round a knife or a stone, with each person describing a way it could be used.

Teaching

Just as stones and knives can be used either for good or evil, so can we humans. We'll look first at how our voices can be used. Think of an example of this, perhaps from current news of lies in public places of power, or an ongoing concern such as tobacco promotion, or doorstep sales pressure.

But it is not just our voices. What about other parts of our bodies which can be offered either to sin as an instrument for evil, or to God as an instrument for good? Do we want to offer some parts of our body to God but keep some bits back for sin? How can we use hands, ears, feet, our gifts, our education and our sexuality for good? How you talk about this will depend very much on the age and culture of your group, but it is an excellent opportunity to address life issues which need to be talked through in the Christian context. Try to cultivate an atmosphere of trust, where real concerns can be raised without embarrassment.

Finally look at the Gospel for today, which reinforces God's recognition of every act of kindness and response to his love, however small or hidden.

Praying

Forth in thy name, O Lord, I go,
my daily labour to pursue;
thee, only thee, resolved to know
in all I think or speak or do.

Activities

There is opportunity on the sheet to unpack the difference between wages and a free gift, so they can see how 'slavery to righteousness' is actually a freely given response to a personal free gift of grace. There is also a puzzle which helps reinforce the words of the Gospel.

FOURTEENTH SUNDAY OF THE YEAR

Thought for the day

To all who are weary with carrying heavy burdens in life, Jesus offers rest for our souls and unthreatening relief.

Reflection on the readings

Zechariah 9:9-10
Psalm 144:1-2, 8-11, 13-14
Romans 8:9, 11-13
Matthew 11:25-30

The first of today's readings, from Zechariah, gives us a clear image of peace and humility, as we hear of a king entering in triumph, but on a donkey. It is an image which Jesus made his own, and it speaks of a king totally in touch with the ordinary people and their needs, an unpretentious king who is unimpressed by the worldly idea of wealth and power, and is not in the business of domination and threat, but openness and integrity.

The psalmist pours out a whole list of God's wonderfully supportive and gracious qualities, in the knowledge that this God-king's kingdom is not like the earthly temporary and fickle ones, but everlasting in its goodness.

So when we meet with Jesus in today's Gospel, what we find is completely in keeping with the discernment of those Old Testament writers who had waited on God and trusted him. Jesus' heart goes out to all who are weighed down in their lives, and his welcoming offer is not to do with domination, or strict rules which terrify with their potential for failure. Instead, Jesus shows himself open and unarmed, offering relief and rest for our souls, through becoming joined, or yoked, with his life in the living God.

It is all so simple in contrast with the complexities we struggle to handle when we are not at peace with God. And this very simplicity, while welcomed with joy by anyone ready to hear it, conscious of their failure to achieve it on their own, is also what brings out the childishness in those who petulantly reject God's help, manufacturing one reason after another to justify their rejection. Sadly, it is often those who pride themselves on their learning or mature, independent thinking, who continue to see Jesus' offer of rescue as a threat and an insult to their maturity and success.

Discussion starters

1. When Jesus chose to enter Jerusalem on a donkey, what was he trying to show the people of Israel?

2. What is the difference between childish and child-like behaviour, and why does being childlike make it possible for us to respond to God's wisdom?

All-stage talk

Bring along four bags or cases, labelled 'Worries', 'Guilt', 'Duty' and 'Wants'. Inside each wrap up heavy bundles, labelled appropriately. Here are some ideas:

Worries

• What if it rains?
• They might crash.
• She hasn't got enough money for that bill.
• He's in with a bad lot of friends.
• I might get it wrong and look silly.
• What if we get broken into?

Guilt

• I'm so ashamed
• God can never forgive me for that.
• I'll never be able to put that right.
• It haunts me every day.
• I'll never forgive myself.

Duty

• I should drive myself even harder.
• I just grit my teeth and wait for life to be over.
• I'll do my duty even if it kills me.
• Day off? That would be lazy!

Wants

• They've got one – I want it too.
• I wish I was rich and could buy whatever I liked.
• I want more freedom.
• I want to look like . . .
• I'd be happy if only I had a . . .

Talk about how hard it is to struggle along carrying heavy shopping bags, or loads of kit and books for school, or a delivery of newspapers, or a supposedly portable laptop computer and printer. Who has ever found their load after school too heavy and given it to someone else (like Mum or Dad!) to carry home, so they can be free to run and play? We all find that carrying heavy loads makes our arms ache, and slows us down. We all enjoy it when we can put that heavy load down, and our arms start lifting up into the air, because they suddenly feel so light!

Today we heard Jesus giving us a wonderful offer. He said, 'Come to me all you who carry heavy loads and I will refresh you. Take my yoke upon you and learn from me, for I am gentle and humble in heart, and you will find rest for your souls. For my yoke is easy and my burden is light.' They are such lovely words to hear for any one of you who feels that you are lugging along heavy loads in your life. Let's look at some of the heavy loads we carry.

Struggle along with the four bags, and read their labels. These are some of the most common heavy loads we carry. What is inside them to make them so heavy? With the help of some volunteers open up each bag in turn. Different people can read out the kind of things that weigh us down so much. It's strange that even wanting things can weigh us down, but it's true. Whenever we are not at peace, we are carrying heavy loads. The good news is that Jesus says we can give those loads to him, so that we are free to play; free to live at peace; free to enjoy life again. (If there is space by a cross, or by the altar, have the bags placed there as you speak.)

When we are yoked, or joined up with Jesus, it is going to be much easier to carry the loads we need, and unnecessary to carry the ones that weigh us down so much.

All-age ideas

• If you have young people present, or the young at heart, play 'Sanctify' – one of the songs from the Delirious? album *King of Fools*, as it deals with the problem of wanting one thing and doing another.

• Before or after the service have someone with a broom-handle who can let some of the children and young people try out being yoked up with them, to see how the yoke helps them do exactly what the partner is doing, without effort.

Prayer of the Faithful

Celebrant
Our loving God is here,
attentive to his children.
Let us pray to him now.

Reader
Father, we pray that your Church
may always be open to receive your love;
keep us swept clear of pomposity,
complacency or self-righteousness;
let us come humbly and simply into your presence
and wait on you,
knowing our dependence on you,
and rejoicing in it.

Silence

As you have called us:
Lord, we come to you.

Father, we pray for all world leaders
and their governments;
for the strength of authority
comes not through force and domination
but through co-operation and mutual respect;
we pray for greater consideration
of the needs of one another and of our planet,
and a desire to right past wrongs and injustices.

Silence

As you have called us:
Lord, we come to you.

Father, we pray for a growing maturity
in our thinking and our loving
that enables us to be childlike;
we pray for healing from all the damage
that prevents us from growing up;
we pray that our children in this church
may be helped to grow strong,
and we thank you for all we learn from them.

Silence

As you have called us:
Lord, we come to you.

Father, we pray for all who cry out for rest and relief,
all who are carrying terrible burdens
that weigh them down,
all whose poverty denies them the chance of healing,
all whose wealth denies them
the chance of knowing their need of you.

Silence

As you have called us:
Lord, we come to you.

Father, we pray for those
who die unprepared to meet you,
and for all who have died recently,
both those well known to us
and those dying unknown and unnoticed
all over the world.

Silence

As you have called us:
Lord, we come to you.

We pray with Mary,
who feels for us in our weariness:
Hail, Mary . . .

In silence now,
we bring our particular petitions
to our loving Father.

Silence

Celebrant
Heavenly Father,
we rejoice in your abundant love for us,
and ask you to hear our prayers,
for the sake of Jesus Christ.
Amen.

TREASURE SEEKERS

Aim: To know that we can tell Jesus all that weighs us down, and he will help us.

Starter

Bring along five or six items which the children can pick up as they choose which is the lightest and which is the heaviest. Make this fairly obvious weight-wise, except that the shapes and weights don't necessarily match up, so they might get a surprise when they expect a large item to be the heaviest and it isn't.

Teaching

Have one of the leaders struggling in with several bulky, heavy parcels. You greet them and comment on how weighed-down they look, and they agree, gratefully letting you unload them so they can feel better and sit down comfortably. They ask what we're doing today, and the children can tell them about choosing the heaviest and lightest parcel. Today we are thinking about carrying heavy loads.

Some loads we can see (like these parcels) but some we can't see – like when we are feeling very worried about something, and we carry our worry around with us and it feels quite heavy. (Pick up a parcel and hold it as you speak.) What kind of things do we sometimes worry about a lot? Ask the children to share their ideas about this, and share with them some of the things you worry about as well, so that you are all in it together.

The lovely thing about knowing Jesus is that we can tell him those worries, and ask him to help sort them out with us. (Have someone take the parcel from you.) And just talking it over with our friend Jesus makes it feel less worrying.

Another load we can't see is being frightened about something. (Pick up another load.) We carry that fear around with us and it can make us scared and sad. What kind of things are we scared and frightened about? Once again, share these together. Well, what's good about knowing Jesus is that we can tell him our fears, and ask him to help us be brave. (Have this load taken from you.) Jesus is never too busy to listen to us, and we can talk to him any time and anywhere. He will always be there for us because he loves us, and doesn't want us struggling along with heavy loads all the time – he wants us to be free to skip and run and play!

Praying

Heavy loads, heavy loads,
  (pretend to carry them)
'I'm worried!' and 'I'm scared!'
  (head in hands, then shake with fright)
'Come to me,' says Jesus,
  (beckon)
'and I will give you rest!'
  (arms out, palms up)
Thank you, thank you, Jesus!
  (jump up and down and clap hands)
You really are the best!
  (both hands up in air)

Activities

Give each child a stone to decorate with paint or stickers which they can put on the mat which they make from the sheet. Then they can use their 'worry stone' to remind them to talk things over each day with their friend Jesus.

PEARL DIVERS

Aim: To look at how being yoked to Jesus helps us.

Starter

Ask the children to get into pairs and fasten their ankles together with scarves. Everyone can try walking about three-legged, or you could stage a three-legged race.

Teaching

Talk together about what it felt like to be joined up together like that. Draw out the point that it made us all learn to work together with one another very well, because when we worked together we got along really well, without falling down.

Now show the children some pictures from library books of oxen yoked together. Explain how farmers will train a young animal by yoking it up

with a good, strong ox who knows what to do. That helps the young ox to learn. Also, the load is not so heavy if two or more animals are sharing it. (You could demonstrate this with two people carrying a handle each of a heavy bag.)

Get a broom handle and lie it along the shoulders of two children. They each hold it in place with both hands. Tell one child to be the leader, and see if they can lead the other child carefully around using the yoke to guide and support.

Now read to the children what Jesus said to all those who are feeling heavily loaded down in life, and they will be able to pick up on the way being yoked to Jesus helps us learn his ways and eases the loads of life.

What are the loads we carry in life? As you talk about some of these, you can pray for people carrying them in a time of intercession.

Praying

Jesus, in you I find rest and peace.
I can talk to you about anything –
my worries and my fears,
my happiness and sadness,
my anger and disappointment.
You always listen and you always understand.

Activities

There is a matching activity on the sheet, working out which loads belong to which bags, and a half-drawn picture to complete symmetrically of oxen ploughing a field. They can also make a load-shaped display of prayer concerns, combining pictures and their own prayers, which can be placed in church to help people pray during the week. Ideas for pictures and prayers are given on the sheet.

GOLD PANNERS

Aim: To look at how we need to be childlike to accept God's love, but not childish.

Starter

Animal, plant, sweet. In a circle someone starts by saying, 'If this person were an animal they would be a . . . ; if they were a plant they would be a . . . ; and if they were a sweet they would be a . . .' Then everyone has to guess who it is. You can either stick to the people in the group for this, or have particular categories such as singers, sports personalities or film stars.

Teaching

We were able to work out some of those (or not, as the case may be!) because the animals, plants and fruit were chosen to sum up what the particular person is like. In the time that the book of Zechariah was written, certain animals had certain images that the people would relate to. A horse, for instance, was a symbol of war and power, and a donkey was a symbol of peace and humility. Read the passage from Zechariah, noticing how the image of a donkey is used, and what idea is being put across by this about the promised Messianic king. Remind them of how Jesus chose to enter Jerusalem many years later, so they can see the connection.

Look at the qualities of God which are listed in Psalm 144, and notice how these link up with the expected Messiah and Jesus riding into Jerusalem. At this point also read Matthew 11:28-30, as this, too, expresses those same qualities in action. (It is a passage that they could learn by heart to have with them at all times.)

Praying

The Lord is gracious and compassionate,
slow to anger and rich in love.
The Lord is good to all;
he has compassion on all he has made.
My mouth will speak in praise of the Lord.
Let every creature praise his holy name
for ever and ever.

(From Psalm 144)

Activities

On the sheet there are animals as symbols associated with God to think about, and they will need dictionaries to look at the difference between 'childish' and 'childlike'. There is also some help with learning Matthew 11:28 by heart, for which they will need a few balloons.

FIFTEENTH SUNDAY OF THE YEAR

Thought for the day

Seed of God's word, sown in good soil, watered by his rain and warmed by his sunlight, produces a good crop of spiritual fruit.

Reflection on the readings

Isaiah 55:10-11
Psalm 64:10-14
Romans 8:18-23
Matthew 13:1-23

We have a wonderful picture of God's faithfulness given to us every year in the round of the seasons, as the bare earth receives the winter weathering before the seed is sown and the growing begins, leading through the warmth of summer to the gathering-in of the harvest in autumn. It is still relatively recently that all this was basic to our everyday lives, and we still get nostalgic about it, even if we have lived all our lives in the centre of a city.

It is not surprising that many biblical images are to do with this annual round and the desperately important blessing of rain. Today's passages from Isaiah and Psalm 64 give us an ancient lesson on the water cycle, beautifully and wonderingly observed. Isaiah uses it to illustrate the way God's word has a habit of being accomplished, working its way down into the human condition and providing all that is necessary for what has been spoken to come about. It may sometimes look unpromising, but, then, so do bare earth furrows unless you have lived through a previous summer. We sometimes need to trust Isaiah's words during our darker, barer seasons of life.

In today's Gospel we are aware that Jesus has been out walking this same earth we inhabit, watching the yearly sowing of seed and hearing the squabbling birds. It speaks to him vividly of the different ways we all respond to the word of God, and, prophet that he is, he tells it out straight as it is. Leaving people to puzzle over his story is an important part of the process of sowing the seed. It gives that seed a good start, wriggling it well down into the hearer's being as curiosity rolls it around before sleep or in conversation in the firelight. What is this seed which takes root and grows fruit in good soil? What was he really telling us? Growing opposition to Jesus' ministry also makes the parable a safer method of teaching. Perhaps it will serve to soften up the ground of defensive hearts in a less threatening way.

The disciples are surprised to hear Jesus using such a learned method of teaching for them and the crowds. Unlike the crowds, they are at least able to ask him to spell it all out clearly for them. Inevitably, they and we are bound to ask ourselves serious questions about where we are, and how we are responding to the word of God. Presumably the ideal is for the Church to be filled with seed growing in good soil, for all that requires is to be open and receptive, nourished and developed in the watering and warming of God's love. And those of us who prepare the ground need to check that we are providing the very best environment for the seed of God's word to grow strong.

Discussion starters

1. What makes some people more receptive to the word of God than others? Is it outside our control, or to do with our chosen attitudes and priorities?

2. Is it easier to believe in a creative sustaining God when we are in a rural setting, living with a rural economy? Is God relevant in the urban sprawl?

All-stage talk

You will need a seed tray filled with seed compost, some large-sized seeds, a dibber (to poke holes for the seeds) and a cloth bag of pearl barley. You will also need to arrange for a broom to sweep up the scattered barley after the talk. Lay down one large piece of paper to represent a rocky patch, and a few footsteps to represent a stony path.

You might like to play a snatch of the *Gardeners' World* theme tune at the beginning, as you set out the seed tray and compost on a table and invite a couple of keen gardeners to demonstrate planting. As the gardeners work, talk with them about why the seed planted like this is more likely to be successful than if we just shake the seeds outside.

Today we heard a story, or parable, that Jesus told, which was all about seeds being sown, and the best growing conditions. Of course, it wasn't just about seeds being planted and growing. Parables are stories with secrets inside, and the secret of this story is that it was really all about us, and how we respond to God's word when we hear it. This is how it works.

Where Jesus lived, it was very rocky, and the farmers had fields with bare rock showing here and there (put down the paper), and stony roads that went right through the middle (put down the footprints). They ploughed the earth in long furrows, like we did here in the seed tray, only much bigger of course, and then the person sowing the seed walked up and down the furrows sowing the seed like this. (Demonstrate with your bag of pearl barley, scattering the seed to left and right.) The problem is that not all the seed goes in the nice soil you have prepared. When God's word is spoken, we are not always ready to accept it. Let's look at where some of those seeds have landed.

Involve a volunteer to look at the stony path and stand over any seeds they find there. Sometimes we read or hear God's teaching and we're more like a stony path than good soil. It just goes in one ear and out of the other, and we hardly notice what we've heard. We might sit here for the readings and our thoughts fly in, like birds, and take away God's message so we don't even remember what was said.

What about the rocky ground? (Send a volunteer there.) Sometimes we hear God's message and get really keen, and take on far too much far too early, so, like plants growing up on rocky soil, we haven't got good roots. We burn ourselves out and drop away.

What about the soil next to the rock? (Send a volunteer there.) Lots of weeds grow here, so there's a lot of competition for the seeds. Sometimes we hear God's message, but there are so many other things going on in our lives, which we consider important, that the really important message of God gets choked and crowded out.

But all the rest is in good soil. We are like good soil when we listen to God's teaching carefully, think about it and what it means, and then live with it. That way we shall certainly grow and produce a good harvest. Let's check this week that we are taking good notice of God's words to us, and giving him proper space and time, so that we grow in his love.

All-age ideas

- For one of the flower arrangements today include plenty of wheat, a bowl of seed and a loaf of bread. Entitle it with Matthew 13:23.

- Invite a group of people to write Bible references on small pieces of paper, and for people to hand these out from baskets, as if they are sowing the word of God. Everyone can be encouraged to look up and read their text each day during the week. Here are some suggestions for texts: Matthew 11:28-30; Matthew 10:29-31; Matthew 10:39; Matthew 11:4-6; Matthew 9:36-38; Matthew 9:28; Matthew 7:7-8; Matthew 7:24.

Prayer of the Faithful

Celebrant
Gathered together as the people of God,
and attentive to his will, let us pray.

Reader
Heavenly Father, may your words of truth
take root in our hearts and grow to rich maturity.
May we hear your will for us and act upon it;
may we take seriously our responsibility
to encourage and nurture one another in faith
at every age and every stage.

Silence

Eternal truth, living God:
your word is life and strength.

Heavenly Father, may every act of selfless giving
and every search for truth
be richly blessed and rewarded;
Disturb assumptions and lead many
to ponder more deeply
the spiritual dimension of their lives.
May the word of God reach all
who are ready to receive it,
and let us set no boundaries here
as to who they might be.

Silence

Eternal truth, living God:
your word is life and strength.

Heavenly Father, make our homes
places of love and growth,
welcoming to all who visit them,
and accepting and forgiving
to all who are nurtured there.
Help us through the quarrels and heartaches
and remind us to honour one another
as your cherished ones.

Silence

Eternal truth, living God:
your word is life and strength.

Heavenly Father, may all whose bodies,
souls or minds are aching
know the comforting and strengthening power
of your companionship,
and the healing work of your love.
May we be more ready to support
and befriend one another
through the difficult times,
in the name and love of the God we worship.

Silence

Eternal truth, living God:
your word is life and strength.

Heavenly Father, we pray for all
who are making the journey through physical death,
as they put down earthly things
and wake to your presence.

Bring us all to share with them
your life in all its fullness.

Silence

Eternal truth, living God:
your word is life and strength.

We pray with Mary,
whose faith grew abundantly:
Hail, Mary . . .

In the silence of a living faith,
we pray for our own needs and cares.

Silence

Celebrant
Merciful Father,
we thank you for providing for us
and for blessing us so richly,
and ask you to accept our prayers,
through Jesus Christ.
Amen.

TREASURE SEEKERS

Aim: To know that God sends the rain to water the
land and make things grow.

Starter

A rainy game. You will need either two tape recorders,
so that you can play 'sunny' music from one and
'rainy' music from the other, or two different types
of sounds, such as a rainstick and a xylophone.
One of the leaders holds a large golfing umbrella.
Play the sunny and the rainy music or sounds to
the children. Whenever they hear the sunny sound,
they skip about in the sunshine, and whenever
they hear the rainy sound, they run to take shelter
under the umbrella.

Teaching

Start with this puzzle song about water, the children
joining in with the chorus. (See Appendix, page 269,
for the music.)

1. You can drink it, swim in it,
   cook and wash up in it,
   fish can breathe in it –
   what can it be?

   It's water!
   God has provided us water!
   Water of life.

2. It's as hard as rock,
   yet it flows down a mountain,
   and clouds drip drops of it –
   what can it be?

3. It's as light as snowflakes
   and heavy as hailstones,
   as small as dewdrops
   and big as the sea.

Show the children a large cut-out cloud, and talk with them about what it feels like to be out in the rain, and what they wear in the rain. What happens to the ground when it rains? Talk about puddles and sloppy mud. What happens to the plants and flowers when it rains? Show the children a daisy or buttercup, still attached to its root, and tell them how the plant drinks up the water through the roots, and that helps it to grow. After a long time without rain the grass looks all dry and brown, but after rain everywhere is lovely and green again.

God sends the rain so that everything can live and grow. We all need the rain – we couldn't live without it! Rain is one of the many ways God showers us with good gifts.

Praying

This is a water cycle prayer as it goes round and round!

Thank you, God, for sending rain,
pitter, patter, pitter, patter,
it makes the grass all green again,
pitter, patter, pitter, patter,
it makes the fruit and veggies grow,
pitter, patter, pitter, patter,
we all need water to live, and so . . .
pitter, patter, pitter, patter,
thank you, God, for sending rain!

Activities

Using the picture on the sheet the children can make a water cycle wheel. They will need to stick it on to thin card and poke a stick or pencil through the middle as shown. They can also have shiny paper raindrop shapes to tie on to string, which they can shake about as they come into church as a refreshing shower of rain. (Arrange this with whoever is leading the worship in church.)

PEARL DIVERS

Aim: To know the parable of the sower and the seed, and its meaning.

Starter

If you are able to go outside, see how many different looking leaves or plants you can find in a patch the size of a hula hoop (not the eating sort!). If this is not practical, bring along a number of garden plants that have gone to seed, and harvest the seeds together in various labelled envelopes which can be taken home and planted, or offered to the rest of the congregation after the service.

Teaching

Beforehand prepare a cloth bag like this:

Use some of the seed gathered in the starter activity, or seeds out of a packet, to show the children how you sow seeds in some earth. Then, as long as they have sunlight and water, they will grow. One of the stories Jesus told was about a farmer and what happened to the seed he sowed in his field. As in the all-stage talk, explain how the fields were full of rocky places (put down some sheets of paper) and there were stony footpaths going across them (put down some footprints).

Place some pearl barley into your cloth bag, and show the children the way farmers in Jesus' country sowed the seed at that time. They walked up and down the field, scattering the seed in handfuls to the left and the right. (They can all try miming this, up and down the room.) It didn't always land on the good, well-prepared soil, though.

In Jesus' story, some of the seed fell on the stony path, where the birds flew down and pecked it up. (They all fly across, cheeping, and pick up the seed on the stony path.)

Some seed fell on the rocky places, where it shot up very fast and then, because it didn't have deep roots, it shrivelled up in the midday sun. (They all crouch down and grow very tall until you show a big yellow sun, at which point they all shrivel up and fall down.)

Some seed fell among thorny weeds at the edges of the field. As it grew, the big tough weeds crowded round it so it never got going. (Name some children as wheat and some as thorny weeds. They all crouch down close together, and the weeds crowd the wheat so that it can't grow properly. No hurting allowed.)

Some seed fell into the good, well-prepared soil that the farmer had ploughed. And here the seed was able to grow up strong and tall, producing a fantastic harvest. (Everyone crouches down and grows up strong and tall, opening out their fingers to be the crop.)

And Jesus didn't tell the people what that story meant. He let them puzzle over it.

Put some quiet music on, and send the children to pick up all the seed that is on the floor, as they puzzle over what the story means.

Praying

Lord Jesus,
some of the things you say
are hard to understand.
But I do know one thing –
God loves us and looks after us
whether we understand everything or not.

Activities

On the sheet the children are helped to understand the meaning of the parable, and also what a parable is.

GOLD PANNERS

Aim: To explore the meaning of the parable of the growing seed, and its relevance to their own life.

Starter

Stage a quick music jury game, playing snatches of current releases, and asking each person to respond either with one of those trumpets you get as stocking fillers, or a whoopee cushion, as appropriate.

Teaching

Point out that we all respond differently to particular music, and to everything in life, including one another. (Which is just as well, or we'd all be fighting for the same partner!) Today we are going to be looking at a parable Jesus told which is really about how we respond to God. The scene is set for us in a passage from Isaiah, which we will look at first.

Read Isaiah 55:10-11 together, picking up on the way the rain comes down, does its job and then goes back to the clouds. The job only gets done because the earth is able and ready to receive the rain and use it. (They may have come across the term 'humus', whose earthy connections are important in the word 'humility'. Humility is rather like being earth, which is open to the sky.)

Before you look at Jesus' parable in Matthew 13, recap on what a parable is – a story with a hidden, deep meaning. Then read Matthew 13:1-9. Brainstorm about the possible meaning, keeping track of the ideas on a sheet of paper, with the main images

listed: sower, seed, stony path, rock, thorns and good soil, before reading the next section of the Gospel, which is the interpretation (Matthew 13:18-23).

Praying

True and living God,
you alone have the word of life
that I need.
All I am interested in is the real truth.
And that's you.

Activities

There is an opportunity on the sheet to record some of the points made in the discussion, and take these into a practical understanding of what various possible responses will mean in their lives. This may well lead into intercessory prayer for people they know and are concerned about.

SIXTEENTH SUNDAY OF THE YEAR

Thought for the day

God's justice is always blended with mercy and loving kindness, so that we have real hope.

Reflection on the readings

Wisdom of Solomon 12:13, 16-19
Psalm 85:5-6, 9-10, 15-16
Romans 8:26-27
Matthew 13:24-43

We are usually quick to complain if something is unfair, provided we or our loved ones happen to be on the losing end. Most shoppers will more readily point out short-changing than over-changing. We watch our children's developing sense of fairness with wry sympathy as they experiment with changing the rules in their favour whenever they start to sense things going against them. It takes maturity to accept fairness whether we gain from it or not. Also, the more complex the situation, the less clear it is to see what is actually fair. Our whole lengthy judicial system is built on the recognition of this.

The Old Testament writers, contemplating God's nature and open to his truth, could discern that in the eternal Being of all truth, justice by itself would be insufficient, and was in fact softened with the compassionate quality of mercy. Mercy can only come from one who has the power, right and authority to punish, since it involves waiving one's right, or even the absolute justice of deserved punishment, in the light of loving concern for the wrong-doer. It is this blend of justice and merciful loving kindness which is a hallmark of the nature of our God.

For a race of beings who know all too well their capacity for making stupid mistakes and deliberate wrong choices, this is all very good news which makes us able to have hope. If we are brave enough to look candidly at our lives we can easily see that justice alone would leave us in a pretty poor state. We would all be poked to death by accusing fingers of absolute fairness accumulated over a good few years of blundering and sin. There would be no hope for us at all.

We catch a glimpse of this inevitable condemnation when we think of the way we are often particularly harsh and critical ourselves about other people's failings which are similar to our own, or about faults we feel we have managed to overcome. What causes this is a large helping of self-righteousness, fuelled by a sense of fairness but lacking in mercy. Thankfully, God holds his love for us as paramount in all his dealings with us, as the life and death of Jesus clearly shows.

In the passage from Romans, Paul's whole argument is grounded in the certainty that we are ultimately safe in the hands of our God, and in Jesus' parable of the wheat and darnel we have a tender picture of God's loving forbearance tempering his justice. How can we, who claim to love such a God, do other than follow this example in our own dealings? Revenge of any sort must be out for us, as must a rigidity of fairness which refuses to look at each individual situation through the eyes of compassion. It is not for us to take God's judgement into our own incapable hands, but to recognise with humility that we all stand condemned, were it not for the amazing merciful love of God, which has dropped the charges and set us free.

Discussion starters

1. How would you answer someone who took all the terrible natural disasters as evidence that God is not merciful but cruel?

2. Can mercy sometimes prevent us from growing up and facing our responsibilities?

All-stage talk

Borrow and bring along one of those toys (Polly Pocket or Mighty Max) which look like a plain box and hold inside a whole miniature world.

Show everyone the toy, and explain that today we heard another of those parables which Jesus told. Parables are a bit like these toys, because they are stories which have secret meanings inside. You need to open up the story to find the meaning. (Open the toy.) First of all, let's look at the story Jesus told.

If you have an OHP you can illustrate the story using cut-outs of weeds and wheat, and the evil enemy based on the pictures below, as these will show up in silhouette on the screen.

Remind everyone of the story, using volunteers to be the farmer sowing his seed (accompanied by music from *The Archers*), and the evil enemy creeping into the field at night to sow the weeds (accompanied by everyone doing a pantomime hiss). When the farmer finds that his field is sprouting loads of weeds as well as wheat, he is faced with a choice (hold a question mark in a thought bubble over his head).

All the servants say, 'Shall we pull the weeds out for you?' (Have this written on a speech bubble so everyone, or a small group, can say it together.)

The farmer shakes his head. (He does.) He knows that if he pulls all the weeds up now he might pull out some of the wheat as well, and he certainly doesn't want to lose any of his wheat. So instead he decides to let both the wheat and the weeds grow together until harvest time, when the weeds can be gathered up and burnt, and the wheat harvested and put in the barn.

That's the parable Jesus told. What's the secret meaning of it?

Here's a clue. The field is the world, and we can all see that in our world there is a lot of good, but also a lot of evil. Why doesn't God burst out of heaven and stop all the evil in the world straight-away, and punish the people who get away with doing cruel and terrible things?

The parable gives us the answer.

If he did that while life is still going on – while the wheat and weeds are still growing – some good might get lost or damaged. It is because God cares about us so much that he won't risk anything that would cause us lasting harm. There's time enough for punishment when the world comes to an end. Then all that is good and honest and kind and thoughtful will be gathered up safely for ever. All that is mean and selfish, cruel and greedy will be completely destroyed for ever. We can trust our God to know the right time to punish and the right time to hold back, because he always acts with love and mercy as well as justice.

All-age ideas

- Make a flower arrangement with wheat and weeds.

- The speech on mercy from Shakespeare's *The Merchant of Venice* has relevance for today's theme, if you have someone with the gift of reading it well. If the reader is appropriately dressed in legal costume, the significance of merciful justice, compared with condemnatory judgement, is highlighted.

Prayer of the Faithful

Celebrant
Let us draw near to the just and merciful God,
and pour out our concerns
for the Church and for the world.

Reader
Lord our God,
as we join the unending cycle of prayer on our planet,
turning through time and space,
we rejoice in your upholding,
your mercy and forgiveness.
In all our small-mindedness
we ask your inbreathing,
so that we learn to look with your vision
and act with your wideness of compassion.

Silence

God of mercy:
hear us as we pray.

Lord our God,
be present at all meetings and negotiations,
where feelings run high,
and many lives are profoundly affected
by the decisions made.
We pray for real communication
which listens to needs and appreciates difficulties,
so that we may live on this earth together
in harmony and peace.

Silence

God of mercy:
hear us as we pray.

Lord our God,
we pray for this neighbourhood
and the particular problems it has;
for communities split apart by conflict
or crushed by tragedy;

we pray for those involved with court proceedings;
may our judicial system uphold your principle
of justice with mercy.

Silence

God of mercy:
hear us as we pray.

Lord our God,
we pray for those who have a raw deal in this life;
for those with ongoing health problems,
and all who are caught up in war and deprivation.
We pray for a just and realistic
sharing of our resources,
and courage, support and healing for all who suffer.

Silence

God of mercy:
hear us as we pray.

Lord our God, we pray for those who have died
and now see their lives as they really are;
we pray for your mercy on them,
and thank you for all their acts
of goodness and love.

Silence

God of mercy:
hear us as we pray.

We pray with Mary
who was filled with the Holy Spirit:
Hail, Mary . . .

God our Father knows our needs;
let us pray to him now
for our own intentions.

Silence

Celebrant
Father, in thankful love
we ask you to hear our prayers,
for the sake of Jesus Christ.
Amen.

TREASURE SEEKERS

Aim: To know that God is fair and kind.

Starter

Split an apple or a bar of chocolate up among everyone so that it is exactly fair, and everyone gets a piece if they want it. In a time of news-sharing, go round the circle in order, so that no one is left out and all are asked if they would like to share some of their news. Don't let anyone get an extra go just because they are noisy or attention-seeking.

Teaching

You will need four puppets, or you can make your own from old socks or wooden spoons. You don't need four hands, though – just pick up the one which is talking at any one time. One puppet is baby-sitting, and trying to give out biscuits fairly, but two of the 'children' are so demanding and noisy that they end up getting more than the other. The third child complains that it isn't fair. Why should they get more just because they're noisy?

Stop the puppets and ask the children what they think should happen. Then have a nearly-action-replay with the baby-sitter telling the noisy ones that the biscuits will be shared out fairly, which means one each, and being noisy won't make any difference.

Now have the puppets being a parent and children buying an ice-cream each. The parent tells the children to be very careful not to drop them. One child does drop the ice-cream, and cries about it. The parent is sympathetic, and says, 'You can share mine!'

God is like a loving mum or dad who is always fair, but very kind as well, and helps us out when we make mistakes.

Praying

Jesus, I'm glad you are always fair.
You love us all, and don't leave anyone out.
And when we make mistakes
you help us put things right again.

Activities

They can give everyone in the picture on the sheet the same things, so it is fair. This can either be done by drawing the items in, or you could provide separate, pre-cut items which they stick on.

PEARL DIVERS

Aim: To know the parable of the wheat and weeds, and its meaning.

Starter

Play a ball (or bean bag) game, first with very unbalanced sides, and then fairly, with equally matched teams.

Teaching

Remind the children of what a parable is, by showing them all one of those sweets which has a surprise in the centre. (Cut it open.) After the story they will get one each, and as they suck on the sweet, they will get to the centre; as they think about Jesus' parable, they'll get to the real meaning of it.

For this story the children will be responding in a particular way whenever certain words are mentioned.

- Farmer – *'Ooh ahh!'*
- Enemy – *'Sssssssss!'*
- Wheat – Rub tummy and say, *'Yum yum!'*
- Weeds – *'Yuk!'*

Make sure you bring all these words into the story fairly regularly, telling it in your own words or following the suggestion from the all-stage talk.

Now give out the sweets as you talk together about what the parable might mean.

Praying

Lord God,
I can see there is evil in this world,
as well as all the good.
Protect us from all evil
and bring us safely to heaven.

Activities

On the sheet there is a pizza to divide very fairly between six children who all like different parts of it. And there is a quiz for them to discover how fair and merciful they are themselves.

GOLD PANNERS

Aim: To know that God's nature is to be both just and merciful.

Starter

Give out a number of crimes, and decide on appropriate punishments for them. Here are some crime ideas:

- Taking the rest of a chocolate biscuit pack that had only had two biscuits previously eaten.
- Borrowing a favourite sweater and getting a mark on it.
- Copying your essay and getting a higher mark for it than it originally got.
- Playing football in the street and accidentally breaking a neighbour's stained-glass window.
- Playing a dud tape in a friend's video so that it dirties the heads and won't play clearly.

Teaching

If you are found guilty in a court, a punishment has to be decided on which is fair and just. Today we are looking at where our desire to be fair comes from.

First read the passage from Wisdom of Solomon. What has the writer discovered about God's nature? That he is both just and kind-hearted; that from his position of power and strength he chooses to act with lenience and mercy. If you have time read part of Psalm 85 as well, which echoes the realisation of what God is like. Talk together about how people came to discover this, before they had met Jesus. (Their own experiences of life, and the great events of the nation, such as the escape from Egypt.)

Since God is obviously just, how come there is so much evil and suffering in the world, much of which seems to go unchecked?

Then look at the parable Jesus told about the wheat and weeds, where, out of loving concern, the evil is allowed to continue at the moment, but it will not be so for ever. Ultimately, all that is good will be saved, and all that is evil will be destroyed. And in one sense, all of us belong to the kingdom now as well as then. God's people are called to right injustice and 'champion the unwanted' here and now.

Praying

Heaven shall not wait
for the poor to lose their patience,
the scorned to smile,
the despised to find a friend:
Jesus is Lord;
he has championed the unwanted;
in him injustice
confronts its timely end.

(From a song by John L. Bell and Graham Maule
© Copyright 1987 WGRG/Iona Community.)

Activities

On the worksheet there are instances of injustices which need righting, and space to plan possible action. They can also discover where they would stand on the 'mercy line'. Are there any suggestions for action within our families, or within the parish community?

SEVENTEENTH SUNDAY OF THE YEAR

Thought for the day

Jesus, the teacher, enables the ordinary, unlearned people to understand God's wisdom – the eternal laws of his Father's kingdom.

Reflection on the readings

1 Kings 3:5, 7-12
Psalm 118:57, 72, 76-77, 127-130
Romans 8:28-30
Matthew 13:44-52

It is with disarming and endearing humility that Solomon prays, as he stands at the starting line of his reign, overwhelmed by the impossibility of the task ahead and very conscious of his lack of experience and the heaviness of responsibility. It is typically at those times when we are acutely aware of our dependence on God, that God can act with power in our lives. The wisdom which Solomon requests is to do with having a heart which is skilled in listening, so that good can be distinguished from evil. In a world where every situation has many facets and interrelated issues, the gift of wise discernment is desperately needed by all with decision-making authority. And, as God's reply makes clear, to desire such a gift is entirely in keeping with his will.

It is a gift which is increasingly recognised and valued by those in management training, so that look-alike versions are marketed to reproduce the actions while bypassing the more costly genuine listening heart.

In Romans, Paul reminds us that God is on our side, if we are on his. That means he is in no way going to condemn or reject us, and there is nothing at all that can ever separate us from his love.

This knowledge, which is heart knowledge, turns lives upside down and remakes them, alters long-held priorities, and opens up all kinds of possibilities for life-spending. We cannot grasp this truth about God's loving personal relationship with us and remain unchanged. In today's Gospel Jesus gives a whole series of images to help us understand what it is like to glimpse the kingdom of God and enter it.

We are told about the excitement and often the surprise of discovering it, upon which everything we presently value seems so insignificant and temporary in comparison that as a matter of urgency we want to give up all that keeps us from owning such a possession. We are told of the way it grows and spreads with astounding effect, so that not only our own lives but the lives of many others are affected for great and lasting good. We are urged to take this teaching seriously to heart, because the consequences of how we lead our lives here are not insignificant or temporary or a matter of personal taste. It is all much bigger than that, and Jesus does not want his hearers, whom he loves, to reach the end of their earthly lives and find they are totally unprepared for the next phase of life and the consequences of living habitually tied to selfish wants.

He hopes for us to cherish both the ancient wisdom of God's guidance through the law and the prophets, and also the new, heady joy of having God's Spirit breathing through our being with the power and forgiveness that makes living good lives an outpouring of thankfulness to a God whose grace alone makes it possible.

Discussion starters

1. Why do many people feel more comfortable learning about Jesus rather than entering into relationship with him?

2. Does it ring true to us to think of our faith as finding treasure in a field for which we dash off and sell everything we own?

All-stage talk

Bring along something that is precious and old, and something that is precious and new. Choose items which your congregation are likely to relate to. (It could be a well-worn teddy and a new Teletubby for a baby, for instance, or an old stained-glass window in the church and someone's new engagement ring.)

First introduce everyone to the old thing, pointing out why it is so treasured and important and valuable. In our faith there are also ancient things which we as Christians value and treasure, such as the stories in the Old Testament which teach us about our God (for example, creation, Noah's flood, the great escape from Egypt, and the teaching of the prophets), and God's law, the ten commandments given through Moses to the people to help them live well and in line with God's will. Although these are old, ancient things, they are precious to us because they help us get to know God and live as his friends. We don't just throw them out because Jesus has come. Jesus valued them himself, and told his followers to go on valuing them.

Now introduce the new thing, explaining why it is treasured, important and valuable. In our faith there are also new things which we as Christians value and treasure. With the coming of Jesus, we are able to have a completely new kind of friendship

with God that had never before been possible. Through Jesus dying, rising and returning to heaven, we are able to have the gift of God's life breathed into our own lives. That means that every new morning of our lives there are new possibilities in our daily friendship with the living God!

Not only are we looking forward to the coming of God's kingdom at the end of all time – we can also enjoy living in it now. In our Gospel today Jesus gave us some ideas of what the kingdom of God is like. Here is just one of them.

It's like some treasure you might find in a field. (You could have an exciting-looking treasure box there.) You're so excited about this precious treasure that you go and sell everything else you have, just so you can buy the field and own the treasure. Let's think about that. If you found a diamond ring, would you go and sell your house and car and World Cup coin collection to get hold of it? Probably not. You'd only bother to sell your house and car and cherished possessions if the treasure you had found was worth far, far more than all the things you already had. Jesus is saying that knowing God in a loving friendship and living in him each day is actually worth far, far more than anything else you own.

I don't think many of us realise that yet. It's as if we dig up a treasure box, look at it and think, 'Oh, that's interesting – a box of treasure. I'll pop over and look at it sometimes.' Then we bury it again and go home to carry on living in the same old way without realising what we're missing out on. Next time you catch a glimpse of what God is really like, and how incredibly wonderful he really is, commit yourself to doing something about it, so you can enjoy that treasure of living in peace and love with him every day of the rest of your life.

All-age ideas

- Have an arrangement of a treasure box, spade and a sign against it which says, 'What is God worth to you?'

- Have an arrangement of advertisements for jewellery and property taken from magazines with the caption, 'Value: £???'.

Prayer of the Faithful

Celebrant
May the Spirit pray through us
as we try to put into words the longings of our hearts
for the Church and for the world.

Reader
Father, we thank you
for all who have helped us to pray

and to grasp something of your great love and power.
We ask your blessing and empowering
for all who teach and minister in your name;
we ask for our Sunday worship to be an overflowing
of our daily walk with you,
an expression of our deepening love.

Silence

Lord of all creation:
teach us your ways.

Father, we thank you for the beauty and diversity
of the created world we inhabit.
We ask for the wisdom to tend it carefully,
respecting the natural laws and sharing the resources,
listening to the weak as well as the strident,
the poor as well as the affluent and powerful.

Silence

Lord of all creation:
teach us your ways.

Father, we thank you
for the candour and innocence of the very young,
and for the joy of friendship;
for all with whom we share our daily life,
and those we love but seldom meet.
We ask for hearts that are skilled in listening,
so that we discern and respond to the real agendas,
and remember that a conversation
is a two-way event.

Silence

Lord of all creation:
teach us your ways.

Father, we thank you
for the advances in medical knowledge
and the hope of new treatments for many diseases.
We pray for all in medical research
and all whose lives are crippled or disadvantaged
by illness, frailty or damage.
Give comfort and reassurance,
healing, wholeness and peace.

Silence

Lord of all creation:
teach us your ways.

Father, we call to mind
all those we have known and loved
who lived among us and now have died.
We pray for all who made that journey
unnoticed and alone.
We ask that they may all know your mercy
and the everlasting peace and joy of heaven.

Silence

Lord of all creation:
teach us your ways.

We join our prayers with those of Mary,
whose wisdom knew no bounds:
Hail, Mary . . .

Trusting in God's loving understanding,
we pray in silence, now,
for our own particular needs and concerns.

Silence

Celebrant
Father, we rejoice in the treasure of your love,
and ask you to hear our prayers,
for the sake of Christ, our Lord.
Amen.

TREASURE SEEKERS

Aim: To know that finding Jesus is like finding treasure.

Starter

Have a treasure hunt where each child experiences the hunting and the discovering. To do this, wrap each 'treasure' in paper tied with a different coloured piece of wool. Give each child a matching piece of wool and send them off to find their own treasure.

Teaching

Talk about what fun it was to find the treasure. Today we are going to hear a story about finding treasure. It is one of the stories that Jesus told.

There was once a man who was digging in a field. He had been digging for most of the morning when his spade hit something hard. At first he thought it was a big stone. He dug around to find the edge of the stone so that he could lift it out. But this hard stone was straight at the edges and very flat at the top. 'What a funny stone!' thought the man, and he bent down and started to scrape away the earth to uncover it. 'This isn't a stone at all!' said the man to himself. 'It's more of a strong box. Whoever would want to bury a box in the middle of a field? How very strange.'

Very carefully he dug all round the edges of the box and brushed away earth until he could get his spade right underneath it. Slowly the box started to come out of the ground. It was heavy work and the man was using all his strength. 'Nearly there!' he kept saying to himself. 'We're nearly there!' Suddenly the last of the box popped out and the man fell over backwards and rolled over. 'Whoopsadaisy!'

he said and crawled back on his hands and knees to see what he had dug up.

It was a strong wooden box with a clasp to hold it shut. The man opened it a tiny bit and peered inside. 'Slugs and earthworms, what have we here?' he gasped. Inside the box was a gleam of gold. It was full of shiny things and sparkling things. The man was so surprised that he slammed the box shut, and then, very slowly, he opened it again so that the sun shone down on all the treasure and the treasure shone and sparkled back at the sun. At first the man could hardly believe his eyes. But he blinked and the treasure was still there. He pinched himself and it hurt. 'Ouch! It must be real and this must be my lucky day!' shouted the man, and he did a little dance all by himself in the middle of the field.

'Now', thought the man, 'what I need to do is to buy this field, and then the treasure will be mine. But fields cost a lot of money, which I haven't got. Let's see . . . I could sell my table and chairs . . . and my old car . . . and my stamp collection . . . and . . . and . . .' The man worked very hard that afternoon. First he buried the box safely back in the field. Then he went home and got together everything he owned and had a car boot sale. He even sold the car boot – with the rest of the car thrown in for free! Then he went and bought the field.

Full of excitement, the man ran back to his field and started digging. It had been well worth getting rid of everything else. This time the box of sparkling treasure belonged to him, and he would be rich for the rest of his life!

Praying

Jesus, you are the treasure of my life!
With your love I am rich for ever and ever.

Activities

On the sheet there is a treasure chest for the children to fill with shiny, sparkling things. Have ready a selection of different coloured sparkling and shiny paper, and gold-sprayed pasta in different shapes, so that they can stick them into the chest.

PEARL DIVERS

Aim: To know that the kingdom of heaven is like a pearl of great value.

Starter

Pearl divers. Scatter some shells or circles of white paper all over the floor. Starting from the edge of the rock (one side of the room), a few children at a time take a deep breath and 'swim' around collecting as many pearls as they can while their breath holds. They must return to the side of the room before taking a new breath.

Teaching

Real pearl divers are often children, who have to swim deep down to collect the shells. There are only pearls in some of the shells, and usually they are quite small, but from time to time you can find a particularly large and beautiful pearl which is worth a great deal of money. They are sold by the pearl sellers to be made into necklaces and brooches. (If you happen to have a pearl necklace, bring it along to show the children.)

Jesus told a story about a pearl seller. In the market all the pearl sellers would have their trays of pearls on show, and everyone would go round looking at them, holding them up to the light, checking for faults, and haggling over the price. (Haggle over the price with either a child or another leader, until you come to an agreement.)

The merchant in Jesus' story was looking around the market for pearls to buy. (Have a child to be the merchant, and others to be selling their pearls. One is holding a velvet-covered cushion and on it is a beautiful 'pearl' – a marble, perhaps.) The merchant went from one seller to another, testing the pearls in the light, and checking them carefully for faults. One of the sellers had a velvet cushion, and sitting all on its own in the middle of the cushion was the most magnificent pearl the merchant had ever seen. (Everyone draws in their breath in amazement at its beauty.)

This pearl had a glow of life about it, and it was large and perfect. The merchant knew that it was far, far more magnificent than anything else he owned, and he wanted to have this beautiful thing. But he didn't have the money to buy it. He thought of everything else he had; nothing seemed as precious to him as this perfect, glowing pearl. So he asked the pearl seller to keep the pearl by for him, and he went off and sold all his other possessions, just so that he had enough money for this one precious pearl. Then he came back with the money and bought it, and was completely happy with what he now had, because it was worth so much more to him than all the other things he had sold.

Praying

Knowing you, Jesus,
is the best thing in my life.
Nothing else is as important
as your love and faithfulness;
nothing else can give me lasting joy and peace.

Activities

On the sheet the children are shown how pearls are made, and there are instructions for making a pearl in a shell prayer. Each child will need a small lump of self-hardening clay, or some salt dough (two cups of flour, one cup of salt, water to mix).

GOLD PANNERS

Aim: To look at how Jesus' teaching about God's wisdom is different from academic learning.

Starter

Mix a little yeast in with some flour and warm water, knead it and leave it in a warm place to see what happens.

Teaching

Say together the first part of the Lord's prayer, up to 'your kingdom come'. We may say these words every day, but what is it that we are praying for when we ask for the kingdom to come? Today we are going to look at some of the ways Jesus explained it to his followers.

Start with reading the Gospel for today, with all the different pictures that are given to help us understand the nature of the kingdom of heaven, and list the images as they occur, or draw them, with the mustard plant and the yeasty flour grouped together, the treasure and the pearl together, and the fish in the net linked with the wheat and weeds from the previous week.

Talk together about the qualities of the kingdom which are being described in each case. (The way it grows and spreads, the way it is so precious and valuable that once we have found it everything else seems less important to us, and the way good and evil are allowed to continue alongside one another until the final gathering-in, when only what is good will last and be harvested.)

Look at the passage from 1 Kings 3, explaining first that Solomon was young and inexperienced, and about to embark on his reign. What does he ask God for? What is 'wisdom'? (Having a heart that is skilled in listening to the real stories, so that we can distinguish good from evil, and understand what is really going on in a situation.) They will be able to see the link between this and what the Spirit enables us to do: God's wisdom is another way of describing God's Spirit, which leads us into all truth, in harmony with God's will.

Could you get a GCSE or a degree in wisdom? Could you write foolproof exam notes for it? No, it isn't a set of rules or a body of knowledge, but

more like a relationship and an attitude to God and other people. The closer we get to God, the wiser we will become.

Praying

There is none like you,
no one else can touch my heart like you do.
I could search for all eternity long
and find there is none like you.

(From a song by Lenny LeBlanc
© Copyright 1991 Integrity's Hosanna! Music/Kingsway's Thankyou Music.)

Activities

On the sheet there is a script for a sketch which highlights the difficulty of discerning what is right and wrong, good and evil.

EIGHTEENTH SUNDAY OF THE YEAR

Thought for the day

God feeds all who come to him hungry, and we, as the Church, are expected to share in that work.

Reflection on the readings

Isaiah 55:1-3
Psalm 144:8-9, 15-18
Romans 8:35, 37-39
Matthew 14:13-21

Supermarkets are very good at placing 'useless' but attractive things right next to the checkout, so that all the children, wheeled past in their trolleys and bored to distraction as the shopping is loaded, crave what is on display at a time when pressurised parents are most likely to give in! Our whole society is skilled at creating inviting displays of things we could well do without, and which encourage us in all kinds of wrong directions. Whether it is the lure to unnecessary spending in an affluent society, to oblivion or happiness and well-being through drugs or alcohol, or the lure to join guerrilla rebellions in areas of instability and poverty, what we are all after is some gratification which is immediate, and we are prepared to ignore the long-term consequences in order to achieve this.

In today's passage from Isaiah, the prophet speaks

out God's yearning for something better for his beloved people. All these short cuts to satisfaction and fulfilment are going to leave us unfed at the deepest level of our humanity, dissatisfied and craving, but too disillusioned to try the only truly satisfying food for our souls – God himself. Psalm 144 marvels at the qualities of this God and the individualised provision he gives us all.

In his letter to the Romans, Paul speaks with great certainty about how, if we focus on Christ, nothing can get in the way – not only the unnecessary things we create, but even the natural problems of life, which are put in their proper place.

The Gospel for today describes the feeding of five thousand people. It is a clear picture for us of God's delight in feeding all who have come to wait on him and listen to him. These people had deliberately set out into the open country to find Jesus. They sensed that he had things to say which they needed to hear. They sensed that he cared about their welfare and their lasting happiness and peace of mind. Jesus was himself in need of refreshment and comfort when he arrived, in the wake of the tragic death of John the Baptist, but still his compassion reached out to a crowd of people who knew their need of him.

As always, in every situation, Jesus takes whatever is made available to him and uses it for great good which far outstrips our expectations. As always, he involves his followers in the work of preparation and distribution. In this act of bodily feeding Jesus teaches the people in a living, three-dimensional parable, about the real, satisfying feeding for the soul which can be theirs, and which is the Father's delight to provide. In order to receive, we have to know our need enough to go out of our way to seek God and listen to him.

Discussion starters

1. Do the physically and emotionally well-fed have more difficulty recognising spiritual hunger?

2. Are we, and how are we, as the Body of Christ, being broken to feed people God's spiritual food?

All-stage talk

Begin by asking people how they like to spend their pocket money. Invite representatives of all ages to join in this. Has anyone ever spent their money on something which has let them down, or been disappointing, so that they end up wishing they had saved their money? Ask a few people to share their experiences.

It may be that you have had to watch as someone you are fond of wastes their money. You can see that it's all going to end in disappointment, or even

tragedy, but they won't listen to you, and all you can do is stand by and wait to pick up the pieces when it all goes wrong, without saying, 'I told you so'! It's our love for the other person that makes us ache to see them wasting their money like that; because we love them we want better for them than to be sad and disappointed by things that aren't worth buying.

That's how it is with our parent God, who loves us to bits, and aches as he watches as we spend not just our money but our time and our love on things which are not going to be good for us, or satisfying or rewarding. He wants better for us than that. God wants us to be aware of our need for his love and power in our lives, and to come to him for it, because he is happy to give it to us free.

Look at all those people in the Gospel story today. Why had they bothered to leave their towns and villages and walk miles out into the country? They bothered because they knew their need of Jesus and were prepared to 'spend' their whole day looking for him and listening to him, hanging on his words. What did Jesus do? Did he let them down or disappoint them? No! He was there for them, ready to heal the sick friends and relations they had brought, ready to reassure them that God loved them, and teach them about how they could best please God in their lives.

And when their tummies started rumbling, and they knew physical hunger as well as spiritual hunger, what did Jesus do? He fed them! All he used was what they had. That's what he always uses. Are you a three- or four-year-old, ready for Jesus to use your life? Then that's what he'll use to make lots of other people really happy. Are you a seventy- or eighty-year-old, ready for Jesus to use your life? Then that's what he'll use to bring blessing and hope to lots of other people. And it's the same with all the rest of us in between.

What about our church? Are we ready to be used by Jesus? If we are, he will use us, and lots of people in this area will be blessed and given hope; if we aren't, and can't be bothered to go and spend time seeking Jesus out and listening to him, then he won't be using us and the people in our area will lose out.

Let's make sure that doesn't happen. Our job is to make ourselves available, and help give out to the people the gifts of God, so that all are properly fed.

All-age ideas

• Incorporate a lunch box of bread and 'fish' in a flower arrangement of water and harvest colours.

• Have a display which on one side has an extravagant restaurant menu with high prices. On the other side have a menu with such 'dishes' as forgiveness, healing, justice, compassion, love, and against each have the price '£ NO COST'.

Prayer of the Faithful

Celebrant
We have gathered here
to meet with our God in worship.
Let us pray to him now.

Reader
Lord, awaken in us our need of you
and make us hungry and thirsty for you,
both as individuals and as the Church of God.
Let no other issues side-track us from seeking you,
and increase our love and compassion
so that we long to serve out your love
to the world around us.

Silence

Bread of heaven:
on you we feed.

Lord, allow our world to see the true value of things,
so that the worthless and dangerous is unmasked
and real needs acknowledged.
Guide our leaders in wisdom and integrity,
and enable us all to co-operate in proper care
and stewardship of the world's resources.

Silence

Bread of heaven:
on you we feed.

Lord, as we eat our food this week,
remind us of your spiritual feeding.
May the meals we prepare and eat together
be opportunities for drawing closer
to one another and to you.

Silence

Bread of heaven:
on you we feed.

Lord, we pray for all who need medical treatment
or are waiting in pain for surgery.
We pray for those who have become addicted
and long to be set free.
We pray for all whose wrong choices
have ended in heartache, disillusion and despair.

Silence

Bread of heaven:
on you we feed.

Lord, welcome into your eternity
all who have spent their lives coming to you
and now come to be with you for ever.
Have mercy on all those approaching death

who do not know you
but reject what they imagine you to be.
May they respond to the true and living God
and know your love for ever.

Silence

Bread of heaven:
on you we feed.

With Mary, who mothered the Son of God,
we make our prayer:
Hail, Mary . . .

In the silence of our hearts,
we pray to our heavenly Father
about our own particular concerns.

Silence

Celebrant
Father of mercy,
you are always more ready to give
than we are to receive;
in thankfulness we welcome your Spirit
into our lives,
and ask you to accept our prayers,
through Jesus Christ, your Son.
Amen.

TREASURE SEEKERS

Aim: To know that Jesus fed a big crowd of people.

Starter

What's in my lunch box today? Have a lunch box, and a number of lunch items laid out on the floor. The children cover their eyes as you secretly choose a few things to put in the box. Then you ask, 'What's in my lunch box today?' Everyone tries to guess or work it out from the items that are now missing from the floor. When everyone has said what they think, reveal the true contents and take them out, ready to start again.

Teaching

Using the same lunch box, place inside it five little rolls and two sardines. (Be brave and go for real ones!) Set out a green bath towel on the floor, with a cut-out shiny blue lake laid on top of it. Tell the children how crowds and crowds of people wanted to be with Jesus all the time, because they could tell that he loved them. It's always nice to be with people who you know are very fond of you. The way they look at you and the way they talk to you makes you feel happy and safe. That's how Jesus makes people feel.

Well, they had heard that Jesus was going over the lake on a boat. (Make a toy boat go over the lake.) The people didn't have a boat, and they were on this side of the lake. So how could they reach Jesus? Yes, they could walk around the lake! So they did. It was quite a long walk but they were so keen to find Jesus that they didn't mind. Move the lunch box round the lake and put it down on the other side.

When Jesus saw them he was tired. He had actually come for a rest. So what do you think he said? 'Go away, I'm tired'? That doesn't sound like Jesus, does it, and he didn't say it. He made the people welcome, and healed the ones who were ill, and forgave the ones who wanted to put right bad things they had done, and he talked to them all in the sunshine.

By the evening they were still there, and they were all hungry. So what do you think Jesus did? He fed them. What with? Yes, one person said Jesus could use their lunch. What was the lunch? Open the box to see.

Jesus took what was offered (take it), thanked God for it (thank God), broke it all up (break it all up), and broke it all up . . . and broke it all up . . . and there was loads of food for everyone there, crowds and crowds and crowds of them! And they all shared it. (Share the food.)

Praying

Loving Father,
give us this day our daily bread. Amen.

Activities

The children can sing the action song about the feeding of the five thousand – 5 0 0 0 + hungry folk.
Here are the actions:

5 0 0 0 + hungry folk,
(five fingers on one hand, make ring with other hand which is shown three times, then rub tummies)
came 4 2 listen 2 Jesus. (cup hand to ear)
The 6 x 2 said O O O,
(use fingers for each number and for the O)
where can we get some food from?
(shrug shoulders and open hands, moving head from side to side)
Just 1 had 1 2 3 4 5, (use fingers)
loaves and 1 2 fishes. (count with fingers)
When Jesus blessed the 5 + 2
(hands face down as if blessing; count with fingers)
they were increased many x over.
(roly-poly with hands going upwards)
5 0 0 0 + 8 it up, (use fingers, then pretend to eat)
with 1 2 3 4 5 6 7 8 9 10 11 12 basketfuls left over.
(count on fingers and stamp each foot for 11 and 12)

(From a song by Ian Smale
© Copyright 1985 Kingsway's Thankyou Music.)

On the sheet they can hunt for the hidden loaves and fish in the picture, and model the loaves and fish from plasticine or playdough to wrap in a small square of cloth (cut from an old sheet or shirt). Here is a recipe for playdough. Mix two teaspoons of cream of tartar, one cup of plain flour, half a cup of salt, one tablespoon of oil and one cup of water to form a smooth paste. Cook slowly in a saucepan until the dough comes away from the sides of the pan and forms a ball. When the dough is cool enough, take it out of the pan, add food colouring and knead for three or four minutes. (Store in an airtight container in the fridge.)

PEARL DIVERS

Aim: To know that Jesus knows our needs and provides for us.

Starter

What do I need? One of the children is given an identity or work label, such as postman or ice-cream seller. The others have to work out the identity by asking them what they would need to do this job of work.

Teaching

Have a number of cards with these words on, illustrated simply, to help with reading: food, air, rest, sleep, hobbies, friendship, water, shelter, fashionable clothes, love, air, TV, chocolate, exercise, God. Have two heading cards: 'Wants' and 'Needs'.

Working together, decide which of these are wants and which are needs. This will mean looking at the things we actually need to survive and the things we think we need but which are only really extras, however nice they are. Sometimes people don't realise what they really need.

Really they need sleep but because they don't want to waste their time sleeping, they have a strong cup of coffee to keep them awake. That's OK sometimes, but if we start to live like it all the time it's bad for us. Really they need to feel loved, but instead of going to God and getting the love they need, they eat loads of sweets to comfort themselves, or drink loads of beer. And if they do this all the time it's bad for them.

(Place a piggy bank on the floor.) Sometimes we get let down or cheated by things we bought because we thought we wanted them and then found they didn't make us as happy as we hoped they would. Sometimes people think that being rich will make them happy, but real, lasting happiness doesn't come from being rich or having lots of things. Real happiness comes from God's love, which you don't even have to save up for, because he gives it to us free. However rich you are and however poor you are, God's love is free and will give you what you really need as a human being. It doesn't cheat you or let you down; it feeds you, just as a good meal feeds your body.

Praying

The Lord is my shepherd,
there is nothing else I need.
He leads me and he feeds me
all the days of my life.
O Lord, my shepherd,
you are all I need.

Activities

On the sheet there is the story of the feeding of the five thousand, told with pictures and code words. There is also a chart to show how God's love can be spread if we start it off, so that many are fed in a way that satisfies. They can also wrap up sweets with messages on and give them away freely just as they were given God's love freely.

GOLD PANNERS

Aim: To explore what it means to be spiritually hungry and thirsty.

Starter

Give everyone a paper plate and ask them to draw on it a really satisfying meal they could eat when they're really hungry. Put the resulting drawings on the table like a feast and enjoy commenting on everyone's tastes.

Teaching

We all know what it means to be hungry for food because it happens to most of us most days. The hungrier you are, the less you are bothered by what you actually eat; as the body's urgency for food increases, anything will do. When your body has been without food for a long time the hunger stops being pleasant and becomes a real, desperate craving, and eventually a matter of life and death. That's how important food is.

This makes a very good picture to help us understand spiritual hunger and thirst. Read together the passage from Isaiah 55. What is the satisfying food and drink being offered here? Have

a wrapped loaf of bread which lists the ingredients, and read these. Then read the list of 'ingredients' of God in Psalm 144 to find out why this spiritual food is so satisfying.

Now look at today's Gospel, with the feeding there, asking yourselves what feeding is going on, and who is hungry. Draw attention to the fact that the people had come here because they needed 'feeding'. Was Jesus able to feed those who had not chosen to come? How might those people eventually realise their hunger and get fed? (Think about the people who had been present at the feeding.) Why did Jesus bother to feed the people?

Think about the local area and any spiritual hunger they can see which is either not being fed or is being fed 'junk food' rather than God's satisfying meals.

Praying

The King of love my shepherd is,
his goodness faileth never,
I nothing lack if I am his
and he is mine for ever.

(From Psalm 23)

Activities

On the sheet they can separate the spiritual junk food from proper, wholesome feeding, and look at signs of spiritual hunger and thirst in our society, thinking through ways the Church can get in touch with this and do the feeding it is called to do as the Body of Christ.

NINETEENTH SUNDAY OF THE YEAR

Thought for the day

God is faithful to us through all the storms of life, yet our faith in God is so very small.

Reflection on the readings

1 Kings 19:9, 11-13
Psalm 84:9-14
Romans 9:1-5
Matthew 14:22-33

In a sense both Elijah and Peter are sinking, and both are given firm-handed rescue by the loving

God. In today's passage from 1 Kings, Elijah is exhausted and worn down, and therefore vulnerable to those nagging negatives which whisper the futility and hopelessness and unfairness of it all. It is a place that many of us will recognise well, and there is rich comfort in the way God responds. First, he has provided Elijah with the basic practical needs of sleep and food, and now comes the spiritual feeding – the teaching that will gather up Elijah and show him new direction and new insights. In contrast to all the turbulence in Elijah's mind and heart, God is noticeable by his absence in the violence of wind, earthquake and fire. The presence of God gradually becomes recognisable in the peace, the intimacy of shared tranquillity.

Still Elijah states his case from his place of misery; God's presence is never kept at bay by such honest aching. But Elijah is now ready to cope with being led out, provided with the new direction and clear instructions he needs. God does not attempt to dissuade Elijah from how he feels, but offers him instead the way forward to view it differently, or as less overpowering and crippling. He does the same with us, taking us through at a pace we can cope with, using where we are as a starting point and gently offering a route of hope.

Peter, too, is suddenly overwhelmed by the sense of his vulnerability, as it dawns on him that he is out in the middle of a huge stretch of dark and angry water, buffeted by the violent wind, and with nothing under his feet except fathoms of cold water. It would be hard to imagine a less secure environment! So how had he got into this precarious and vulnerable place? By responding to Jesus' calling. How vividly this matches the experience of many Christians, responding in joy and enthusiasm to the call of Jesus to trust him and come to him, only to be thrown completely at the realisation of where this places them.

It is all very well to say that, like Peter, we need only to fix our gaze and concentration on Jesus for everything to be fine. But the truth we are shown in today's readings is that there will be moments when we are made desperately aware of our vulnerability. When we take that decision to climb out of our neatly constructed lives and follow Jesus, we open ourselves up to an environment where Christ is our only and total security; the truth of our existence is that we are out on deep water without a boat, and it is only at the moment of this realisation that we begin to learn what faith is all about.

Thankfully, Jesus is always there to grasp us firmly, in our lack of faith, and bring us back to where we feel safe. It is a learning process, and we progress at a pace God knows we can manage. If we compare Peter's performance here with the Peter who boldly proclaims the Gospel in spite of being insulted and thrown into prison, we can see dramatic growth in faith. The environment is no less stormy or insecure, but it is matched by the working knowledge that dependence on the faithful God is all the security we need.

Discussion starters

1. What kind of things build up our faith, and what knocks it about?

2. What can we learn from Elijah and Peter about God's reaction to people at the low and vulnerable points of life?

All-stage talk

If you know a juggler, invite them to come and juggle. Failing this, give out some balloons to a group of older children and ask them to keep them in the air, in as controlled a way as possible, using hands, head, knees and feet.

As the juggler or children perform, draw attention to the way they need to concentrate and keep their eyes on the balls or balloons if they are to be sure of catching them under control. Notice how the moment they lose concentration, or lose balance, things go wrong.

Today we heard in the Gospel about some people in a boat, weathering a terrible storm. It was the disciples, and Jesus had sent them off home while he himself went off to pray on his own after he had fed all those five thousand people. He needed to be alone with his heavenly Father to talk that over, and give special thanks for all that had happened. The waves were churning, and the boat was rocking and the disciples were frightened – especially when they saw Jesus walking across to them. This was water, and you can't walk on that! We are told they thought Jesus must be a ghost, and they got more scared than ever.

Let's look at what Peter did next. He called out to Jesus, 'If it really is you, then tell me to come to you over the water.' Why did he say that? What was he doing? It sounds as if he was testing whether Jesus was real or not, like us saying to a friend, 'If you've really been up in space, show me a photograph to prove it', or 'If you really love me, how about helping with this washing-up'.

Jesus knows he isn't a ghost, and he takes Peter up on what he's asked. 'Come on, then!' he says. There's no way out now! Peter concentrates on Jesus, like the juggler concentrated on the balls. He gets as far as climbing out of the boat, and he starts to walk towards Jesus, still concentrating on him, and then suddenly it all hits him. 'This is crazy! This is impossible! The water can't possibly be holding my weight! Rationally I know I ought to be sinking!' And as those doubts make him panic and lose his sight of Jesus, he does just that – he starts to sink and has to shout out in terror to Jesus to save him. And, of course, Jesus reaches out to him and gets him to safety straightaway.

Trusting Jesus is keeping ourselves concentrating on him and his love, underneath everything else that we do. Suppose you're buying some sweets. At the same time you're aware of Jesus and his love. What difference does that make? You will probably buy without being greedy, and you'll probably end up sharing what you get. Suppose you are travelling to work, and you've also got your eyes on Jesus. That will affect the way you drive, and the way you treat other commuters.

Today Jesus is saying to each of us, 'Yes, it is OK for you to put your total trust in me. Just keep that in mind and all the things which make you feel frightened and insecure will not let you sink – you can walk straight over them, confident in my love and power.'

All-age ideas

• Involve a group to make some sound effects as a background to the reading about Elijah. Having read the passage through together, good ideas may well be suggested, but here are a few to start you off:

Wind – breathing and shakers, getting louder and then softer.

Earthquake – Drums, shaken tray or hardboard, large cartons being banged with wooden spoons.

Fire – Crunching up cellophane, and plastic bags, and shakers.

Still, small voice – Very quiet triangle or shaker fading into silence.

• Using music such as the storm in *Noye's Fludde*, have a group of dancers to whirl and leap around like a raging sea in a storm, and gradually calm to gentle movements and stillness. You could dress them in sea-coloured tabards, on the shoulders of which are sewn thin strips of blue and green. These will then fly out as they move. Otherwise they could wave large flags and long streamers of sea-coloured fabric.

Prayer of the Faithful

Celebrant
Trusting in our faithful God, let us pray.

Reader
Faithful God, we pray for the gift
of deeper faith in you,
so that we trust you in a way
that alters our dependence on everything else,
and allows us clearer vision

as to the direction and role of the Church.
Remind us that it is your Church, and not ours;
your work, your power and your kingdom.

Silence

Lord our God:
let only your will be done.

Faithful God, as we call to mind
the stormy areas of our world,
the raging and the insecurity,
the confusion and bewilderment,
the restlessness and fear,
let your calming and reassuring presence
be sensed and recognised,
bringing peace and goodness,
righteousness and hope.

Silence

Lord our God:
let only your will be done.

Faithful God, come to us in the storms of life,
when we let one another down,
mishandle opportunities
and come to the end of our strength or patience;
and bless us with the love that never lets us down.

Silence

Lord our God:
let only your will be done.

Faithful God, we place into your loving keeping
all those who have died,
knowing their dependence on you
and your limitless mercy.
We thank you for them and their gifts to the world,
and ask that we may, in our turn,
come to you across the waters of death
and live in your company for ever.

Silence

Lord our God:
let only your will be done.

We pray with Mary,
who listened with all her heart:
Hail, Mary . . .

As God's stillness fills our hearts,
we name any we know
who especially need our prayers.

Silence

Celebrant
Merciful Father,
hear us as we pray,
for the sake of Jesus, our Saviour.
Amen.

TREASURE SEEKERS

Aim: To know that God can cope with our bad days as well as the good ones.

Starter

What's the time, Mr Wolf? The children creep up on Mr Wolf, who sometimes pleasantly tells them the time, and sometimes decides it's time to eat them.

Teaching

Use a few instruments – such as simple shakers and bells, saucepans and wooden spoons, and hand tapping and clapping – as you talk about the different moods of the weather. Sometimes it seems wild and cross, with the wind racing round and blowing everything over, and the rain lashing down. (Make the sounds.) Sometimes it seems in a quiet and gentle mood, perhaps when it's a bit hazy and misty, and there isn't any wind, or when the snow is quietly falling. (Make those sounds.) And sometimes the weather seems all happy and smiley, with the sun shining in a clear blue sky and just a little breeze, and everywhere warm and bright. (Make these sounds.) Sometimes it seems sad, with dark grey clouds and steady rain. (Make these sounds.)

It's the same with us. We have times when we feel all wild and cross, and we grumble and snap at everyone and make ourselves as horrid as possible. Sometimes we have quieter times, when we just want to sit and cuddle up to someone who loves us, and read a story, or watch television, or go to sleep. And sometimes we feel all sunny bright and happy, bouncing around with lots of energy and being friendly and helpful.

Which of those times do you think God loves you best? Answer with a simple 'No' to every suggestion until someone says that God loves us all the time, and celebrate that truth together. Sometimes what we do makes God sad, but he is loving us all the time, in all our different moods.

Praying

Sometimes the weather is wild and cross.
   (shake fists and stamp feet)
Sometimes the weather is quiet.
   (lie down still)
Sometimes the weather is sunshine happy.
   (trace big sunshine smile)
Sometimes the weather is sad.
   (make fingers into trickling rain)
Sometimes I feel wild and cross.
   (shake fists and stamp feet)

Sometimes I feel quiet.
   (lie down still)
Sometimes I feel sunshine happy.
   (trace big sunshine smile)
Sometimes I feel sad.
   (fingers make trickling tears down cheeks)
And ALL the time God loves me!
   (stretch arms out in wide circle all around)
God loves me ALL the time!
   (reverse the wide circle)

Activities

The sheet can be made into a weather chart for the children to set each day. They will each need a split pin, and you may like to make the pointers in advance, from different coloured paper. The chart can be strengthened by sticking it on to thin card.

PEARL DIVERS

Aim: To know the story of Jesus on the water, and Peter walking to him.

Starter

If the weather is fine, have a paddling pool outside and some toy boats, or floating tubs to play with. Otherwise, have a number of washing-up bowls on plastic sheeting indoors.

Teaching

One way of telling today's story is with a parachute. Everyone stands around the edge and the parachute becomes the sea, which can be made very still and calm, and various other stages of roughness to a roaring storm. Practise this with the children first, giving a clear signal for following the leader's instructions, so that they get good at all responding together. As you tell the story, use the parachute sea and its natural sound effects, with everyone shouting above the storm: 'Help! It's a ghost!'

Or you can get everyone making the sound effects of the storm and waves with percussion instruments, rubbing their palms together, tapping fingers on palms and using voices. For this have most people sitting in the form of a boat, and rocking in unison as the waves get worse, and a few, including Peter, inside the 'boat'. Then Peter can climb out of the boat towards Jesus.

Praying

Be with me, Lord Jesus, through the storms in my life, through the times when I'm frightened or angry or sad.
Teach me to trust you with all of myself through the good times and through the bad.

Activities

On the sheet there are instructions for making a working model of a stormy sea. The children will need thin card to strengthen the model.

GOLD PANNERS

Aim: To look at that sinking feeling, and Jesus' rescue.

Starter

Provide some bowls of water and see how much cargo floating tubs can hold before they sink. This could be done in two teams, to see whose boat stays afloat longest.

Teaching

First today we are looking at a prophet with that sinking feeling. It's Elijah, who has done wonderful things which witness to the truth of the living God, and is at present exhausted and dejected and fearful. Read 1 Kings 19:9, 11-13, imagining how Elijah might have felt when at last he knew God's presence in the still small whisper.

Now look at today's Gospel, jotting down the details under the following headings: Who? Where? When? What? How? Then think about 'why'. (What did Peter and the others learn from the incident? What new light does it throw on Jesus' identity?) Draw attention to the way you can often do things you would think impossible if you are following the instructions of a dynamic teacher or instructor. (Think of those TV documentaries about scary rescues, where ordinary passengers need to take over the flight controls and are talked safely down to landing by trusting the instructor in the control tower enough to do exactly as they say.) Jesus sees it all as a question of faith – the sort of faith which would make us quite naturally take an umbrella with us to pray for rain. This sort of faith expects real results, and, says Jesus, the results will happen. It's often our lack of real, practical believing in God which prevents his work from happening.

Praying

Lord, increase my faith
so that if you tell me
to step out more towards you,
I'll step out trusting you.
And if you tell me to stop, I'll stop,
and if you tell me to wait, I'll wait.
Lord, increase my faith;
Lord, increase my faith.

Activities

Stage an interview with Peter. Instructions and guidelines are provided on the sheet. Other activities encourage them to think through some of the reasons why people do get that 'sinking' feeling, and how God helps us come to terms with it.

TWENTIETH SUNDAY OF THE YEAR

Thought for the day

The good news of salvation is not limited to a particular group or nation but available for the whole world.

Reflection on the readings

Isaiah 56:1, 6-7
Psalm 66:2-3, 5-6, 8
Romans 11:13-15, 29-32
Matthew 15:21-28

The idea of God's salvation being for all nations did not emerge as a new concept of the Early Church. It had been there, intrinsic to that first promise to Abraham, and today's reading from Isaiah is representative of what all the prophets proclaim. In fact, the whole reason for Israel being called as a nation of light is so that other nations can see their way to the true and living God. Zechariah's song at the birth of his son, John the Baptist, sets it all out clearly.

Paul, with a passion for spreading the good news to the gentile world, is equally strong in proclaiming hope for his own people of promise. God is never fickle, and if his promise has been made, it will, in good time, be fulfilled. He can even see how God can bring blessing out of their rejection of Jesus, the source of hope. What that does is to place even the chosen people of promise in the position of receiving God's mercy, spelling out to them his amazing forbearing love.

In today's Gospel we are given an example, a foretaste, of those putting their faith in God who are gentiles. Not only the centurion (who was obviously closely involved with the Jewish people, since he had built their synagogue) but also this Canaanite woman (belonging to a country which was the traditional enemy to God's ways) is recommended by Jesus for her remarkable faith, which touches his heart and impresses him. It is seen in sharp contrast to the 'experts' – the Pharisees who are able to see Jesus at work and hear his teaching with all their background of promise behind them, and are still blinded to the truth of fulfilment.

Such tunnel vision not only makes it unlikely that they will relate to anything Jesus says, but also creates terrible obstacles for other people coming to faith, and that is what disturbs Jesus so much. Self-righteousness, self-sufficiency and cynicism are excellent for stubbing out flickering flames of faith. On the other hand, as we see in the tenacity of the Canaanite mother, perseverance, trust and hope, even in the face of opposition and difficulty, is excellent for building up faith in others.
Exactly how much faith we really have in the true God will be shown not by what we say or claim but by the way we respond and act.

Discussion starters

1. What have today's readings to teach us about those who have not yet been introduced to the one true living God?

2. Was Jesus just being narrow-minded when he declined to help the Canaanite woman, or very traditional, or was he making a deliberate teaching point here?

All-stage talk

Ask everyone who is a Brownie to stand up. That means that everyone left sitting down is a non-Brownie. Do the same with various other groupings, such as Scouts, servers, the short-sighted or cocopops-eaters. Each time we become a member of a group, there are lots of others who are not included.

Remind everyone of the promise God first made to his friend Abraham, whose family the Bible traces right back to Noah. What was it that God promised to Abraham? God promised that (1) he would make his family into a great nation, and (2) all the people on earth would be blessed by this nation which was starting with Abraham. That's quite a promise! And because God always keeps his promises, it came true. Abraham's grandchildren and great-grandchildren and great-great-great-grandchildren did grow into a great nation of God's chosen people.

The people of Israel (as the nation came to be called) were rightly proud of being God's chosen people. Like the groups we had standing up, they thought of themselves as God's chosen, and everyone else was outside and not included. They called all the outsiders 'gentiles'. Probably most of us here are gentiles.

So much for the first part of that promise to Abraham: 'I will make you into a great nation.' But there was a second part, wasn't there? What was that? It was that *all the people on earth* would be blessed by the nation which God had started with Abraham. All through the Old Testament there were prophets like Isaiah who reminded the people of this bit of the promise. 'This is not just for you, remember,' they'd say. 'We are called to bring blessing to all the other people on earth eventually!'

It was true. Starting with the chosen nation, God wanted all the people on earth to have that special friendship with God which Abraham had. It isn't just for a few people, or for one particular nation, but for people of every age, country and time. It's for all the Brownies and the Scouts and the short-sighted and the servers and everybody else, because with God not one person is left 'on the outside'. God's loving is for everybody, everywhere, every time.

If that's how it is for God, then that's how it must be for us as well. We must make sure that in all our loving we don't leave people out. Think about that when you are playing or working in a team, or chatting in a group. Check whether there are people we deliberately avoid. Do we assume some people are not worth telling about Jesus? Would we rather some types of people didn't come to our church?

If God had thought that about us, most of us wouldn't be here. It's his love for us that brought us, and he has love for lots of others who need us to show it to them, and love them into the kingdom.

All-age ideas

• Give the church an international flavour today, with banners and flags representing different countries, and a globe or world map surrounded or dotted with candles.

• Have a display with 'Jesus is Lord' written in as many different languages as possible.

Prayer of the Faithful

Celebrant
In faith let us pray to the God
who is Lord of all the earth.

Reader
Holy God, may the worship of your Church
throughout the world
be attentive and expectant,
ready to be set on fire again and again
with the outrageous foolishness of loving,
without exceptions and without limits.

Silence

Servant God:
let us honour you with our lives.

Holy God, may all that encourages people
in goodness, honesty and compassion
be blessed and grow;
may all that encourages self-seeking and cruelty,
prejudice and deceit
wither and be exposed for its futility.
May we learn from one another's cultures
and respect one another's differences.

Silence

Servant God:
let us honour you with our lives.

Holy God, we thank you for the joy of human love,
and for all those among whom we live and work.
We pray particularly for loved ones
who worry us with their health,
or circumstances, or life direction.
We pray for those among our friends and families
who do not know you,
or whose faith has been shaken.

Silence

Servant God:
let us honour you with our lives.

Holy God, we pray for all whose backgrounds
make belief in a loving God difficult.
We pray for all
who suffer mental or emotional anguish
and those who despair.
We pray for those facing another day of pain,
another day of hunger, another day of fear.

Silence

Servant God:
let us honour you with our lives.

Holy God, gather into your eternal kingdom
all who have come to the end of this earthly life
and rejoice to see you as you really are.
We remember all
whom we love but can no longer see,
and thank you for your overarching love
and undergirding faithfulness to us.

Silence

Servant God:
let us honour you with our lives.

Holy God, we remember with gratitude
all who gave up so much
to bring the good news to our country,
and pray that with us it may continue to be spread
until the whole earth knows of your truth and love.

Silence

Servant God:
let us honour you with our lives.

We make our prayer with Mary,
faithful Mother of Jesus:
Hail, Mary . . .

Upheld by God's peace,
we pray now in silence
for any who especially need our prayers.

Silence

Celebrant
Father, we trust in your unswerving love,
and bring you these prayers,
through Jesus, our Saviour.
Amen.

TREASURE SEEKERS

Aim: To know that God loves everyone in the
whole world.

Starter

The world is turning. Make a circle and choose some
children to be birds, some planes and some clouds.
Walk round singing to the tune of *The wheels on
the bus*:

The world is turning round and round,
round and round,
round and round.
The world is turning round and round
all year long.

As you sing it and walk around again, all the birds
can fly around the moving earth. Then the planes
can zoom around. Then the clouds can drift lightly
around.

Teaching

Bring along either a large globe beach ball, or a
globe, and spin it around, pointing out where on
our planet earth we are. (Although this age group
is too young to understand maps, they can begin to
get an idea of living on a round world.)

Talk about the different places on our world
where people live. Some children live where it is
very hot all the time, and some where it is very
cold all the time. Some children live where it rains
and rains every day, and some where it hardly ever
rains. Some children have never seen snow, and
some live in snow all the year round. (Calendars
are often a good source of pictures, or you can show

them pictures from library books, or photographs you have taken.)

Some of the world is very flat, and some has high hills and mountains. Some children go to church by boat, and some by donkey. Lots of children all over the world walk to church and lots drive or cycle.

And all that goes on at the same time on our round, spinning world! (Spin the globe again.) You know that God loves each of you? Well, he also loves each and every person living in the world. No one is left out.

You can sing the prayer today.

Praying

He's got the whole world in his hand,
he's got the whole wide world in his hand,
he's got the whole world in his hand,
he's got the whole world in his hand!

Activities

The children can make their sheet into a turning world. Beforehand use the land mass shapes as templates and cut these from green and white paper. Also cut out blue circles to fit the basic shape shown. The children can then stick these on. Punch a hole in the place shown so the children can thread a pipe-cleaner through it, and twist the ends together. They can then make the world turn by pushing it along a surface, holding the pipe-cleaner.

PEARL DIVERS

Aim: To know that the Gospel is for all nations.

Starter

Tell the children a selection of different greetings, and set them off walking around to music. Whenever the music stops, call out a nationality, and everyone goes round greeting one another appropriately. Here are some suggestions for greetings:

British – shake hands and say, 'How do you do?' 'How do you do?'

Japanese – hands together and bow to each other

American Indian – raise hand and say 'How!' or rub noses

Australian – 'G'day!'

French – kiss both cheeks or say, 'Bonjour!'

Teaching

Bring along a world map and a selection of books on different life patterns in various countries, with tasters of various foods from around the world.

(Many supermarkets have quite a wide selection of breads; other items might be dates, bananas, yams, rice and raw cane sugar.)

You could either introduce these in the circle or have it set up more as a 'market place' with the children walking round looking and sampling while music from other cultures is playing. Then come back and see where some of these places are on the world map. If the map is placed on a table they can be marked with nightlight candles.

Remind the children of how the whole world is God's, and he made it. Use the cut-out sections of the diagram below to explain how God made a promise to Abraham long before Jesus was born: that he would make his family into a chosen nation, and that through this nation the whole world would be blessed. When Jesus came, the second part of that promise started to come true, and it's still coming true now, as more and more of the world hears the good news of God's love.

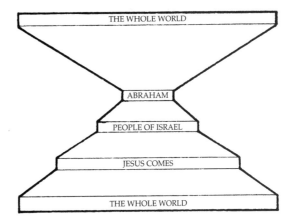

It hasn't been completed yet though. That's why we all pray in the Lord's prayer, 'Let your kingdom come'. There are still people in our world who do not know and need telling. It may well be that some of the children here will spread the Gospel, so that eventually everyone will know.

Praying

God, bless our world.
Help us to look after it
and to look after one another.
Let your kingdom come in our world
and let your will be done,
so it is filled with peace and love. Amen.

Activities

Through coded puzzles on the sheet the children are taken through from the promise to Abraham up to the hope for all the world. They are also encouraged to pray for the world Church and make links with a group of Christians in another part of the world.

GOLD PANNERS

Aim: To look at the implications of today's Gospel about the healing of the daughter of the Canaanite woman.

Starter

Odd one out. Place a series of several objects down together and decide which are the odd ones out in each case. For instance, if you put down at random an umbrella, a pen, a CD and a chocolate bar, you may decide that the CD is the odd one out because it is more curved than straight; or that the chocolate bar is the odd one out as it is the only one that is edible. The more random the objects, the more brainwork there needs to be to find connections and misfits.

Teaching

Look first at today's Gospel, Matthew 15:21-28. Draw attention to the parts of the episode which do not seem to fit in with the character of Jesus as we know it, or any areas that puzzle them. Initially they may well feel that Jesus was being unwelcoming and rude to the woman in her need. From where they are standing, what did it matter that she came from Canaan?

We need to put the story into context. Remind them of the original promise God made to Abraham because of his faith (Genesis 12:2-3), and how that led to the making of the chosen people. Jesus was born into this nation, and his mission was to gather up the chosen people and lead them, so that through them the rest of the world could be blessed. If Jesus had gone straight out during his earthly ministry to preach to the gentiles, what would that have said to the Jewish people? Jesus was concerned to stay obedient to his calling. This woman is not part of that chosen people; in fact, she comes from a people traditionally held to be the enemy of God's ways.

So we find here a very human picture of Jesus, struggling with what is the right course of action in a very difficult situation. He doesn't immediately reject the woman, and we can imagine the conflict in his mind as he says nothing. The bit about not giving the children's food to the dogs is probably a proverb like 'Charity begins at home', and so not nearly as rude as it sounds in translation. But the woman's reply makes Jesus realise that although she is not a 'flesh and blood' descendant of Abraham, she is certainly his descendant through faith, and all doubt in his mind disappears about whether to include her in his ministry to the chosen people or not.

Praying

May God be merciful to us and bless us,
show us the light of his countenance and come to us.
Let your saving ways be known upon earth;
your saving health among all nations.
Let the peoples praise you, O God,
let all the peoples praise you.

(From Psalm 66)

Activities

There is help on the sheet for exploring Romans 11 in the light of today's teaching, and an activity to encourage them in thinking through our calling to continue spreading the Gospel, with suggestions of opportunities for doing this in their lives.

TWENTY-FIRST SUNDAY OF THE YEAR

Thought for the day

The Church is the Body of Christ, built on strong rock of faith and energised by the living Breath of God.

Reflection on the readings

Isaiah 22:19-23
Psalm 137:1-3, 6, 8
Romans 11:33-36
Matthew 16:13-20

It is part of being human to ask questions. As soon as children can speak they badger their parents with the constant 'Why?' questions, and that is the way we all learn to make sense of the world we live in. The deep, spiritual questions are searching for the meaning of identity and the meaning of life itself, and it is these questions which are at the heart of all faiths and systems of belief. They surface particularly at times when a people has its sense of identity shaken.

For us as the Church, standing at the start of a new millennium, there are bound to be questions about our identity and our calling. We cannot look back over all the terrible costly mistakes without regret and sadness, nor at the divisions and lingering anachronisms which still cripple the spread of the liberating Gospel today. But today's readings are full of inspiration and real hope for the Church.

In Romans, Paul tells us to start by marvelling at

the wonder of God – his wisdom and knowledge, which are far greater than anything we can imagine. God is where it all comes from, and where it is all going.

And the Gospel reminds us to look back to our roots for further encouragement. We, too, share the faith ancestry of Abraham, and all the prophets, and Jesus talks of the Church which he will build on the rock of discerned faith in the revealed God, as spoken out by Simon. Symbolically, he is given the name of 'Rock' to mark the importance of this recognition. The Church is to last, through all kinds of attacks and dangers, cosmically safe in the keeping of the eternal love of God, constantly renewed and equipped for its work in every age.

Discussion starters

1. What do you think had helped Simon Peter realise the true identity of Jesus?

2. In what ways is the Church of today a real, living body?

All-stage talk

Beforehand, ask a few people of different ages to provide you with a photograph of them when they were very young, and have these pictures duplicated, or shown on an OHP. Don't identify them, but say they are all members of the church community. When people have had a go at guessing the identities, ask the people to come to the front. This narrows the choice, and makes it easier to see who's who. We might have a hunch about someone, and can ask them directly. They will tell us whether or not we are right, and then we'll know for certain. (Invite people to do this.) Once we know the true identity, it's often easier to see the likeness!

In today's Gospel, Jesus knew that people had all sorts of ideas about who he was. Some ideas were close to the truth, some were wide of the mark, and Jesus always wanted his followers to make the discovery for themselves. Discovering something for ourselves means that we always remember it far better than when we have simply been told things. (People may remember discovering for themselves that fire burns, for instance, that cement hardens into a solid lump, or that overloading a computer can cause it to crash.)

No doubt Jesus sensed that the disciples had almost got to the point of discovering that he was not just their friend and teacher, but also the promised Messiah, the Son of God. This conversation, starting with what other people think, will help them tip over into that 'Aha!' of learning, that point when you suddenly know something and everything falls clearly into place.

It is Simon, the fisherman, who comes out with it for the first time. 'You are the Christ,' he says, 'the Son of the living God.' It must have been a bit like when you first say the words 'I love you' or 'I'm three'. It's the first time you have ever said it and as you say it, you know it is really true, and your life will never be quite the same again.

All-age ideas

- Have a display with unfamiliar or disguised pictures of well-known people with the caption, 'Who am I?' Have also a large picture of Jesus with the caption, 'Who do you say I am?'

Prayer of the Faithful

Celebrant
Gathered as the Church of God,
members of the Body of Christ,
let us pray together.

Reader
Fill your Church, O Lord,
with life and energy, spiritual health and vitality.
As we feed on you, may we grow more like you;
may we exercise your loving,
minister with your tenderness,
serve with your humility
and co-operate with your vision.

Silence

In you, O Lord:
is all meaning and truth.

Fill your world, O Lord,
with wonder at creation,
recognition of our mutual human responsibility,
desire for reforming what is at fault,
and hope in the possibilities of living at peace
with God and with one another.

Silence

In you, O Lord:
is all meaning and truth.

Fill our homes and neighbourhoods, O Lord,
with the generosity and trust that allows space
but is always ready to encourage and support.
May we cherish our bodies, minds and spirits
as temples containing your Spirit,
and honour one another as people of your making.

Silence

In you, O Lord:
is all meaning and truth.

We pray for all who are ill at home or in hospital,
for all in emergency surgery or in casualty;

for those who have just discovered
that they have injuries or illnesses
that will change their lives.
We pray for the work of all who heal and comfort,
all who visit the sick and counsel the distressed.

Silence

In you, O Lord:
is all meaning and truth.

We pray for the dying and those who love them;
we pray for those who have completed this life
and have made the journey through death.
We pray for the work of those
who comfort the bereaved.

Silence

In you, O Lord:
is all meaning and truth.

We pray with Mary,
Mother of the Church:
Hail, Mary . . .

We pray in silence, now,
for our own particular needs and concerns.

Silence

Celebrant
Heavenly Father,
we want to fix our lives
on your unending love,
and we ask you to accept this prayer,
for the sake of Jesus Christ.
Amen.

TREASURE SEEKERS

Aim: To know that the Church is made of people.

Starter

Who can it be? Have some large pictures of familiar things, people and places, and start with a picture completely covered up. Gradually uncover it. The children say what they think it is and can see if they're right when it is totally revealed.

Teaching

Have a picture of Jesus healing, or with the children. This could be an illustration in a children's Bible. Start with it fully covered, as in the starter activity, and tell the children that this picture is someone they have never seen, but who they know and love. As you talk, giving verbal clues, uncover the picture so they can see that it is Jesus. They are getting to

know Jesus better and better as they hear more about him and as they talk with him in prayer.

Now show a large outline picture of a church. What do we do in church? We pray to God, we sing together to thank God and praise him, we give our money to God, we hear about Jesus, we share a meal, and we play in the children's corner.

What's inside our church? Coloured windows, an altar, candles, flowers, chairs and books.

All those things are there to help us worship God, and to give him our best, as a thank-you for everything God has given us. There are people in church at the moment, and we are all here as well. And there are grown-ups and children all over the world in their churches today. They are all there to worship God and say thank you by giving him their best singing and their best living every day.

Praying

The Body of Christ needs eyes and legs
and feet and hands and mouth.
We are the Body of Christ on earth –
God's eyes and legs
and feet and hands and mouth!

Activities

On the sheet there are puppets to make which the children can work by pushing their fingers through the holes. They can also draw in the missing bits of body.

PEARL DIVERS

Aim: To know about Peter's confession of faith.

Starter

Who am I? Stick a picture of an animal or person on someone's back. This person turns round so the other children can see the picture. The volunteer asks questions to determine his/her identity, to which all the other children can only say 'yes' or 'no'.

Teaching

Give clues about a particular child in the group until the identity is guessed correctly – for example, this person likes Irish dancing . . . wears glasses . . . has a wobbly tooth . . . and is seven. It must be Rory! Today we are going to hear about someone else. See if you can work out who it is.

Imagine you live in a village. Not far from your house is a sea, and your dad is a fisherman. You often walk down to the beach and help him sort out the fishing nets, and mend any rips in them. Over the past year or so life has changed in your village because of a man who walks around the country with a group of friends. Everyone in your village knows about him. One person used to be so deaf she couldn't hear a thing, but she went to this man and now she can hear as well as you. Your next-door neighbour couldn't walk very well, but he can now because this man made the leg better.

Every so often someone will come running into your village shouting that this man is talking by the lake, and suddenly everyone comes out of their houses, or stops what they're doing, and you all set off for the beach, just because this man is going to be there. And when you get there, you find crowds of other people from other villages have come as well, settling themselves down on the beach and the grass, looking towards a man who is sitting in one of the fishing boats. He doesn't look anything special. He's just wearing ordinary clothes, and he isn't shouting or waving his arms around or anything.

But everyone feels good when he's there. He has this strange way of making you feel important and special and yet able to be really yourself. People are kind to each other, making room for one another and helping the old ones sit down. This man seems to make you all want to behave well, just because he is so lovely himself. He tells stories, and gets you thinking about what life is really all about, and then he starts walking quietly around, praying with people, laying his hands on them and making them better, listening to them and comforting them. Some people have brought food, and often it all turns into a picnic, with the man enjoying the food he's been given, talking and smiling with you, interested in you.

When he has to move on to another area, you all wave and walk with him away from the beach, before going back to work as usual in the village. But the day seems happier and brighter because the man has been to visit you. Who is this man – is it John the Baptist? Is it Elijah or one of the prophets? The man is . . . Jesus, the Christ, the Son of God.

Praying

Lord Jesus, I can see
that you must really be
the Son of God our Father,
because you speak God's word
and live God's love,
and there is no one else like you.

Activities

The sheet helps them to look at Simon Peter's confession of faith and the things that made him realise who Jesus was. There is also a code sum to change Simon into Peter and discover the meaning of his new name.

GOLD PANNERS

Aim: To look at the Church in the light of its roots and heritage.

Starter

Who's who? They will need Bibles for this. Working in pairs, discover who's who from a list of clues. Here are some suggestions:

- this person killed his brother – Genesis 4:8
- this woman drove a tent peg through an army commander's head – Judges 4:21
- this person caused a great temple full of people to collapse – Judges 16:29-30
- this person was so excited to find Peter knocking at the door that she left him there outside – Acts 12:13-16
- this person escaped by being let down over the city wall in a basket – Acts 9:25

Teaching

Look first at today's Gospel, up to verse 14, and see who people thought Jesus was. Why might they have thought he was John the Baptist or Elijah or one of the prophets? In what ways was he behaving like them? What reasons are there for thinking he wasn't any of these people?

Then look at what the disciples thought, and Simon said (15-16). What might have brought them to this conclusion? What had they seen Jesus doing which convinced them?

Now look at Jesus' response to Simon's reply (17-20). Notice Jesus' joy and excitement that Simon has finally got to the point of real faith which Jesus had been longing for. The new name he gives him to mark this event and prophesy Simon's leadership role in the church is often translated as 'Rock', though in the Greek it has the sense of great boulder! It certainly makes him bolder. (Sorry.) The church is to be established on the firm bedrock of Jesus, the Christ, the Son of God, which Simon Peter has just confessed, and it will be led by the human Peter, with strong faith in that truth.

This is the first time 'Church' is mentioned in the New Testament, and it must have come as quite a shock to the disciples, who had been thinking of a kingdom with a king on a throne, to hear that it was planned to be more like a community or society of equal people. It doesn't seem to be just earthly, either. Jesus sees it standing firm against all kinds of evil attack, from outside and in, being constantly renewed and revived through all the centuries, touching both heaven and earth.

And that is the same Church which we belong to now, in this parish, in this country!

Praying

Lord Jesus, you are the Christ,
the Son of the living God!
Revive your Church in our generation
so that the whole world benefits.

Activities

The teaching is reinforced on the sheet with an exploration of where the Church does show these important roots, and where today's readings challenge us as church members.

TWENTY-SECOND SUNDAY OF THE YEAR

Thought for the day

As Jesus prepares for the necessary suffering of the cross, he is tempted, through well-meaning friendship, to avoid it.

Reflection on the readings

Jeremiah 20:7-9
Psalm 62:2-6, 8-9
Romans 12:1-2
Matthew 16:21-27

The harder we hit against God's will for us, the harder that will appears to be. Today's readings prepare us for the serious business of committed following, and we need to listen very carefully if we are not to be thrown by what can seem impossible demands while we are in the wrong place, and yet which suddenly turn into blessing as soon as we approach them differently.

Jeremiah is thoroughly fed-up with his impossible position. He knows God's hand is on him to be a prophet and speak his word to the people, and he feels that he has made a very good job of sacrificing the pleasures of life in order to be obedient. Yet what has he got in return? Only misery and loneliness, rejection and insult. He complains bitterly, full of self-pity (which always comes from self-righteousness) that it simply isn't fair. God is not that sympathetic, suggesting that he gets himself back to the right place and starts speaking some sense instead of all the moaning, so that God can use his mouth once again to proclaim what needs proclaiming.

It is so easy to get into the worldly habit of trading where spiritual matters are concerned; so easy to start totting up the noble sacrifices we have made, and the time or money we spend for God, expecting tangible returns of our own choosing. Even our intercessory prayer can so easily turn into a kind of bullying of God, or bribery, and, of course, as soon as this happens, we have actually swung round with our backs to the Lord we claim to love.

There is another danger, too. Peter has genuine love for Jesus, and his horrified denial of the necessary suffering is so very understandable. Would we not all react in the same way at the prospect of a loved friend having to go through that? Yet Satan has hijacked this human friendship to tempt Jesus as powerfully as he possibly can: 'Avoid the cross and gain the crown without having to go through all that agony of body and spirit. How will you or your dear friends cope?' Jesus' reply shows us how sharply the temptation has stabbed him, and how deeply he must have yearned, in his humanness, for Peter to be right. But he recognises in it Satan's cunning, and shows Peter that he is, in this instance, not a rock of God's strength but a rock for Jesus to trip over, with all the terrible consequences of that for the whole world.

The suffering has to be. There is no other way. Jesus braces himself for the way ahead, in the certainty that it is for great and permanent good, and that is also the message he needs us to hear and understand. Any cross laid on us will be heavy, and it will hurt, but the loving God lays it on us with such tenderness and as gently as he can. Any cross laid on us is not to do with us only, but has far-reaching effects which we will never realise until we reach heaven and see there the value of the painful journey we have lovingly travelled in God's company.

Discussion starters

1. How can we ensure that our well-meaning friendship never becomes a stumbling block to another's spiritual growth?

2. Are we prepared to accept the cross God needs to lay on us, or are we trying to remain in control and choose our own?

All-stage talk

You will need two lengths of bramble, and gardening gloves to handle them. If you can get hold of a length of chain as well, this would be excellent; otherwise, rope, or a paper chain will do fine.

Lay the two lengths of bramble to form a cross

on the floor, explaining what you are doing for the benefit of those who will not be able to see this. Make the point that you are wearing protective gloves as the brambles are painful. Explain that the brambles represent all the suffering and pain of the cross. Ask for a volunteer to stand at the top end of the cross. This person represents all of us humans, chained up in all the sin and selfishness that stops us from living freely. (Chain their hands together.) Ask another volunteer to stand at the foot end of the cross, some distance from it. This person represents Jesus at the point of today's Gospel.

Last week we heard how Simon Peter was ready to speak out the truth he had realised about Jesus – that Jesus was the Christ, the Son of the living God. Jesus knew his friends had to be sure of this before they could cope with the next stage of the plan. Now that was in place, and it was time for Jesus to get his friends ready for what had to happen next.

Jesus couldn't just go on working in one part of our world, because he had come into the world to save all of us. That would mean walking a very painful road – the way of the cross. The pain of giving his life on the cross was the only way for Jesus to be able to reach us and set us free. He couldn't get round it; he had to go through with it, even though he knew it would hurt.

Ask the person who is representing Jesus to take their shoes off and start walking towards the cross. Before they get there, stop them as you remind people how Simon Peter couldn't bear to think of his friend going through all that pain, and said, 'Never, Lord! This shall not happen to you!' But if Jesus had listened to him (walk round to the representative human in chains), we would never have been set free from the sin that imprisons us. Never. There would have been no hope for us any more.

(Go back to 'Jesus'.) The good and wonderful news is that Jesus loved us far too much to let his own suffering stop him from saving us. Today we won't make (Lawrence) walk barefoot over those brambles, but as we think of Jesus gladly stepping out to Jerusalem, where he knew he would meet terrible pain and suffering, let's thank him in our hearts for loving us so much that he was prepared to do it anyway (walk round to the human in chains) so that we could all be set free. (Set the person free.)

All-age ideas

- Have a photo/picture display, taken from news-papers and magazines, under the caption 'Take up your cross', of people who are carrying substantial burdens in their lives.

- Have the bramble cross placed on the floor near the altar so that people see it and are reminded of its meaning as they receive communion.

Prayer of the Faithful

Celebrant
As followers of Jesus Christ,
let us pray to our loving Father in heaven.

Reader
Father, help us all in your Church
to understand what it really means
to love and serve you.
At the times of testing, strengthen us,
at unexpected or undeserved suffering, support us,
at the end of our energy, revive us
and teach us through it all
the inexplicable peace and joy
that comes from doing your will.

Silence

We look to the cross:
and see your love for us.

Father, have mercy on us for the misdirected use
of time, money and resources in this world.
In the struggle against evil and sin, empower us,
so that justice and righteousness are established,
upheld and celebrated,
as hearts rejoice in the freedom of all that is good.

Silence

We look to the cross:
and see your love for us.

Father, renew our commitment to your loving
in all our relationships, our work and our prayer.
In the hard choices, give us wisdom,
in the painful decisions, affirm us,
and may our words speak your truth,
whether that is to encourage,
to comfort or to challenge.

Silence

We look to the cross:
and see your love for us.

Father, bring healing and wholeness
to those who suffer, in body, mind or spirit.
In the sleepless nights and endless days of pain,
give the grace to persevere with patience,
and turn these dark times
into places of spiritual growth.

Silence

We look to the cross:
and see your love for us.

Father, may those who have died
rest in the eternal peace of your presence,
their burdens laid down and their suffering ended.

Silence

We look to the cross:
and see your love for us.

Mindful of Mary's quiet acceptance of God's will,
we join our prayers with hers:
Hail, Mary . . .

We pray our private petitions now
in the silence of God's attentive love.

Silence

Celebrant
Father, we thank you
for your constant loving provision for us,
and want to become better able to do your will;
please hear our prayers,
through the pleading of Jesus, your chosen one.
Amen.

TREASURE SEEKERS

Aim: To know that Jesus is willing to suffer for us
because he loves us.

Starter

Have ready some bean bags or rolled socks to
throw about, and a basket or bag to put them in.
Throughout the throwing activity, ask children by
name to do things – 'Ben, will you give everyone a
bean bag?' 'Noah, will you throw your bean bag as
far as you can?' 'Julian, will you throw your bag as
high as you can?' 'Eleanor, will you go round with
the basket, and, everyone else, will you put your
bag in the basket?' Give lots of praise, thanks
and encouragement throughout. Catch them being
good as much as possible, tactically ignoring the
inappropriate behaviour as much as you can.

Teaching

Explain that the reason they all helped so well during
that activity was that they were being kind. If they
were selfish they wouldn't have done it. Being kind
is doing things for other people, even when it isn't
what we like doing best. Sometimes being kind is
nice (Will you help me eat up these last biscuits so I
can wash the tin?), and sometimes being kind is
not so much fun (Can you help me by putting your
toys away now?). Collect ideas about times they
have been kind and celebrate these.

Tell the children that whenever they are kind
they are being just like Jesus. He loves us so much
that he was ready to give up everything for us, and
put up with lots of hurts. Jesus was kind when he
made people better, and when he made them feel
safe and happy. He was kind because he helped
people and set them free from worrying all the
time. He was kind when they were sorry for what
they had done wrong, and Jesus forgave them.

It is good to practise being kind, whether we are
boys or girls, men or women, and when we do, it
makes Jesus very happy.

Praying

Thank you, God, for those I love
and all they do for me.
Help me to be kind as well –
I really want to be!

Activities

On the sheet there are situations for them to look at
and think how they could be kind here. They are
also encouraged to celebrate the ways other people
are kind to them. Also, the children can do something kind today, making some chocolate cornflake
cakes to give away.

PEARL DIVERS

Aim: To look at why Jesus set his face to Jerusalem.

Starter

All change! Set the children walking or hopping or
jumping, and every time you clap your hands they
change direction, and the method of movement
also changes.

Teaching

Draw the following outlines on thin card to be road
junctions, and have a toy car to drive along them.

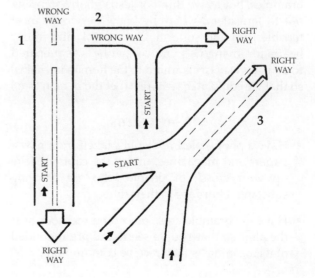

If you are driving along in the wrong direction, you can make a U-turn to go right round and go back the way you came (1). Sometimes you come to a junction, where you have to choose whether to go to the right or the left (2). And sometimes the road you are driving on turns into a new, important road, with more lanes to it, and all you do is carry on in the same direction for this next stage of the road. (3)

These things happen to us in life as well. If we are living wrongly, it's like driving in the wrong direction, and we have to make a U-turn to get right again (1). Often in life we are at those junctions, where we have to choose whether to go one way or another, whether to do what is right or please ourselves and do what is wrong (2). (And if we make the wrong choice, we'll be back at that U-turn!)

Jesus seemed to be at one of those junctions (2) just after Peter had recognised him as the Christ, the Son of the living God. He knew that he had been sent to earth to save us all, and he knew that would be expensive. Not in money, but in life. Jesus knew that the only way he could set us free was to suffer and die for us. So here was the junction – was he willing to go through all that for us . . . or not? The Gospel of Matthew tells us that he was willing, and he started getting his disciples ready for the terrible things that would happen to him at Jerusalem.

In fact, his road had just turned into a new stretch of road (3) – all Jesus was doing was carrying on with the same loving direction he had always had. But now Peter was at a junction (2). He didn't like to hear Jesus talking about having to suffer and die – he didn't want his good friend to suffer at all! Yet if Jesus was saying it, then it must be all part of God's good plan. Peter couldn't cope with that at the moment, so he chose the other way and said to Jesus, 'Never, Lord! This shall never happen to you!'

So now Jesus was at a junction (2). What do you think would have happened if he had agreed with Peter, instead of going on with God's plan? We could never have been set free! So it was a rather important choice for Jesus to make. He chose the loving way – to go through with the saving plan, even though he knew it would be terribly painful and cost him everything. That's how much he loved us. And what about Peter, still driving along the wrong way (1)? Jesus helped him to make a good U-turn so he was back in the right direction again.

Praying

Jesus, it must have been very hard to go to Jerusalem, knowing you would be going to lose your life there. Thank you for loving us enough to do it.

Activities

On the sheet there are the different road shapes so that if you provide microcars (or buttons) they can decide which road is which for the suggested situations in life. There is the possibility for discussion here about friends leading and being led in wrong directions, and leaders need to be aware that some children may need practical help in standing up for what they know is right in difficult circumstances.

GOLD PANNERS

Aim: To look at why Jesus had to suffer and why Peter's advice was rejected.

Starter

Give out road maps and ask them to find a motorway route to Manchester from London which will avoid Birmingham in the rush hour. (They will find this is virtually impossible without a vast detour!)

Teaching

Today we are looking at how some things have to be faced and can't be avoided, however much we would like to side-step them. First tell them about a prophet called Jeremiah, who never found it easy to be God's spokesman but knew that was his calling. Today's reading finds him full of doubts and fears, pouring his heart out to God. Do they ever feel like this? Is it OK to talk to God like this? Yes, it is! God wants us to come to him 'real', wherever we happen to be. Part of prayer is working through our feelings of anger and resentment, with God who can help us with them.

Now read today's Psalm. See how God is always with us, as he would have been with Jeremiah. We are never expected to work on our own, but always with God to help us, and that eases the load.

Now look at today's Gospel, where Jesus, in his human nature, is dreading and fearing the suffering of the cross, while at the same time, in his divine nature, he can see it as the glorious plan of salvation which will bring hope to the world. He can't afford to be tempted to side-step the suffering which is all part of the package.

Praying

Lord, my God,
may I love with sincerity,
hate what is evil
and cling to what is good.
May I be joyful in hope,
patient in affliction
and faithful in prayer. Amen.

Activities

On the sheet there is a short sketch to read or act out, which looks at our willingness to offer ourselves but our surprise at being expected to put up with some costly giving as part of the deal. Also they are encouraged to pray for those having doubts and misgivings, and those going through a time of testing.

TWENTY-THIRD SUNDAY OF THE YEAR

Thought for the day

It is our responsibility to encourage and uphold one another in living by the standard of real love.

Reflection on the readings

Ezekiel 33:7-9
Psalm 94:1-2, 6-9
Romans 13:8-10
Matthew 18:15-20

It is never easy to tell someone you think their behaviour is out of order. It is particularly unpleasant to do this to a loved one, or to a member of your parish community. At the mere thought of it, we are bombarded by fears of judgementalism and hypocrisy, and the possibility that picking someone up on their behaviour runs counter to the Christian principles of compassion and accepting love. It is a difficult path to tread, but that is no reason for dismissing it, and for too long we have been content to do so.

Obviously, we are to love one another with God's love, and that will guide us to approach anyone with respect and honour, regardless of what they have done or failed to do. But we do one another no kindness by turning a blind eye to behaviour which is clearly contrary to God's way of living, or excusing and accepting standards of behaviour which are against his law of love. There are many cases of people who, having waded through great suffering as a result of their sin, have heartily wished that someone had been courageous enough to challenge them about their behaviour at the outset. Through Ezekiel we are warned that any of us who opt out of such challenging, however difficult it might be for us, are actually held partly responsible for any evil that results.

Today's Gospel has some practical advice for us in this delicate area. Matthew places it in the teaching Jesus gives his followers about the kingdom. He has just been telling the story of great love and compassion about the way a shepherd searches for one lost sheep until he finds it. It is in the context of this total concern for each individual, and God's loving commitment to the idea of rescue, that we are told to take one another discreetly aside and talk over the problem with them. This is no judgemental confrontation, then, but it is a recognition of our concern, the concern of the Church, and, most importantly, God's concern for the well-being of a loved sheep.

This meeting may be enough, especially if it happens early enough, to bring about a change of heart, or a realisation of the dangers, and a change of direction before the situation gets totally out of control. So often, this is the stage we miss out on, with serious and often tragic consequences for all concerned.

We are given a graded list of courses of action, which, in principle, allow as much opportunity as possible for the matter to be treated discreetly and calmly, so as to avoid the damaging public humiliation and self-righteous hysteria which the media revel in and which is so alien to the concept of Christian love. In the event of all approaches being deliberately rejected, there is the need to recognise where the person is. It is both pointless and dangerous to pretend that what is sinful is acceptable and right. Someone who is deliberately placing themselves outside God's care is doing just that. What they then need is our honest acceptance of where they are, and our continued love and prayer.

Discussion starters

1. Why do we instinctively draw back from facing someone with their sin and talking through it with them? Should we have a special ministry for this, or is it everyone's concern?

2. Where does welcome and acceptance of the sinner turn into a lack of concern for their behaviour which is damaging for them and the community?

All-stage talk

Ask a number of volunteers to get themselves into a line in order of size. When they have achieved it they can be applauded. Draw attention to the way they helped each other in the task, and showed one another if they were in the wrong place, whenever that was noticed. Because they were working on the task as a team, no one got terribly upset by seeing they were in the wrong place – they just moved into the right place.

Today's Gospel gives us all some teaching about helping one another to keep in order as we live as Christians. The good thing about being a Church is that we are all in the same team, God's team, and we can help one another along. But we're not always very happy to do this. The truth is that we are all going to make mistakes and be in the wrong place with God sometimes, so we need to get used to reminding one another and being reminded without getting too upset about it.

Let's look at what we mean by being in the wrong place with God. (Ask some volunteers to stand facing the cross.) Explain that when we are facing God we are living in his love, and whenever we don't live lovingly, we are turning our backs on God. (Ask the volunteers to turn and face the cross when you say something which is loving, or turn their backs on it when you say something which is unloving.) Here are some suggestions: telling lies, telling the truth, looking after someone, being friendly, grumbling about everything, making sure you get your own way, being generous in your giving, telling dirty or unkind jokes, being bossy and pompous, listening carefully, cheering someone up.

And this is the way we want to be as the Church, with all of us facing God's way. It's our job to help one another keep facing that way, and to help them turn round if they are facing the wrong way.

Supposing we are behaving in an unloving way, then, turning our backs on God? (Turn one of the volunteers around and make up the wrong behaviour they are involved in.) How can the rest of the church help?

In today's Gospel we heard what Jesus said: 'Go and take him to one side and talk it over with him.' (Let one of the volunteers tap him on the shoulder and lead him off a short way from the others, pretending to talk with him.) The point is that we don't always realise that we're in the wrong place, and it is kind to let one another know, so that we can do something about it.

We actually ought to be grateful if someone takes us aside and says, 'Look, I've noticed that you've got really snappy lately. Is anything the matter?' We may have thought we were hiding our worry very nobly, and it will help us to talk it over and recognise that we've been taking our problems out on other people. Or perhaps someone is kind enough to take us aside and say, 'I don't suppose you realise, but you never actually look at people when you are saying hello, and it makes them think you aren't interested in them.' Or 'Have you noticed that every time I say anything at all you contradict me? Have I offended you in some way?' Or 'I've noticed you are always nasty to Paul whenever Steven and you are playing, and that's

not very kind. What do you think you could do to stop that happening?'

It may not be a wonderful feeling to know that our faults and failings are noticed, but if it's going to help us put things right, then let's practise being thankful instead of offended, and be ready to help one another up whenever we fall down.

All-age ideas

- Make the Penitential Rite, or a penance service, a chance for a real checking of any selfish or unloving habits we may have slipped into. Here is a possible form for this:

Leader How is it that we are called to live?

All We are called to love God and to love one another.

Leader In that case, let us think about the times we would prefer God to be closing his eyes or blocking his ears.

What would we prefer God not to see us doing?

(Silence for reflection)

What would we prefer God not to hear us saying?

(Silence for reflection)

What would we prefer God not to know us thinking?

(Silence for reflection)

God desires not the death of a sinner but rather that he may turn and live.

All O God, you see all things, hear all things, know all things, and we are ashamed of the unloving way we sometimes act, speak and think. Have mercy on us and forgive us, and enable us to put things right.

- Display three large signs or posters with an eye, an ear, and a thought bubble, and the words: *'Does God hear you speaking with love?' 'Does God see you acting with love?'* and *'Does God find you thinking with love?'*

Prayer of the Faithful

Celebrant
In our need and human weakness,
let us come to Almighty God with our prayers.

Reader
Unchanging God, change us from the heart
until the whole Church awakens to your love
that reaches out, nurtures and celebrates,
neither holding back from what is difficult,
nor rushing where angels fear to tread.
We pray for sensitivity and courage.

Silence

Lord, take us by the hand:
and lead us.

Almighty God, give us such love for the world
that we may pray with longing and desire,
'Your kingdom come.'
Give our leaders the grace to see
their work as service and their role as stewards;
and sharpen both the recognition of needs
and the commitment to just provision.

Silence

Lord, take us by the hand:
and lead us.

Merciful God,
break all habits of destructive behaviour
in our homes and families, our friendships
and in all the homes of this parish.
Develop our ability to celebrate what is good
and face what is not with honesty.

Silence

Lord, take us by the hand:
and lead us.

Healing God, lay your hands on those who suffer,
so that they may know the support of your presence
and find wholeness and peace in your love.
We pray especially for those who are locked
into the conviction
that they are beyond your forgiveness.
May they quickly discover
the freedom of your acceptance.

Silence

Lord, take us by the hand:
and lead us.

Eternal God, in your unchanging love
receive all those who have died in faith,
that they may rejoice in you for ever.

Silence

Lord, take us by the hand:
and lead us.

We make our prayer with Mary,
the Mother of our Redeemer:
Hail, Mary . . .

In silence,
as God our Father listens with love,
we name our own particular cares and concerns.

Silence

Celebrant
Father, we ask you to gather up
these prayers of your people,
through the merits of Jesus, our Saviour.
Amen.

TREASURE SEEKERS

Aim: To know that God forgives us.

Starter

Provide enough potatoes and spoons for everyone,
so that they can try getting from one end of the
room to the other and back as quickly as possible,
trying not to drop the potato. If the children are at
the older end of the age-range you could make this
into a race, but that isn't necessary, as it is the
exercise in balance and sorting out mishaps which
is important. Support those who are hesitant or
timid, so they get used to picking the potato up
and trying again when things go wrong.

Teaching

Talk about the potato and spoon runs, and how
hard it was to manage without getting it wrong
and dropping the potato. What did they do to put
things right when their potato dropped? They didn't
stand and do nothing and they didn't give up.
They went after the runaway potato, picked it up and
put it back in the spoon. Then they could carry on.

In our life we sometimes make mistakes. Sometimes we choose to do what we know is wrong.
Both children and grown-ups sometimes choose to
do what they know is wrong. We might have been
told to stop drawing on the wall, but we choose to
do it anyway. We might see our baby sister is asleep,
and we choose to wake her up and make her cry.
Lots of the time we choose to do the right thing, but
what can we do to put things right when we have
done what is wrong?

We can say sorry. Saying sorry means that we wish
we hadn't been unkind or disobedient, and we want
to put things right. We can say sorry to grown-ups, to
our big brothers and sisters or our little brothers and
sisters. We can say sorry to our friends. And we can
say sorry to God. When we have said sorry, and
meant it, God will help us to put things right, and
then we can carry on happily with our life again.

Praying

Jesus, when people say to me, 'No!'
and I think, 'I'm still going to do it,
whatever they say',
I know that isn't good, and I'm sorry, Jesus.
Thank you for helping me put it right again.

Activities

On the sheet there are all kinds of things and people in the wrong places, and the children can try sorting out where they ought to be. They can also make a puzzle which can be put together wrongly, but they put it right.

PEARL DIVERS

Aim: To know we are to help one another live in God's way.

Starter

Give everyone a building brick (all different sizes and colours) and a drawn plan of the tower they are all going to build. They help one another to get the bricks in the right places, so the tower is completed. They can each only handle their own brick.

Teaching

Have an outlined person cut from thin card or paper, which is split into chunks as shown below.

Point out to the children how they all helped one another in the tower building, and if someone noticed that a brick was in the wrong place they helped to change it. We all belong to the Church of God, and we have to work together, helping one another so that the church can be what it is meant to be – the Body of Christ (fix the body together so everyone can read it).

(Put down a pair of binoculars.) If I want to look at the moon, and see it clearly, I can use these binoculars to help me. Suppose I was looking at a group of Christians. The binoculars I'd be looking through would be magic ones, so that I could see not just what they looked like but what they were really like as people, and how they behaved. (Look through your binoculars at the group.) What do you think I would see?

Collect all their ideas, which may include such things as looking just like everyone else, going to church, praying, reading the Bible, loving God, helping people, loving people, trying to be good and making mistakes but wanting to put them right. It's true that people with magic binoculars should be able to look at Christians and see that we are loving, honest, kind and friendly, but most of all they should be able to see that we know we are loved and forgiven by the God who made us. They should be able to see that we know and love the true God.

How can we help one another to be like this? (Get the bricks and build them up as the ideas are mentioned.)

- We can pray together and for one another.
- We can cheer one another out of bad moods.
- We can say if we think something is wrong.
- We can be keen and join in at church so others can see we mean it.
- We can listen and look so we notice if someone is sad or worried.
- We can be a good example by how we behave.

That way we will be working in God's team, as he has called us to do, helping and encouraging one another so that as a church, as the Body of Christ, we can all be used to make the world a better and happier place.

Praying

Here I am, Lord.
Help me to live your way
and help me to work with others
so that we can all be part of your team.

Activities

On the sheet the children can work out which qualities are the ones we want to build up in one another, and which we want to have sorted out. They can also put into practice the prayer-partner idea, using the form provided.

GOLD PANNERS

Aim: To explore our responsibility as Christians to encourage and uphold one another.

Starter

Play 'pick-up-sticks', using either the bought game, or drinking straws or sticks. Having tipped all the sticks on to a table, each person has to try and remove one without any of the others moving.

Teaching

What made it hard to move one stick on its own was that all the sticks were holding one another up. As Christians, we need to be holding one another up like that, in an interconnected heap of God's love and care, so that we can't easily be tempted away from living in God's promise.

Read the passage from Ezekiel 33. There are two important things to look at here:

1. If we don't warn people and encourage them to turn back to God when they are in the wrong place, we will be held responsible to God for them.
2. The last thing God wants is for people to perish, and he will always forgive; no one is ever a hopeless case.

It's a bit like those sticks again – if evil is trying to pull someone away, we need to start moving, supporting them so they are safe.

Now read today's Gospel, with Jesus picking up on the teaching in Ezekiel and giving us guidelines for dealing with situations where people need to be approached about how they are behaving, or about wrong attitudes. Have the process drawn out like a programme sequence (see below) and trace it through together.

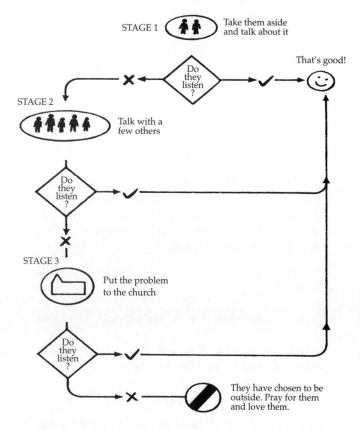

Then look at the passage from Romans, to remind ourselves of what we are aiming at, and what those right attitudes are.

Praying

Lord God, give me understanding
to keep your law of love
so that I walk in the path of your commandments,
for that is what I really want to do.
Help us to encourage one another in living your way
and protect one another from falling.

Activities

The programme sequence is shown on the sheet and this can be used as a basis for a role-play. Suggestions are given for this. They are also encouraged to put in place any practical ideas for mutual support, and their ideas may be valuable for the whole parish community.

TWENTY-FOURTH SUNDAY OF THE YEAR

Thought for the day

Forgiving is a natural result of loving, so it is not an option for us but a command.

Reflection on the readings

Ecclesiasticus 27:30-28:7
Psalm 102:1-4, 9-12
Romans 14:7-9
Matthew 18:21-35

All the readings today make us think about forgiveness: the forgiveness that God gives to us, and the forgiveness expected from us. This theme is found in the reading from Ecclesiasticus, where we first hear that to forgive others for the hurt they do to us, is to open the way for the forgiveness of our own sins.

Psalm 102 celebrates the wonder of God's forgiveness, extending naturally from his loving and compassionate nature and his genuine longing for us to be set free from the hold of sin. In today's section from Romans, Paul points out that God is the one to whom we are all answerable in the end, and since Jesus is Lord of both life and death, there is nowhere that he isn't, or that his mercy isn't.

In today's Gospel, it's Peter again as spokesman, voicing the thoughts of the disciples about forgiveness, and a fair slice of self-righteousness colouring their thinking. Peter would have been considering himself generous to be suggesting forgiveness that stretches to the seventh offence, but, as ever, Jesus shocks him, and us, with a glimpse of God's ideas about things. Suddenly we are in a whole new dimension, placed in the position of the one on the receiving end of mercy, rather than thinking of ourselves as the noble one dishing it out to those inferior to us.

Rather like Nathan the prophet, when he used a story to show King David the reality of his sin, Jesus tells a story which begins by making us identify with the servant who owes millions of pounds and has had that whole debt cancelled. Peter, who had fallen to his knees when he first met Jesus and said, 'Go away from me, Lord, I am a sinful man!' would realise immediately that he was like the servant in the story, owing so much and yet totally forgiven. If we imagine Jesus looking into our eyes as this part of the story is told, we are similarly shown what God has let us off.

From this place, the concept of forgiveness is very different. How can we dare to treat others without forgiveness in view of what God has done in us? It isn't a question of totting up scores against us any more, but simply a natural effect of loving.

Discussion starters

1. To 'forgive and forget': how easy is it to do both?

2. If only God can forgive sins, how can we be expected to do it?

All-stage talk

First ask anyone who has never done anything wrong, *ever*, to raise their hand. Make it quite clear that doing wrong doesn't stop when you grow up, and it's a problem that we all have to deal with. In which case there's going to be another problem we need to deal with. What about when people do things wrong which hurt and upset us? It's bound to happen, and today we are given some very useful teaching from our Lord Jesus to help us with it.

Suppose someone lets you down, cheats on you, loses their temper with you and says some cruel unkind things, lets you down again, steals from you, makes you look stupid, and breaks something you've let them borrow. (Count on your fingers seven typical offences.) Peter goes to Jesus and says, 'Is seven times about the limit for forgiving someone? It seems fairly generous to me. You might as well give up on them after that, don't you agree? Or am I being a bit over-generous – more forgiving than is good for me?'

Jesus says, 'Actually, seven times isn't nearly enough! You need to keep on forgiving until you've lost count and just do it anyway.' And then he tells one of his stories to explain what he means.

Give a volunteer a sign to hold which says 'IOU millions'. The story is about a servant who owes loads and loads of money. He has a wife and children, and he's borrowed so much and has been using his plastic money facility so much that he's stacked up a huge debt to his master, which he can't pay off. The master calls for him (use another volunteer and give him a mobile phone or a smart jacket) and demands the money. The servant kneels down and begs (he does this) to be given more time to pay. The master feels sorry for the servant and lets him off the whole debt! Just like that! (Master draws a thick black line through the IOU.) How do you think the servant feels? (Collect ideas.)

Now that is what God has done for each of us. Ask them to think of all the things they've done wrong, perhaps which no one else knows about except them and God. Think of all the meanness, selfishness, pride, hypocrisy and so on that we have been forgiven completely by God. It's just as if we owed God millions of pounds (hold up the IOU) and God has drawn that line through it, setting us free from the debt.

So here is this happy, free servant, who finds a fellow servant owes him a few pounds. (Give another volunteer a sign with 'IOU a few pounds' on it.) And the same thing happens. The servant goes on his knees and begs (he does this) to be allowed more time to pay. But what does the servant do? He grabs him by the neck and shakes him (not too realistically) and has him thrown into prison until he pays up. What Jesus wants us to ask ourselves is this: Is it fair or right for the servant to behave like this? What do we think?

Next time we are not wanting to forgive someone, let's remember how God has treated us, and pass on that loving forgiveness time and time and time again.

All-age ideas

- In a discussion group, or with children, the Gospel could be acted out, either by miming while it is narrated or by different people taking the parts and saying their words.

- Place the cancelled 'IOU millions' sign in a place where it can be seen as a reminder of what God has done for us in releasing us from our sins.

Prayer of the Faithful

Celebrant
In the knowledge of all God has done for us,
let us bring to him our concerns
for the Church and for the world.

Reader
Thank you, Father, for the love
which forgives again and again,
and is prepared to trust us
with the care of your people
even after we have let you down many times.
Teach us to minister to one another's needs
with compassion, sensitivity and discipline,
so that all are affirmed and encouraged.

Silence

The Lord is full of compassion:
his love lasts for ever.

Thank you, Father, for the order and variety,
simplicity and complexity of this universe.
Thank you for all that humankind is able to do;
may all these gifts be used wisely and well,
for the good of all, including those as yet unborn.

Silence

The Lord is full of compassion:
his love lasts for ever.

Thank you, Father, for what we have been forgiven
and for the opportunities we have each day
to learn the joy of forgiving others.
Smash through our self-righteousness
and keep us learning in humility at your feet.

Silence

The Lord is full of compassion:
his love lasts for ever.

Thank you, Father, for all those who care for the sick,
the unstable, the ungrateful and the difficult.
We pray for all who are on the receiving end
of hate, deceit, suspicion or abuse,
and for those who cause others pain
and distress of any kind.
We pray for your healing and transforming.

Silence

The Lord is full of compassion:
his love lasts for ever.

Thank you, Father, for those whose living and dying
have taught us much about love.
Freed from their pain and restrictions of age or injury,
may they enjoy for ever the life of heaven.

Silence

The Lord is full of compassion:
his love lasts for ever.

With Mary, the Mother of our merciful Lord,
we make our prayer:
Hail, Mary . . .

Now, in the space of silence,
we bring to God, our forgiving Father,
our private petitions.

Silence

Celebrant
Heavenly Father,
we know that in you we shall be safe;
give us courage to do your will gladly,
and hear our prayers in mercy,
through Christ, our Lord.
Amen.

TREASURE SEEKERS

Aim: To know that we are to love as God loves us.

Starter

Sit in a circle. One person does something and the next person does the same, then the next until everyone has done it. This might be standing up, turning round and sitting down again, clapping a rhythm or blinking twice. Everyone changes places, and then you start the round again with a different person and a different action.

Teaching

Tell the children that you are going to give them all a present, and that you want them to share the present they are given with everyone else. Make sure they are all clear about this expectation and then give every child a little pack of chocolate buttons, smarties, jelly babies or raisins. It's nice to have a variety, and only have a few sweets in each pack. Now play some music while the children can go round offering other children sweets from their packs. Encourage them to say 'thank you' for what they are given.

Sit in the circle again and talk about the fun of having things given to us, and the fun of giving to others which they have just enjoyed. God gives us his love all the time in so many ways, and we are to do the same – we are to be loving and giving.

Praying

Thank you, Father God,
for the love you give to me.
Teach me how to be like you,
happy to love and give.

Activities

There is space on the sheet for some printing, which passes on a picture all over the place from the master design, and so reinforces the generosity of God's giving. The children will need potato wedges cut into designs as shown, and some flat trays of thick paint mixed with a little washing-up liquid. Ensure their clothes are well protected and have washing-up bowls with warm soapy water and towels at the ready for afterwards.

PEARL DIVERS

Aim: To know the parable of the unforgiving servant and explore its meaning.

Starter

Help everyone to feel their heartbeat or pulse. Explain that we are going to do an experiment and find out what happens to our heartbeat when we do exercise. Then lead them in running on the spot, star jumps and frog hops for a while, or dance to some praise music. Now everyone feels their pulse again. Is it any different? What have we discovered? That when we move about fast, our heart beats faster.

Teaching

The natural result of moving about is that our heart beats faster. What is the natural result of sitting in the sun? We get hot. What's the natural result of putting the plug in a washbasin and turning on the taps? We get a basin filled with water. What's the natural result of climbing into a swimming pool? We get wet. Lots of things happen naturally as a result of something else.

Wanting to forgive is the natural result of loving. It's what happens. God forgives us because he loves us so much. We're not always so keen to forgive when people have done things to upset us, and Jesus told one of his parables (his stories with secret meanings) about it to help us.

You will need three puppets, made from socks or paper bags as shown.

Give the script to three children to read, and sit them down behind a table placed on its side, so the puppets show over the top.

Narrator	In this story there is Mr Boss the master . . .
Mr Boss	Hello there!
Narrator	Servant Sam . . .
Servant Sam	Hi!
Narrator	. . . and Servant Ben.
Servant Ben	Good morning!
Narrator	Servant Sam had borrowed loads and loads of money from Mr Boss and one day Mr Boss called him in and demanded that the money should be paid.
Mr Boss	You owe me millions and I want my money back NOW! If you can't pay me, then you and your wife and children will have to be sold.
Servant Sam	Oh, Mr Boss! I haven't got the money to give you yet. Please, please, just give me time and I will pay it all.
Narrator	Mr Boss felt sorry for Servant Sam so he let him off.
Mr Boss	OK, Sam. I will let you off. It is a lot of money but you are free. You do not have to pay it.
Servant Sam	You mean I will never have to pay it?
Mr Boss	Never.
Servant Sam	Oh, thank you, thank you, Mr Boss! You are so kind. Yippee – I'm free!
Narrator	Servant Sam was very grateful and very happy. But later on he met Servant Ben who owed him a little money, and he got hold of Ben round the neck and shouted at him to give the money back.
Servant Sam	Come on, Ben, hand over my money. Hand it over NOW! I want it back!
Servant Ben	Oh, Sam, it's only a little bit of money, but I haven't got it to give you. Please give me time and I will pay it all.
Narrator	But Servant Sam wouldn't listen. He had Ben thrown into prison.
Servant Sam	Off to prison with you!
Narrator	When the other servants told Mr Boss about it, he was very upset and very angry, and he went to find Servant Sam.
Mr Boss	Sam, how dare you do that to Ben! You owed me loads of money and I felt sorry for you and let you off. But you did not let Ben off at all. So now I will throw you into prison!

Narrator Servant Sam was kept in prison until he had paid every last penny.

Praying

Father, if you are so kind
and forgiving to us,
we need to be kind and forgiving
to one another.
Please help us.

Activities

On the sheet there are a couple of maths machines to work out, and a puzzle to help them explore why we find it hard to forgive, and how we can learn to do it better.

GOLD PANNERS

Aim: To look at what forgiving is and what it isn't.

Starter

Backwards. Ask each group to work out a series of actions, first doing them forwards and then in reverse, such as washing and drying up, or taking an exam.

Teaching

Today we are going to look at what forgiving is all about. Like our forward and reverse sequences, forgiving is rather like giving in reverse. In the Lord's Prayer we ask for God to give us our daily bread and to forgive, or take from us, our sin, rather as you can suck out the juice from an ice lolly. Forgiveness is something we have to have done for us by the forgiver. We are completely dependent on their kindness and mercy, and if they choose not to forgive us, then we won't be forgiven by them. You can't force someone to forgive you.

Look at Matthew 18:21-22. How is Peter thinking of forgiveness if he feels seven times is quite enough? Probably from the point of view that we don't deserve to be treated badly by people that much, and shouldn't put up with it. Look at the first part of Jesus' story, up to verse 27. That is the true situation with each of us and God. We've had taken from us a debt which we had no hope of ever repaying, and out of love for us God chose to cancel that debt through the sacrifice of Jesus on the cross.

Now read on to verse 35. That's how small-minded we are when we fuss about forgiving other people. Our two great rules of life are to love God and love one another as ourselves. Loving leads us to want to forgive, so it follows that forgiving is not

something we have a right to choose, according to circumstances, but something that, as Christians, we are required to do as part of the rule of love.

Praying

Give us today our daily bread
and for-give us our sins,
as we for-give those who sin against us.

Activities

On the sheet there are some situations to look at where forgiveness is costly, and a look at the differences between forgiving, forgetting and excusing.

TWENTY-FIFTH SUNDAY OF THE YEAR

Thought for the day

We have no right to be envious at the generosity and mercy God shows to others.

Reflection on the readings

Isaiah 55:6-9
Psalm 144:2-3, 8-9, 17-18
Philippians 1:20-24, 27
Matthew 20:1-16

There is a wonderful candour in the way the Bible records people's relationships with God, warts and all. There is a hint of such variety of human weakness in the reading from Isaiah. The prophet tells us that the Lord is always there, ready to forgive with a forgiveness quite beyond our understanding. The Psalm takes up the same theme, 'The Lord is close' – we just have to call him.

Time and again in his teaching, Jesus tries to help us grasp something of the nature of God's loving, which is so much wider and more far-reaching than we seem to understand. Today's parable of the hired workmen is a case in point. The first lot are happy to agree a day's wage, but they cannot cope with the employer being generous to those who started work near the end of the day. Naturally it is not those paid first who complain, but those who see the arrangement as a raw deal for themselves and resent it. If our basis for reckoning in life is simply what we're worth on an hourly rate, then the longest working labourers have a point.

But the owner is looking at it quite differently, and sees the holistic needs of all the men in the market place, just as God sees all people with their needs and is concerned to provide for them all. Whenever we see God's generosity in evidence, however much of a surprise it is in view of our perceived suitability of the recipient, we have no right to question or quibble, but should be rejoicing with the angels at the amazing love of our God.

Discussion starters

1. Are we happy to do God's work, or would we rather do our work, maintaining our control, and offer it to God complete?

2. Are we still expecting God to keep to our rules and guidelines? How can we avoid this in all our planning and church activities?

All-stage talk

Today we might usefully think about being grumpy and sulking, something most of us do from time to time. (Have one or two volunteers to give a really sulky, grumpy face.) Did they notice how sulky and cross Jonah was in our first reading? Do we do this if we have a row? – remembering things that were said at other times and throwing them back at the person we want to upset, and saying, 'I knew it would end up like this! If you'd listened to what I said, this would never have happened!' We feel quite at home here! And if we're a loving parent on the receiving end of all the anger and resentment, which we know comes from a lack of understanding or experience, perhaps we can sense something of how God feels, loving this very hot-headed, angry person shouting at us, and knowing that our job is to stay calm, stay loving, and pick up the pieces once they've got over it.

What is it that makes us sulk, usually? (Collect answers.) Usually it's when we feel hard done by, as if we have been unfairly treated and been given a raw deal, or when we see others get off lightly.

Jesus told a story about some sulking workmen, which we heard today. The ones who worked all day agreed their wage, and at the end of the day they got it in full. Why were they sulking? Because some other workmen, taken on much later in the day, were paid the same wage. So they sulked. And we often behave in the same way. (Sulky faces.) In Jesus' story the owner helps the workmen to understand why they are sulking. He asks them, 'Are you jealous because I am good to these people as well?'

We all need to understand that God doesn't split us up into some who are OK to be saved and some who aren't worth bothering with. We shouldn't get jealous or angry if Christians of another church or tradition seem to be having God's blessing as well as us, or if people who have made bad mistakes in the past are allowed to be part of our fellowship. If we are loving, like God loves, this will make us not sulky (sulky faces) but happy (happy faces).

All-age ideas

- On large notices or posters, stuck on the walls or pillars, display the qualities of our God which today's readings emphasise: gracious; full of compassion; slow to anger; of great goodness; rich in love.

- Mime the parable of the workmen while it is being narrated, or have a group act it, expressing the dialogue in their own words.

Prayer of the Faithful

Celebrant
Let us come with openness
to express our concerns
for the Church and the world,
to the God of compassion
and gracious understanding.

Reader
Loving Father, whenever we start to get offended
by your generosity or open-mindedness,
give us the grace to repent and join your rejoicing.
Guard the Church against self-righteousness
and all rules and limits which you would not own,
but keep always before us the rule of love.

Silence

Not our will:
but your will, Lord, be done.

Loving Father, increase in us love
not only for the victims but for the perpetrators
of evil and violence in our world;
for all governments
which run on corruption and fear.
We pray for a change of heart and attitude,
an awakening to a better way of living,
and the courage to reject wrong principles.

Silence

Not our will:
but your will, Lord, be done.

Loving Father,
may our closeness to family and friends
make us never exclusive, shutting others out,
but always inclusive, welcoming others in.
Encourage us in outgoing hospitality
and keep us from becoming possessive
with those we love.

Silence

Not our will:
but your will, Lord, be done.

Loving Father, we pray for all offenders in prison,
that on release they will not re-offend
but find enough support
to start a new life in the community.
We pray for all who are vulnerable
and unable to cope with the demands of life,
for alcoholics, drug addicts
and all who are sick in mind.
We pray for proper, compassionate help for them.

Silence

Not our will:
but your will, Lord, be done.

Loving Father, we pray for those
who have died alone, unmourned and unnoticed.
We pray for those who have committed suicide
or died in accidents of their own making.
We commend them to your merciful love.

Silence

Not our will:
but your will, Lord, be done.

Loving Father, thank you for helping us to pray;
deepen our loving
so that as we pray through this week
we may do it with your heart of compassion.

Silence

Not our will:
but your will, Lord, be done.

We make our prayer with Mary,
who was always open to God's will:
Hail, Mary . . .

In silence, now,
we approach our loving Father
with our private petitions.

Silence

Celebrant
Merciful Father,
you alone give meaning to our lives;
help us live in closer communion with you,
and accept these prayers,
through Jesus Christ.
Amen.

TREASURE SEEKERS

Aim: To know that God is generous, and when we are generous, we are being like him.

Starter

Play shops, with empty packets and cartons, play money and shopping bags and baskets.

Teaching

When we go out shopping we look out for things that are on special offer. (Show the children some things you have bought this week because there were two toilet rolls for the price of one, or because you got free chocolate bars with your tea bags.) The people who own the shop like to be generous and give things away sometimes so that we shoppers are happy and go back and buy more next time. They end up making more money if they are sometimes generous.

God is generous. He gives away free sunshine and free showers of rain. He gives us free sea and free clouds and free hills and rivers. He gives us life, so we can live in his lovely free earth and enjoy it. God doesn't give us all this because he makes money out of it. God doesn't make money at all. He generously gives us all this just because he loves us. He likes to see us enjoying his gifts, and there's something else he really likes to see.

God loves it when he sees his children being generous like him; when they share and give things away free, and are happy for their friends to have a nice time as well as having a nice time themselves.

When we are generous, we are being like God, and if we get good at giving, we'll end up much more happy than if we tried to keep everything for ourselves.

Praying

Father, you have given us a bright new day
and we would like to spend it in the very best way.
Help us to be generous, giving it away,
helping one another in all we do and say.

Activities

The children can make rubbings of coins so that there is money in the drawn purse on the sheet, and they can make a posy of flowers to give away free.

PEARL DIVERS

Aim: To know the parable of the workmen in the vineyard and explore its meaning.

Starter

Vineyard. Go through the following actions with the children first: vine-planting, watering, weeding, grape-picking, grape-treading, and bottling, appointing a particular area of the room for each task. Call out the tasks and everyone runs to the place and mimes it. Make the change-arounds from task to task quite speedy, and use each task any number of times and in any order. The last person to start doing the job each time is 'fired' until the winner is left.

Teaching

Today's parable is all about some people who worked in a vineyard. As they already know, there's a lot of work to do in vineyards! Tell the story as it is in Matthew 20, involving the children to act it out as you tell it. The ones who are employed can do the actions from the starter activity, with the odd break session included. Make it quite clear that the workers and the boss were happy to agree on the day's wage before they started work.

Did the workers get what they had agreed was fair for a day's work? Yes, they did. Jesus was showing the people that God will always treat us fairly, giving us what we need, but if he wants to be generous we shouldn't get grumpy about it. The vineyard owner wanted to see everyone who needed a job being able to work, so he was happy to pay them all a fair day's wage, rather than just the first ones.

Praying

Lord, help me to be generous like you,
wanting the best for everyone,
and not just for me and my friends.

Activities

On the sheet the children can check whether they get grumpy at other people's blessings, and the parable of the vineyard can be acted out with puppets made from the sheet. Each child will need a card frame or a shoe box.

GOLD PANNERS

Aim: To look at the nature of God's generosity.

Starter

In a circle pass round a twenty-pound note (or a Monopoly equivalent). As it gets to each person they say how they would spend it if it was theirs, and next time round they say who or what they would give it to and why, if they were going to give it away.

Teaching

Look at the parable Jesus told in Matthew 20. It can be read as a group, with parts being taken by different voices. Had the workers agreed a fair wage before they started? Why were they grumbling, then? Point out that it was the owner's right to be generous with his money – and the all-day shift were not losing out. Jesus wanted his hearers to see that whether people came to faith early or late in life, God was simply overjoyed that they were saved. We don't earn our right to everlasting life in any case; new life is a freely given gift, and we shouldn't ever begrudge people having it, even if we feel we have worked harder for God or our church than they have.

Praying

Christ's is the world in which we move,
Christ's are the folk we're summoned to love,
Christ's is the voice which calls us to care,
and Christ is the one who meets us there.

(From a song by John L. Bell and Graham Maule
© Copyright 1989 WGRG/Iona Community.)

Activities

The sheet looks at the significance of 'the last shall be first and the first shall be last' and helps them think through ways of being generous in God's terms, without the limitations and parameters we usually fix in place.

TWENTY-SIXTH SUNDAY OF THE YEAR

Thought for the day

God longs for us to die to sin and live, but it has to be our choice, too.

Reflection on the readings

Ezekiel 18:25-28
Psalm 24:4-9
Philippians 2:1-11
Matthew 21:28-32

However much we may long for our loved ones to go to the doctor, do their homework or take a holiday, we all know from experience that, unless they share our concern, they won't get round to doing what, to us, seems so sensible and good for them. We may nag or drop hints, threaten or cajole, but in the end it is up to them and we can do nothing about that.

It must be rather like that for God, as he sees what would be such lasting good for the children he loves, and yet must watch us all making disastrous choices, never getting round to tackling our habitual sins, wasting opportunities, and taking no notice of all his hints and teaching, his examples and offers of help.

We can sense that longing for our good and grief at our turning away from it, all through the Bible, in both the Old and the New Testaments. Ezekiel is just one example of the way God keeps speaking to his people through the voice of the prophets, to urge them to look seriously at the consequences of wrong choices and the joyful hope of right ones. Time after time he explains that he is not out to shoot them down, or to condemn; no way does God find pleasure in anyone perishing as a result of leading a life of evil and wrong choices. At the same time, being of nature ultimate truth, goodness, love and justice, it is impossible for God to have deep life companionship with evil, deceit, hypocrisy, corruption or impurity.

We are each of us only responsible for the choices we ourselves make. It is very important to understand that God will never hold us to blame for any evil committed by our parents or ancestors, and any guilt we may be carrying as a result of another's abuse of us is guilt that belongs to them, not us. It is God's will that we should be freed of such unjust burdens.

The truth is that God promises to teach us how to make good choices, and through Jesus he is working within us, inspiring both the will to do good and the act of carrying it out. What the religious leaders in today's Gospel needed to see was that talking about it is not enough; a good choice is completed in the action. It is the son who gets round to doing the work who is recommended, rather than the one who airily talks about it but does nothing.

So we are involved in the kind of caring, encouraging relationship with God which really does enable us to tackle those wrong areas in our life. We are never too old, too set in our ways or too busy to take God up on his offer of live-in help.

Discussion starters

1. Does a loving and merciful nature mean that God will overlook all evil, or should we be looking at the prospect of judgement far more seriously than is fashionable?

2. Why did the religious leaders not recognise what God was doing? Can this still happen today?

All-stage talk

Bring along the details of a children's colouring competition, and also one of those junk mail promotional letters which tell you that you have already been selected as a winner.

Begin by sharing this exciting letter with everyone, reading out some of the blurb, and getting a volunteer to scratch any secret messages included. No doubt many of us receive these kinds of letters. When we do so, we have a choice: are we going to bin it (or preferably recycle it), or will we take them up on their wonderful offer and claim our prize? What we decide will depend on all kinds of factors, such as how busy we are, how desperate for winnings we are, how many previous disappointments we have experienced, and whether we actually believe them.

But one thing is certain. Unless we decide to return our reply slip, we have no chance of winning anything at all. It's the same with colouring competitions. A prize is offered and anyone has a chance of winning. But if you don't get your felt-tips or paints out and do the colouring, and send it off in time, you will have no chance of winning a prize, however good you are at colouring.

Today we are being reminded by God that he has great prizes and gifts for us, which he longs for us to enjoy. He wants to see us all as winners, happily receiving the gift that has been reserved specially for us. But . . . and it is a big 'but' . . . unless we choose to turn to God and take him up on his offer, we will have no chance at all of winning. If we choose wrong instead of right, evil instead of good, and self instead of God, we cannot have the joy and peace and life that God longs to give us. We don't just get it anyway, however we live. Lots of people think that is what happens, but it isn't because God isn't like that. He is a God of goodness and love, truth and kindness. Do we want to go along with that? We have to choose it, then, and start doing something about it.

As soon as we choose it, God can give us all the help we need, and he will, because all he wants is for us to know complete and lasting happiness with him.

All-age ideas

• As people come into church give everyone a copy of the form shown below, and provide time for them to fill it in. Actually ticking the boxes emphasises their commitment, and the forms can be given with the offering and presented for God's work.

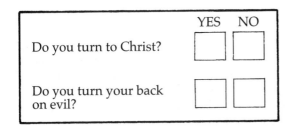

	YES	NO
Do you turn to Christ?		
Do you turn your back on evil?		

- Everyone can say these words from Philippians to one another, as words of encouragement:
    It is God who works in you to will and act according to his good purpose.
    It is God who works in you to will and act according to his good purpose.

Prayer of the Faithful

Celebrant
God has called us;
as we gather in his name
let us bring to him our prayers
which come from our love and concern.

Reader
Lord, we thank you
for all the help and encouragement
we are given from the Church –
from its worship, teaching and fellowship;
from its faithfulness in prayer.
Bless and further all loving ministry
in word and sacrament
throughout the world Church;
inspire us all to want your will and to do it.

Silence

O God, work in us:
inspiring both will and deed.

Lord, we pray for the world,
where the misery and tragedy of wrong choices
grieves your heart of love.
Let there be wisdom and compassion
in all negotiations and decisions;
let there be humility in leadership
and responsibility for right action shared by all.

Silence

O God, work in us:
inspiring both will and deed.

Lord, we bring to you the joys and worries,
the frustrations and accomplishments of this week
in the lives we have met and shared.
As we pray, let your light shine into all these lives
for fresh directing and lasting good.

Silence

O God, work in us:
inspiring both will and deed.

Lord, we bring to you those we know
who are ill or suffering in any way.
Give them healing, restore them
in body, mind and spirit,
and provide them with your indwelling.

Silence

O God, work in us:
inspiring both will and deed.

Lord, we remember in your presence
all those who have died,
and particularly those we have known and loved.
Thank you for them,
and thank you for your promise
of eternal life and peace.
May we comfort one another through your love.

Silence

O God, work in us:
inspiring both will and deed.

As we join our prayers with those of Mary,
may we learn from her example
of true humility:
Hail, Mary . . .

Let us whisper to our heavenly Father
our particular burdens of prayer.

Silence

Celebrant
Father, in you we hope and place our trust;
please accept these prayers,
and help us to do your will,
through Christ Jesus.
Amen.

TREASURE SEEKERS

Aim: To know about making good choices.

Starter

Beforehand cut out blobs from different coloured paper and also a set of small blobs of the same colours. Have the small set laid out on a table at the side of the room and the others scattered all over the floor. Put on a praise tape and let the children all dance around. When the music stops they choose a colour to stand on. One child has been standing with her back to the others, facing the table of colours. She chooses one of the colours and the children standing on that colour blob get a sweet or a sticker. Then another child becomes the selector.

Teaching

Prepare a Y-shaped road junction from paper and lay it on the floor. In one direction have a full pot of honey hidden, and in the other direction an empty pot of honey. Introduce a bear who walks along the road until he comes to the fork junction. He says to himself, in a growly voice, 'Now which way shall I choose? I can go this way or that way. Now let me see.' Invite the children to help the bear choose. They can ask you where the roads go to, if that will help the bear to choose wisely.

When they ask, show them (but not the bear) that one way leads to a full pot of honey and the other way to an empty pot of honey. Now they can talk to the bear, giving him their help and advice. He talks back, wondering if they are really, really sure, and just supposing they are wrong . . . and having other misgivings that a bear might worry about. In the end the bear decides to take the children's advice and finds the full pot of honey, which makes him very happy.

When we have difficult things to choose, God will give us help and good advice. God is good, so what he tells us is always going to help us make a choice that is good.

Praying

Help us, dear God,
to choose the good
and loving way. Amen.

Activities

On the sheet they can make their own road for a bear at home to try, drawing in something nice at one end of the road and something nasty at the other. They can also choose their favourite colours to decorate today's prayer.

PEARL DIVERS

Aim: To know we have to choose whether to work with God or against him.

Starter

Beforehand prepare a number of pieces of drinking straw holding rolled-up numbers. Half these numbers (all of which are in the same colour straw) end with a 0. The children choose a straw and see if it has a 0 in the number. If it has they can have a sweet or a sticker. Draw their attention to the colour of the winning straws. Have enough winning ones for everyone to have one if they choose the right colour.

Teaching

Talk about the choices we make all day long – what to have for breakfast, whether to brush our teeth or pretend we have already brushed them, whether to play football or chat with friends, whether to share our crisps or eat them all ourselves, whether to work hard or waste our time. Some of these choices don't matter much, but when they are choosing between good or bad, kind or unkind, then they matter very much.

One of the parables Jesus told was about two brothers. Their dad was yet another vineyard owner – there are a lot of vineyards in Israel (you could have a bottle of wine from that area to prove it) so that is why Jesus used them a lot in his stories. Today he would probably talk about owners of video shops or supermarkets. Anyway, the dad went to one of his sons and said, 'Off you go and work in the vineyard, son.' And his son turned round and said to his dad, 'No, I'm not going to.' But later on he changed his mind, and went.

Then the dad went to his other son, and said the same thing to him: 'Off you go and work in the vineyard, son.' This son jumped up and said to his dad (very politely), 'Yes, sir, I will!' But he didn't actually go.

Which of these two brothers did what his father wanted? When the children have told you, find the place in Matthew 21 and show them how they have just answered the question Jesus asked the people listening to his story. And it's the right answer. What is Jesus telling us all in this parable? Who is the father? It's God. Who are the brothers? All of us. When are we like the first brother? When are we like the second brother? What is most important to God – hearing us say we will follow him and do his work in our life, or watching us choosing to do something about it?

Praying

Lord, teach me to choose good, not bad,
to choose kindness, not cruelty,
to choose honesty, not lies,
to choose right, not wrong. Amen.

Activities

There are instructions on the sheet for making a paperweight which they can use to think about their actions and whether they are working with God or against him. Each child will need a small lump of self-hardening clay or some salt dough (two cups of flour, one cup of salt, water to mix). It is also made quite clear that God knows they are not to blame for someone else's wrong, and they need never feel to blame for something bad which someone might have done to them. Be sensitive, here, to any children who are living with this kind of guilt.

GOLD PANNERS

Aim: To look at our choices and their consequences.

Starter

Consequences. Pass round sheets of paper so that each line is added by a different person. If it's a long time since you played this, here are the sections, to refresh your memory:

1. Boy's name
2. Girl's name
3. Place
4. He said to her . . .
5. She said to him . . .
6. The consequence was . . .

Then all the versions are shared and enjoyed.

Teaching

Today we are looking at the choices we make, and the consequences of them. First read the passage from Ezekiel, where the prophet is speaking out God's concern for the people. Although God loves them and hopes they will turn to him, if they deliberately turn away then the terrible consequences will not be God's fault but their own. Think about some present-day examples, but also notice the important message that God doesn't want anyone to perish – he's not trying to catch us out so we fail. Also, notice how it's our own responsibility that counts; we are not to blame for wrongs committed by anyone else against us.

Now read about Jesus' confrontation with the religious leaders. Use the parable of the two sons to see what Jesus was trying to show these leaders, and what they were refusing to hear.

In complete contrast, look at the beautiful words in Philippians about Jesus, so that we can all benefit from this amazing example of humility and chosen obedience. That can inspire us, and, as Paul says, Jesus promises us live-in help to make right choices in life.

Praying

Lord, may our attitude be the same
as that of Christ Jesus,
who, being in very nature God,
did not consider equality with God
something to be grasped,
but made himself nothing,
taking the very nature of a servant,
being made in human likeness
and being found in appearance as a man,
he humbled himself and became obedient to death –
even death on a cross!

Activities

The sheet includes a choices activity, and they are encouraged to think through the possible consequences of wrong and right choices. They could also work with music and mime to bring the Philippians reading to life and share this with the people in church.

TWENTY-SEVENTH SUNDAY OF THE YEAR

Thought for the day

God does everything possible for our spiritual growth and well-being, but still we can choose hostility and rejection.

Reflection on the readings

Isaiah 5:1-7
Psalm 79:9, 12-16, 19-20
Philippians 4:6-9
Matthew 21:33-43

Following on from last week, we hear today how Jesus responds to the challenge of the religious leaders to name his authority and qualifications. First he had met their confrontation with a return question, which directed them both to the answer and to their unwillingness to accept it. Now he follows this up with a parable drawn directly from their own familiar tradition. As soon as they hear the beginning of it, they are bound to tune in to the passage from Isaiah, which is also our Old Testament reading for today. There is a good chance, therefore, that they will already be looking out for God's loving exasperation with his people, in whom he has invested so much and whose fruit is so disappointing that exile and suffering are inevitable.

However, although the two parables begin in a similar way, Jesus' story suddenly changes direction. If the religious leaders are going to hear anything, this is surely the time their ears should prick up and their hearts be challenged. Before, God had found bad fruit instead of good, and the tenderly planted vineyard was abandoned to the encroaching wilderness. In this story the owner does not come in person but sends his servants, who meet an appalling reception of hostility and rejection. Anyone already familiar with identifying God as the vineyard owner would perceive that his servants must be God's prophets. So when the story goes on to talk about the owner sending his own son, and the vineyard managers choosing to plot his death, Jesus is telling them in as clear a way as he can about his own identity and authority.

Yet what do we find? The smug reply of the Pharisees shows that they are not yet willing to take on board the implications of this parable for themselves, even though Jesus has brought them to the very brink of understanding. Yes, they can see what a terrible thing it would be to treat God like that, but, no, it can't have anything to do with them, for they are bastions of the faith, are they not?

It is a warning for all of us. We cannot assume that just because we were born into a church-going family, have been to church for years, are on the Parish Pastoral Council, or live in a so-called Christian country, that we are immune from the responsibility of making a personal choice to follow Christ each day of our lives. As Paul says in Philippians, we must keep on doing the things we have been taught, the things that bring us closer and closer to God.

One of the reasons we reject God is because he will insist on telling us the truth, and we prefer the flattery and indulgence of self-deception. Yet if we can be courageous enough to allow ourselves to hear him, we gain so much.

Discussion starters

1. How might knowledge of the Isaiah parable enable those listening to Jesus to grasp the significance of his version?

2. Paul was also a Pharisee. How can we account for the astounding difference in outlook between the Pharisees in today's Gospel and the letter to the Christians at Philippi?

All-stage talk

Bring along a watering can, secateurs, a gardening fork and some slug pellets. Show everyone these things and have any gardeners in the group (both young and old) explain to you what they are all for. Ask if anyone has been using these this year, and what has been grown and eaten.

All gardeners can feel in good company, because one of the often-used pictures of our God is as a gardener. In our reading from Isaiah, God is imagined as a gardener planting vines in a vineyard – digging the ground, and getting it all ready, planting carefully, weeding and watering regularly, supporting the branches and pruning, and really caring for this vine so that it may bear a wonderful juicy crop of grapes. Gardeners are always fond of what they grow – that's why they'll go to any lengths to protect their plants from things like slugs and greenfly. We can imagine God caring like that (only more so) for his people, and wanting desperately to protect them from evil and sin.

But when this gardener comes to pick the crop of grapes which he has grown so carefully, he finds they are not delicious and sweet but bad and sour, and the lovely vineyard ends up all overgrown and wild. Like a gardener, God has looked for the good fruit of justice in his people but found only bloodshed; he has looked for the good fruit of righteousness and found only the cries of those who are treated badly. What kind of fruit does God the gardener find in us, in his Church, or in our society? Does what he finds in this church and this world put a smile on his face, or does he find instead sour fruit which makes him sad?

We all know the kind of thing that delights God. He loves to find such fruits as love, joy, peace, patience, kindness, goodness, gentleness and self-control. He loves to see justice, mercy, right living, purity and honesty. May this garden grow a bumper crop of such fruits, that will gladden the heart of God and bring blessing and healing to our town.

All-age ideas

- Incorporate grapes and secateurs in one of the flower arrangements.

- Have the parable section of the Gospel mimed as it is read. Use clear, unfussy and stylised movements. Have the owner at the back of the action, facing the congregation, with his hands on the shoulders of the son until he sends him off. As two farmers grab the son and throw him out of the vineyard, they both pull his arms so that for a moment the son is stretched as if on a cross, and at the back the owner assumes the same position. At verse 40 the group freezes in attitudes of hatred and rejection. As the owner approaches, arms by his sides, they turn and see him, cover or avert their eyes, and creep away.

Prayer of the Faithful

Celebrant
Let us pray trustfully to the God
who has loved us into being
and cherished us all our life.

Reader
Loving God, guide your Church
into ways of spiritual beauty and gracious wisdom.
May your word be spoken out with passion
and heard with humility and joy.
Sustain and feed us
so that we bear fruit in abundance.

Silence

Root your people:
firmly in your love.

Loving God, may justice and righteousness
flourish in this neighbourhood,
this country, this world.
Bless those who work to right what is wrong
and mediate where there is conflict.
Raise up leaders who are happy to serve
and protect them from power's corruption.

Silence

Root your people:
firmly in your love.

Loving God, we thank you
for the nurturing we have received,
and pray for our children and young people
as they grow.
Protect them from evil
and strengthen them in faith;
may they continue to be yours for ever.

Silence

Root your people:
firmly in your love.

Loving God, give comfort and healing to all
who are in any kind of need, sorrow or pain.
May they sense your reassuring presence
and know that you are there with them,
wherever their journey takes them.

Silence

Root your people:
firmly in your love.

Loving God, we pray for those
who have died to this earthly life,
and now see you face to face.
We remember your mercy
and commit our loved ones
to the safety of your keeping.

Silence

Root your people:
firmly in your love.

Loving God, we thank you for all the care
and attention that you lavish on us;
make us worthy of our calling
and continue your ongoing work in us.

Silence

Root your people:
firmly in your love.

With Mary, who so calmly
made herself available to God's will,
we join our prayer:
Hail, Mary . . .

Now, in the space of silence,
we bring our private petitions
to the Lord of the vineyard.

Silence

Celebrant
Father, we thank you for your steadfast love,
and ask you to accept these prayers,
through Christ our Lord.
Amen.

TREASURE SEEKERS

Aim: To know that God helps us grow in all kinds
of ways.

Starter

Plant some bulbs, either in pots to be flowering at
Christmas time or outside to bloom next spring,
brightening up a patch of ground near the church.

Teaching

Bring a selection of fruit and vegetables, preferably
with a piece of the plant they came from, and let
the children look, handle and smell them. You
could also eat some. Talk about all the growing that
had to go on before the plant gave us this fruit, and
the hard work of the farmers or gardeners who
looked after the plants so they had enough water,
food and light.

We take quite a lot of careful looking after as
well. All that eating and drinking we need, all
those cuddles and games, all that washing and
ironing, tooth-brushing, and comforting after nasty
dreams.

God is in all the loving care that we get and give,
and he hopes we will grow up to be:

- healthy and strong in our bodies, so we can work
  and play and help
- healthy and strong in our minds, so we can think
  sensibly and wisely
- healthy and strong in our souls, so we get to know
  God as our friend.

Praying

Dear God, thank you for making us grow
big and strong in your love
so that our lives are fruitful.

Activities

The children can make salads or fruit salad with the fruit and vegetables, and use some, such as cabbage and carrot and potato, to print a large picture which has the prayer stuck on to it.

PEARL DIVERS

Aim: To know the two parables of the vineyard and their meanings.

Starter

Come and sit on my friend's chair! One person goes out of the room, and the others arrange themselves in a row, each standing behind a chair. They agree on which chair is going to be the 'right' one to sit on. When the person comes in, everyone tries to encourage them to sit on their friend's chair and the person chooses one and sits down. If it's the 'right' one, they get a cheer and applause; if it isn't, they get tipped off and a thumbs-down. Then it's someone else's turn to go outside.

Teaching

Today we are looking at some people who found it very hard to recognise the truth when they saw it, and we'll be looking at what it feels like to be chucked out and rejected.

To help tell this week's parables, prepare some cut paper shapes of appropriate colours, as shown below.

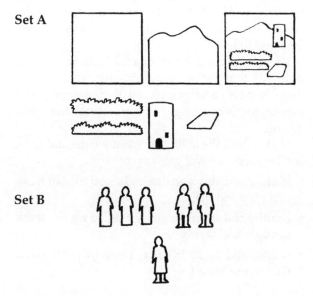

Set A

Set B

As you tell the parable from Isaiah, place the shapes from set A, one by one, on to a sheet of plain paper. In the Isaiah story the pieces will then be gradually taken away again until there is nothing

left. Help the children to work out who's who in this story, and what it might mean. Then put down the words of verse 7 and everyone can read them together:

The vineyard belonging to the Lord is the nation of Israel,
his carefully planted garden is the people of Judah;
the Lord looked for justice but all he found was killing;
the Lord hoped for right living but there were only cries of pain.

Explain that many generations later, Jesus was trying to get the religious leaders to recognise who he was, but he was having a hard time getting through to them because they didn't want to hear. (Like us when someone calls out that it's bedtime and we accidentally on purpose don't hear them and carry on playing!) Jesus chose a story they would already know, as the children will see, but at one point it changes. See if they can spot where this is. As they listen to the story, they can pretend they are the religious leaders, who don't approve of Jesus, and have just challenged him to tell them who on earth he thinks he is.

Use the shapes again, building up the picture just as before, but go on to the shapes in set B. See if anyone has spotted the point of change, and then draw out what they think this parable means, and what the leaders would think as they listened to it. (The vineyard and planted vine are still the same, the servants are God's prophets, sent to speak out God's words, and the son is Jesus, God's Son. Being thrown out and killed is being rejected and crucified.)

Praying

Keep our ears open, Lord,
to hear what you want us to hear.

Activities

The sheet can be made into a stand-up model of a vineyard so that the children can build it up as they go over the parable.

GOLD PANNERS

Aim: To look at the vineyard stories and their meanings in context and for our own time and situation.

Starter

Make toffee apples. Push sticks into the apples and dip them into the toffee, which has been mixed beforehand and just needs the cooking. Alternatively, use melted chocolate for dipping. Leave them to harden on greaseproof paper.

Teaching

Remind them of the situation Jesus was facing in last week's Gospel, with the Scribes and Pharisees confronting him while he was teaching the people and demanding to be told by what authority he was doing so. Having told them through the parable of the two sons that they needed to get their act together and start putting their own words into action, Jesus now starts to tell them a story they would already know. (We are sometimes less threatened and more ready to listen to familiar things.)

First read the parable as it is in the Old Testament, in Isaiah. The 'who's who' is also made clear here. They have just experienced the satisfaction of good fruit; God is saying he has lavished care on this vineyard, but it has only produced bad, disappointing spiritual fruit, and cannot avoid becoming overgrown and overrun with weeds. National misery is bound to come to a people who have rejected their God.

Then go on to the parable Jesus told the religious leaders, picking up on the similarities and the differences. (It is often helpful to people if these are noted in two columns.) Read up to verse 39. What do they think the message is now? Who is the owner, who are the farmers and the servants?

Once you have discussed this, look at the question Jesus asks, and the answer he gets (verses 40-43). Do you think the leaders realise that they are the farmers in the story? Jesus follows the parable with direct teaching, explaining their situation to them, and it hits them that Jesus was talking about them, but that didn't make them change their hearts – it only made them more determined than ever to get rid of this teacher.

Praying

Turn now, O God of hosts, look down from heaven; behold and tend this vine,
preserve what your right hand has planted.
Restore us, O God of hosts;
show us the light of your countenance (face)
and we shall be saved.

(From Psalm 79)

Activities

On the sheet there are questions to answer about both 'vineyard' stories.

TWENTY-EIGHTH SUNDAY OF THE YEAR

Thought for the day

We are all invited to God's wedding banquet, but in accepting we must allow the rags of our old life to be exchanged for the freely given robes of holiness and right living.

Reflection on the readings

Isaiah 25:6-10
Psalm 22
Philippians 4:12-14, 19-20
Matthew 22:1-14

There is a lot of rejoicing in today's readings, the kind of rejoicing which is born of relief and victory, such as was experienced when peace was declared after the Second World War. The images used in the passage from Isaiah emphasise protection and safety in the middle of turmoil, as, for instance, 'shelter from the storm' and 'shade from the heat'. The well-loved Psalm 22 echoes this sense of all being well in God's company, even if we are walking through the valley of the shadow of death, and in both these readings the banquet is prepared by God for his loved ones as a feast of celebration in full view of those who mean harm, emphasising their powerlessness and God's complete victory over evil.

In Philippians, Paul is able to talk about rejoicing in the same breath as suffering. He has trusted God as you might trust ice you have tested, and has found with relief and joy that God does not let us down. In that case, all our time spent worrying anxiously about what might happen is rather a waste of time. Paul suggests that instead of filling our heads with such anxious thoughts we would do better to spend our time contemplating the wonderful glory of God.

We so often slip into the habit of worrying and complaining, rather than rejoicing. At those moments of joy and relief after a difficult or dark patch, we may say to ourselves that we'll never grumble or worry again, because we are at present full of thankfulness; but it doesn't take long before we're back into our old habits. Yet what a lot we miss by failing to rejoice, whatever the circumstances. Rejoicing is a result of trusting God to be the shelter in the storm, and really knowing that he will not let us come to ultimate harm, so that we have, ultimately, nothing to fear.

The parable Jesus tells about the wedding feast

once again features the rejoicing and celebration with God which happen even in the face of violent opposition and rejection. All of us can count ourselves among the guests who have accepted the invitation once it is thrown open to those walking in any direction and with a good or bad past life. And it is quite a celebration, stretched over all time and space, heaven and earth. We can afford to savour that rejoicing, rather than rushing on immediately to the next section of the story.

Wedding garments would have been provided, free of charge, so there is deliberate insult in the guest who has decided not to wear his, but remain in the filthy rags of his old life. Jesus wants his hearers (and Matthew his readers) to be under no illusion. Accepting the honour of a place at the banquet obliges us to accept also the grace to be renewed and transformed. Living with our former outlook, attitudes and behaviour is not on, and places us alongside those who have chosen to reject the invitation.

Discussion starters

1. What does it say about a guest if he accepts the King's invitation but not his freely given new clothing of holiness?

2. Why do you think Jesus made it a wedding feast, rather than any other celebration?

All-stage talk

As people come into church make sure that everyone is given a small picture or cut-out paper shape of a robe of righteousness, with this title on it:

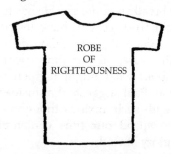

ROBE
OF
RIGHTEOUSNESS

Probably we have sometimes looked into our wardrobes before a party and decided that we have nothing suitable to wear. However jam-packed the wardrobe is, with all that extra junk stuffed in to keep it out of sight, we can't find anything we want to wear! Prepare to be impressed: the wardrobe space of today's teaching is quite something.

Mention the piece of paper they were all given when they came in, checking for any who have been missed and providing for them now. Everyone has been given a beautiful wedding garment! That's what used to happen when guests were invited to palaces. It was the practice for kings to provide thousands of guests with a suitable robe each from their vast wardrobes in which thousands of garments were kept ready specially for such occasions. (Dress a volunteer up in a clean white robe – a surplice is fine.) They had special servants to be in charge of those huge wardrobes.

In Jesus' parable of the wedding feast we can imagine all the poor and the dirty straggling along to the palace in their smelly rags, and the people in charge of the king's wardrobes fitting up everyone with a clean, beautiful robe to wear, before ushering them into the grand dining hall. No doubt they felt different dressed like this – perhaps they even walked taller and were more polite to each other than usual! Then the king comes in to inspect his guests. (Perhaps everyone sits up straighter, like you do when someone important walks into assembly.) He is glad to see the palace full of guests who have accepted his invitation, because the original guests had refused to come. Everything is light and warm and happy.

Suddenly the king finds a guest who has accepted his invitation but rudely refused to wear the proper clothes provided. He's still in the filthy rags he came in, and the king has him put outside in the darkness with those who had chosen to turn down his invitation.

What is Jesus teaching us in this parable? One thing is that God is very happy to invite all of us to the Church of Christ and feed us here with love and rejoicing. So we can be happy together in God's company and enjoy ourselves in our worship. The other thing is that if we say yes to God, we do need to let him reclothe us, and not expect to go on wearing the rags of bickering and fighting, lying and cheating, self-indulgence and lack of self-control which we came in. That's why we always start our worship by saying sorry to God, and hearing his forgiveness, letting him clothe us with robes of righteousness.

All-age ideas

- Have an arrangement of golden flowers set inside a treasure chest labelled 'Holiness'.

- Try this sketch in which a reporter is interviewing some of the guests.

Reporter Well, I'm standing here in the great hall; it's filled with the warm glow of candle light, the smells of delicious food and the sound of crowds of people enjoying themselves. Quite a wedding feast! Excuse me, sir, may I interrupt your meal a moment and ask how you came to be invited to this banquet?

Guest 1   Yes, sure. I was trimming my hedge.

Reporter   Trimming your hedge?

Guest 1   That's right – crazy isn't it! One minute I was trimming my hedge, feeling hungry, and the next this servant from the palace comes along and says I'm invited to the king's banquet! It seems the original guests had turned it down. So I'm here with the wife and kids, and we've never enjoyed ourselves so much, isn't that right, dear? I've never been to a banquet before, but I tell you, I could get used to it!

Reporter   And here's a very senior citizen. Good evening, madam.

Guest 2   Eh?

Reporter   *(Shouts)* Good evening, madam! how are you liking the banquet?

Guest 2   Oh, it's wonderful, dear! Just wonderful! We're being so well looked after – and I've never felt so loved and honoured in all my life. Just think – me being treated like this! It makes me feel young and beautiful again.

Grandchild   You are beautiful, Gran!

Guest 2   What's that, my chicken?

Reporter   Well, as you can see, the atmosphere here is amazing – so much joy and happiness for so many people! And none of them bought a ticket. When the original guests turned it down, the king just had all these ordinary, poor folk invited and brought in from the streets and farms, and gave them each a wedding garment to wear so he'd have a full gathering to celebrate his son's wedding. And I must say, it's the most happy and extraordinary wedding celebration ever. I'm going outside now . . . it's dark and cold out there, and there's a whole lot of people who sadly don't realise what they're missing.

Prayer of the Faithful

Celebrant
Invited by our God, we have gathered here.
Let us now voice our prayers
for the Church and for the world.

Reader
Father, when either the traditional or the progressive
blinds us to the truth of your will,
clear our vision and speak through our prejudices
until we are once again open to your changing.
May we be, before anything else, your people,
sharing your concerns and desires.

Silence

As you have called us:
Lord, we come.

Father, we recognise how powerful
the influences are in our world
which distract many and lead away from your truth.
We pray for the quiet whisper of your wisdom
to be noticed and acknowledged in many lives;
we pray for widespread discipline of the heart,
a new openness to generosity of spirit.

Silence

As you have called us:
Lord, we come.

Father, may our homes and daily schedules
be part of the territory of your kingdom,
where it is your will which guides
and your love which rules.

Silence

As you have called us:
Lord, we come.

Father, our hearts rail against the cruelty
and unfairness of suffering and disease,
and we kneel now alongside all in pain
and weep with them, crying out to you
for comfort and the healing of your love.
For you are no bringer of evil to our lives,
but share our sorrow and give us the grace to bear it.

Silence

As you have called us:
Lord, we come.

Father, as death takes from us those we love
and we find it hard to live without them,
take from us all bitterness of heart and
let us share with them the peace you give
over which death has no power at all.

Silence

As you have called us:
Lord, we come.

With Mary, bearer of God's Son,
we make our prayer:
Hail, Mary . . .

We pray in silence, now,
for those known to us
who have particular needs.

Silence

Celebrant
Lord, in thankfulness
for all your rich blessings to us every day,
we offer you our prayers,
through Christ our Saviour.
Amen.

TREASURE SEEKERS

Aim: To know that God invites us to his party.

Starter

Either make party hats as shown below or decorate the room with streamers and balloons.

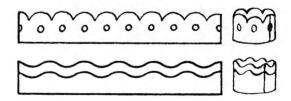

Teaching

Talk about the kind of things they like about parties, and then gather all these things into the happiness of enjoying ourselves together. God's kingdom is like being invited to God's party. He's invited us because he likes us, loves us and wants us to be there with him and all his other friends. Being in God's party is lovely because we are all together with God, enjoying ourselves.

Put on a praise tape, give out some instruments and streamers, and all enjoy worshipping God in a praise party, wearing our party hats.

Praying

Dear Father God,
thank you for inviting me
to your party.
Yes, please, I want to come!

Activities

On the sheet there is a picture of a party to colour, with some hidden things to look for, and a party game to play – putting the tail on the donkey with your eyes closed.

PEARL DIVERS

Aim: To know the parable of the wedding feast and begin to look at its meaning.

Starter

Can I come to the party? Everyone sits along the wall at one end of the room, taking turns to throw a dice. When someone throws a six, everyone stands up and calls out to the leader at the other end, 'Can I come to the party?' The leader calls back, 'Only if you're wearing blue and white/had no breakfast/have a sister . . .' Then those allowed to come to the party go into the middle for a short, loud snatch of music and dancing, before returning to the wall and continuing to throw dice.

Teaching

Bring along enough pieces of fabric, towels, sheets and scarves for everyone to be given one. They are all helped to dress in these and then sit down to listen to the story.

Tell the children about the way kings used to have wardrobes full of special clothes for visitors, so that whenever people were invited to a party at the palace, they would be given one of the king's robes to wear just as we have all been fitted out with a robe today. That was all part of the invitation.

Jesus told a parable about a king who threw a party. It was a wedding party for his son, and all the guests were invited. But they all refused to come; they didn't want to celebrate the prince's wedding, and they made feeble excuses, and went off to make money instead. The king was very angry and punished them all. But he still needed guests for the party. So he sent his servants out to stand at all the crossroads and invite the ordinary people passing by to come to the grand celebration as guests of the king.

In they all came, crowds of them. Some were good people, some were bad; the king didn't mind – he wanted to invite everyone, with no one left out. As everyone came in with their old, scruffy clothes on, the servants in charge of the king's wardrobe sorted out a wedding garment for them all, and shooed them into the great hall which was all decorated, loaded with food and drink, and well lit with candles at all the tables.

The ordinary people were thrilled – they'd never thought they would ever be invited to a party at the king's palace, and they really enjoyed themselves. The king came in and looked around, glad to have the great hall filled with happy guests, celebrating his son's wedding. As he walked around, he suddenly had a shock. One of the guests was insulting the king who had invited him to this honour. He was not wearing the special robe he had been given, but was sitting there in dirty rags. The king went up to him. 'Friend,' he said, surprised, 'how come you aren't wearing a wedding garment at this important wedding party?' The man was speechless, and the king had him thrown outside. How dare he expect to be part of the celebration if he couldn't even be bothered to change.

So inside the great hall, all the invited guests had the time of their lives. They danced and sang and ate and drank and laughed. And outside, in the cold darkness, stood those who had refused to be part of the celebration, even though they had been invited.

Praying

Father God, you have invited us,
just as we are, to your kingdom.
You forgive us our sins
and clothe us in your robes of goodness.
You satisfy our hunger and our thirst,
and make us happy.
Thank you, Father God,
for all your goodness to us.

Activities

On the sheet the children are led to work out what the secret meaning of this parable is, both for the people listening to Jesus at the time, and for us today. They can use the pictures to show the story on a matchbox television (instructions included), and also enjoy a festive time of praise and dancing, with streamer and flag waving, and some taped praise songs to sing along with.

GOLD PANNERS

Aim: To explore the implications of the wedding feast parable both for the people of Israel and the members of the Church.

Starter

Rules of the game. Give them a ball and a bucket. They are going to use these to invent the rules for a new game, and play it.

Teaching

In their game, as in all others, abiding by the rules is essential. If you choose to play any sport, it's understood that you will get sent off if you deliberately break the code laid down. Today one of Jesus' parables invites us to look at this in relation to the kingdom of God.

First read the Isaiah passage. It is full of praise and thanks, and also looking forward to a time of complete victory and joy. Then read the passage from Romans, with its rejoicing and security in God's love which helps us concentrate on all that is lovely, noble, right and good, even when there is great anxiety all around.

Now comes the parable of the wedding banquet in today's Gospel. Place it in its context of Jesus speaking both generally to the people and also directing a particular, hidden message to the Pharisees who were out to destroy him. Explain the custom of giving out wedding garments from the palace to all guests; otherwise the full insult of the guest is not understood. Then, using one sheet headed 'Pharisees' and the other 'Riff-raff', jot down their ideas about the message in the parable for each.

Praying

You prepare a table for me
in the presence of my enemies;
you anoint my head with oil, and my cup overflows.
Surely goodness and mercy shall follow me
all the days of my life;
and I shall dwell in the house of the Lord for ever.

(From Psalm 22)

Activities

On the sheet they are encouraged to look at the symbolism of old and new 'habits', and the difference between being expected to change on our own, and receiving the freely given grace which makes it possible. They also look at the kind of Pharisaic attitudes that are just as likely to happen now as then.

TWENTY-NINTH SUNDAY OF THE YEAR

Thought for the day

All leaders and rulers are subject to the ultimate authority and power of God, the living truth.

Reflection on the readings

Isaiah 45:1, 4-6
Psalm 95:1, 3-5, 7-10
1 Thessalonians 1:1-5
Matthew 22:15-21

One of the difficulties students have is when there are exaggerated expectations of emotional returns on money contributed by parents towards their keep and education. But, of course, they are dealing with different currencies here, and the confusion is what causes the frustrations and disappointments. Today we are looking at another such clash of currency; our duty and responsibility towards God and to 'Caesar'.

The Pharisees had simply contrived the question in order to catch Jesus out, picking one of those 'Catch 22' situations where you can't win. If Jesus said they should give their taxes to Caesar, it would be an insult to the national pride of his followers, and if he said they shouldn't, the Roman authorities would be able to sort him out for them. We can imagine the quantities of midnight oil spent planning the scheme.

Jesus sees exactly what they are planning, and deftly counters the attack by means of stating the truth. He points out that in fact the two are different currencies. This challenges his hearers to check their balance and commitment both to earthly and heavenly citizenship. It completely avoids the confrontation hoped for, and alienates neither the people nor the authorities, so the Pharisees, impressed but no doubt furious, can only withdraw and leave Jesus alone.

It conveniently allows us to learn from Jesus about authority and those in charge. Both the Isaiah reading and Psalm 95 are grand and glorious, proclaiming the total and ultimate authority of God over all creation and all peoples, including their rulers, and in Thessalonians there is the same sense of God's authority as the living truth. These are concepts of cosmic proportion, and remind us of the transcendence of the God we worship. Human authority and empires shrink as we contemplate the reality of God's glory and power. Yet the Son of God, breaking into our human system of life, chooses to walk among the ordinary people in the squalor of their need, and enter the holy city on a donkey.

What does this tell us about giving to God what is God's? Certainly it burns into our consciousness that the great almighty God, source of everything we have, including life itself, is not to be 'paid off' with our small change, either in money or time. He is worth nothing less than everything – all that we are, our past, present and future, freely given back in gratitude and love to the one who has given us so much.

Immediately it becomes clear that our commitment to 'Caesar' is a completely different type of giving. However much earthly rulers may like to think of themselves as close to divine, we are in fact all equal in human status before the majesty of God, and our governmental structures are matters of convenience and useful order to be respected and upheld where they express God's will, and challenged wherever they do not.

Discussion starters

1. What is 'Caesar's' and what is God's?

2. It is sometimes said that we end up with the leaders we deserve. Do we expect more of our leaders than we are willing to give ourselves?

All-stage talk

Unless the size of your congregation makes it far too expensive, give everyone a penny. Invite everyone to look at their coin. On one side there is a picture of someone's head. Whose head is it? It belongs to Queen Elizabeth II. She is there, just as Caesar's picture was on the coin Jesus looked at, because she is the Head of State and we are her subjects. In our country there are taxes to pay to make sure that everyone, both rich and poor, can have schools, roads and hospitals. There are laws to keep, so that we can all live safely and peacefully, and there are police to check that we keep the laws. Those who break them are sent to prison or charged a fine.

Each country works out its own way of organising all this, and some are fairer than others. Each country has leaders – people who are in charge – and the country Jesus lived in was ruled by the Romans.

Now invite everyone to hold their coin in the palm of one hand. This penny is not very big. It won't buy very much. It sits here in your hand, and your hand is here in this church building. It's only a very little part of all the space in here. As you hold your penny, your hand is surrounded not just by the space of this building but by the whole universe. Now God is greater than the universe, because he is the One who thought and loved our universe into being.

There's a huge, huge difference between the kind of power and authority human leaders have, and the kind of power and authority God has. We are to give to God what is God's. What is God's? Is there anything God doesn't know? No. Is there anywhere God can't reach? No. Is there anything or anyone God doesn't care about? No. God is much greater and more wonderful than we can imagine, and he holds all creation in the palm of his hand, like you are holding the little penny in the palm of your hand.

No wonder we've all chosen to come and spend some time praising him this morning! God is worth everything we can ever give him.

Of course, we are to respect our leaders, and keep the laws. We are to be good citizens, just as our Christian rule of love tells us. But we also need to remember who is ultimately in charge, and put God first. We need to be prepared to make a fuss if any laws are passed which are against God's law, and we need to do what we can to help our leaders uphold the authority of the God who made us all.

All-age ideas

- Use the coins as a focus for prayer, praying for all leaders and rulers as we look at the monarch's head; for the world, as we see the roundness; for the blind and spiritually blind as we feel its edge; for the imprisoned as we see the portcullis; and for the rich and the poor.

Prayer of the Faithful

Celebrant
Let us focus our gaze
on the great God of our making,
as we pour out to him our prayers.

Reader
Lord of all,
give your Church such maturity and wisdom
that we may not be swayed
from our purpose and calling
by trivialities or worldly pressures,
but know increasingly
our dependence on you in all things
and proclaim your Gospel
with steadfastness and joy.

Silence

You, O Lord:
are the ground of our being.

Lord of all, give to all monarchs,
leaders and heads of state
graciousness and integrity,
that all in power and authority
may undertake their duties in a spirit of humility;
that the oppressed may find a voice,
and the nations work together
for the good of the world.

Silence

You, O Lord:
are the ground of our being.

Lord of all, give to our homes
and places of work and leisure
your harmony and peace;
give us grace to respect one another and ourselves
in the way we talk and think,
and in the way we behave.

Silence

You, O Lord:
are the ground of our being.

Lord of all, speak your peace into the hearts
of all who are agitated, anxious or confused.
Lay your hands of healing on all who are ill
and let them know your reassurance and love.

Silence

You, O Lord:
are the ground of our being.

Lord of all, welcome into your kingdom
all who have kept faith
and now can lay their burdens down.
May they rest in your peace for ever.

Silence

You, O Lord:
are the ground of our being.

We make our prayer with Mary,
who joyfully poured out her thanks and praise:
Hail, Mary . . .

Together in silence,
we name those known to us
who need our prayers.

Silence

Celebrant
In joy, Father,
we offer you our prayers and our praise,
through Jesus Christ,
our Saviour and our brother.
Amen.

TREASURE SEEKERS

Aim: To celebrate that God's in charge.

Starter

In a circle have a 'news time', passing round a coin, so that whoever holds it is allowed to speak without interruption.

Teaching

Tell the children this story.

'Here she is!' shouted Ali. She was looking out of the window, and could see the baby-sitter walking up to the front door. 'Ding, dong!' went the door bell. Mum opened the door.

'Hello, Vicky,' said Mum. They've had their baths, and they know they have to go to bed once this programme ends. Oh, and I've left the mugs for a drink. Sometimes they like hot chocolate, but Jonathan may want a cold drink. Don't let them eat anything after they've brushed their teeth.'

'Vicky, come and see the dead mouse that Molly brought in today,' said Jonathan.

'Sounds great,' said Vicky. 'Hi, everyone! Did your cold get better, Ali?'

'Yep,' nodded Ali. 'But I've got a plaster on my knee. Look!'

'Right, my loves, I have to go now,' said Mum. 'Where did I leave my car keys?'

'You're holding them,' said Jonathan. 'When will you get back?'

'Quarter to eleven,' said Mum. 'Now remember, Vicky's in charge. Look after her and give her a nice evening. Show her where those chocolate gingers are in case she wants some with her coffee. And don't you bring that dead mouse inside again or there'll be trouble! Must go. Love you lots! Bye, everyone, and thanks, Vicky.' Mum hugged and kissed Ali and Jonathan, and Vicky took them upstairs so they could wave from the window.

They watched Mum unlock the car and climb in. She waved back to them and then Vicky helped them make a drink each. Vicky had coffee with one sugar. Ali had hot chocolate and spilt a bit on the cat, who licked it off. Jonathan had apple juice. And they all had chocolate ginger biscuits.

Talk about people being in charge, and how we can help those who are in charge of us, and how they can help us. God is in charge of the whole universe, and he loves us, and looks after us.

Praying

Lord Jesus,
bless us and keep us safe
now and for ever. Amen.

Activities

On the sheet there is space for the children to draw those who are in charge of them, and instructions for making an orb – the world with a cross on it. Each child will need an orange or apple, two sticks and a wire bag fastener.

PEARL DIVERS

Aim: To look at Jesus' teaching about giving to God what is God's and to Caesar what is Caesar's.

Starter

Price tags. Give out a selection of play money to each small group of children, and have some objects for them to 'buy'. Then call out a price tag: 'Here's a pair of scissors and it costs twenty pence.' The first group to come up with the exact money gets the pair of scissors. The group with most items bought is the winner.

Teaching

If you have any old or foreign coins, bring them along and pass them around, and also show the children pictures of Roman coins from library books. Draw their attention to the pictures on the coins. Who are the pictures of and why are they there?

Remind the children of how the Pharisees were becoming more and more keen to get rid of Jesus, and how they tried to catch him out with a cunning plan. In order to understand the trap, they will need to know something about the Romans. Using the books, tell them how the Roman empire covered lots of countries. The Romans would fight their way into a country and take it over, ruling over the people there. They needed money to build the roads and market places, the aqueducts to carry water and the public baths. Where did the money come from? All the people in the countries the Romans ruled over had to pay tax. Do you think they were happy to pay tax to the people who had taken over their country? No, they weren't. In fact they hated it!

Now that you know this, you will see what a clever trap was set to catch Jesus out. The Pharisees went up to Jesus with the crowds all around him and asked him a question. First they buttered him up. 'We know you are a good person,' they said, 'and you always tell the truth, even if it isn't what people want to hear.' (That's what had happened to them, wasn't it!) Then came the question (show this so they can all join in with asking it): 'Is it right to pay tax to Caesar or not?'

Now that was a tricky question. If Jesus said, 'Yes, it's right to pay tax to the Romans', what would the people who hated the Romans think? (They might think Jesus was sucking up to the Romans and not standing up for his own country.) And if Jesus said, 'No, it isn't right to pay tax to the Romans', what would the Romans do? (They would get him into big, big trouble.)

So what did Jesus do? He knew it was a trap. He asked to borrow a coin (pick one up) and he showed it to the people. 'Whose picture is on this coin?' asked Jesus. 'Caesar's,' they answered. Then Jesus said this: 'Then give to Caesar what belongs to Caesar and give to God what belongs to God.' (Have these words written out and all join in saying them.)

Clever, wasn't it? The Pharisees had set out to teach Jesus a lesson and trick him, but Jesus ends up teaching *them* and challenging them yet again to give God the honour he deserves.

Praying

Great is the Lord who has made heaven and earth.
He is our God and we are his people.
Lord God of earth and heaven,
we worship and adore you.

Activities

The children can make rubbings of some of the coins brought in, and use the world picture to make a car hanging. They will need to mount it on thin card, punch a hole in the top and have thread provided.

GOLD PANNERS

Aim: To look at issues of authority and leadership from a Christian perspective.

Starter

Give everyone some newspaper with which to make a hat in five minutes.

Teaching

The newsprint represents the events considered of world importance by the media, and they have made them into head-gear. Today we are going to look at those who head countries and states, and at how this fits in with God's authority.

First read the passage from Isaiah 45, where the prophet sees God's hand in the political events of time, with even other national leaders being used by the God they do not worship. The crucial sentence is 'I am the Lord', and God's total authority is established clearly.

You could also look at the Thessalonians reading, which reinforces the understanding of God being the living truth.

Now explain how the Romans taxed everyone in the countries they occupied, and the taxes were naturally disliked and distrusted. Have a coin to look at and read today's Gospel from Matthew 22. Explore the possible responses to the question put to Jesus by the Pharisees and then look at what Jesus managed to say about it in his reply. He is suggesting that the giving to God is in a different 'currency' from our civilian duties and loyalties. Our responsibility to God arises from our recognition of his total authority, and our loving response to his gifts to us.

As far as our political and national responsibilities are concerned, we are dealing with other human beings. Loyalty and respect are important, along with the willingness to question injustice and challenge corruption.

Praying

You are worthy, our Lord and God,
to receive glory and honour and power.
For you have created all things,
and by your will they have their being.

Activities

Supply headline stories from the newspapers which show conflict and violence resulting from nationalism, and instances of oppression and injustice where not only the leaders of one country but the historical legacy of empires cause suffering and degradation. There is space on the sheet to draw some of these discussions and challenges together.

THIRTIETH SUNDAY OF THE YEAR

Thought for the day

We are to love God with our whole being, and love others as much as we love ourselves.

Reflection on the readings

Exodus 22:20-26
Psalm 17:2-4, 47, 51
1 Thessalonians 1:5-10
Matthew 22:34-40

If any proof were needed that Jesus had come not to condemn but to save, it is here in today's Gospel. Jesus' response to the Sadducees, putting them right in an area of understanding, had the effect of making some of the Pharisees much more open to Jesus, and this time they come not to trick him but examine him, to sound out more of his teaching on the law, in which they considered themselves expert. They ask Jesus what kind of commandment is the greatest, and this would have arisen from the debates they were used to having with the Sadducees about emphasis. From the Gospels and Letters we can see that current debate must have centred on such matters as right observation of the Sabbath, right giving and tithing, and the question of purification and circumcision. Where did Jesus stand?

Typically, Jesus takes them back to the heart of the matter, quoting a specific commandment, the first, which they would have been assuming intellectually, but which in their lives was being crowded out by all the detailed laws and rules. Jesus was willing to stand alongside the Pharisees as soon as there was the faintest hint of openness, and he shows respect for what they have got right: the law's importance. From the fairly obscure book written for the Levite priesthood, and revered by the Pharisees, Jesus draws out the summary of the law: love given to God first and, by extension, to our neighbour, using the measuring stick of self-love to help us understand its meaning. At least the Pharisees have it in their heads, even if not yet in their hearts.

Answering their agenda of detailed differences with this broad sweep of general principle, taken from writings they cherished, opened up the possibility of truth dawning on these over-conscientious law-keepers. As with old paintings, the years of familiar yellowed varnish needed removing so that the original vibrant colours could once again shine. Jesus patiently chips away, flake by flake. He asks

them to look again at the Messianic promises, looking deeper than the traditional snap responses towards a curious questioning which might lead them to look at wider possibilities of fulfilment than they have previously dared.

With Jesus we are always being drawn forwards, deeper into the love and meaning of God, and he will use all our doubts and experiences of life to help us. We need not be afraid to question where God is concerned, for that is how we learn.

Discussion starters

1. What advantage is there in a general summary of the law over the detailed rules system?

2. How does this summary of the law affect the way we live?

All-stage talk

Hold a large edition of the Bible, and tell everyone that today we are all going to read the whole lot as part of our talk!

Explain that today we heard Jesus giving us a summary of the whole of the Bible, in a couple of sentences. (Reader's Digest can eat their heart out!) He was saying that everything in all the law and the prophets was an exploring and working out of this. (Have Matthew 22:37-39 written out large, and invite everyone to join you in reading it out.) There – we've read the Bible! Or, to be more precise, we have read the subject matter of the whole Bible, because everything in it is to do with what we just read – people learning to love God with their whole being, and their neighbours as themselves. It's the story of their learning, their mistakes and failures, and of God's great love helping us make the impossible possible. (Well worth reading the full-length version!)

Let's look at what it means to love others as we love ourselves. How do we love ourselves? Invite a couple of friends to come and help show us. Get one to stand behind the other, with the front person putting their hands behind their back, and the back person providing them with substitute arms by pushing their own arms through the front person's. Have someone offering them a wrapped chocolate which they eat, and give them a brush so they can do their hair.

All day long we look after ourselves like this, feeding and washing and scratching ourselves whenever the needs arise. Even if we don't admit to loving ourselves our actions show that we do. If we start getting too hot, our body kindly makes us sweat to cool us down. If we're threatened by the cold, our helpful body sets us shivering and raises our hairs to warm us up again. And if there's a real emergency (the children can make an ambulance siren sound), the body shuts down some systems and kicks in with others to keep us alive as long as possible. That's love for you!

So if we are to love others like that, we'll be attentive, looking out for one another's well-being and ready to help when we see someone in need. We'll be doing what we can to feed the hungry and look after those with problems. We'll scratch where it itches but not where it doesn't. We'll be ready to drop everything and be there for people if there's an emergency and they need us. We'll do everything we can to help them feel better and get through the difficult times.

And where does all this love come from? From our wonderful God, who made us all in the first place, and loves to see all his children caring for one another like this.

All-age ideas

• Sing this summary of the law to the tune of *London's burning* in a round with actions. Then the whole of the law is being celebrated in voice and action, just as people are doing in real life twenty-four hours a day around our planet earth.

You shall love the
  (hands on heart)
Lord your God with
  (arms raised)
all your heart and
  (hands on heart)
all your mind and
  (hands hold head)
all your strength! All your strength!
  (show muscles in arms)
And love your neighbour,
  (arm round neighbour on one side)
and love your neighbour.
  (arm round neighbour on other side)

• Make decorated banners or posters, proclaiming the summary of the law.

Prayer of the Faithful

Celebrant
In love and trust, let us pray to our God.

Reader
Holy God, give us the courage
to tell out your truth without fear,
and to work for your kingdom with joy.
Thank you for the support
and love of other Christians,
and the richness of our varied traditions.
May we focus our attention on you with such love
that all unnecessary divisions between us crumble.

Silence

You are the Lord:
there is no other.

Holy God, we pray for our law makers and keepers;
may our laws work to uphold what is just and true.
We pray that we may live
in godly peace and goodwill
through choice,
rather than through fear of punishment;
through the desire to live well,
rather than avoiding detection.

Silence

You are the Lord:
there is no other.

Holy God, in all our day-to-day living
may we reject deceit and flattery,
so that our motives and behaviour are honest,
and our love for one another clear as the day.

Silence

You are the Lord:
there is no other.

Holy God,
we pray for all law breakers and their families;
for those in prison
and those returning to the community.
We pray for those imprisoned by guilt or shame,
or trapped by physical frailty, illness or paralysis.
We pray for those whose lives are tragically disrupted
by war and famine, poverty and disease.

Silence

You are the Lord:
there is no other.

Holy God, we remember those who,
dying in faith, rejoice to see you as you are.
We thank you for their example
and commend them to your peace for ever.

Silence

You are the Lord:
there is no other.

Holy God, we give you thanks for the love
poured out to us each moment of each day,
and ask of you the grace to live our gratitude
and give freely of what we have freely received.

Silence

You are the Lord:
there is no other.

We make our prayer with Mary,
Mother of the Lord of Love:
Hail, Mary . . .

Trustingly we pray to our loving Lord,
for our own needs and cares.

Silence

Celebrant
Father, we ask you to work your love in our lives,
and accept these prayers we have brought to you,
through Christ, our Lord.
Amen.

TREASURE SEEKERS

Aim: To know the summary of the law: Love God,
love one another.

Starter

Play 'Here we go round the mulberry bush'. It is a
'looking after yourself' kind of song, so you could
have such verses as these: brush our teeth, take a
shower, eat a pizza, and wrap up warm.

Teaching

As we sang in the song, we are good at looking
after ourselves and caring for our bodies. Our arms
are like big machines that we train to pick things
up for us and take them over to our mouths. (They
can try this with some crisps.) We love ourselves,
and that's why we make sure we are comfortable
and well fed.

In the Bible we are told two rules:

1. Love God.

2. Love others as much as you love yourself.

When we love others as much as we love ourselves,
we look out for *their* needs as well as ours, and want
them to be happy and comfortable as well as us.

Praying

Dear God,
you have given us life – thank you!
You have given us a lovely world
to live in – thank you!
You have given us people
to look after us – thank you!
You have given us friends – thank you!
You have given us two rules to help us:
'Love God' and 'Love one another'.
Thank you, God!

Activities

Get a drum beat going (a biscuit tin and wooden
spoon works well) and clap hands to it. Over this,
chant the words: 'Love God; love one another!'
until it has become second nature and the children
know it off by heart. Then they can colour the two
arm or ankle bands drawn on the sheet, and either
cut them out themselves or have help with this.
Fix them round their wrists or ankles and try the
chant again.

PEARL DIVERS

Aim: To know the summary of the law.

Starter

Tape some lengths of wool to the floor, criss-crossing the circle where you are all sitting. Choose four
or five people to cross the circle at the same time,
walking along the lines. The rule to avoid collisions
is that whenever you meet someone else, both of
you get off the line, swap positions and carry on.
Point out how useful the rule was; keeping it made
life easier and better for everyone.

Teaching

You will need a full sheet of blue sugar paper as the
background, yellowy green hills, a blue river, a
brown trunk and branches, green foliage and red
and yellow fruit. As you talk, gradually the picture
is built up, sticking one layer over another. The
completed picture should look something like this:

In the countries where lots of rain falls all the year
round, the trees have plenty to drink, so their
leaves grow well and stay green in the summer.

The tree grows lots of juicy fruit. In places where there isn't much rain at all, like this picture, the grass gets yellowy and dies in the heat of the sun. The trees can't survive either. *But,* suppose there is a river flowing through the dry grass (stick it on) and suppose a tree grows up right beside the river (put on the trunk and branches). The roots of this tree can drink up the water from the river, so this tree grows lovely green leaves (put on the foliage) and they stay green. The tree beside the water can grow so well that it starts to have fruit – lots of fruit (stick on the fruits). Even when there are times when it doesn't rain, this tree beside the water is going to be fine, and have lots of fruit for the people and animals and birds to eat.

In the Bible, we are told how to live in the very best way, like trees planted beside streams of water. The Bible tells us that the river we need to live by is this:

To love God, and to love one another. (Write this in on the river of the picture.)

Live by this, and we'll grow and live strong and tall, with lots of good fruit in our life. Read the summary of the law, now that they know its outline.

Praying

Help us, Lord, to keep your law,
loving you with all we are,
loving other people too,
that's what we will try to do.

Activities

Sing the summary of the law with actions in a round. This is sung to the tune of *London's burning*, and the words and actions for this are in the all-age ideas. Provide the children with the different shapes of coloured paper as shown on the sheet so they can make their own collage of the tree planted beside the water, with the summary of the law written on the river.

GOLD PANNERS

Aim: To see how the whole law and teaching of the prophets are summarised in Jesus' words.

Starter

Put some paper cups filled with water on a table and get everyone to try and drink from them with their hands behind their backs. It makes you realise how clever we are at training our arms and hands to provide lovingly for our every need.

Teaching

Every day we get our arms to feed and dress us, switch on the television and the toaster, and open doors. That is a caring consideration, or love, that comes as second nature to us. We are told in the Bible that we are to love God, and love our neighbour as we love ourselves.

Start by reading the Gospel, Matthew 22:34-40. Notice how Jesus says that on these two commandments hang all the law and the teaching of the prophets. Show them a parcel with this summary on the label. If you unpack this (do so), you are looking at the whole word of God. (There's a Bible inside.)

Did Jesus make this summary, or was he quoting from somewhere in the Old Testament? He was actually quoting from the book of detailed instructions on ritual and practice for the Levite tribe of priests. This is found in the Book of Leviticus.

Why does loving others as we love ourselves incorporate all those other laws? It's because if we showed to others the kind of attentive caring we lavish on ourselves, there would be no lying, stealing, murder, adultery, envy or lack of respect. All those things happen because we are not thinking considerately of the other person or people.

How does the first commandment fit in? As we love God, establishing him as number one in our lives, his love pours out to us, enabling us to love others in this attentive, considerate way.

Praying

Lord, have mercy upon us
and incline our hearts to keep this law.

Activities

The questions on the sheet encourage them to look at the pros and cons of a positive summary of the law, rather than loads of specific negatives. There is also a suggestion for a short sketch in which the body attentively cares for its needs and wants.

Thirty-first Sunday of the Year

Thought for the day

Our lives need to reflect our faith; we are not just called to tell the good news but to live it as well.

Reflection on the readings

Malachi 1:14-2:2, 8-10
Psalm 130
1 Thessalonians 2:7-9, 13
Matthew 23:1-12

Jesus came into contact with all kinds of sinners, and the overwhelming impression we get from his encounters with those who knew themselves to be out of step with God's law is one of deep compassion and encouragement, affirmation and affection. But the one thing which Jesus seems to have found exceedingly difficult to cope with is hypocrisy. This is what elicits Jesus' strongest language and exasperation, his frustration and anger.

In keeping with all the prophets before him, Jesus tries many times to break through the defences of those who are preaching one message and living another. It goes completely against the whole un-divided nature of our faith in the one true God to have any hint of double standards, or that spiritual blindness which cannot detect personal wrong from preached righteousness.

It seems that religious people are particularly prone to it, so we all need to be scrupulous in our spiritual hygiene, and keep regularly in touch with those who would be kind and honest enough with us to alert us to early warning signs we may have missed. It is easy to see why it happens. Religious people, conscientious in their practice, cannot bear to think of themselves as displeasing God; rather than recognise this horror, they start the practice of pretending to themselves, and argue their own sin into being part of God's will.

The Pharisees in today's Gospel, for instance, have persuaded themselves that it is their duty as guardians of the faith to be seen praying and wearing their God-given honour proudly; but in reality they are simply enjoying the fame and power for themselves. They are horrified at the thought of being seen as hypocrites, since they have effectively hidden this knowledge from themselves, and take great offence at some upstart who starts undermining their complex persona.

In his letter to the Christians at Thessalonica, Paul's affection and genuine concern is obvious; he draws attention to they way they can see his intentions for them were good because of the way he and his helpers looked after them, rather than just preaching at them. And this points us to the key difference: it is love. If, through God's love, we are genuine in our love for others, we will be far less likely to split ourselves off from them and start seeing ourselves as superior and above the usual temptations. Once we have stepped off the self-made pedestals it will be less difficult for us to admit our failings to ourselves, and that will encourage us to spend time in humility before God each day, recognising our need of his grace and forgiveness.

Once we are in that realistic position of knowing our need of God, we are open to God's healing love.

Discussion starters

1. How can we preach the good news without words?

2. Hypocrisy starts when those who value what is right find the idea of themselves doing wrong quite abhorrent. Rather than going down that damaging road of self-deceit, what should be done?

All-stage talk

Bring in an ordinary mirror. Also make a distorting mirror using a sheet of the very shiny wrapping paper or cooking foil. It can either be stuck on bent card or simply held by two volunteers. Invite a few people to see themselves in both mirrors, or walk the mirrors round the church reflecting people here and there. Which reflection looks most like them?

Sometimes we are like good mirrors, when we reflect God's loving by being loving to others. Or we may reflect God's forgiving nature when we forgive someone who has been unkind to us. Or we may reflect God's faithfulness when we are trustworthy and faithful ourselves.

But sometimes we are like bad mirrors. We distort God's loving into possessiveness of other people; we distort relaxing into laziness; we distort honesty into critical gossip, or pleasure into greed. Worst of all, we distort trust. We are designed to trust God and depend on him, and when we start trusting things or our own image instead of God, our lives get twisted and misshapen, and we can no longer reflect to other people the truth of our God. We may tell others about God but our lives will only reflect a distorted picture of it, so they end up thinking God is a slave driver, or without any compassion and forgiveness.

How terrible if even one person has been stopped from putting faith in the living God because they have been put off by the distorted image of God they see in our lives! We need to be like mirrors that are straight and true, with our lives reflecting the true loving God we say we worship.

All-age ideas

- This dance expresses getting our lives sorted out and our agendas untangled so that we can be open to God. While the choir or congregation sing *O Lord, your tenderness* quietly and prayerfully, a group of about six people of all ages get completely tangled up together. Slowly they get untangled, raising their arms upwards in thanks and praise as they do so, and then helping to free those who are still 'knotted'. During the repeated 'O Lord, I receive your love', they slowly form first a circle facing inwards with their arms raised to God, and then a circle with their arms extended to one another and out to the congregation, expressing the truth that when God fills us with his love it enables us to reach out in love to other people.

Prayer of the Faithful

Celebrant
Let us bare our souls before God as we pray.

Reader
We pray for those in ordained and lay ministries;
for a deepening of our own commitment to Christ,
and a cleansing of our lives,
so that the Church is a true image
of the Body of Christ.

Silence

Lord of truth:
light our way.

Heavenly Father, we pray for all
who are fearful of being their true selves;
all who cannot face the truth of their sin
and dare not admit it,
either to themselves or to God.
We pray for courage,
and the humility to see ourselves as you see us;
our actions and our motives as you see them.

Silence

Lord of truth:
light our way.

We thank you for those in our families
who prevent us from taking ourselves too seriously,
and for all who know us and accept us as we are,
recognising our weaknesses and failures
as well as our strengths.

Silence

Lord of truth:
light our way.

We pray for those who are going through difficult
or confused times at the moment;
those whose lives feel full of pain and darkness;
those who do not realise their need of you;
those who have rejected you through being shown
a false image of your nature.

Silence

Lord of truth:
light our way.

We pray for those who have died to this life
and see you face to face.
May your merciful love surround them
and bring them safely to your eternity.

Silence

Lord of truth:
light our way.

Encouraged by Mary's example of integrity,
we join our prayers with hers:
Hail, Mary . . .

We name our particular prayer burdens now,
in silence filled with love.

Silence

Celebrant
Father, in your love accept our prayers,
through Christ our Saviour.
Amen.

TREASURE SEEKERS

Aim: To know that we can preach the Gospel by how we live.

Starter

Sing an action song such as 'In a cottage in a wood' where the actions can take the place of some of the words.

Teaching

Tell the children to look happy, sad, surprised, cross, hungry and tired. Now have them guessing how you are feeling from how you look, giving them a choice of two each time – for example, 'Am I happy or hungry?' or 'Am I cross or am I tired?'

We show each other how we are feeling by how we behave. How do we show that we love someone? We may give them a hug or a kiss, we may look after them and play with them, we may do something nice for them like painting them a picture or helping them. If we said we loved them, but did our best to be horrible to them, that would be silly, wouldn't it?

It's the same with God. We are never too young to tell people about God. We can show people that God is loving and giving by being loving and giving ourselves. We can show people that God is kind by being kind ourselves. We can show people that God is fair by being fair.

Praying

I show I'm happy by smiling.
I show I'm cross by frowning.
I show I love you, Jesus,
by loving those I meet.

Activities

On the sheet they can draw themselves showing God's love by doing something kind, helpful or thoughtful.

PEARL DIVERS

Aim: To know that Jesus wants our lives to reflect our faith in God.

Starter

Cut some stencils of simple shapes from card, or use bought ones, and have lengths of lining paper for the children to cover with shapes using paint and sponges. Protect their clothing thoroughly, and have washing-up bowls of warm soapy water and towels so that the cleaning-up process is straightforward.

Teaching

Admire the completed length of paper. How come the shapes are all the same, even though different people were making them? The stencils made it possible for all the children to reproduce the designs faithfully and exactly, so that they could make this patterned wall hanging.

Today we are going to look at how the pattern of our living can be shaped by God guiding us. Pick up one of the stencil shapes. If I want to make this shape exactly, I have to use it. That's like us in our Christian life. If we want to act in a loving, right way, we need the loving righteous God to live by. Just as I have to get in touch with the stencil shape to use it, we have to get in touch with God each day to be like him. That's called *praying*. (Display a sign of praying hands and the word 'Praying' with it.)

Just picking up the stencil won't make the shape, though. I have to use it. Fill a sponge and stencil a shape. As you do so, talk about the way you are keeping to the shape and trying not to go over the edges. It's the same with our Christian life. When we have got in touch with God, we go and live through the day, keeping to God's guidelines of love and truth. That way, whatever colours the day gives us, whether they are bright ones or dark ones, we'll be able to make with them the pattern of God's loving nature. The way we live will be showing other people the love we know God has for us and them.

Praying

Lord Jesus, may my life
be a pattern of your loving,
your truth and your faithfulness,
so that others can see
that I am your friend and follower.

Activities

There is space on the sheet for some more printing, using some bright and some dark colours, so that the children see that God's pattern of loving can be shown in both happy and sad times, both easy and difficult times.

GOLD PANNERS

Aim: To look at the necessity for living our faith and not being hypocritical.

Starter

Play 'Cheat'. Deal out equal quantities of a pack of cards to everyone. The aim is to be the first to get rid of all your cards. This is done by laying down cards in numerical order around the circle, using any suit, so that the first person may place (face down) the ace of spades, the second person the two of diamonds and the third the three of hearts. If you haven't got a suitable card, you can pick any of your cards and lie about what it is as you put it down. If you are challenged and found to be cheating, you take both your cards and those of the challenger. If, when challenged, you are found to be correct, the challenger takes yours and their own cards.

Teaching

It isn't only in cards that we cheat. Often in life we pretend things, either to others or to ourselves and to God. Today we are going to look at God's view of this.

Start by reading the passage from Malachi. Like all the other prophets, Malachi was trying to get the people to be honest to the God of truth. If the priests claim to worship the one true living God, they have got to live that out, rather than leading people astray by their teaching and example. God hates this kind of false religion.

Look in contrast at the kind of ministry shown in 1 Thessalonians. What evidence is there here that the leaders were acting out their faith, rather than leading people astray?

Now read today's Gospel. Why is Jesus angry at the behaviour of the Pharisees? How are they seen as false guides? Notice how it is Jesus' love and compassion for the people that makes him so concerned about the leaders guiding them away from the loving God. That links with the way the Thessalonians have been cared for rather than preached at.

Use the sheet to think about the guidelines Jesus gives for all leaders and teachers of the faith.

Praying

Lord, show me the path of life
and fill me with joy
in your presence.

Activities

There is space on the sheet to explore Jesus' guidelines for teachers and leaders, and examples of hypocrisy in times past which we can see now but which people didn't recognise at the time. They are encouraged to look at any areas in our own church or society where there are double standards which need addressing.

THIRTY-SECOND SUNDAY OF THE YEAR

Thought for the day

We need to keep ourselves awake and prepared so that the Day of the Lord does not come to us as darkness rather than light.

Reflection on the readings

Wisdom of Solomon 6:12-16
Psalm 62:2-8
1 Thessalonians 4:13-18
Matthew 25:1-13

Most of us see in ourselves what we want to see, and have blind spots about areas we do not wish to change. The human brain is immensely good at self-deception, packing in layers of psychological wadding to protect us from truths we do not wish to hear. This is why, if someone trespasses anywhere near the truth we are avoiding, we tend to react with what seems like irrational anger and irritability. In fact, it is exceedingly rational, since we are protecting ourselves from discovering that hidden core. With the light of wisdom we can come to see the truth about ourselves more clearly. The hidden core is revealed but with a light that helps us to see the good and the bad in perspective. It is a light that also helps us see the way forward.

The risks of living without self-knowledge, however, far outweigh the attractions. The less we live a lie, the more integrity we have as people, and that has benefits for the society in which we live, and for our local church community. A whole group of people with self-knowledge can bring about great good and widespread healing.

The unprepared bridesmaids in today's parable alert us to the terrible possibility of being shut out of the kingdom by default. As we consider the tragic, eternal consequences of living in denial of God's law of love and truth, we need to be brave about those areas we may have hidden from ourselves, perhaps for many years, and ask for God to reveal them to us, so that we can have them healed before it is too late.

Discussion starters

1. Why is the way of justice and righteousness a better way for a society to be run?

2. How can we ensure that we have enough oil in our lamps for when they are needed?

All-stage talk

Beforehand prepare some sticks with red paper flames stuck on the end.

Begin by asking who has ever been a bridesmaid or a page-boy at a wedding. Were any of them late for the wedding? Today we heard a parable Jesus told about some bridesmaids. Some were ready when they were needed, but some weren't.

Show the 'torches' which were used at that time. Material was soaked in oil and tied on to the end of sticks. When you set light to them they would burn well, so the bride and bridegroom, coming from the bridegroom's house in the evening of the wedding, could have their way lit by the bridesmaids' torches. (Have a bride and groom and some bridesmaids to show this, holding their torch sticks.) At least, they could if the bridesmaids had their oil with them.

The problem in Jesus' story was that half the bridesmaids hadn't checked their oil supplies, so when the bridegroom needed their torchlight, they were rushing off to buy more oil, and ended up being shut out of the wedding feast.

What is the hidden message in this parable? What is Jesus wanting us to understand?

He wants us to be ready, and have our oil supplies topped up, so that whenever the bridegroom returns, even if he takes longer to arrive than we were expecting, we will be there waiting, shining brightly in the darkness. Then the bridegroom can lead us all into the celebrations and the feast.

Fill the oil lamp and light it. God's Spirit is like the oil we need to keep us burning brightly with God's love. If we stop keeping ourselves 'topped up' by forgetting to pray and read the Bible each day, our lives will stop shining, just as the girls' torches went out. Then, if Jesus suddenly returns, unexpectedly, either at the end of time or in a situation where our bright Christian love is badly needed, we won't be able to help.

So Jesus is telling us to keep praying, keep listening and keep loving. That way, we'll be all ready whenever he needs us.

All-age ideas

- Have an oil lamp and bottle of oil with some bridal flowers and a veil as one of the flower arrangements today.

- Give out small squares of foil or shiny paper to everyone as they come in. Invite everyone to look at their 'mirrors' and imagine them reflecting back their spiritual rather than physical state. Allow everyone space and time to recognise any areas which need bringing to God's love for forgiveness and healing.

- Invite a group of people to mime the parable in the Gospel as it is read.

Prayer of the Faithful

Celebrant
In the power of the Spirit,
let us pray to the Lord.

Reader
Heavenly Father,
anoint your Church all over the world
with the oil of your Spirit,
so that we burn brightly,
lighting the dark world with your love and truth.
Keep our church communities from error and sin,
and supply us all, through word and sacrament,
with all our souls require.

Silence

Waken us, Lord:
to understand your love.

Heavenly Father, take the false values of our world
and upend them;
take the oppressed and free them;
take the leaders and inspire them;
take the past and redeem it,
the present and fill it,
the future and guide us in it.

Silence

Waken us, Lord:
to understand your love.

Heavenly Father, it is in our homes and daily tasks
that you train us in loving obedience.
We pray for those who have to live and work with us
and are familiar with our habits, gifts and faults.
May we make the most of the opportunities
to love, to forgive, to stand back and to reach out.

Silence

Waken us, Lord:
to understand your love.

Heavenly Father, as we pray for all who are ill
in body, mind or spirit,
surround them with your love and healing,
your reassurance and peace.
We pray for those
who are too weak or exhausted to pray,
but simply know they ache for your comfort.

Silence

Waken us, Lord:
to understand your love.

Heavenly Father, as real and living for the dead
as for those of us walking through time,
we commend to your mercy and love
those who have died in your faith and friendship;
may we all share in the joy
of Christ's coming in glory.

Silence

Waken us, Lord:
to understand your love.

With Mary, Mother of Jesus,
let us pray:
Hail, Mary . . .

In a time of silence,
we share with God our Father
our personal burdens, joys and sorrows.

Silence

Celebrant
Father, whose character is full
of mercy and compassion,
accept these prayers
for the sake of Jesus, our Saviour.
Amen.

TREASURE SEEKERS

Aim: To know that we are called to shine like lights
in the darkness.

Starter

Close the curtains, if practical, and give two children
torches so that they can help the others to find
some hidden milk bottle tops around the room.

Teaching

Point out how useful it is to have some shining
lights when we have lost things in the dark. Show
the children an oil lamp, fill it with oil and light it.
We can shine like lights in the darkness, when we
are kind and friendly, thoughtful and generous,
when we tell the truth and help each other, when
we cheer one another up. That makes the world a
happier place for everyone to live in. Like this
lamp, we need to be soaked with God's love so that
we burn brightly.

Praying

Jesus, keep us shining
like lamps in the darkness,
shining with your love
in the world.

Activities

The sheet can be made into a lantern. Provide shiny
red paper for the children to push inside so that it
shows through the slits.

PEARL DIVERS

Aim: To know the parable of the unprepared
bridesmaids and its meaning.

Starter

As they come in, the children can make torches by
fixing shiny red flames on to sticks with rubber
bands or sticky tape.

Teaching

Jesus was telling his friends about the future, and
what would happen at the end of the world when
he would come back in glory. He told this parable
to help them understand. It's set at a wedding. If
any of them have been bridesmaids or page-boys
they will remember that there's a lot of waiting
around to do at weddings, and the wedding in Jesus'
story was just the same. Explain how in Jesus' time,
the bride and groom would go to the bridegroom's
house, and then come out in the evening for the
party. All the bridesmaids would wait around near
the bridegroom's house until they came out, so
they could light the bride and groom's way to
where the wedding feast was held.

The torches they carried were like ours – sticks
with flames on the top. They soaked some material
in oil and tied it on to a stick before lighting it, so
they needed to have spare oil with them, ready for
when the oil was used up.

In Jesus' story there were ten bridesmaids waiting
for the bridegroom. Five had plenty of oil for their
lamps and five hadn't been keeping themselves
ready. When eventually the bridegroom was ready
to go, the five unprepared bridesmaids panicked.
'Give us some of your oil!' they said. 'Ours is running
out!' But the other five couldn't give their oil. If they
had done that there wouldn't have been enough light
from any of the lamps, so they sent the unprepared
bridesmaids to buy some more oil.

By the time they got back, the bride and bridegroom had been led through the night by the
lamps of the other five bridesmaids, and the whole
wedding party had gone in to the feast. The five
unprepared bridesmaids weren't recognised when
they hammered on the door, so they missed out on
the party, all because they hadn't kept their oil
supplies at the ready.

Jesus said to his hearers, 'So you keep awake

and keep prepared, because you don't know when the bridegroom will be returning, and if you aren't ready, you'll find yourselves shut out of the celebrations on the last day.'

He was talking about the time when he will return in all the glory of God at the end of time. And we all need to keep our lamps topped up with oil ready for that.

Praying

Give me oil in my lamp, keep me burning,
give me oil in my lamp, I pray,
give me oil in my lamp, keep me burning,
keep me burning to the break of day.

Activities

On the worksheet there are instructions for making jam-jar lanterns. Each child will need a nightlight, a jar, some garden wire and some string. There is also a waiting activity using a clock face.

GOLD PANNERS

Aim: To explore the meaning of the parable of the bridesmaids and Jesus' teaching about the Day of the Lord.

Starter

Who can count a minute? One person has a watch or clock, and when they are ready they say, 'Go!' Everyone imagines how long a minute is and puts their hand up when they think a full minute has passed. The person checking notes who is closest to real time.

Teaching

Time is quite elastic and drags if you are waiting. Today we are going to look at some bridesmaids who had a long time to wait.

Go straight to the Gospel, reading it as a group with different people taking different parts. What is this parable really talking about? What event is the bridegroom's return that the girls are waiting for? (Jesus coming back in glory.) Who are the bridesmaids, waiting for his return to welcome him? (The Church; Christians.) What is Jesus telling us by the bridegroom taking longer to arrive than expected? (The second coming may not be as close as they thought.)

So what does it mean about some of the brides-maids letting their oil run low so that their lamps are not shining when the bridegroom returns? (As Christians we need to make sure we are keeping

ourselves filled with God's Spirit, so that our lives shine with God's love.)

Praying

O thou who camest from above,
the pure celestial fire to impart,
kindle a flame of sacred love
on the mean altar of my heart.
There let it for thy glory burn
with inextinguishable blaze,
and trembling to its source return
in humble prayer and fervent praise.

Activities

On the sheet they are looking at the reading from Thessalonians and its implications, and there are references to help them see the significance of oil and fire, together with the traditional practice in weddings at the time, so that they can place the parable in context.

THIRTY-THIRD SUNDAY OF THE YEAR

Thought for the day

The Day of the Lord will hold terror for the wicked and unprepared, but rejoicing for those living in God's light.

Reflection on the readings

Proverbs 31:10-13, 19-20, 30-31
Psalm 127:1-5
1 Thessalonians 5:1-6
Matthew 25:14-30

People speak sometimes of being petrified by fear; they are so terrified that the fear paralyses their bodies, and they are, momentarily, 'turned to stone'. There are passages in the Old Testament which give stark descriptions of the Day of the Lord, full of wrath and anguish, trouble and ruin. It is like the shock tactics used in documentaries to terrify us out of speeding, and it pronounces unrelieved condemnation, justly deserved. It is good that these Old Testament readings are tempered with the positive, though still serious, words of the letter to the Thessalonians. Certainly the Day of Judgement will come 'like a thief in the night', at a time we are not expecting, but that need not make us over-fearful if we are people of daylight. Christ's coming and his saving work have given us access to the necessary protection against evil, and, provided we make use of it, we do not need to live in terror. We are reminded that it is certainly not God's will that any should perish, and what he longs for is that we should all be saved.

Accordingly, we need to spend our energies as the Church more in encouraging one another, and loving sinners to repentance, than coming in heavy with scaremongering and condemnation. We should not behave as 'daylight dwellers' through terror of eternal punishment, but through a natural thankfulness as the extent of God's love dawns on us, and his ways of love and truth become increasingly attractive to us.

This carries with it not terror but peace and joy, together with the maturity of responsibility. The kingdom of God is not about people terrorised into submission; part of salvation is being given the grace to grow up. Today's parable of the talents and the passage from Proverbs exalting the special gifts of character remind us of this expectation in our new life. God expects us to make the most of all we have been given, rather than hiding our gifts away, either out of a mock modesty or a fear which insults the loving justice of God. All these gifts we have been provided with can be used and enjoyed, both for the encouragement and building-up of the Church and in the service we are called to give in the world.

Discussion starters

1. There are many in our time who assume God is impotent to do either good or evil. In the light of prophecies about the Day of Judgement, should we be so accepting of this, or should it spur us into fervent prayer and urgent action?

2. Has the pendulum swung too far from the 'fire and brimstone' terror sermons to the point where we are complacent about the possibility of punishment?

All-stage talk

Beforehand place three boxes of different colours around the church. In the red box put five one-pound coins (cardboard ones are fine!), in the blue box put two one-pound coins and leave the yellow box empty.

We know that one day the world as we know it will come to an end. We know that life as we know it will finish. All the prophets and Jesus teach us in the Bible that there is going to be a Day of the Lord, when we will see Jesus in all God's glory, and all

that is evil will not survive. That includes people. How we live now in our lives will affect what happens to us that day. We do need to know that.

When will it happen? We don't know the time or date; in fact, what we do know is that it will happen suddenly, without us having loads of time to change. That's why we need to live every day as if it were our last.

But God doesn't want us so scared of the last day that we can't enjoy life here. Jesus came to set us free from that fear, and, if we are walking through life as Jesus' friends, there is nothing to be frightened of, because it's only the evil and bad and selfish that will be destroyed; everything that is good and loving and honest will be gathered up safely for ever.

Jesus told one of his stories with secrets – parables – about making the most of all the gifts God has given us, and we need three people to help us with it. (Make sure that the third servant chosen has been warned beforehand that she will be told off in the story, and is confident enough to cope with that.)

In Jesus' story, a man is going on a long journey and, before he goes, he gathers his servants together and entrusts his property to them to look after. (Give five coins to one servant and send her off to find the red box. Give two coins to another servant and send him off to find the blue box. Give one coin to the last servant, and send her off to find the yellow box.) The man went off on his travels, and after a long time came back home. He called the servants to him to settle accounts with them. (Call the volunteers together with the boxes.) Let's see how the first servant has got on. (She opens the box and counts out to the owner ten coins. Be very pleased. Everyone can clap.) What about the second servant? (He opens the box and counts out four coins. Praise and applause.) What about the third servant? Tell everyone how this servant told the owner she was too scared to do anything with her gift, so she just hid it as it was. (She gives it back.) The owner was not pleased at all because the servant had not made good use of the gift she had been given. (Tell the servant off, and thank all the actors for their help.)

We all have gifts God has enjoyed giving us. Some of us are good at being friendly and welcoming, some good at looking after animals, working out money, ironing, or thinking out solutions to difficult problems. Whatever our gift is, we need to enjoy using it and making the most of it for the good of everyone.

All-age ideas

• Have a display of paintings and photographs which show people in ordinary situations, with the title: 'Flower where God plants you.'

- As well as an offering of money, suggest people give an offering of time. They can be given circles of paper as they come in, and commit themselves to a daily prayer time. The circles are then collected and offered to God.

Prayer of the Faithful

Celebrant
Gathered as God's people, let us pray.

Reader
Holy God, if we are presuming on your mercy,
alert us and shatter our complacency;
if we are doubting your mercy,
affirm in us the reality of your forgiveness.
May we, as the Church, encourage and warn,
but never condemn;
acknowledge sin, but never judge.

Silence

Christ will come again:
make us ready to meet him.

Holy God, raise up prophets to speak out your truth,
and draw attention to whatever needs changing
in our world, our expectations and assumptions,
our management of resources and finances,
our systems of government and our attitudes.
May all peoples come to recognise your truth.

Silence

Christ will come again:
make us ready to meet him.

Holy God, fill our homes and places of work
with so much love
that tensions and barriers melt away,
conflicts are resolved
and troubles lightened by being lovingly shared.
Open our hearts to hope again
where we had given up.

Silence

Christ will come again:
make us ready to meet him.

Holy God, may all in misery and despair
turn to find you close beside them in their heartache,
not condemning but loving them in their pain.
May all who are locked in terror or guilt be set free,
and may those whom long-term illness wearies
be strengthened to persevere,
freed from resentment.

Silence

Christ will come again:
make us ready to meet him.

Holy God, Lord of the living and the dead,
we commend to your mercy all who have died,
and thank you for that eternal healing
which frees us from all pain and suffering.

Silence

Christ will come again:
make us ready to meet him.

Holy God, we thank you for the gifts and talents
you have given us.
Give us the courage to use them
for the good of the world.

Silence

Christ will come again:
make us ready to meet him.

We make our prayer with Mary,
who used all her gifts in God's service:
Hail, Mary . . .

God our Father loves us:
in silence
we make our private petitions to him.

Silence

Celebrant
Heavenly Father, grant these prayers
which we bring before you,
in the name of Jesus Christ.
Amen.

TREASURE SEEKERS

Aim: To know that God enjoys giving us gifts and wants us to enjoy them too.

Starter

Pass the parcel. Pack it with a sticker at each layer and make sure that everyone receives a gift.

Teaching

When do we give presents to people? Talk about birthday, Christmas and 'just because' presents that we give to people we love. What makes us happy is seeing they enjoy what we have chosen for them, and enjoy using it.

That's what it's like with God. God loves giving, and he enjoyed giving us the things we are good at. Some people are good at being friendly, or playing football, or cheering people up, or saving their money, or listening, or painting, or learning. Go round the group with the children saying, 'I'm happy that God made me good at . . .' God is happy to see us making the most of the gifts he has given us, and enjoying using them. We can all use these gifts to make the world a better and happier place.

Praying

Thank you, God,
for making us good at things.
Help us to use these gifts
to make people happy.

Activities

There is space on the worksheet for the children to draw themselves doing whatever they are good at, and God smiling to see them enjoying the gift he has given them. They can also fill in the card to give someone else, to encourage them.

PEARL DIVERS

Aim: To know the parable of the talents and its meaning.

Starter

I am the music man, I come from down your way. There are lots of instruments the music man can play, which are 'played' by everyone in this song.

Teaching

Point out how talented the music man was in that song, able to play lots of different instruments. Today we are going to look at the gifts we have been given, and how God hopes we will enjoy them and make the most of them. Talk about the sort of gifts God gives us, such as being good at particular sports or skills, being thoughtful and kind, making people feel comfortable, helping them when they're ill, using money wisely, being able to work out answers to tricky problems, listening well, leading, or helping people make up after an argument. Some of us are given the happiness and security of a loving home, and others are given the gift of being cheerful even when life is difficult for us. All these things can be used to help the world.

Go round the group in circle time, with everyone saying, 'I'm glad God made me good at . . .'

Jesus told a parable about being responsible about our gifts, and using them, rather than hiding them away and ignoring them. As they will see, God expects us to make good use of whatever we are given.

Give out a copy of this script to four people, who can act it out.

Owner	I have to go away for a long time. I will put my servants in charge until I get back. Servants, come here!
Servants	Yes, sir, what do you want?
Owner	I have to go away for a long time and I am going to put you in charge until I get back. Servant Jack, I am giving you five bags of money to look after. Look after it well for me.
Servant Jack	OK, I will.
Owner	Servant Molly, I am giving you two bags of money to look after. Look after it well for me.
Servant Molly	OK, I will.
Owner	Servant Luke, I am giving you one bag of money to look after. Look after it well for me.
Servant Luke	OK, I will.
Owner	Now I am off. Use that money well and see what you can do with it. I will see you later. Good bye.
Servants	Good bye!

Later

Owner	Here I am! Come on, servants. Let's see how you used the gifts I gave you.
Servant Jack	Here you are. You gave me five bags of money and I have worked to make it ten.
Owner	Well done, you good and faithful servant. I will reward you.
Servant Molly	Here you are. You gave me two bags of money and I have worked hard to make it four.
Owner	Well done, you good and faithful servant! I will reward you.
Servant Luke	Here you are. I haven't done anything with the bag of money you gave me. I just hid it. You can have it back again now.
Owner	Just one bag of money? You lazy servant! I put you in charge of that. You should have used it, not just hidden it. I will give this one bag of money to servant Jack. He made very good use of the gifts I gave him. Out of my sight, servant Luke!

Praying

Lord God,
thank you for giving us gifts and talents.
Help us to enjoy them and use them well
for the good of the world.

Activities

There are instructions on the sheet for making some wrapping-paper, and the children will need plain coloured paper and an assortment of biscuit cutters to print with. There is also a wordsearch to reinforce the teaching of the parable, and a quiz to help them with the meaning of it.

GOLD PANNERS

Aim: To look at the prophesied Day of the Lord, both from the point of view of judgement and mercy.

Starter

Fix a sheet of paper to everyone's backs and provide pens. Everyone goes round writing on the sheets of paper things they appreciate and enjoy about each person. Then the sheets are taken off and given to their owners to read.

Teaching

Read the first part of the passage from 1 Thessalonians and consider why people might be frightened about the end of time (the Day of the Lord).

Now look at the rest of the passage from Thessalonians, where it is still recognised that there will be a Day, a Day of Judgement, but through Jesus there is hope of salvation for us. Jot down the words which describe how we should behave.

Finally read the parable of the talents, with different parts being taken by different people. God wants us to be responsible about the gifts we are entrusted with, and not waste them, hide them, or be too frightened to use them. He wants us to enjoy using them to the full.

Praying

Lord, you have been our dwelling-place
throughout all generations.
Before the mountains were born
or you brought forth the earth and the world,
from everlasting to everlasting
you are God.

(From Psalm 89)

Activities

There are examples on the sheet of people who have used their gifts to the glory of God and for the good of the world, and they are encouraged to look at their own gifts and how they could be used to the full in their life.

CHRIST THE KING

Thought for the day

In total humility, at one with the least of his people, Jesus, the Messiah or Christ, reigns as King, with full authority and honour for eternity.

Reflection on the readings

Ezekiel 34:11-12, 15-17
Psalm 22
1 Corinthians 15:20-26, 28
Matthew 25:31-46

There is a glorious contrast between the high office, power and authority given to the Messiah and the tender humility in which he acts with his people. This high office is not of the worldly kind, which tends to take promising people away from the practical caring and isolate them in managerial offices where they can easily lose the common touch.

The Messiah finds his true identity in searching for the lost, bringing back the strays, binding up the injured and strengthening the weak. Ezekiel the prophet proclaims the humility of this Servant King, whose mercy and loving kindness soothes aching souls and reassures us all. It is not that sin is excused or ignored, but that God longs to mend whatever is broken in us, and to gather us up, even after our own foolishness has caused our scattering. Psalm 22 echoes the image of us belonging to God and his kingdom as sheep belong to the shepherd and his pasture.

In the reading from 1 Corinthians, Paul talks of the great power at work in raising Jesus from the dead, which places him in the position of eminence, King of earth and heaven, and which is also the cause of our hope. In becoming one with Christ through faith in him, we are brought into the everlasting kingdom where he reigns, and can rejoice that it is so, since it is not earned by works but freely given through grace.

In the Gospel we reach the end of the series of parables in Matthew dealing with the Day of

Judgement. We have seen it from the viewpoint of the Church (the bridesmaids), the leaders with responsibilities (the talents), and now those who live and die without knowing the revealed truth. As all these people of other faiths and none are gathered before the throne of God, it is shown to them how, in their human goodness and thoughtful service to others, they have unknowingly been serving the God of love, and therefore belong to his kingdom, whatever name they may have given it before.

Of course, the reverse is also true, and it is not simply doing harm to others which marks out our rejection of God's ways. It is the goodness we fail to do, the needs we do not notice and ignore. Such blindness works in opposition to the law of love and places us outside the kingdom. The separation of sheep from goats is not so much judgement and punishment as sorting out those already shown to belong to the kingdom of God by their life's intent from those who are already shown to belong to the kingdom of darkness.

Discussion starters

1. What does today's Gospel say to those who claim that they have never done anyone any harm?

2. If we are to be in nature like the Christ, how do today's readings suggest we should be living?

All-stage talk

Bring along a crown and robe, some pretend bags of money, a dish of fruit and two fans on sticks as shown below. Drape some cloth over a chair.

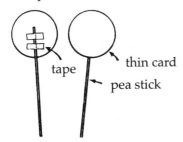

tape

thin card

pea stick

Tell everyone that today we are celebrating that Jesus Christ is King for ever. Ask a volunteer to come out and dress them up in the grand robe of very costly material, hand-embroidered by expert craftsmen, and the solid gold crown, studded with real diamonds and rubies. Sit the king on a grand throne covered in pure silk and made from finest marble, and provide him with some servants to stand around and wave him with fans, bowing before him. Give him bags of money on a table nearby, and provide a dish of fresh fruits for him to snack on between banquets.

Is this right? Is this what King Jesus is really like? No, it's all wrong! Although Jesus has been given all power and majesty and honour, and is King of all time and space, he is a very different sort of king. He lays aside his majesty (help the king up from his throne), lays aside his robe and his crown (take them from him), lays aside all wealth and comfort (the servants move the table), so that he can be one with us (he shakes hands with the servants) and live among us, caring for us, searching for the lost, and binding up the injured. (Thank the servant and the king for their help.)

Now if that's how our king behaves, then that's how we are to behave as well. If we worship and honour a Servant King, who doesn't greedily look after his own needs all the time but makes a point of looking after other people's needs, then that's what we have to do! Our wealth and treasure will be in loving service, wherever we're needed. That's how Jesus will recognise us as his people, when we get to the gate of heaven.

All-age ideas

- Have the crown and robe and the other props near the altar as people come up to communion, with the title 'The Servant King'.

- Have the parable mimed during the Gospel. To help everyone understand that the sorting is checking existing citizenship of the kingdom, give all the 'sheep' a cross on their foreheads, which the king looks for as they are chosen and welcomed.

Prayer of the Faithful

Celebrant
Let us humble ourselves in the presence of God and pray to him for the Church and for the world.

Reader
Loving God, in all our ministry as the Church,
both laity and clergy,
on Sundays and on weekdays,
may we give glory to you
and further your kingdom.
Direct us to those who are searching
and give us the wisdom to know
how best to draw them to your love.

Silence

We are your people:
the sheep of your pasture.

Loving God, may we actively seek to do good,
to stand up against injustice and work for peace;
Lord, rid the world of the terrible evils
that result from unvoiced objections,
and unspoken misgivings.
Give us the courage to act as true citizens of heaven.

Silence

We are your people:
the sheep of your pasture.

Loving God, may the ways we manage our homes,
decisions, time and money
be in keeping with our calling
as inheritors of the kingdom.
May your love undergird all our loving.

Silence

We are your people:
the sheep of your pasture.

Loving God, search for the lost,
bring back those who have strayed,
bind up the injured,
and strengthen the weak;
help us all to share in this work of loving care.

Silence

We are your people:
the sheep of your pasture.

Loving God, welcome into your kingdom
all whose lives show them to be your servants,
whether or not they have known you by name.
Prepare us all to meet you with the confidence
of sins confessed and forgiven.

Silence

We are your people:
the sheep of your pasture.

With Mary, Mother of Christ the King,
we make our prayer:
Hail, Mary . . .

We make our private petitions now,
in the knowledge that God our Father
listens with love.

Silence

Celebrant
Trusting in your great love, dear Father,
we lay our prayers before you,
and ask you to hear our requests
through Christ Jesus.
Amen.

TREASURE SEEKERS

Aim: To know that Jesus is the greatest King of all.

Starter

Pass the crown. When the music stops, whoever is
wearing the crown sits still while everyone stands
up and bows or curtsies to them.

Teaching

Take along a globe and point out where you all live,
and a few other places they might have heard of, such
as the USA and Africa. Show the children a picture of
our Queen and some other heads of state. These are
all very important people. But there is one King who
is over everyone who has ever been alive and who
will ever live. His kingdom is not a place on a globe.
Who can this important King be? It's our friend Jesus!
We are friends with the most important King ever.

Praying

Jesus, you are my friend
and you are my King.
You are the King of love.
I want to serve you for ever.

Activities

On the sheet there are instructions for making a flag
to wave. Each child will need a stick to fix it on.
There is also a picture of Jesus washing his disciples'
feet, and the children can spot the hidden crowns.

PEARL DIVERS

Aim: To know the parable of the sheep and goats,
and its meaning.

Starter

In teams the children pass a crown from head to
head down the line, and the person at the end runs
up to the front to start again. The first team to get
back to the starting order wins.

Teaching

Jesus is like a Shepherd King, who looks after us all
as his sheep, and searches for us when we are lost.
Although he is King of the whole world and all time
and space, he is always looking after our needs,
more like a servant. Today we celebrate Christ as the
humble King he is, full of glory but also full of love.

If we are going to be his people, we will act like
him in our lives, and that is how he will recognise
us as his people. Every time we do something kind
or loving, or help someone, we are actually serving
our King Jesus. Every time we are unkind and
thoughtless, and don't notice that someone needs our
help we are turning ourselves away from our King.

Jesus told one of his stories to help us understand. Place some carpet tiles, sheets or towels on
the floor as the background for the story, and use

cut-out pictures such as those shown on the sheet. You will need about twelve people. Move the pictures around on the background as you tell the story.

Jesus is talking about all the people standing before the throne of heaven who have not known him or been told about him during their lifetime. He says that the king is standing there and the people all stand in front of him. Just like a shepherd sorts out his sheep and goats he'll look at the people and put them into two groups, one on his right and the other on his left. To the ones on his right he will say, 'Welcome to my kingdom! I can see from your lives that you belong to my kingdom of love. When you were alive, you gave me food when I was hungry, drink when I was thirsty, you welcomed me when I was a stranger, you gave me clothes when I needed them, and you visited me and helped me when I was ill and in prison.'

Very puzzled, the people looked at each other and at the king. (Show the question mark over them.) 'We don't remember doing those things to you,' they said, 'When did we help you like that?'

The king explained to them that whenever they had done any of those kind things to anyone, they had been doing it to him. Their kind way of living showed, and that's how he could tell they were members of his kingdom of love.

Then he turned to the other group. 'I can see that you don't belong to my kingdom,' said the king. 'The way you lived your life shows up now. I was hungry but you never fed me, I was thirsty but you never gave me a drink. When I was a stranger you never invited me in, and when I needed clothes you didn't give me any. When I was ill and in prison you never came to visit me.'

The people were very surprised. (Show the question mark again.) 'We didn't do any harm in our life,' they protested. 'And we don't know what you mean – we don't even know you; when did we not help you?' The king looked at them sadly. 'I was there when you ignored the needs of those all around you and you just got on with your own lives without even noticing their pain and needs. When you failed to do good to those around you, you were failing to do good to me. That's how I can tell you don't belong in this kingdom of love. So you'll have to leave.'

And those people were sent away. Suddenly they realised that there is more to good living than just not hurting people. Good living is noticing needs and caring for them.

Praying

O Jesus, our King and our friend,
help us to live as your people,
aware of others' needs and ready to help.

Activities

Have the letters of 'Christ the Servant King' drawn on separate sheets of paper and let the children colour them all in, so they can be strung on to a length of wool and displayed in church. On the sheet is a pop-up card to make.

GOLD PANNERS

Aim: To look at the nature of Jesus' kingship.

Starter

Have the names and dates of the kings and queens of England written on separate pieces of card and work together to put them in order.

Teaching

Today we are going to look at Jesus as our King, and what kind of King he is.

First look at the passage from Ezekiel, making a note of the image he uses of a shepherd. (Who else was a shepherd who became a king?) This picture fits in well with the Jesus we know from the Gospels. (How?)

Look at the passage from 1 Corinthians and notice the images here of power and authority. When was this given to Jesus? After the Resurrection, once sin and death were conquered.

Then read the parable of the sheep and goats. Before you read it together, explain that 'all the nations' uses a word referring to those who do not know of Jesus and have not yet heard of him. Share out the different parts in the reading. Notice how the second group had not actively done anything wrong but had failed to do active good.

Praying

Come, let us bow down in worship,
let us kneel before the Lord our Maker;
for he is our God
and we are the people of his pasture,
the flock under his care.

(From Psalm 94)

Activities

The sheet further explores the kingship of Jesus as a servant, full of humility. And there is a wordsearch of the different titles of Jesus from different references, for which they will need a Bible.

SPECIAL FEASTS

MARY, MOTHER OF GOD – 1 JANUARY

Thought for the day

Jesus Christ, the Son of God, is born of a woman.

Reflection on the readings

Numbers 6:22-27
Psalm 66
Galatians 4:4-7
Luke 2:16-21

Mothering a child is one of those miracles which is no less wonderful for happening in villages and cities all over the world every day. The delicate balance and timing which makes it possible for a living being to grow from one cell to a baby capable of surviving outside the mother's body is quite amazing, and few of us can think of it, or witness the birth of a baby struggling into the world, without being deeply moved. Those who have experienced the privilege of carrying a baby through the months of pregnancy to birth know the extraordinary sense of parenting and responsibility which seems to grow as the baby grows; the being housed by your body and kicking strongly into your rib cage is both part of you and separate from you. All subsequent parenting throughout that child's life will be coloured by that dual responsibility – to care for as your own and to give the space to fulfil the separate nature.

No one can have been more aware of this than Mary, chosen by God to mother his Son and bring that vulnerable gift of salvation through the months of pregnancy to the moment of birth, and on to the parenting which brought her such joys and such pain. Jesus was her son to love and care for, but he was also the Son of God, born as human in order to save the world. Mary was told of this mission right at the beginning, and still she said, 'Yes'. All through Jesus' life she had to be there loving and caring, but never possessing, never demanding what could not be given. The Son of God belonged to the world, and Mary must have found this difficult at times to cope with.

Luke tells us that Mary was one to treasure things in her heart, and mull them over in her thoughts and prayer. We can imagine her listening and watching with that openness and lack of defensiveness which God had seen and nurtured in her. If it made her vulnerable to pain, it also made her open to joy, and enabled her to be, above all things, real.

The Church, as the Body of Christ, can enjoy the same mothering of Mary as Jesus knew, and we must expect it to be both loving and unpossessive, so that we are enabled to grow into maturity as Christians, for, as the Body of Christ, we too are here for the good of the world, and that may well take us into areas of suffering. Mary's example of positive willingness to co-operate with God, wherever it led, can inspire us at the start of another year.

Discussion starters

1. Why was it so important for the Saviour to come into the world as a human baby, born of a woman?

2. How can Mary's example of carrying, bearing and parenting the Christ help us in our own relationship with Christ?

All-stage talk

Ask everyone to raise their hands if what you say applies to them. (For example, they are sitting on the end of a row, ate cornflakes for breakfast, watch *Coronation Street*, and, finally, were born of a mother.) Although the first few things would have applied to some but not to others, everybody on earth in every generation, however young or old, has been born of a mother. That is something we all share as humans. We were all carried around inside a woman, where we were provided with all we needed until we had grown big and strong enough to survive out in this world. That's when we were born.

Over Christmas we have been celebrating Jesus being born into this world, and today we are looking at that from the point of view of Mary, his mother. It was through Mary saying, 'Yes!' to God that Jesus, the Son of God, could be born into the human family as a baby, born from a woman. It is when *we* are prepared to say, 'Yes!' to God, as Mary did, that God can use us and work through us for the good of the world.

We have such a lot to thank our mothers for. All that time we were in the womb, growing in the darkness, our bodies taking shape, it was our mothers' bodies that kept us safe and healthy, protected from the outside world, warm and nourished, so that when we needed energy, particular minerals or vitamins, we got them. As we got larger, our mothers found it quite tiring and needed to put their feet up sometimes. As we took up more space, our mothers found it harder to bend down and could feel us kicking about inside.

And then it was time for us to be born, and our mothers worked, or laboured, hard at that with us, so that we could live out here in the world we now know so well. The mothering didn't stop there, of course; when you are a mother you go on with the loving and caring for the rest of your life, helping your children gradually to grow into the independent persons God planned them to be.

So as we think today of our own mothering, and thank God for it, we remember with love and affection Mary, the woman who agreed to mother the Son of God. It was in the darkness and security of her womb that Jesus Christ grew and developed; it was through her labour that he was born, and it was her mothering that enabled him to become the adult who was and is the Saviour of the world.

All-age ideas

- Have mothers and their young children taking the collection and offering the gifts today.

- Make a collection particularly for children who need mothering, or for women and children in refuge homes.

- Decorate with flowers the Lady Chapel or a statue of the Mother and Child.

Prayer of the Faithful

Celebrant
Let us still our bodies and souls
as we gather to pray to the God
who made us and loves us.

Reader
As the Church we are the Body of Christ;
we thank you, Lord God, for Mary's mothering
which we share with Jesus.
We thank you for her love and faithfulness
and her example of willing co-operation.

Silence

Your will, Lord:
be done in us.

Out of love for the world
God sent his Son into the world;
we pray for all who live in the darkness of sin,
for the places where evil and corruption flourish,
where the problems and troubles
seem almost too entrenched to be solved.
We pray for hearts to be healed of hatred
and hope to be rekindled.

Silence

Your will, Lord:
be done in us.

As we remember with gratitude
Mary's mothering in the home at Nazareth,
we pray for our own homes and families,
for all expectant mothers,

those giving birth and the children being born,
that they may be surrounded and upheld
with love and affection.

Silence

Your will, Lord:
be done in us.

As we call to mind those we know
who are in trouble, need or sorrow,
we pray for comfort and healing,
refreshment and encouragement.

Silence

Your will, Lord:
be done in us.

We thank you, Lord God, that through the Cross,
death no longer has the victory;
we pray for those mothers who have died to this life
that they may know the fullness of joy in heaven.

Silence

Your will, Lord:
be done in us.

We pray with Mary,
our spiritual mother:
Hail, Mary . . .

Meeting our heavenly Father
in the stillness of silence,
let us whisper to him
our particular burdens of prayer.

Silence

Celebrant
Father, we bring these prayers
through Jesus Christ, our Saviour.
Amen.

TREASURE SEEKERS

Aim: To know that Mary is both Jesus' mother and the mother of the Church, the Body of Christ.

Starter

Sit in a circle and pass round a teddy. When each person holds the teddy they say why they love their mum. Then everyone says, 'Thank you, God, for Darren's mum.'

Teaching

Build on the starter activity to celebrate all that our mothers are for us and all they do for us. If you can draw stick people, make quick drawings to represent these ideas on a large sheet of paper, or, having talked about it, give everyone crayons to draw what they love about their mother on a communal sheet, and then share the ideas on it.

What were we celebrating last week? Christmas! Whose birthday was it? Jesus' birthday. Who was Jesus' mother? Mary. It was Mary who carried Jesus inside her until he was ready to be born, and Mary who looked after the baby Jesus, and fed him and kept him clean, and washed his clothes, and cuddled him when he fell over and hurt himself.

We are all part of the Church, the Body of Christ, so Mary is the Church's mother as well as being Jesus' mother. Mary wants us to follow Jesus and get to know him well, and she is always ready to help us get closer to him. Show some pictures of statues where Mary is always showing us her Son. 'Look,' she says, 'this is my Son Jesus. He's the one you need. Do what he says!'

Praying

Thank you, God, for my mother
who loves me and looks after me.
Thank you for Mary, Jesus' mother,
who loves all of us in the Church
and leads us to Jesus.

Activities

There are some pictures of mothers and babies from around the world to colour, and a picture of Mary with Jesus as a small boy, with some parts in dot-to-dot, to be completed by the children.

PEARL DIVERS

Aim: To celebrate our own mothers and the mother of Christ.

Starter

Have a rough-cut collection from catalogues and mission magazines of pictures of mothers and their children. The children cut round the pictures and mount them on coloured paper to make a collage entitled: 'Thank you, Lord God, for our mothers.'

Teaching

Looking at the collage, talk together about the things mums do for us, and how they love and care

for us. What could we do to let them know we love them and appreciate all they do? Write their ideas down on another sheet of paper and suggest they all try one of those ideas to do something for their mums today or during the week.

Talk with the children about Christmas, and all the family festivities, remembering what we were all celebrating. Today we are looking at the woman who said, 'Yes!' to God so that Jesus could come into the world as a baby, born like all the rest of us. Who is this woman? It's Mary. What sort of things would she have had to do to look after the baby Jesus? Talk about these, and how Mary was happy to be the mother of God's Son, even though she knew there would be times when it would be very hard and sad.

Praying

Thank you, Lord God,
for our mothers and all their love;
thank you for Mary,
and all her love.

Activities

On the sheet they are celebrating the mothering they have from their own mothers. There is a picture of Mary and Jesus to colour, and instructions for making a gift. If possible, ask a new mother to come in with her baby to talk to the children about mothering, and answer their questions.

GOLD PANNERS

Aim: To appreciate Mary's special calling as the mother of Christ.

Starter

Choose a trustworthy and sensible person and take them aside. Tell them to try and convince the others that they have won a thousand pounds. Back in the group, this person says they have won a thousand pounds, and weathers the scorn and disbelief, sticking to their story. Have a show of hands as to who is convinced and who isn't, and ask the 'prize winner' how it felt to be disbelieved and thought of as a liar. Today we are looking at Mary's special calling to be the mother of Christ, and some of the problems it must have caused for her.

Teaching

As part of our celebration of Christmas we are celebrating Mary's willingness to co-operate with God in his saving work by becoming the mother of Christ. Read together the passage from Numbers, remembering how Gabriel had greeted Mary at the Annunciation, calling her 'blessed among women'. Mary, in her humility, knew her need of God and so was open to his will, ready to be used in bringing Life itself to birth as a human baby.

Read the passage from Galatians, drawing attention to the need for the Son of God to enter into the full experience of being human and Jewish, in order to do the work of redeeming from the 'inside'. Also, since through Jesus we are made children and heirs, in a spiritual sense we share with Jesus Mary's mothering. Her calling to be his mother extends to being, in that spiritual sense, the mother of the Church, in every generation.

Now read today's Gospel, noticing how Mary, this young mother given such a great responsibility, absorbs everything and treasures it all in her heart. She is still open to God and his meaning, still attentive to hear what he is saying in all the events of her baby's birth. It is that openness and attentive listening to God which makes it possible for God to use her for such an important role. She never draws attention to herself or tries to bask in Jesus' glory, but always directs our attention to Jesus Christ, her Lord and her Son.

Praying

Father, we give you thanks
for the openness and willingness of Mary
to do your will
and take on the mothering of your Son.
We ask that her prayers may direct us
to attentive listening and openness to you,
so that with Mary we may say:
'Let it be to me according to your word.'

Activities

There are examples on the sheet of people who have experienced Mary directing them to Jesus Christ, her Son, and some questions to encourage them to think seriously about their own calling in life and their openness to God.

THE PRESENTATION OF THE LORD (CANDLEMAS) – 2 FEBRUARY

Thought for the day

In accordance with Jewish tradition, the Light of the World is presented as a first-born baby in the temple at Jerusalem.

Reflection on the readings

Malachi 3:1-4
Psalm 23
Hebrews 2:14-18
Luke 2:22-40

We have probably all experienced praying for something, supposedly open-mindedly, and then finding ourselves surprised by the way God answers our prayer in quite an unexpected way. Our surprise shows us that we must have actually had preconceived ideas we were not aware of. The people of Israel had been looking forward to the coming of the Messiah for generation after generation. The prophets had been foretelling his coming, and every Jewish young woman hoped that she might be going to bring the Messiah into the world. Today's reading from Malachi speaks of the messenger coming to prepare the way, after which the Lord himself will suddenly enter his Temple.

Today, as we hear that prophecy in the context of Jesus being presented by his parents as a young baby, brought into the temple in Mary's arms, we are aware of God's word being fulfilled in a way which did not exactly tie in with expectations of style, and yet it is obviously the right and natural way for the Lord to enter his temple: as an orthodox and humble Jewish baby, born into that faithful remnant of God's people.

Simeon and Anna are wonderful examples of the elderly faithful who have stayed spiritually flexible and alert throughout their long lives. Simeon has been told by God that he will see the Messiah in person before he dies, and we can imagine his excitement as, on this particular day, he feels drawn to go to the temple court. His trust in God is such that he will not be thrown by anything unexpected, and as soon as he sees this unremarkable little family walking in with their baby, he knows beyond all doubt that this is the child he has been waiting all his life to see.

Simeon has no problem with Jesus being the light for the whole world because he has never allowed legalism to hide or quench the flame of truth. But this perception also enables him to see something of the inevitable suffering-servant role the Messiah will have as he reveals people to themselves. Some will find this the key to new life, while others will prefer to reject the light of truth. Simeon can see that an intrinsic part of saving through love and truth is making enemies and meeting conflict and suffering; suffering this young woman, his mother, is bound to share.

It is important that God's Son identifies with his faithful people in every way, meeting them where they are. At Candlemas we look both back to the Incarnation and forward to the events of Holy Week, as Jesus, 'God with us', is presented to the Lord.

Discussion starters

1. Why was it necessary for Christ to become one with the human race and with the faithful remnant of Israel in order to save the world?

2. How was Simeon able to recognise this particular baby as the Christ? Do we expect God to tell us things?

All-stage talk

Today is a good opportunity to celebrate the elderly faithful and build relationships between young and old. Beforehand arrange for an elderly man and woman to sit at the front with a microphone to answer a few questions put to them by the children about what life was like when they were children. Gather the children round their feet and introduce the elderly people. Since they have been alive a long time they have picked up lots of wisdom. They have lived through things the younger ones here have heard about in history. Invite the children to find out what it was like being a child 70 or more years ago – they can ask about clothes, toys, school, church or food, for instance. After a few questions thank the volunteers and have the children escort them back to their seats.

In today's Gospel we heard about Joseph and Mary bringing the baby Jesus into the temple. All Jewish families did this when their first son was born. They came to give a present, or offer a sacrifice to God and dedicate the child. We've had two wise, elderly people answering questions today. And when Mary, Joseph and Jesus came into the temple there were two wise elderly people there. Their names were Simeon and Anna. They had both loved God all their life, and if any of us do that, we will end up wise and lovable in our old age. You can't love God all your life and end up crabby and narrow-minded.

Jesus didn't have a big label tied round his

swaddling clothes saying 'I am the Messiah'. Joseph and Mary didn't wave flags or shout to everyone, 'Look! This is the baby you've all been waiting for!' From the outside he looked just like any other baby, and Mary and Joseph looked just like an ordinary, fairly poor set of parents, rather dusty after the journey.

So how did Simeon and Anna know that this baby was the one they were waiting for?

Simeon had been told that he would see the promised Messiah in person before he died. He had been listening to God all his life, and because he was used to listening to God, he was able to recognise that this particular baby was the Messiah, God's chosen one.

When we spend a lot of time with another person we get to know how they think, and we understand them better and better. If we spend time with God every day, starting from today, and carry on doing that right into our old age, we will get to know him better and better, and it won't be long before we are able to hear what he speaks into our hearts. It is astounding that the powerful creator of this universe is happy to communicate with individuals like this, but that's God for you. He's hoping there will be some wise and faithful elderly Christians in the future – twenty, thirty, forty, fifty, sixty, seventy or eighty years from now. There could be. It could be us.

All-age ideas

• Have a grandparent and grandchild bringing up the offertory gifts.

• Act out the Gospel as it is narrated, using a young family with a real baby if you have one available!

• Have a display of photographs of those who regularly receive communion in their homes, with space for people to sign their pledge to pray for a particular person daily. It is important that these frail and elderly faithful do not become forgotten by the rest of the church.

Prayer of the Faithful

Celebrant
As we gather in Christ's name,
let us bring to mind those
who particularly need our prayer support.

Reader
We remember those who teach the faith
throughout the Church and throughout the world.
Keep them close to your guiding,
and open the hearts of those they teach
to hear and receive your truth.

Silence

Show us your ways:
and help us to walk in them.

We remember those in positions
of authority and influence
in this country and in all societies,
that needs may be noticed and addressed,
good values upheld and all people respected.

Silence

Show us your ways:
and help us to walk in them.

We remember those who looked after us
when we were very young,
and those who have no one to love and care for them.
We remember all young families
and all the children in our parish,
that they may be introduced to the one true God
and live their lives in his company.

Silence

Show us your ways:
and help us to walk in them.

We remember the elderly faithful
and especially those who are housebound
and can no longer join us to worship in person.
We thank you for their example
and ask you to increase our love for one another
across the age groups.

Silence

Show us your ways:
and help us to walk in them.

We remember those who have finished
their lives on earth
and commit them to your everlasting care
and protection.
We ask you to keep us faithful to the end of our life.

Silence

Show us your ways:
and help us to walk in them.

We offer our prayers with Mary
who took on the joys and sorrows
of mothering Jesus:
Hail, Mary . . .

In silence, let us bring to our God
the concerns of our own hearts,
knowing his love for us all.

Silence

Celebrant
Father, through the light of life
we are enabled to pray,
in the assurance of your faithfulness.
We offer our prayers
through Christ, the Light of the World.
Amen.

TREASURE SEEKERS

Aim: To know that Simeon had been waiting for the Saviour and knew it was Jesus.

Starter

A waiting game. Everyone gets into a space and sits down. The leader calls out, 'Ready . . . steady . . . hop/jump/walk!' and the children mustn't move until they have heard the full instruction. You can make it harder by sometimes giving the instruction quickly and sometimes slowly. Today we are going to meet someone who waited all his life for something, but at last he got it.

Teaching

Dress up one of the leaders as Simeon, or just tell the children we have a visitor today, and put on a headdress and white beard as they watch. When you are ready, resume eye contact with them and say, 'Hallo, children, my name's Simeon. Can you say, "Hallo, Simeon"?' Say you want to tell them about something exciting that happened to you. Tell them how old you are, and explain that you love God and know you can trust him. You knew that one day God was going to send someone to save and rescue people, and God had told you that you would see this Saviour in person before you died. Go on to tell the children what happened on that day in the temple when Joseph and Mary brought Jesus in. Chat your story, involving the children, and try to get across your excitement at actually meeting the Saviour God had promised.

Praying

Leader	Simeon knew he could trust God.
All	We can trust God, too.
Leader	Simeon loved God.
All	We love God, too.
Leader	Simeon knew that Jesus had come to save us.
All	We know Jesus came to save us, too.

Activities

The worksheet goes over the story with a sequencing activity involving cutting and sticking. If you have nativity dressing-up clothes suitable for the children they can 'play' the story through in costume.

PEARL DIVERS

Aim: To see that Jesus was being shown to those who were close to God and wanted to see.

Starter

Piecing the story together. Have a large-scale floor jigsaw and give the pieces out to everyone in the circle. One person starts by putting down their piece, and then you go round the circle adding pieces bit by bit until the picture is complete. This may well mean that some people can't go until someone else has added another piece. Since the feast of the Epiphany we have been looking at Jesus being shown to the world. All the different stories come together to give us a clearer picture of who he is and why he came.

Teaching

Have Anna and Simeon chatting together in the temple after Jesus has been taken home. They are talking about what has happened, and how they knew this particular baby was the promised Messiah. The children are listening in to the conversation. In the conversation bring out their age and their hopes, the way God has shown them the Saviour and their joy at recognising him. After the story get out two sheets, headed 'Simeon' and 'Anna'. Build a factfile about the two people we have just met, under the following headings:

Age Group (Young/Middle aged/Old)

Prayer Life (Prayed from time to time/Prayed if they felt like it/Close friendship with God)

Hope (The Messiah coming/Meeting the Messiah/ Recognising the Messiah)

What they thought of Jesus (A cute baby/An ordinary baby/The promised Messiah)

Praying

Simeon's prayer of praise. This translation from the *International Children's Bible* is a suitable one to use:

Now, Lord, you can let me, your servant,
die in peace as you said.
I have seen your Salvation with my own eyes.

It is Jesus.
You prepared him before all people.
He is a light for the non-Jewish people to see.
He is the glory of your chosen people.
I believe that Jesus is my Lord and Saviour.
Amen.

Say it line by line with the children repeating.

Activities

The worksheet extends the teaching to include what Simeon foretold about Jesus and his ministry. There are also instructions for making a prayer diary for the children to develop their own prayer life.

GOLD PANNERS

Aim: To see how Simeon and Anna's faithfulness and trust were rewarded, and relate this to our own faith.

Starter

Play a trust game, such as making a close circle around one person who allows themselves to fall in any direction. The circle of people around them prevents them from getting anywhere near the ground. Today we are looking at two people who knew they could really trust God.

Teaching

Read the Gospel passage together, with different people taking the parts of Simeon and Anna. Using the format provided on the worksheet, discuss *who* was involved, *what* happened, *where* it happened, *when* and *why*. Draw out the fact that both Simeon and Anna had been faithful in prayer for many years, so that they were able to recognise what God was saying to them, and trust him to do what he said. They had also learnt to be obedient. (Suppose Simeon had decided not to act on God's nudging to go to the temple that day.)

On a sheet of paper, write in the middle: 'What about us?' Around this question jot down what Simeon and Anna can teach us about good practice in our own lives. (This may include such things as the value of regular daily prayer, getting to know what the Bible says, listening to God as well as talking to him, doing what God asks straight away, trusting God, being patient, being prepared for God to answer our prayers in unexpected ways.)

Praying

Use the sheet you have completed and go round the ideas, asking God to help us grow in each of these areas.

Activities

Give each person one of the ideas to express in mime and present this with a reader as part of the service. Alternatively, write and illustrate each point and make a display for the church or for the magazine headed 'Learning from Simeon and Anna'.

SAINT JOHN THE BAPTIST – 24 JUNE

Thought for the day

John is born with a mission to prepare the way for the Messiah by calling people to repentance.

Reflection on the readings

Isaiah 49:1-6
Psalm 138
Acts 13:22-26
Luke 1:57-66, 80

Since God works with full knowledge of everything in time and place, he is in a position to orchestrate events with perfect timing, even though the individuals involved may only see their own particular part. Isaiah is aware that God has called him right from before he was born, and also that in a sense he is representative of the people of Israel, chosen and called into being for the bringing of light to the entire world. With hindsight, we know that Zechariah and Elizabeth were to enable John the Baptist to come into the world, preparing the people for the Messiah. Yet at the time of her pregnancy, with her husband unable to communicate, Elizabeth may at first only have been thankful that God had answered her prayer to mother a child.

So we, too, may be one small part of a great plan in God's heart at the moment; but unless we go along with him in our section, the plan will take far longer to be realised. We need to cultivate Mary's art of saying, 'Yes' to God straightaway, and that ability is in direct proportion to the extent we trust him.

When the baby is born all the neighbours are simply happy to rejoice at God's kindness to Zechariah and Elizabeth; yet the full extent of God's kindness will only become apparent as people discover that this child is there to alert the people to their need to sort out their lives in readiness for the coming of the Messiah. Every person in every age has this same need – we shall not be able to

receive the Christ with joy unless we have faced the truth about who we are, where we are going, and where our lives need changing. Repentance is the key to new life in Christ.

Discussion starters

1. Why did Zechariah lose his power of speech until the naming of John?

2. In what way is John the Baptist like the prophet Elijah?

All-stage talk

Begin by explaining that to prepare for the talk today you will need everyone in each row to sit in reverse order from how they are sitting at the moment, so that those nearest the centre will end up nearest the sides. And they will have to do it cheerfully! (Give everyone some time to organise this. It should create mild chaos for a while which gradually settles into order again.) Thank everyone for their co-operation.

What they have just experienced is an important truth – when God prepares his people for his coming, that is bound to cause disturbance. Prophets are there to cause disturbance. The Holy Spirit disturbs us in order to prepare us and change us.

Today we are celebrating the birth of a great disturber: John, known as the Baptist because of the way he baptised people with water as a sign of their washed and changed lives. His calling was to alert people to the way they were living and to challenge them to sort themselves out in line with God's standards. When our own lives are challenged like this we have to set about checking the way we are living – are we in line with God's way of love and God's values?

There may be drastic changes needed (as there were today for those sitting on the ends of rows), or there may be minor changes and fine tuning to be done (as there were for those few who have ended up sitting in the same place as before). But either way we need to get up, spiritually, both individually and as a community, and take a candid look at the way we speak to people, and how we spend our time and our money. We need to look at our relationships and our attitudes, and at the extent we allow our Lord to reign in us.

Now, as they realign themselves in their rows, ask them to do so in silence, opening up their lives, both in thankfulness for John the Baptist, and in readiness to be realigned with God's will.

All-age ideas

- In the entrance to the church have some large display boards with such signs as 'Get ready to meet God's Son!', 'How does your way match up with God's way?' and 'You can be free – God's love can set you free!'

Prayer of the Faithful

Celebrant
Let us pray together in the presence of God.

Reader
Father, into every situation of doubt
and despondency among your followers
breathe your faithfulness.

Silence

Prepare us, O Lord:
to walk in your ways.

Father, into our strongholds of ambition
and defensiveness
breathe your humility.

Silence

Prepare us, O Lord:
to walk in your ways.

Father, into the prisons of guilt and revenge
breathe the grace of forgiveness.

Silence

Prepare us, O Lord:
to walk in your ways.

Father, into the darkness of pain and fear
breathe your reassurance.

Silence

Prepare us, O Lord:
to walk in your ways.

Father, into our complacency
breathe your zeal.

Silence

Prepare us, O Lord:
to walk in your ways.

Father, into our homes and places of work
breathe your fellowship and love.

Silence

Prepare us, O Lord:
to walk in your ways.

Father, into the whole of your creation
breathe your joy and peace.

Silence

Prepare us, O Lord:
to walk in your ways.

We make our prayer with Mary,
who rejoiced with her cousin Elizabeth
over the birth of John the Baptist:
Hail, Mary . . .

In silence, let us bring our private prayers
to the loving mercy of God.

Silence

Celebrant
Father, like John the Baptist,
may we courageously prepare the way
for the coming of the kingdom.
Through Christ, our Lord.
Amen.

TREASURE SEEKERS

Aim: To know that today we celebrate the birthday of John the Baptist, Jesus' cousin.

Starter

Messages. Have leaders and helpers standing around the room with notepads and pencils and each with a number of other things visible beside them. These can be anything you like, such as a Treasure Seekers book, a cup and saucer, a bucket, clock, sellotape or tape player – whatever is available. Send the children with messages from one leader to another, like this: 'Kevin, take this clock to Katherine, with my love – here's a note to take with you. It says, "With love from Susan."' or 'Esther, take this note to Kate. She's over there by the window. It says, "Please can I have the Treasure Seekers book? Love from Susan."' Everyone can be trotting backwards and forwards with messages at the same time, and the leaders will be able to see what they can and can't ask for.

Teaching

Thank everyone for all their help in taking those messages – what a busy lot of messengers the Treasure Seekers are today!

God likes using his friends to take his messages to people, and today we are celebrating the birthday of one of God's special messengers. His name is J-O-H-N (sound it out) – John. John's mum and Jesus' mum were cousins, so John and Jesus would have played together when they were little, like some of you play with your cousins. (You might even have some cousins at Living Water.)

God needed John as a special messenger to tell his people an important message. The important message was this: use the same notebook you were using for the starter activity and write on it 'Get ready to meet God's Son!' Read this out to the children. When John grew up to be a man, he waited for God to tell him when to tell the people his important message. At last God said, 'Now!' and off went John, telling his message to great crowds of people: 'Get ready to meet God's Son! Get yourselves ready, everyone!'

Lots of people listened to John, God's messenger, and they started to put right the things in their lives that were bad and selfish. John washed them all in the river as a sign that their lives were made clean again. So when Jesus came, many people were ready to meet him.

Praying

Thank you, Father,
for sending John
to get people ready for Jesus.

Activities

On the sheet there is a large picture of John and Jesus playing together as boys with their mothers. This can either be coloured with paints or crayons or made into a collage using stuck-on coloured paper and fabric.

PEARL DIVERS

Aim: To know the events leading up to John the Baptist's birth, and why we celebrate him.

Starter

The message game. Everyone has a partner, and they all sit in two rows at either side of the room, opposite their partner. One of each pair is given a short message to shout across to their partner, and at the words, 'Ready, steady, speak!' they shout their messages. When the listeners are sure they have received the message accurately they go and tell the leader, who checks it.

Teaching

Today we are celebrating the birth of one of God's special messengers – John the Baptist. On a long roll of wallpaper or lining paper have the following things written and drawn (see ideas below):

- God makes the good world
- Sin spoils and damages
- The rescue plan: Abraham, Moses
- God is coming in person to save us
- He is coming very soon; get ready!

Have the paper rolled up, and gradually unroll it as you go through the events from the creation of a good world, and the sin which spoils and damages. But this wasn't the end of everything – God had a great rescue plan. Starting with one faithful man, Abraham, he chose a whole family, and that built up into a whole chosen people, who Moses led out of slavery in Egypt to freedom in the promised land. Gradually this chosen people learnt about their God, and the prophets did their best to keep them following God's ways. One day, they said, God will come in person to save us.

All through many generations the people waited for this to happen.

And then, at the right time – God's time – a messenger was born to bring a new message to the chosen people. John did not just say, 'One day God will come in person to save us'; he had been born to say, 'It's time to get ready, everyone! God is coming in person to save us very soon – any day now!' So, when Jesus came, many people were ready to recognise him and welcome him.

Now hang the names of Elizabeth and Zechariah round the necks of two children. This is John's mum and this is his dad. Zechariah had been told by an angel that his wife Elizabeth would have a son who would be God's messenger. But Zechariah had found that very hard to believe because he and his wife were very old. So Zechariah was suddenly unable to speak (tie a gag around his mouth) until the baby was born and had been named John. How did Zechariah name him if he couldn't speak? He mimed for a writing tablet, and wrote on it, 'His name is John'. (Bring Zechariah a clip board with paper and pencil and let him write the message on it.)

As soon as the baby was named, Zechariah could speak again, and he was very happy, praising God for the way he had brought John into the world as his messenger, and excited that his own son was the one chosen to get the people ready for the Messiah, who had been promised and expected for so long.

Praying

Blessed be the Lord God of Israel,
for he has visited his people
and set them free,
just as he always promised he would!
John was the person chosen to prepare the way,
and Jesus was the promised Christ,
come to save the world.

Activities

There is a series of pictures to colour and mount in the right order to link with the story text. The children will need coloured paper for mounting, and this could be made into a zig-zag or conventional book form.

GOLD PANNERS

Aim: To see how the coming of John the Baptist was essential preparation for the coming of the Messiah.

Starter

Melt some chocolate and pour it into little moulds, or coat things with it, such as biscuits, marzipan or fruit. Leave to dry on greaseproof paper or foil.

Teaching

We couldn't have made these delicious things unless we had prepared the chocolate by melting it to make it flexible. Today we are celebrating the birth of John the Baptist, who urged people to prepare their lives, so they would be ready to receive the Messiah when he came. Like our chocolate, they needed God to soften them and make them warm and responsive to his love, so they could be made new.

Read the passage from Isaiah, where the chosen people are called to be the light of the nations, so that God's salvation may reach to the ends of the earth. Pick up on this expectation and collective calling, and the hope of the Messiah.

Now read Luke 1:5-25, followed by today's Gospel, to get the full picture of the circumstances surrounding the birth of John the Baptist. Although this is quite a lot of reading, it is sometimes valuable to look at a complete section of a narrative like this. It makes clear that the prophecies are being fulfilled, and the pace has quickened; there is an urgency of preparation like the 'Scramble!' command or the red alert which gets everyone suddenly extra attentive and poised. God is about to come among his people and John is the 'outrider'.

We are all important 'members' of Christ's Body, the Church. When we are 'tuned in' to God he can work with us and through us, and we are the only ones who can do the particular work God needs us to do.

Praying

O Lord, you search me out and you know me,
you know my resting and my rising,
you mark when I walk or lie down,
all my ways lie open to you.
For it was you who created my being,
knit me together in my mother's womb.
I thank you for the wonder of my being,
for the wonders of all your creation.

(From Psalm 138)

Activities

On the sheet there is a John the Baptist factfile to complete, and an opportunity to explore their own area of calling and work within their life situation at the moment.

SAINTS PETER AND PAUL – 29 JUNE

Thought for the day

Through the dedication of the apostles Peter and Paul, the Gospel of Jesus Christ spread and the Church was rapidly established.

Reflection on the readings

Acts 12:1-11
Psalm 33
2 Timothy 4:6-8, 17-18
Matthew 16:13-19

It is good that we celebrate these two great saints of the early Church together on the same day. In their ministries we are given a wonderful example of the united body of the Church in good working order; their gifts and their vocations provide the balance and stability always needed, and the two saints complement one another as they work for the coming of the kingdom, united in their love of God and their openness to him.

In the Gospel we hear of Peter's confession of faith as he speaks out boldly on behalf of the other disciples, recognising the true identity of Jesus as the Messiah, the Son of God. Jesus appoints Peter as leader of the Church about to be born, and renames him 'Rock'. It will take time for Peter to grow into his new name, and Jesus was willing to build his Church on Simon Peter, well knowing his weaknesses and fears. What he could see was openness and receptivity to the things of God, and that, coupled with Peter's natural gifts of leadership and training as a skipper, made him the right person for the difficult task ahead.

In the reading from 2 Timothy, we see Paul thinking back over his turbulent life, with all the adventures and difficulties encountered as part of his calling, and celebrating the wonder of God's unfailing provision through it all. If anyone can say with conviction, 'God is always with us', Paul can, because he has so much experience of it in such unpromising circumstances. From the moment he finally recognised Jesus as the Messiah, he was his devoted slave, open to his guiding and zealous in spreading the good news far and wide. Like Peter, Paul had his weaknesses and hang-ups, but Jesus was able to use this man because of his availability to God, which transformed his natural gifts and good education for the growth of the kingdom of heaven.

While Peter gathered the faithful flock of the people of Israel and nurtured them, enabling them to be built up into the Body of Christ, Paul began the spread of the Gospel to the Gentiles, fulfilling the prophecies and setting up church communities all over the Roman world. Both men allowed themselves to be so in-breathed by God's Holy Spirit that even their natural faults and failings could be used, and through them the young Church was established quickly and strongly.

This is the kind of miracle God can work in anyone who makes themselves open and available, willing to lay aside all other ambitions, misgivings and sub-agendas in committed service to the one true faithful God.

Discussion starters

1. How did the twin ministries of Peter and Paul complement each other?

2. What can we learn from Peter and Paul's adventures and letters about effective evangelisation?

All-stage talk

Bring along a length of cotton and a length of rope. Around the church place some keys, a fishing net with fish in it (a piece of net curtain is fine), a writing pad, envelopes and pen, and a map.

Today we are celebrating two great saints together – Saint Peter and Saint Paul. It is largely thanks to the work of these two that we are all here today, because when the Church was very young and very new, Peter led it and Paul spread it!

Send some volunteers to find and bring back the keys and the fishing net. What do these have to do with today? Simon Peter was a fisherman when Jesus walked along the beach and talked to the people there. He was impressed by what Jesus said and did, and Jesus called Simon to fish for people instead of fish. Instead of casting his nets into the water, and bringing in lots of fish, he would be working where Jesus led him and in charge of bringing lots of people into God's kingdom.

What about the keys? Later, when Jesus asked the disciples who they thought he was, Simon knew: 'You are the Messiah,' he said, 'the Son of God.' And Jesus gave him a new name – Peter, or Rock. He said that on this rock he would build up the new Church. As leader, he would be in charge, and a good sign of being in charge is having the keys. Peter was going to be in charge of who should be let into the kingdom of God, and that's a very responsible job.

Send other volunteers to find the notepaper and the map. What do these have to do with today? Paul travelled a lot, all around the Mediterranean sea, sometimes on land by foot and sometimes by ship. He was shipwrecked three times, and was often in danger. Why did he spend his time doing that? He was spreading the good news about Jesus, setting up small churches in all the main cities and teaching them the faith. Once they were strong enough, off he'd go to start another church somewhere else, but he kept in touch with all these church communities by letter, helping them grow and sort out their problems.

(Hold the cotton.) Both Peter and Paul were ordinary people, with their faults as well as their strengths. They had made big mistakes in their lives and let Jesus down. (Break the cotton.) But what made it possible for God to use them for so much good was that both of them were open to God and willing to learn; they were prepared to trust God with their whole life. (Hold the rope.) They knew that, however much they had let God down, God would never let them down. (Tug the rope to show that it holds.) By the end of their lives they could both say that, although they had been through such a lot of adventures and so much danger, and faced lots of angry people, their God had always been there, and never let them down.

And when they were eventually killed for their faith in Jesus, they were welcomed into the joy of heaven for ever.

All-age ideas

- Have the symbols from the talk displayed near the altar so that people are reminded as they come to receive communion.

- Have twin flower arrangements side by side, one expressing and celebrating Peter's life and the other Paul's life.

Prayer of the Faithful

Celebrant
Gathered as the Church of God,
let us pray.

Reader
Heavenly Father, as we celebrate
the life and work of Peter and Paul,
we give you thanks for our Church
and its faithfulness through the ages.
We ask your blessing on the Pope
and all leaders, pastors and teachers in the Church,
that they may be always open and attentive
to your guiding Spirit.

Silence

In all things, Father:
may your will be done.

Heavenly Father, as we recall the opposition
and persecution experienced by Peter and Paul,
we pray for all who are persecuted and threatened
for their faith today,
and for those working to discredit and crush
the influence of the Church.
We pray for the leaders of the nations
and those who advise and support them,
that they may seek what is right and good,
and bear in mind the needs of those they serve.

Silence

In all things, Father:
may your will be done.

Heavenly Father, we pray
that in our daily prayers and conversations,
our daily work and service,
we may remain true to your teaching
and love with your compassion,
whatever the cost.

Silence

In all things, Father:
may your will be done.

Heavenly Father, we pray for all who are imprisoned,
whether physically, emotionally or spiritually;
free them to live in the freshness of your love
and the security of your faithfulness.

Silence

In all things, Father:
may your will be done.

Heavenly Father, as we recall with gratitude
the willingness of Peter and Paul
to risk their lives in your service,
we pray for all who have died in faith
and thank you for their love and commitment.
Welcome them into your eternity;
may they know your peace and joy for ever.

Silence

In all things, Father:
may your will be done.

We join our prayers
with those of Mary our Mother:
Hail, Mary . . .

In the stillness of God's peace,
we bring our personal prayers
to our loving Father.

Silence

Celebrant
Father, accept these prayers
for the Church and for the world;
we pray that in all things
your kingdom may come.
Through Jesus Christ our Lord.
Amen.

TREASURE SEEKERS

Aim: To know that Peter and Paul worked together for God.

Starter

Sit in a circle and give the children tasks to do, two by two. Here are some ideas:

- Give one child blue bricks and the other red ones, and ask them to work together to build and red and blue tower.

- Give one child a jug of water and the other a tray of four or five plastic cups. Ask them to work together to fill the cups.

- Give both children a heavy bag with two handles. Ask them to work together to carry the bag across the room.

Teaching

Point out that for all those jobs, both the children were needed. Working together is friendly, and it gets the jobs done better. Talk about those people who all do their own jobs so that together they make a block of flats, run a hospital or a bus. What sort of different jobs are there to do that? (The bus driver, the bus maker, the bus cleaner, the painters, the mechanic and, sometimes, the conductor.) God likes to see his friends working together, like we are now. Talk about the other people who help this to be possible, like the cleaners, builders, helpers, writers, artists and publishers, and our mums and dads.

Today we think of two people who worked together with God to spread the good news about Jesus and lead the Church when it was still very new. Their names are Peter and Paul. Peter was a fisherman and Paul was a tent maker. God wanted both of them to work with him to build the Church of God. And they did. God hopes we will work together in his Church too.

Praying

Thank you, Father,
for working with Peter and Paul
to tell everyone about your love. Amen.

Activities

There are two pictures to colour, one showing Peter and the other Paul. When they have been coloured, they can stick the pictures back to back, punch a hole through and thread wool to hold it by.

PEARL DIVERS

Aim: To know about Peter and Paul being available for God's plans.

Starter

Draw a plan of the room set up in a particular way with chairs facing certain directions and people sitting on them. Display the plan on the wall and tell the children to work together to set the room up as it is in the plan. Let them make mistakes and right themselves as far as possible, rather than butting in, as this is all part of working together. Even if they fail to do it exactly right, point out to them what they have done well, and look out for any good examples of co-operation which you can mention and praise.

Teaching

We had a plan, and at first that's all it was – a drawing on the wall. But because they all made themselves available to work with it, we ended up with the plan being put into practice.

That's what it was like with Jesus' plan for the new Church. Both Peter (who was called to lead it) and Paul (who was called to spread it) were happy to spend their lives working on God's plan so that it all happened. The Church grew very fast all over the Roman world, and the faithful flock were looked after and fed.

Show the children two sheets of paper, one with a Peter-shaped space cut out of it and the other a Paul-shaped space. (Keep back the Peter shape and the Paul shape with their names written on.) On the first have written: 'WANTED – Rock person to help people be built up as living stones into the Church of God.' On the second have written: 'WANTED – Pharisee to preach and teach the faith to the Gentile world.' These were the jobs that needed filling. There were two people who filled the need. (Fit the named Peter shape into his space and the named Paul shape into his.)

God has jobs that need doing now. There are jobs that can only be filled by our particular shape of life and character. If we don't agree to work with God to do them, they will not be done.

Praying

Heavenly Father,
here I am, ready to do your will.
Wherever you lead me,
wherever you need me,
I am here, to do your will. Amen.

Activities

On the sheet the names of Peter and Paul are drawn with pictures of their lives. Either the children can colour the complete words and string them on to a length of wool, or you could enlarge the letters so that the whole thing is on a larger scale and it becomes a group project, with the names strung up and carried into church, where they can be hung along the walls.

GOLD PANNERS

Aim: To look at how the ministries of Peter and Paul balanced and complemented each other in the early Church.

Starter

Provide a varied assortment of objects, a broom handle, string and two matching containers. The task is to fill the containers with varied loads which exactly balance each other.

Teaching

We have just seen how very different things can balance each other, and today we are looking at the very different ministries of Peter and Paul and how they balanced each other so that God's plan for the early Church was accomplished.

Have two large outlined drawings, one of Peter and one of Paul, with their names underneath. Collect from discussion any facts or characteristics they know about Paul and Peter already, and write these on the spaces. Add to these so that you include the following information:

Peter
• Placed in charge of the early Church
• Ministry to the faithful Jewish people
• Martyr

Paul
• Preacher, teacher and letter writer
• Spreading good news to the Gentiles
• Martyr

Now read today's Gospel, followed by the passage from Acts 12. Draw attention to the way Peter's commission (Matthew 16) was showing up in his behaviour and trust in God (Acts 12). You could also look up the references on the sheet.

Now look at the reading from 2 Timothy, and use some of the references on the sheet to pick up on what experiences had led up to Paul claiming that the Lord has stood at his side and given him strength.

Praying

Loving Father, as members of your Church
we offer ourselves for your work
in this generation.
Make us strong in faith
and happy to give ourselves away
in serving you.

Activities

On the sheet there are Peter and Paul profiles with identikit characteristics to build up on each. These include mistakes and weaknesses, and the way God can use and transform all our faults as well as our strengths, as long as we open up to his life-giving Spirit.

THE TRANSFIGURATION OF THE LORD – 6 AUGUST

Thought for the day

Jesus is seen in all God's glory, and as fulfilling the Law and the prophets.

Reflection on the readings

Daniel 7:9-10, 13-14
Psalm 96
2 Peter 1:16-19
Matthew 17:1-9

To claim that Jesus, the itinerant teacher and healer from Nazareth, was nothing less than Lord and Messiah, would have shocked and disturbed many. As Christians today we hear references to Jesus as 'incarnate God' or 'God made man' so much as a normal part of church language that we can sometimes be anaesthetised from the original shocking nature of the claim. How could the great transcendent God walk about on feet that got travel sore, in a human body that yawned, sneezed, hungered, thirsted and slept?

There has always been a tendency for some Christians to find the humanness or the divinity of Jesus too much to cope with, and in every generation there are attempts to wriggle out of the shocking nature of the Incarnation by denying either the full divinity or the full humanity. This great feast of the Transfiguration is a celebration of God's glory shining visibly in the person of Jesus, showing him to be both human and divine, the promised Messiah and the Lord, the Son of God, worthy of all our love and worship.

Peter is anxious to clear this point up in his letter, replying to the rumours that the good news of the Gospel may be in reality some cleverly invented myth. By way of evidence he describes that glimpse of glory given to them in person on the mountain, when they saw and understood something of the full majesty of God's anointed, and heard God's voice claiming Jesus as his own beloved Son. Peter, James and John were actually there at the time; they were eye-witnesses on that holy mountain.

The experience, particularly in the subsequent light of the Crucifixion and Resurrection, leave them in no doubt about Jesus' identity. They pass on the good news to everyone who will listen, knowing it to be extraordinary, yet knowing with utter joy that it is true.

We sing regularly, 'Heaven and earth are full of your glory.' We need to cultivate sensors to perceive and recognise God's glory all around us, both in the great and wonderful events of our faith, and also in the little glimpses of glory in ordinary living. We can praise God as we enjoy eating each mouthful of good food given from the earth and prepared by human hands. We can thank God for his glory shown in everyday pleasures like a hot shower or a morning cup of tea, smiles exchanged with shop assistants, and opportunities to give like putting someone else's name on a raffle ticket we buy.

The wonderful truth is that the Holy Spirit of our glorious transcendent God lives in us and with us through the saving power of Jesus, the Christ.

Discussion starters

1. How would the Transfiguration strengthen the disciples for the scandal of the cross?

2. Is transfiguration something that happens, to some extent, in all who pray?

All-stage talk

Bring along a piece of coal.

Show everyone what you have brought – a lump of black, hard shiny stuff which burns well. It's called coal. Coal is dusty and dirty and not that wonderful to look at. It used to be burnt in people's fireplaces and in steam engines and steam ships and factories all over the world as fuel. To get coal, the miners are taken deep down under the ground into coal mines to cut or blast the coal from the rock. They are covered in dirty coal dust when they come up at the end of their work and need hot showers and lots of soap to get them clean again.

So it is quite a surprise to find that a diamond, like you get in jewellery, is made of the same carbon that coal is made of. Ask people to show around to one another any diamonds they may be wearing, especially so that all the children can see the clear sparkling nature of diamonds. Sometimes the light splits into lovely rainbows through a diamond, and they cost a lot of money to buy. They are precious jewels, and they play with the light like clear water, yet they're so strong that they are sometimes used in industry to cut things that nothing else can cut.

Why are we looking at coal and diamonds today? Today we are celebrating the Transfiguration – the time when Jesus took Peter, James and John up the mountain, and while he was praying with all his heart and soul, he suddenly looked completely different. The disciples saw him not as the human friend and teacher they knew well, but filled with all the bright glory of God, shining with God's majesty, power and love. If we imagine seeing a familiar piece of coal suddenly shining and sparkling like a diamond, and we suddenly realise that actually both coal and diamond are the same thing, that's a bit like how it must have seemed for Peter, James and John when they suddenly saw that Jesus was both human *and* the Son of God.

As we think today of that experience they had on the mountain, we can see, with them, Jesus, the wandering teacher and healer from Nazareth, shining with all the glory of the living God! It would not always be showing in that way, but even during the terrible, humiliating process of crucifixion, the glory would still be there, seen in the beauty of love and forgiveness that goes on and on and never gives up on us.

All-age ideas

- Have lots of candles, flowers and reflected light in church today.

- At one point read *The glory of God* by Gerard Manley Hopkins.

Prayer of the Faithful

Celebrant
Let us quieten ourselves
in the presence of the living God,
as we pray.

Reader
Father, you know us better than we know ourselves,
and are well aware of the needs
and pains in your Church.
We lift them now to your healing love.

Silence

Father, we love you:
open our eyes to see your glory.

In our world there are decisions to be made,
countries to be governed and people to be honoured.
We lift them now to your grace and wisdom.

Silence

Father, we love you:
open our eyes to see your glory.

In our neighbourhood and in our homes
there are celebrations and tragedies,
times of hope, weariness and tenderness.
We lift them now to your parenting.

Silence

Father, we love you:
open our eyes to see your glory.

In our hospitals and clinics there are many in pain,
many who are fearful,
and many who have lost hope.
We lift them now to your comfort and protection.

Silence

Father, we love you:
open our eyes to see your glory.

As each day others die and enter your presence,
we ask your mercy
and commend them to your safe keeping.

Silence

Father, we love you:
open our eyes to see your glory.

We pray with Mary
who saw in her Son the glory of God:
Hail, Mary . . .

Let us be still and silent in God's presence
and pray in faith to our loving Father.

Silence

Celebrant
Father, as the disciples saw your glory
revealed in Jesus,
so may your glory be revealed in us.
Through Christ our Lord.
Amen.

TREASURE SEEKERS

Aim: To see God's glory in all things.

Starter

If you have access to an outside area, go on a 'glory trail', wandering around looking at things and thanking God for them all. This doesn't just have to be natural things, of course; you can praise God for the people who worked hard to make the path, for those who will be collecting the rubbish from yesterday's wedding party, and for the kindness of the person who mended the broken fence.

Teaching

Sit in a circle and talk about all the places you found God's glory, sometimes hidden and sometimes unexpected.

Give everyone some coloured cellophane to look through so that all the world is a different colour because of how they are looking. Explain that the whole world and all of life is filled with God's glory, but we need to look out for it and listen out for it – otherwise we can miss it.

Praying

Open my eyes, Lord,
to see your glory all around me.
Open my ears, Lord,
to hear your glory in all the sounds.

Activities

The sheet is used to decorate cardboard tubes so that they can focus their gaze on anything and spot the glory in it.

PEARL DIVERS

Aim: To know the story of the Transfiguration.

Starter

Decorate some household candles with coloured wax crayons. SAFETY ALERT! This needs very careful and attentive supervision. Protect everywhere thoroughly and strip the paper from the coloured crayons. Warm them over a lighted night light, standing in a saucer of water, and drip the colours on to the household candle.

Teaching

First remind the children of two people who come into today's Gospel: Moses, who led the people across the Red Sea out of slavery in Egypt, and was given the ten commandments for the people to live by, and Elijah, who was a prophet, speaking out God's words to the people.

Take the children quietly to a safe area where there is a cross, flowers, and lots of votive candles standing on foil and backed with foil so that there is a sense of beauty and wonder and reflected light. Gather the children around this as a focus as you tell them how Jesus took Peter, James and John with him up the mountain, where Jesus prayed and was suddenly seen shining with all the glory of God. If you use a suitable version you can read it straight from Matthew 17:1-9. Have music playing quietly as Jesus is transfigured and fade it out again as the disciples look up and see only Jesus there.

Praying

(This prayer can be sung)

Jesus, Jesus, let me tell you what I know,
you have given me your Spirit,
I love you so!

Activities

On the sheet there are things to spot in the picture, and words to spot in the wordsearch. They can light their decorated candles as they sing the prayer and say the words on the sheet.

GOLD PANNERS

Aim: To look at God's revealed glory in the Transfiguration and his glory in our world.

Starter

Give out some sweets which have centres different from the outside. People may be able to guess what they taste like because they've eaten other ones that look very similar. But the only way to know what this particular sweet is really like, through and through, is to eat it, very slowly, noticing the way it changes as you get through to the different layers, and paying attention to the different textures throughout the experience. (The sweets are now savoured, with people jotting down any words that describe the different experiences of texture, flavour and so on.)

Teaching

Usually we tend to rush through even pleasant things like eating sweets, without really appreciating them, and it's a good idea to give these ordinary things our full attention sometimes, as we can use all these little things to give us glimpses of God's glory, as well as the more dramatic things.

Today, as we celebrate God's glory being revealed in Jesus at the Transfiguration, we are also reminded of the way the whole of earth, as well as heaven, is filled with glory, if we have our senses open to notice.

Read the passage from Daniel, where he is trying to describe the full glory of heaven in human language. Even though this is pretty much impossible, the passage does set off in our minds some sense of that brightness and majesty of a totally loving and powerful God.

Now read the account of the Transfiguration from the Gospel, so that they can see how it is like seeing the glory of heaven but on the earth, in Jesus. What does that tell us about Jesus' identity? Look at what the voice of God is heard to proclaim. How did the experience make the disciples feel (a) immediately (b) at the events of the Crucifixion and Resurrection?

Read the letter from Peter to see how the amazing experience had stayed in his mind right through to the early Church.

Praying

The Lord is king, let earth rejoice,
let all the coastlands be glad.
Cloud and darkness are his clothing;
his throne, majesty and might.
For you indeed are the Lord,
most high above the earth,
exalted far above all spirits.

(From Psalm 96)

Activities

Give out large sheets of paper (lengths of wallpaper, perhaps) and sponges to paint with so that they can express the glory of the living God on a large scale.

THE ASSUMPTION – 15 AUGUST

Thought for the day

The Almighty has done great things for me!

Reflection on the readings

Apocalypse 11:19; 12:1-6, 10
Psalm 44
1 Corinthians 15:20-26
Luke 1:39-56

When Christ was raised to life on the first Easter Day it was, as Paul says, like the first fruits of resurrection new life, the start of a whole stream of faithful people throughout the generations, redeemed and saved, as at the end of time we are all brought to share the fullness of eternal life. Somehow, and in a way we do not need to worry about, our whole nature, body and soul, will be transformed into the immortal nature of those believing in the resurrected Christ and belonging to him. If Christ had not been raised from death we would be crazy to live with this hope, but with the Resurrection having happened, the prospect of eternal life is a natural consequence of living each day in Christ's company.

As today we celebrate the assumption of Mary into the glory of heaven we are reminded, with her joy, of that glorious hope we all have, and in which we also live while in our earthly life. Living in Christ is like living both here and in eternity at once, as we are gradually transformed more and more into God's likeness. It is like being clothed with his righteousness which increasingly works on us until our own nature becomes not only fully itself but also freed from all that is self-seeking and self-motivated.

Today is another opportunity to thank God for the beautiful example of Mary's humility and openness, and her self-giving which enabled her to have growing within her body the Son of God; God's indwelling, twenty-four hours a day. The clothing of Christ's nature, as we live faithfully the Christian life, and the regular feeding on his life through the eucharist enable us to share in love's transforming until, at the time of accomplishment, when we are perfectly restored, we shall take our place in the glorious worship of God in heaven, surrounded by Mary and all the saints.

Discussion starters

1. What holds us back from total self-giving?

2. If the Church is to be truly the Body of Christ, what do we need to learn from the life and example of Our Lady?

All-stage talk

Ask if anyone ever dreams, and collect a couple of examples of dreams. What about daydreams and wishes? Collect some examples of these, too. We all have wishes that are close to our hearts, whether they are ones we are brave enough to share in public or not! Sometimes a dream can spur us into action. If we dream of being a supermodel, we'll probably start experimenting with clothes and make-up – and with our expression in front of a mirror to perfect that essential pouty look! If we dream of becoming a rock climber, we might start on the stairs, going up three or four at a time. If we dream of joining a band, we might start practising by singing loudly in the bath. Often it is those whose dreams keep them focused who end up by achieving what at one time seemed almost impossible.

As Christians, we have a great and wonderful hope – that we will one day come to know for ourselves the glory of heaven, and live with God in that life which lasts for ever, sharing with Our Lady and all the saints the joy of worshipping God with our whole being, at one and at peace with our Creator and Redeemer, and with one another in the community of heaven.

As with our other dreams and hopes, this hope may sometimes seem a long way off. Perhaps we are tired and scratchy with the children; perhaps we are winding our brothers or sisters up and can't seem to stop; perhaps we have once again let slip our habit of daily prayer, and there seems so little time to fit God in. Will we ever make it to that dream of heaven?

Today's celebration of the Assumption reminds us to hope again. As we think of Mary, our spiritual Mother, taken into the glory of heaven, the full impact of Christ's resurrection hits us with all its power. Christ raised from death spells victory! It is not we who are going to earn that place in heaven, but Christ who has won it for us and graciously offers it to us. All we have to do is trust Christ, hang on to Christ with our hopes and dreams, and let him clothe us with righteousness and new life. It is God's pleasure to give us the kingdom, and he will use every opportunity this life provides to transform us into heavenly citizens, so that, one day, we shall be able to realise that dream, and join Mary and the saints in the full joy of heaven.

All-age ideas

• Have several arrangements of flowers moving upwards from dead wood at the bottom to gradually increasing colour, so that the top arrangement is a burst of colour and joy of new life.

Prayer of the Faithful

Celebrant
As children of our heavenly Father,
let us gather ourselves to pray.

Reader
Lord our God, on this feast of the Assumption,
we praise and thank you
for the mothering love of Mary,
Mother of Christ and his Body, the Church.
We pray for each member of the Church of God,
both lay and ordained,
in their ministry to encourage one another
as loving servants to the needs of the world.

Silence

Lord of life:
may your kingdom come.

We pray for the world Christ died to save,
with its diversity of cultures and beliefs,
expectations and memories,
and its shared resources and human needs;
we pray for those who lead and govern,
for responsible stewardship
and wise decision-making.

Silence

Lord of life:
may your kingdom come.

We pray for our parents and our own families,
for all those we love and all who love us;
we pray for our friends and neighbours,

our colleagues, employers and employees;
we pray for those on either side of us now.

Silence

Lord of life:
may your kingdom come.

We pray for those who are in pain,
sorrow or distress,
that they may know your presence
and receive your comfort and healing.

Silence

Lord of life:
may your kingdom come.

We pray for those who have died
and all who grieve for them;
we pray for those dying alone and unnoticed,
we pray for those dying unwanted and unborn.

Silence

Lord of life:
may your kingdom come.

We pray with Mary,
our Mother in heaven:
Hail, Mary . . .

In the silence of eternity,
let us bring to our loving Father
the concerns on our own hearts.

Silence

Celebrant
Father, with Mary we know
that you give us abundant blessing;
hear these prayers in mercy and love.
Through Christ our Lord.
Amen.

TREASURE SEEKERS

Aim: To know that heaven is our home and Mary is
there with Jesus, her Son.

Starter

Prepare a number of different home shapes, drawn
on slips of paper – for example, a house, bungalow,
flat, caravan, house boat, tent, tree house, castle
and cottage. Lay them all out and look at each in
turn. Say you are thinking of a particular home,
and they can point to it when they think they know
which one you mean. Start by saying something
like: 'I'm thinking of a home which is made of
wood . . . has one window . . . and is reached by
climbing up a ladder.' Carry on giving clues until
most children are pointing to the right home.

Teaching

Homes are where we belong. They are where we
go back to when we've been out, and we keep our
favourite things there. Talk together about what
they like about home.

As well as our ordinary homes that we live in on
earth, heaven is our home, where one day we and
all our loved ones will live for ever with Jesus. We
don't know what it looks like, but we do know
that it will be lovely, without any pain or hurts or
sadness, and we will be completely happy and at
home there.

Jesus' mother, Mary, is there already and will be
there to welcome us home.

Praying

Hail, Mary, full of grace,
the Lord is with thee:
blessed art thou among women,
and blessed is the fruit of thy womb, Jesus.
Holy Mary, Mother of God,
pray for us sinners now,
and at the hour of our death. Amen.

Activities

The sheet can be coloured and folded so that Mary
is first seen at home on earth and then in the glory
of heaven.

PEARL DIVERS

Aim: To know that Mary is in the glory of heaven,
and that one day we hope to share that with her
and all the saints.

Starter

Pass a rose around the group to enjoy it, with each
person noticing something different about it.

Teaching

Have a rose hip, and empty the little hairy seeds
from it on to some paper. That lovely rose we have
been enjoying came from a seed a bit like these. To
become a beautiful rose there was first a lot of
growing to be done, and then it became a tightly
closed bud, before it opened out in the warmth of
the sunshine to this beautiful rose.

Our lives are rather like this. We have the
possibility, like this seed, of being transformed into
people who are colourful and lovely, expressing
the love of God our Creator. But first there is a lot
of growing to be done spiritually. One day, as Jesus
has promised us and shown us by the Resurrection,
God's love can transform us so that we bloom into

the new life of heaven for ever, like fresh flowers that never fade.

That can happen if we are open to Jesus and happy to let him into our lives to do the transforming. And we have a wonderful example of someone who was willing for God to work in her – it's Mary, Jesus' mother. Sometimes she is described as a beautiful rose, because her lovely openness to God meant that God could work beautifully in her. Today we celebrate Mary being taken into the glory of heaven and look forward to the time when one day we will all be together in God's lovely heaven, our whole selves brought to blossom in the joy of God's love for ever.

Praying

Hail, Mary, full of grace,
the Lord is with thee:
blessed art thou among women,
and blessed is the fruit of thy womb, Jesus.
Holy Mary, Mother of God,
pray for us sinners now,
and at the hour of our death. Amen.

Activities

The sheet can be coloured and made into a basket of roses which can be laid in front of a statue of Our Lady, either in church or at home.

GOLD PANNERS

Aim: To know the hope of resurrection as we celebrate the assumption of Mary.

Starter

Have a picture of Mary, cut into wet mud or clay on a board, and a selection of small leaves and flower petals of different colours. They press the petals lightly into the wet clay to complete the picture.

Teaching

Today we celebrate Mary being taken into the glory of heaven; it is a wonderful celebration both of Mary's openness to God's will and of the great hope of full resurrection for everyone who believes in the risen Christ.

Begin by reading today's Gospel, where Mary is greeted by her cousin Elizabeth as the mother of her Lord, and which includes the Magnificat – Mary's song of praise and joy which traces God's promise of salvation and his faithfulness. Next look at the passage from 1 Corinthians, where Paul is celebrating the great Christian hope of resurrection, shown and promised by the Resurrection of Jesus Christ in his victory over death. Paul is looking

both at the new life we live in Christ here and now, and also at the hope of that time of fulfilment and accomplishment at the end of time, when all the faithful will be gathered and, made perfect, live in the full glory of heaven for ever.

Finally read the passage from Apocalypse together. In Mary we have a wonderful example of what openness to God's will can do. In the Christly love she pours out we have a picture of the Church being filled with the love of God and pouring it out in loving service for the good of the world. We look forward today to that resurrection promise for which our receptive openness and commitment is the only necessary qualification, since it is God's good grace which saves us.

Praying

Hail, Mary, full of grace,
the Lord is with thee:
blessed art thou among women,
and blessed is the fruit of thy womb, Jesus.
Holy Mary, Mother of God,
pray for us sinners now,
and at the hour of our death. Amen.

Activities

On the sheet there are different aspects of Mary's openness and commitment which encourage us in our spiritual journey. Any suggestions for loving outreach which come from today's discussion can be noted and put into action by the parish or in the neighbourhood.

THE TRIUMPH OF THE HOLY CROSS – 14 SEPTEMBER

Thought for the day

Through Christ's loving obedience, even to death on a cross, he has opened up the way for us to eternal life.

Reflection on the readings

Numbers 21:4-9
Psalm 77
Philippians 2:6-11
John 3:13-17

Today the Church reflects on the great mystery of God's salvation through suffering; the Triumph of the Cross. To speak of 'triumph' and 'cross' in the same breath is at first sight utmost foolishness. How can a crude instrument of torture and execution, and the innocent death of the Son of God, be in any way considered a victory or triumph? What on earth are we talking about here?

The key to the mystery is love. What we are celebrating today is God's victory over sin and death. Having submitted to the complete, punishing result of all sin, and having continued loving and forgiving, sinless throughout, Jesus displays the limitless extent of God's love, which is willing to give up everything – human dignity, recognition of success, common thanks and respect, life itself – rather than give up on the loving. If this inevitably brought the Son of God to be hanging, despised and in agony, naked on a Roman gallows, then that is what he would be prepared to do. Full, costly loving was the only way to set us free, and that is what God's nature of love and mercy would naturally do.

Through that glorious love, Jesus cannot be held in by death, but is transformed into new life which has no end. The love shown on the cross has enabled us to have a new and full relationship with God which was not previously possible. That is a triumph, a glorious victory over all that is destructive, mean-spirited, self-centred and evil. Full, glorious life is not to do with selfish gratification but with sacrificial loving and generosity of spirit, with goodness, honesty and unlimited forgiveness.

The victory of the cross only makes sense when viewed from the vantage point of Easter. Whereas on Good Friday we were wrapped in the grief and pain of the cross before the explosion of light and new life on Easter Day, today we can celebrate the triumph of the cross as we look back at that suffering through the glory of the Resurrection, rejoicing in the conquering of evil and the victory of love.

When we are baptised we pledge our allegiance to Christ, showing by our 'immersion' in water that we share his death, dying to our sin and desiring it to be killed off in us. Then, as we rise up from the water, we show that we are sharing in the triumph of resurrection, living now not for ourselves but in the power and Spirit of the God of love. At each act of Communion, we take into ourselves the power of love over death, and proclaim it by the lives we lead, nourished by that spiritual feeding.

Discussion starters

1. How can the horror of an innocent young man being crucified be counted as 'triumph'?

2. What can we learn from the cross that will help us when faced with the problem of suffering?

All-stage talk

Beforehand cut a number of teardrop shapes out of paper and leave one of these on each row. Also have a bunch of flowers, hidden until later.

Today we are celebrating the Triumph, or victory, of the Cross. Direct everyone's attention to a crucifix. When we look at the cross what we see is the good Jesus, nailed on the cross in great pain. How can that be a victory, when it looks like a terrible, evil thing happening to such a good and loving person? It doesn't look much like a victory. The cross seems to be about pain and disappointment and failure.

Sometimes we feel disappointed with God, too. Perhaps he doesn't answer our prayer in the way we would like him to. Perhaps things aren't working out for us in the way we hoped they would, and we feel God could have done something about it. Perhaps there has been a tragedy or natural disaster, and we feel God should have stopped it happening.

One thing the cross shows us is God, suffering. We don't worship a being who sits a long way off from our real, painful world and isn't interested in whether we are hurting or sad. The true God loves us so much that he came to join us and join our suffering, whatever it is. It would not be loving to control us completely, so that we were like robots. God knows that the best kind of world means we will sometimes suffer, and not understand why. His answer is to be there for us and with us with unlimited loving, which we can see in the cross.

Ask people to find the teardrop on their row and, as they pass it along to the aisle, to look at it and think of their own personal disappointments and regrets. Have a couple of people to collect the teardrops in a basket and walk up in silence to lay them at the foot of the cross. In a way, that is what is happening as Jesus hangs dying there.

Send a young volunteer to get the flowers and stand holding them in front of the cross. The great triumph of the cross is that this love, which goes on and on and never ends, manages to turn death into life, and bring good out of evil.

All-age ideas

- Surround a cross with garlands of Michaelmas daisies.

- Use the following for the Penitential Rite:
Love stretched out on the cross exposes our indifference.
Lord, have mercy.
Lord, have mercy.
The generosity of the cross shows us our meanness of spirit.
Christ, have mercy.
Christ, have mercy.

The humility of the cross challenges our vanity
and pride.
Lord, have mercy.
Lord, have mercy.

Prayer of the Faithful

Celebrant
In the knowledge of the extent of God's love for us,
let us pray.

Reader
Father, we pray for all in your Church
whose journey through life is hard,
dangerous, exhausting or confused.

Silence

Lord of love:
you have won the victory.

We pray for those whose lives
are disrupted, oppressed or devastated
by war, famine or political unrest.

Silence

Lord of love:
you have won the victory.

We pray for our families, friends and neighbours;
all who cause us concern
and all in need of your peace.

Silence

Lord of love:
you have won the victory.

We pray for those whose lives
are filled with pain, resentment or hatred;
for all who are trapped in addiction or despair.

Silence

Lord of love:
you have won the victory.

We pray for those who have died
and for those who miss them;
we thank you for saving us through the cross
so that we can hope to share the glory of heaven.

Silence

Lord of love:
you have won the victory.

We join our prayers with those of Mary,
who witnessed the tragedy
and the triumph of the cross:
Hail, Mary . . .

As we kneel at the foot of the cross,
trusting in its power to save,
let us bring to the Lord our own prayers.

Silence

Celebrant
Father, you gave us the gift of your Son;
accept these prayers and transform our lives.
Through Christ our Lord.
Amen.

TREASURE SEEKERS

Aim: To know that the cross is a sign of God's love
for us.

Starter

Make three signs – one circle coloured in green, one
circle coloured in red and one circle with an arrow
inside. Have some music to move around to, and
while it plays show a series of the signs. They stop for
the red circle, go for the green, sit down if the arrow
is pointing down and stand up if it is facing up.

Teaching

Talk about signs being useful in our game, as they
are on roads. Go over what the red and green lights
mean at road crossings, and one or two road signs
they have seen.

Have a look at the sign of the cross on various
places – such as round a neck, on a building, on a
Bible or hymn book. Help everyone to make the
sign of the cross on themselves. Why do Christians
have this sign? Show the children a crucifix. Jesus
is on the cross. He loved us so much that he was
even willing to die for us on a cross. Did he stay
dead? No! He came to life for ever; he's alive now
and will always be alive. The sign of the cross says:
God's love is stronger than death. God's love lasts
for ever.

Make the sign of the cross again, saying, 'God's
love lasts for ever.'

Praying

O God, your love goes on and on and on,
your love will always be.
I sign myself with the sign of your cross,
the sign of your love for me.

Activities

On the sheet there is a bookmark to make in the
shape of a cross. Each child will need three strands
of coloured wool.

PEARL DIVERS

Aim: To help them understand how Jesus' death on the cross brought life and victory.

Starter

Have pictures of the following road signs: roundabout, bendy road, dead end, and T-junction. Making driving noises, they drive around watching out for the road signs. If the roundabout shows they drive round and round; they steer a windy course for the bendy road; change direction, either right or left, for the T-junction; and stop if you make a police car or ambulance noise.

Teaching

Explain how we use lots of signs when we are driving. They are quick, short ways of giving us important messages.

Show a cross. Today we are celebrating the triumph, or victory of the cross. The cross is a sign for Christians of the love God has for us, which was shown more than anywhere by Jesus dying for us on the cross, before he was raised to life on Easter Day.

Explain how that pain and suffering was the way God showed that he will always go on loving us without getting tired of it. There isn't any limit to the love and forgiveness of our God. When we sign ourselves with the sign of the cross, we remember this great love of God which is stronger than death and evil.

Praying

We adore you, O Christ,
and we bless you
because by your holy cross
you have redeemed the world.

Activities

The sheet can be coloured and folded to show the glory and hope of the cross from the viewpoint of Easter. Also, the children can break pieces of jelly in a bowl. When you have poured hot water over this they can all help stir before the melted jelly is poured into small pots to be taken home, set and eaten.

GOLD PANNERS

Aim: To explore the triumph of the cross.

Starter

Have some magnifying glasses or a microscope to look at things, noticing the things that are hidden until you look at them this closely.

Teaching

Our faith is about deep and holy things, so we'd expect some of these to be full of mystery. As humans contemplating the all-powerful God, there are bound to be some things our minds can't grasp. Some things we sense and 'know', rather than being able to set out as clear evidence. Thinking of the cross as a triumph is quite a mystery, but the mystery draws us deeper into the mind and heart of God.

First read the passage from Numbers, where the bronze snake is lifted up by God's friend Moses, so that all those who are dying from snake bites may draw healing and life from looking at it. How is that rather like a picture of Jesus on the cross? Those who are mortal, and know their need of healing, can gaze at the Christ, dying out of love for us, and find there peace and healing and new life.

Read today's Gospel next, linking the Old Testament passage and having everybody reading John 3:16. Notice that there is no sense of Jesus coming to condemn, but to save us. Read the Philippians passage to see how Paul sees Jesus' mission, and notice the total self-emptying, humility and obedience to God's loving will.

Having read these passages, use the sheet to record in what ways the cross stood for failure, and in what ways for victory. Help them to see that the failure and degrading nature of the Crucifixion was all part of the self-giving love which triumphs over evil and death.

Praying

Alleluia, sing to Jesus,
his the sceptre, his the throne;
alleluia, his the triumph,
his the victory alone.
Hark, the songs of peaceful Sion
thunder like a mighty flood;
Jesus, out of every nation,
hath redeemed us by his blood.

Activities

On the sheet they can tease out some of the reasons we see the cross as the supreme victory, even as we recognise its failure and degradation. There is also a cross to complete with the aid of Bible references.

ALL SAINTS – 1 NOVEMBER

Thought for the day

Lives that have shone with God's love on earth are filled with joy as they see their Lord face to face.

Reflection on the readings

Apocalypse 7:2-4. 9-14
Psalm 23:1-6
1 John 3:1-3
Matthew 5:1-12

Saints are not a special breed or caste. They do not possess a certain prescribed blend of skills, and emerge out of particular sets of circumstances. There is really only one thing which marks out a saint from the rest: they are the ones who know, without doubt, that they need God, so they do something about it, and go to him, just as they are and open to receive from him.

Psalm 23 obviously comes from experience when the psalmist reflects that those who go to the Lord for help will have every good thing, and the saints would agree. In the vision of heaven in the Apocalypse we find them utterly filled with joy and peace as they lose themselves in worship and praise. Describing heavenly things in earthly language is naturally difficult, but this passage gets close to touching the heavenly in us, and draws us into a sense of heaven's fulfilment, where there is no more pain or hunger and all tears are wiped away for ever.

Here is the reward promised in the Beatitudes – reward in the sense that it is the natural outcome of living so knowingly dependent on God's goodness, love and guiding. We are all called to be saints, and become so in direct proportion to the extent we desire God. That is linked with the way we perceive him. There are so many who reject a god they wrongly assume to be the God of living truth, and if only they were introduced to the real person would have a very different response. There are others who lavish attention and time on false images they think are true, so that desire for the real Person of the true and powerful, living God is treated with suspicion and renounced.

The wonderful thing about our God is that he searches for us, wherever we are, listening for our bleating, lifting us on his shoulders and carrying us safely home. It doesn't matter where we have been, how bedraggled and smelly we are, or how long we have been lost. As we bleat in our brokenness and long for our Shepherd-God to give us all we need, we begin the path to sanctity, and only lose our way again if we start to lose sight of the truth of our dependence on God's grace, and his unwavering provision.

As John writes in today's reading, to be really Christlike is to see things as they really are, with our perception healed. And that takes us back to the saints in heaven, gazing on the Lord they have been drawing close to throughout their lives, and whom they now recognise clearly. That integrity of perception drenches them in the beauty of holiness, and their eternity is filled with worship and praise.

Discussion starters

1. What factors prevent us knowing our need of God?

2. What prevents us from trusting God with our deepest needs?

All-stage talk

Today we are celebrating the festival of all the saints of God. Saints are God's close friends, and there are lots of them around, as well as all the famous ones like Our Lady and Joseph, Peter and the other disciples, Francis, Benedict, Clare and Catherine.

What makes a saint?

Suppose your car breaks down on the motorway, and, as you drive skilfully on to the hard shoulder, smoke pours out of the bonnet. At this moment there is no doubt in your mind about it – you know that you need the AA or the RAC to sort you out. Suppose you've fallen down in the playground and find you can't move your ankle without terrible pain. At that moment you know without doubt that you need some help from the teacher on duty and the first aid people in the school office.

Show everyone a large arrow on which is written 'We know our need'. As soon as we know our need that points us towards getting it sorted. (Have 'Get help' written on a large piece of paper or card.) But what if we don't know or realise our need?

Suppose you have got some spaghetti sauce on your chin and you are just going out to meet an important client, or a new boyfriend or girlfriend. If we realise we have the sauce on our chin (show the arrow), then we'll probably go and wipe it off. (Show the 'Get help' sign.) But if we aren't aware of the sauce on our chin (show a sign without an arrow which says, 'Don't know our need') then we won't do anything about wiping it off. (Turn the 'Get help' sign over so it's a blank sign.)

If we don't realise our need of God (show 'Don't know our need') then we won't go to him for the help we urgently and desperately need. (Keep the blank sign up.) But if we *do* realise how much we need God (show the arrow) then that will lead us to seeking God's help in our lives. (Turn over the 'Get help' sign so it shows.)

Saints are ordinary people like us who realise their need of God (show the arrow) and spend their lives close to him so that he can help them in all they do. (Show the 'Get help' sign.)

All-age ideas

• For the reading from the Apocalypse, ask several people to read it chorally, preparing it prayerfully and deciding how their voices can best express the sense of the heavenly.

• Ask different groups and clubs to prepare banners celebrating different saints, so that the church is full of their witness and example.

Prayer of the Faithful

Celebrant
Knowing our dependence on God in all things, let us pray to him now.

Reader
Glorious God, as we celebrate the lives of those Church members who have shone with the brightness of your love, we offer you ourselves and our lives in fresh commitment and conscious awareness of our need for you in this parish and as individual Christians.

Silence

Just as I am:
I come.

Powerful God, may your kingdom of love and peace be established in this world and grow.
We pray for both the influential and the ignored, both the popular and the disliked, both the ambitious and the vulnerable.
Teach us all your ways and your values.

Silence

Just as I am:
I come.

Loving God, we call to mind our families and friends, neighbours and colleagues, thanking you for all the loving care and forgiveness, and asking your light to shine in all areas of hurt and misunderstanding.

Silence

Just as I am:
I come.

Healing God, we bring to you those whose lives are darkened by pain, fear or weariness.
Come to our aid; help us to bear what must be carried, and take from us all resentment and bitterness, replacing it with the abundance of peace.

Silence

Just as I am:
I come.

Eternal God, we thank you for all the saints – those recognised by the Church and those known only to a few, and to you.
We praise you for their example and rejoice that they live in your heaven with every tear wiped away.
In your mercy may all who have died in your friendship know your lasting peace.

Silence

Just as I am:
I come.

Gracious God, you can take us as we are and transform us by your life in us.
Clear our lives of all that is not of you, so that we let your goodness shine through the colours of our personalities and gifts you have given us.

Silence

Just as I am:
I come.

We join our prayers with those of Mary and all the saints:
Hail, Mary . . .

In a time of silence and in the presence of all the saints in heaven, let us pray for our particular concerns.

Silence

Celebrant
Father, as we celebrate the joy of those whose wills are united with yours, we commend to you our lives and our hope of heaven, through Christ our Lord.
Amen.

TREASURE SEEKERS

Aim: To know that saints are Jesus' friends and followers.

Starter

Sing Oh when the saints go marching in, marching around the room together.

Teaching

Bring along a family or parish photo album and look through the pictures together, recognising some and hearing about others. (This is my grandad who shouted at me when I climbed the cherry tree, and who loved his old dog called Judy. Here's the Brownies at the May Fair, with Mrs Phillips who sells birthday cards after church sometimes. This is Timothy's dad when he'd broken his leg playing football with the youth club.)

All these people are part of the big family of God. We're all God's friends.

Now look with them through another photo album, made up in advance from an enlarged Pebbles worksheet. These saints are all part of the family, too, who have lived good lives as specially good friends of God. Talk about them as you did about the family and parish people, without any 'holy language' reserved for saints.

Praying

Thank you, God,
for all the saints,
your good friends.
Thank you for being
my friend, too.

Activities

The pictures on the sheet can be made into a book of saints, and the cover made from a piece of coloured paper with tissue stuck into it as shown, so that they hold it up to the light and see the light shining through.

PEARL DIVERS

Aim: To celebrate All Saints' Day, looking at the example of some of the saints.

Starter

Get in an 'expert' to help everyone learn to juggle. Give out rolled socks for this. If you have no jugglers to draw on, just pick some other expert, such as a cat's-cradle person, fitness trainer, Irish dancer or cartoonist. Looking at their example helps the rest of us get the hang of whatever we are trying.

Teaching

When we looked at the example of someone who had been practising for a long time, it helped us pick up the skill. Today is the day we celebrate a festival – all the saints who have been God's good friends down through the centuries, and now live in heaven, happy for ever in God's company. We thank God for their lives and their example to us.

They all started off as ordinary people and any of us could be saints. All it takes is to realise that we need God, and to walk with him closely through our lives. Let's look at where that took some of God's friends. Either draw as you talk, or have different children to be the saint in question.

- Saint Alban (a Roman soldier)
- Saint Margaret of Scotland (a queen)
- Saint Benedict (a monk)
- Saint Helena (an elderly lady)

Praying

Thank you, Lord God,
for the example of all your saints.
They knew they needed you
and they trusted in you.
Help us to do the same.

Activities

On the sheet there is an illustration to trace, so the children will need tracing paper (or greaseproof paper) and paper clips. There is also a saintly wordsearch.

GOLD PANNERS

Aim: To explore sanctity and the heavenly reward.

Starter

Provide each group with a diary which gives saints' days, together with a book of saints to use as a reference book. Give each group a list of dates, and they have to discover whose saint's days these are, and what each saint is remembered for. Here are some dates to choose from:

- 1 March: Saint David
- 17 March: Saint Patrick
- 23 April: Saint George

- 19 May: Saint Dunstan
- 9 June: Saint Columba
- 22 June: Saint Alban
- 11 August: Saint Clare
- 27 August: Saint Monica
- 4 October: Saint Francis
- 11 November: Saint Martin
- 16 November: Saint Margaret, Queen of Scotland
- 30 November: Saint Andrew
- 6 September: Saint Nicholas

Then they can tell one another what they've dis-covered.

Teaching

All through the year we celebrate the saints, and today we remember all of them, together with all those unknown to us but known to God for their special friendship. What is saintliness? Is it a demure, holy expression on a painting or in a stained-glass window? The readings for All Saints show us that these are ordinary people, made extraordinary by their openness to God and their dependence on him.

Read the Gospel passage. These 'Beatitudes' or the 'blesseds' are aptly named, since they do stress the natural happy outcome of living in the way of God's love. It is knowing our need of God that opens us up to receive all the gifts he longs to give us. The Beatitudes are like the saintly handbook, and in the Psalm we do some saint-spotting too.

1 John 3:1-3 looks forward to the hope which is seen in the vision of the Apocalypse, chapter 7. Explain the difficulties of expressing heaven in images of time and human experience, and list the qualities of heaven that this passage hints at.

Praying

Amen!
Praise and glory
and wisdom and thanks and honour
and power and strength
be to our God for ever and ever. Amen!

Activities

The prayer is set out on the worksheet with space to illustrate the joy and peace of heaven, and they are encouraged to think about what a saint is, drawing general principles from a series of potted 'CVs' of saints.

FEASTS OF THE DEDICATION OF A CHURCH

Thought for the day

The church building symbolises the spiritual temple, being built of the living stones of God's people.

Reflection on the readings

2 Chronicles 5:6-11, 13-6:2 or Acts 7:44-50
Psalm 83
1 Corinthians 3:9-13, 16-17
John 4:19-24

All over the world there are holy places, soaked in the prayers of the faithful for generation after generation. In one sense, of course, the whole universe is holy, thought into being by the loving intention of the creative God, and there to be valued and reverenced. The people of Israel had sensed God's presence travelling with them on their journey out of Egypt, and, until Solomon built the temple, it was the more mobile Ark of the Covenant which symbolised God's presence with his people in the midst of their community.

It is a very human thing to wish to build God a house to live in. It is a symbol of the hospitality and welcome, acceptance and honour which we want to lavish on the One we worship. The account of the dedication of Solomon's temple emphasises the great holiness of God which cannot be contained by any building, and also the tender humility of the mighty God who is gracious enough to choose to dwell in this man-made house. The beautiful imagery of Psalm 83 expresses the soul at peace in God's presence in terms of being at home in his house, where holiness and security give unburdened joy.

We are not to be bound by place, of course, nor any rigid structures which tempt us away from the heart of worship, for God is to be worshipped in spirit and in truth, and, when we hold fast to that calling, the significance of all other issues is seen in proper proportion.

Our own church buildings are places hallowed by daily prayer and corporate praise and worship. It is here that at every celebration of the Mass the life of the parish, the troubles and joys of the people, are gathered and offered and given back transformed by the love of Christ. It is here that the people are fed and built up to be the Body of Christ in the world, so that the holiness of God is spread out in all directions his people walk, into every room they enter and into every conversation they share.

Discussion starters

1. What do you particularly thank God for on this anniversary of your church's dedication?

2. What are the advantages for a community of having particular buildings dedicated to God?

All-stage talk

Draw attention to the decoration of the church. Today we are celebrating the anniversary of our church being dedicated. In (1900) a lot of bricklayers, masons and glaziers, plasterers and painters created a space which was set apart for God. At that first service of dedication the people of this area gathered. Talk about the kind of things they might have been wearing, how they might have travelled and so on, to build a picture of that day when the church began its life.

One of the most important things those people did that day was to offer the building for God's work and dedicate themselves to be the living stones of Christ's Church here. Now we are here today, still gathering to worship God, still dedicating ourselves to his service in this area. And the church building is like a picture of what we are all called to be – built up as living stones into the spiritual temple of God.

Week by week we bring in with us all the people and situations we have met and enjoyed and wrestled with; all the griefs and joys, heartaches and hopes of those we have talked with and whose lives have touched ours. Here we offer all that in the Mass, and it is gathered up with our praise and love to be accepted and transformed. So we do not worship here for ourselves alone, but on behalf of all who are not here and would never think of coming; on behalf of all those our lives have brushed against. Through our worship, their worries and fears are brought into the healing love of God.

The name of our church reminds us that the whole Church includes the saints in heaven as well as all of us on earth, and they are here with us, too, cheering us on and praying for us as we worship God in our prayers and our work each day. As we thank God for this place, which holds precious memories for many of us, we dedicate ourselves freshly to living as God's people, and ask God's blessing on our neighbourhood and all who will visit this place during the coming year.

All-age ideas

- Have banners and posters showing the date of the church's dedication and other significant dates in its history, together with reminders of the saint in whose name the church is dedicated.

- Gather a collection of photographs and have an exhibition celebrating the ministry of the church both in the past and in the present.

Prayer of the Faithful

Celebrant
Gathered as the Church of Christ in this place,
let us pray together in his name.

Reader
Father, we give you thanks for this church building
and the privilege of worshipping you without fear.
We thank you for all
who have prayed and ministered here,
and ask that you keep us attentive to your voice,
worshipping you in spirit and in truth.

Silence

Take us, Lord:
renew us and use us.

Father, we pray for this area and its problems,
for all who live, work and raise their families here.
We thank you for all that is good and hopeful,
and ask you to bless and guide those in authority.

Silence

Take us, Lord:
renew us and use us.

Father, may the homes we represent
and all the homes of this parish
be filled with your light and love,
your warmth and welcome,
your comforting and peace.

Silence

Take us, Lord:
renew us and use us.

Father, may all who come to this place
in distress of body or soul
find here your healing and refreshment,
and touch the beauty of your holiness.

Silence

Take us, Lord:
renew us and use us.

Father, we commend to your love
all those who have worshipped here in the past,
both those we remember
and those known only to you.

Silence

Take us, Lord:
renew us and use us.

We make our prayers with Mary,
the Mother of the Church:
Hail, Mary . . .

In a time of silence, filled with God's peace,
we bring our personal prayers and petitions,
in the assurance of God's love.

Silence

Celebrant
Father, hear these prayers
which we offer as your people,
and build us as living stones
into a spiritual temple.
Through Christ our Lord.
Amen.

TREASURE SEEKERS

Aim: To celebrate the building of the church.

Starter

Provide lots of building bricks and/or cartons and boxes, and have a free time of building.

Teaching

Talk about what the children have been building, and then tell them that today we are thinking about a special building where we all come to worship God. It's our church (St. Helen's), and it's now (sixty) years old!

All through the years babies have been baptised here (everyone mimes holding a baby and pouring water over the head), lots and lots of people have come to pray (everyone puts hands together), and been to Mass (hold out hands). People have come here to weddings and been very happy (look happy), and they have come here to requiems when their loved ones have died, and felt very sad (look sad). At our church we've learnt about God and grown to love him.

Which bit of the church do they like best? As they mention things, try drawing them on a blackboard or sheet of paper (they don't have to be expert works of art!), and then thank God together for the church building and all the things that go on there.

Praying

Thank you, Father, for our church
and all the people in it.
Help us to love you
and love one another.

Activities

The sheet can be coloured and folded to make a stand-up church, and if you have pre-cut some people, these can be stuck on to it.

PEARL DIVERS

Aim: To know what the Dedication Festival is and why we are celebrating.

Starter

Cut out the shapes below in different coloured paper, and prepare a chart which shows what number needs to be thrown for each section of the church. Sit in a circle (or several if you have more children) and pass round a jumbo dice, made from a cubic box with stickers on. As each correct number is thrown that section of the church is added, until the whole church is built up. The basic rectangle (costing a six) has to be put down first, and the tower (worth five) must come before the clock. Other than that, any order is fine.

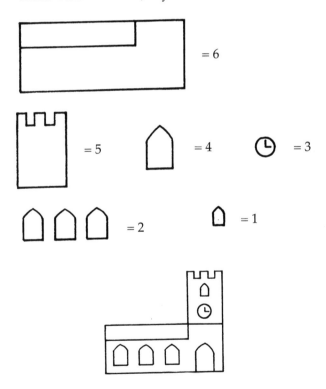

Teaching

Adapt the facts of the following story for your own situation. One person tells the events and another does the actions. For the building they all do the actions.

A hundred years ago (show the number on a card) some people in Westcliff decided to have a new church built. They looked at some designs and plans (show some rolls of paper and a local map), and they checked how much money they had (tip out some money from a money bag or purse). They did lots of sums (scribble some and pretend to work them out), they did a lot of thinking (hold head and concentrate), and they all talked to each other about what the church should be like (everyone talks to each other about their ideas for a church building).

At last it was all agreed, and the building of St Alban's started. They dug deep trenches for foundations (everyone digs) and filled them with strong concrete (pour the concrete in). The bricklayers built the walls (build walls) and the glaziers put glass in the windows (fit panes of glass). They climbed up ladders and scaffolding (climb ladders) and fixed the roof on top (hammer nails in). They screwed doors into the doorways (twist screws in) and built an altar of stone (build it). They plastered and painted the walls (plaster and paint), and brought in the new chairs (carry pretend chairs). They laid the carpet (roll and tack down carpet) and they brought in the font and the lectern (carry them).

Now the new church of St Alban's was ready. The people were very pleased to have a new church. They packed into the building and praised God for it, thanking him for all those who had worked so hard to make it and pay for it. The building was dedicated, given over to God, so that it would always be used to God's glory. It would be a place where the children and grandchildren and great-grandchildren of the people there would know they could always come to pray to God.

And here we are, a hundred years later, still worshipping God at St Alban's in this building which was dedicated to be a place of worship a hundred years ago today.

Praying

Thank you, Father, for this church
where people have come to worship you
day by day, week by week, year by year.
Keep us faithful in your love
and bless the work of our church
in the coming year.

Activities

The sheet can be made into a card which opens to show the inside of the church, in which they can draw and colour the people worshipping God.

GOLD PANNERS

Aim: To look at what it means for the transcendent God to dwell in a building.

Starter

Set a timer for two minutes and ask everyone to write down the names of all the people they know, the towns and countries they have visited, and the subjects they have had lessons in at school. When the two minutes are up, ask them to look over their own lists. That represents just two minutes of thinking, and if the room could now be filled with all the people and places mentioned there, it would be pretty crowded. Each of us holds a huge landscape of places and people inside our heads.

Teaching

We have seen how we are really far bigger than we look. Today, as we celebrate the dedication of our church, we are thinking about how the great God of earth and heaven can dwell in a church building. Of course, our God is far too great to be contained in a building, because both heaven and earth are full of his glory, and all that exists is contained in God, the source of all creation. But, rather like all the ideas, memories and knowledge we have in our minds, God's presence dwells in the church building dedicated to him, where daily prayer and offering makes it hallowed as a meeting place for God and his gathered people.

Read the passage from 2 Chronicles or Acts, which recognises both God's transcendent greatness and his closeness and humility; our God travels with his people and stands among them where they are. (How does that link up with the Christmas story?)

Now read the Gospel, looking out for any guidelines Jesus is giving us for how we should be worshipping God. What does it mean to worship in spirit and in truth? Do we do this? How does our church building help us to do it?

Praying

Father, in this holy place
we sense your presence with us.
Build us up like a strong building,
firm in faith and ready to be used.

Activities

There are different parts of the church building to label and write in their value, and there is also space for looking at how the church building is used for God's work.

APPENDIX

You can drink it

2. It's as hard as rock,
   yet it flows down a mountain,
   and clouds drop drips of it –
   what can it be?

3. It's as light as snowflakes
   and heavy as hailstones,
   as small as dewdrops
   and big as the sea.

Text: Susan Sayers
Music: Susan Sayers, arr. Noel Rawsthorne